FORGOTTEN HORRORS

Vol. 10:
The Missing Years

Vol. 10: The Missing Years

MICHAEL H. PRICE

WITH

VAN CLIBURN

• • •

GEORGE E. TURNER

CREMO STUDIOS • LOWER KLOPSTOKIA

ALSO BY
Michael H. Price & Accomplices
• Forgotten Horrors ET SEQ.
(with John Wooley, Geo. E. Turner, ET AL.)
• The Ghosts & Girls of Fiction House
(with Craig Yoe & Clizia Gussoni)
• Mantan the Funnyman:
The Life & Times of Mantan Moreland
• Thick Lights, Loud Smoke & Dim, Dim Music:
The Honky-Tonk Badlands of Texas
• Forgotten Horrors Comics & Stories
• The Comics from the Gone World Series
• The Big Book of Biker Flicks
(with John Wooley)
...AND OTHERS TOO HUMOROUS TO MENTION

Cover & Interior Design: Meatwood Flack, Cremo Studios, Inc.
Crucial Technical & Aesthetic Assistance: John Wooley
Copr. © 2016 Michael H. Price

Essential research derives from the work of George E. Turner and Michael H. Price during 1968–2000 on behalf of the *American Film Institute Catalogue of Feature Films*. The *Forgotten Horrors* books have been designated as Standard References by the American Film Institute.

In memory of Phil Hardy (1945–2014), and with grateful acknowledgments to: Gary D. Rhodes • Mike Gold • Mark Evan Walker • Josh Alan Friedman John Wooley • Bill Chase • Ellis Goodson • Rachel Pilcher • Jennifer O. Henderson • Tom Huckabee • Tim Paxton • Steve Felton • Keith Randal Duncan • Drew Friedman •   Stephen R. Bissette • Jim Vance • Mark Martin • Barret "Dr. Demento" Hansen • Gabriel Horn • David Hickey Kerry Gammill • Betsy Pepper • Mark Lamberti • Keith & Patrick Reardon Perry "Buck" Stewart • Rob Bosquez • Rogelio Agrasanchez • Allan Turner David Colton • Robert Tinnell • Joey Hambrick • Mark A. Nobles • Todd Camp • Doug Hopkins • Paul Crawford • Craig Yoe • Tillmann Courth Jasper Bark • Clizia Gussoni • Larry D. Springer • J. Ben Sargent • the American Film Institute • Turner Classic Movies • Hoblitzelle Archive, Harry Ransom Center, the University of Texas at Austin • the Fort Worth Public Library Foundation • the Rondo Awards • the Ghastly Awards

ISBN–13: 978-1530932788
EAN–10: 1530932785

TABLE OF CONTENTS

Roy Crane
(Page No. 182).

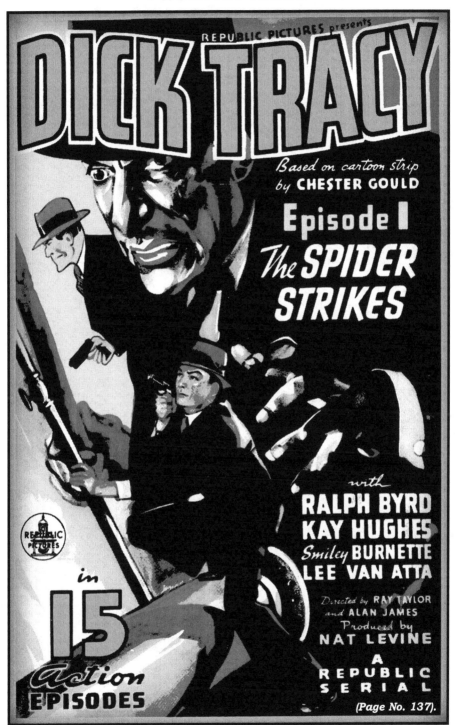

(Page No. 311).

THE CUSTOMARY WORDS TO THE FORE

From MICHAEL H. PRICE

This 10TH volume of the *Forgotten Horrors* series breaks ranks significantly with its predecessors to present a wider range of genres, in a wider context of mostly larger studios, quite beyond the smaller-studio emphasis that has defined the books since 1979. All during our original collaborative span of 1968–1999, founding author George E. Turner and I worked as generalists in the movie-scholar trade while seeking to give the (purportedly) lowlier horror movies a dignified representation on a par with that accorded the romantic comedies, historical epics, high-minded dramatic exercises, and other such (purportedly) more respectable genres and idioms. George and I scarcely gave a Flying Damn whether we might be typecasting ourselves in the process.

For we had meant to stake out a signature territory, and the low-budget spookers provided that haven. Scarcely anyone else among the tribe of Film Theorists was paying attention to the Poverty Row chillers. George and I might have preferred to concentrate upon slapstick comedy, or Westerns, or the major studios' Gothics, or the silent-screen age, but such colleagues as William K. Everson and John McCabe and Kevin Brownlow had staked out those more visible territories with such style and authority that George and I could see no purpose in poaching on anyone else's preserve. George's prior book, *The Making of King Kong* (1975), had already (unwittingly) provoked an outbust of envy from Everson—"That's the book *I* had wanted to write," he informed Turner—and George's and my approach was such that we preferred cordial alliances over potential rivalries.

George and I also dealt all along in the greater sweep of filmmaking, as film reviewers for our Texas-based newspaper. For the Public Library System of Amarillo, Texas, and the Amarillo Art Center, we curated film-festival programs that (usually) dealt in pictures of a broader general interest: The likes of Orson Welles' *Citizen Kane*, John Ford's *The Searchers*, and Howard Hawks' *His Girl Friday* were perennials with our provincial audiences. Only rarely would we sneak in a *White Zombie* or a *Vampire Bat*—usually to popular acclaim, notwithstanding that city's underlying Bible Belt resistance to the darker forms of entertainment.

The original *Forgotten Horrors* took shape amidst an outpouring of newspaper commentaries on the mainsteam films, new and old, and a Turner–Price research project for the American Film Institute. And so it goes with this present volume, which reproduces not only my Turner-influenced observations on a wealth of large-studio chillers but also my curatorial notes for metropolitan museum and film-festival screenings; my observations on indigenous music, Fine Art and Commercial Art; comic strips and comic books; and the occasional straightforward historical essay.

An unlikely but compatible collaborator is the Great Pyrotechnical Pianist, Van Cliburn, for whose influential Cliburn Piano Competition I have produced various curatorial exhibits of films devoted to classical music. The Cliburn program book of 2001 is reproduced at Page Nos. 327 *et Seq.*—and of course I managed to smuggle in the occasional horror-movie reference, despite Van's professed distaste for the genre. As though the lives of the Great Eurocentric Composers were not riddled sufficiently with the horrors of madness, of treacherous intrigues, of murder and mayhem.)

Context is everything: The diehard tunnel-vision monster-movie enthusiasts can only gain a greater apprecation of their favorite realm by studying films and books and comics and music outside that narrowly defined genre. Got yer Broader Context, right here...

The chapters thus arrayed derive from a variety of published sources, including the magazines *Midnight Marquee Monsters* and *Mad about Movies*; program guides for Baltimore's FanEx festivals; and the upstart publishing empire known as ComicMix. The commonality is that these have never before been collected into a single volume. Pointless to cherry–pick my two years' worth of ComicMix columns for a concentration upon spooky movies when even the off-cinema entries help to establish a greater Cultural Context. Not to mention that I've got a mess of pages to fill, here, so Waste Not, Want Not, already.

This No. 10 volume also is a jump-the-gun entry in the *Forgotten Horrors* series: At this writing in the springtime of 2016, John Wooley and I are in the midst of an original research regimen for *Forgotten Horrors Vol. 9: Into the Ectoplasmic Spasmochasm*—a book whose manuscript has barely been started. Much as John's and my *Forgotten Horrors to the NTH Degree* (2013) breaks stride with a strict chronology to collect our long-running *Forgotten Horrors* column for *Fangoria* magazine, so the present book darts back–and–forth in time from the wartime 1940s to periods even earlier, and then again to more nearly recent years. And all to the better for that. Sez me. Thank you.

—*M•H•P*
ON THE TRAIL OF
THE LONESOME PINE

REDISCOVERIES

This rambling prefatory array (through Page No. 109) derives from the many spinoff articles that George E. Turner (1925–1999) and I had begun compiling as early as 1968 in connection with our work for the American Film Institute, the American Society of Cinematographers, and of course the *Forgotten Horrors* project. Each original venue of publication is noted where relevant and/or/if/as though appropriate.

'CAT PEOPLE' AND THE ORIGINS OF THE VAL LEWTON STYLE

The grander days of the American horror film were a distant memory by the beginning of the 1940s. The genre had turned generic in less than a decade, despite a resurgence and a return–to–form (more commercial than artistic) during the late 1930s. And although such pictures remained viable at the box office, only the occasional example of finer artistry surfaced from a morass of Superfluous Redundant Overkill.

We would hardly deny our fondness for the period's greater body of such films, and to speak otherwise would be a betrayal of our own arguments in the *Forgotten Horrors* books (1979 and onward), and of our friend William K. Everson's enlightened findings in 1990's *More Classics of the Horror Film*. (The fashionable notion of the Guilty Pleasure is a cowardly sham, calculated to allow *dilettante* enthusiasts to enjoy low-brow delights while pretending to dismiss them.) The rediscovery of numerous Depression-into-wartime pictures—both outright horrors and subtler variations—invariably turns up moments of brilliance, even in clear-cut instances of Mass Production. But the period lacked a vision capable of lending uplift or sustenance. The rare hint of visionary lustre served chiefly to nurture a hope that some artistic heir to James Whale or Tod Browning—both of whom were by now in decline as casualties of big-studio treacheries—would herald a rebirth.

That arrival required an assertion of mastery from someone purposeful enough to break ground in defiance of the established Lay of the Land, someone willing to ditch the shopworn conventions for the sake of fashioning Something Entirely New. Hence Val Lewton.

With his first picture, *Cat People*, in 1942, RKO–Radio Pictures' upstart discovery, Vladimir "Val" Lewton, declared a small-scale revolution–*cum*–renaissance. His follow–throughs would prove comparably assertive. For Lewton was less concerned with tearing down the traditional forms than with subverting or snubbing them outright while developing from scratch an agenda of narrative standards, driven by a willingness to allow his productions to interact with an Absorbed Audience. The stagnant pond of horror films turned fresher as a consequence, even among the rival studios. And many of the parties responsible would in turn develop a participatory influence upon filmmaking as a class, ranging beyond the atmospheric pictures of the Lewton unit at RKO. Not so for Lewton himself, for his own career can be boiled to an essence within just a five-year span at that one studio.

Of course, the racket cares little for any renaissance on mere visionary grounds, and Corporate Hollywood tolerates innovation only on condition of moneymaking potential. Lewton's production unit was created in a chain of managerial upheavals. These tremors were caused by the failure of expensive, middlebrow-to-highbrow produc-

Simone Simon.

tions to crank the profits. The most conspicuous recent example at RKO was Orson Welles' *Citizen Kane*, whose box-office belly–flop (contrary to the studio's extravagant expectations) had supplied a convenient scapegoat for broader problems on a companywide scale.

A veteran movie-theatre executive, Charles Koerner, was brought aboard early in 1942 as vice president for production. From his advantageous box-office perspective, Koerner knew that RKO was losing money on many prestigious big-budget features and turning robust profits on the so-called B–pictures, which at RKO meant those made on budgets of $150,000 and less. (The *B* stands for *budget*—not for some schoolmarmish grading system.) The balance sheets proved Koerner correct.

Koerner also knew that one entrenched rival, Universal Pictures, was making so much money on its B–unit horror pictures that the Front Office had termed them "Midas productions." Koerner decided that RKO must establish a low-budget production unit dedicated to the proposition of sure-seller horror movies. These efforts would be conceived as sensationalistic titles—the cornerstone of High Concept project development—and tested as such upon a prospective audience before even a synopsis could be written. *Would you pay to see a movie called* Cat People? *Well, then, we'll whip up a picture to go with the name.*

Val Lewton at 37 had settled in H'wood, where the former RKO executive David O. Selznick—long since turned Big Shot Independent—had brought him from New York nine years previously with hopes of turning Lewton's Russian literary flair to the service of a film based upon Nikolaj Gogol's Cossack swashbuckler, *Taras Bulba*. That project never materialized under Selznick, but assignments in publicity, research, and story–editing for MGM and Selznick–International kept Lewton visible until the unanticipated development at RKO could occur. Charles Koerner and Lewton met informally, at a dinner party in Beverly Hills. Burly and good-

humored, a raconteur at ease with himself and his listeners, Lewton impressed Koerner as a showman in need of a show. Koerner acted upon instinct and offered Lewton the job as RKO's horror-movie expert. Lewton went onto the payroll in March of 1942 at $250 a week. He took a bawdy delight in informing his friends that he was listed on the studio's roster of abbreviated titles as an "Ass. Prod." Lewton's immediate superior was Lou Ostrow, a hard-nosed "Exec. Prod." and diehard champion of the *Status Quo*.

Lewton, a prolific if hardly famous novelist, found himself impressed with Koerner's professed literary conceits as the two considered properties worth adapting; they looked in particular at Algernon Blackwood's "Ancient Sorceries." Koerner, however, let slip a more annoying Populist attitude after he had attended a party and accepted moviemaking suggestions from the civilian guests. Someone there declared that vampires and werewolves had been done to death, but "nobody has done much of anything about cats." Koerner shelved the Blackwood tale and suggested a title in search of a story: *Cat People*. Lewton found the title absurd, but he promised an elaboration.

The title had come easier than a story that would fulfill such lurid possibilities and still sit comfortably with Lewton's narrative values. Lewton spent months examining cat yarns, including Cornell Woolrich's *Black Alibi* (presently to be developed into *The Leopard Man*, at Lewton/RKO); Bram Stoker's "The Squaw," about a mother–cat's vengeance for a slain kitten; and Ambrose Bierce's "The Eyes of the Panther." Lewton leaned briefly toward a true-to-Poe adaptation of "The Black Cat" but was dissuaded by the reminder that Universal had exploited that title in free-handed twists as recently as 1934 and 1941. A likelier possibility lay in Margaret Irwin's "Monsieur Seeks a Wife," which Lewton described in a memorandum as "a fetching little tale about a man who meets two sisters who are not really women, but cats." With this notion in mind, Lewton abandoned all pretense of adapting any known story and set out to draft an elaboration of his own.

Our diggings through the RKO files during 1978–1981 yielded this embryonic *Cat People*: The story opens in a snowbound Balkan village under invasion by a Nazi Panzer division. By day, the local denizens seem somnolent and unconcerned. By night, these citizens transmogrify themselves into great cats and attack their captors. (Hence the term *nocturnal*: They *turn* on the oppressors and *knock* them down.) One girl of this village escapes to New York, where she falls in love with an ordinary American male human being. But her heritage follows.

In the inescapable gulf between visualization and realization, Lewton had planned to have the girl speak directly. He advised: "I thought we might let our cat–girl only speak in long shots. You hear the murmur of her voice, you never hear what she is saying, and if it is necessary to give her words' meaning to the audience, I think we can always contrive to have some other character tell what the girl said." This proposal—the earliest surviving evidence of Lewton's radical willingness to involve an audience in the very telling of the story—was rejected out–of–hand, but the head office warmed to the basic concept.

Lewton also proposed an ending unlike the one eventually filmed: "Most of the cat/werewolf stories I have read and all the werewolf stories I have seen on the screen end with the beast ... turning back into a human being after death. In this story, I'd like to reverse this process. For the final scene, I'd like to show a violent quarrel between the man and woman in which she is provoked into an attack on him. To protect himself, he pushes her away, she stumbles and breaks her neck... The young man, horrified, kneels to see if he can feel her heartbeat. Under

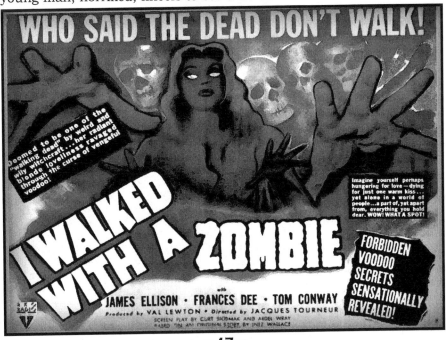

Not one, not two, not three . . . but ALL of the famous creeper characters you ever heard of, plus some new ones, in the wildest nightmare of terror thrills that mind can imagine! . . Cat People, Zombies, Leopard Men, beast-women and bat-men, blood-curdlers by the dozen . . . all in a merger of monsters that will make anything else in this line look like a Sunday School picnic!

"THEY CREEP BY NIGHT"

An exhibitor-trade promotional herald for the Lewton pictures (1944–1945) summarizes the sensationalism that Lewton avoided in his productions.

his hand, black hair and hide come up, and he draws back to look down in horror at a dead black panther."

The more iconoclastic innovations did not survive the concept-by-committee sessions, but the memoranda suggest important elements of the final version. Lewton wrote, for example, that he wanted "a man, possibly a doctor, who always gives the scientific or factual explanation for any phenomena ..., brushing the supernatural aside, and yet who is always proved wrong by the events on the screen. This device, I believe, will express the audiences' doubts even before they are fully formulated in their minds and quickly answer them, thus lending a degree of credibility ..., which is going to be difficult to achieve."

Another idea, envisioned in pre–production and translated to the screen, is the scene in which leading man Kent Smith squires Simone Simon, as the cat–in–human–form named Irena, into a pet store. Wrote Lewton: "Here, I'd like to show the chattering fear that arises upon her entrance. At the very height of the uproar, I would like to have a little black cat come down the center aisle ..., very calmly, and rub affectionately against the girl." (In the finished product, however, the cat seems as terrified as the other creatures.)

Lewton dropped the Balkan framing sequence in an extreme reaction against the Eurocentric trappings of many of the Universal chillers. He chose instead a modernized, workaday American setting. After the success of his approach had been established, Lewton would write in a studio press release of 1944: "The characters in the run-of-the-mill [*read:* Universal] weird films were usually people very remote from the audiences' experiences. European nobles of dark antecedents, mad scientists, man-created monsters, and the like cavorted across the screen. It would be much more entertaining if people with whom audiences could identify were shown in contact with the strange, the weird and the occult. We made it a basic part of our work to show normal people—engaged in normal occupations—in our pictures."

Lewton made patent his admiration of Alfred Hitchcock, already an acknowledged master at showing the consequences that result when the Extraordinary intrudes upon the Ordinary. Lewton also expressed a fondness for the documentary-styled, strange-but-true short subjects of MGM (including early directing assignments for Lewton associate Jacques Tourneur) and, particularly, for an often horrific series of shorts and featurettes from Warner Bros., issued during the late 1930s under the blanket title of *Your True Adventures.*

Lou Ostrow, Lewton's boss, was a pragmatist who preferred to Leave Well Enough Alone and rankled at any suggestion that cinema might become art. Ostrow, typical of the RKO Suits, considered Lewton too ostentatious and fussy to make the grade as a producer for the masses. (This is a familiar conflict of Old Hollywood, crystallized in a 1992 film from the Coen Bros., *Barton Fink.*) Only Koerner's intervention rescued *Cat People* from turning into an exercise in formula— if not from being abandoned outright. Ostrow approved the basic idea and then lay in ambush for another opening, ordering the Accounting and Security departments to watch for irregularities in protocol. Lewton installed DeWitt Bodeen, a research assistant at Selznick–International, as the first screenwriter within the new unit.

Val
Lewton.

Bodeen told us during the early 1980s: "Before Val departed for RKO, he asked me to call him as soon as my work for Selznick was completed. I 'phoned him two weeks later, and he made arrangements for me to be hired as a contract writer at the Guild minimum of $75 per week. I had never written for the screen before."

The occasion for our visits with Bodeen, then 74 and just six years away from death, was a matter of gauging his reactions to Paul Schroeder's 1982 remake of *Cat People*, with Nastassja Kinsky inheriting the Simone Simon role. Bodeen was the only member of the original Lewton team to receive a screen credit on the revamp. Bodeen found that the new script "follows the original fairly closely as to the incidents, but of course it is very modern and very—*very*—sexy. I didn't really like that part, and I suspect Val would not have been pleased at the lack of suggestive restraint, but I'm glad they gave me a credit."

The drill in 1942 called for Lewton and Bodeen to read all they could find as to the habits of cats. They screened what Bodeen called "a marathon of horror pictures, most of them from Universal," in search of clichés in need of avoiding. Lewton assigned Bodeen to compose a 50-page story—not as a scenario or a script, but as if for magazine publication. The result was a first-person narrative, written in the voice of a woman named Alice, who loves the man who has married the cat–girl. Bodeen arrayed many essential elements, most

notably the sequence wherein Alice (played by Jane Randolph) is men-aced by a shadowy, catlike presence at a darkened swimming–pool. The idea sprang from grim experience: "I'd almost drowned, once, as a youngster, while out swimming alone," Bodeen recalled.

Jacques Tourneur, son of the great French filmmaker Maurice Tourneur, joined the company at Lewton's behest. Having worked in France and America on features and short subjects, Tourneur had met Lewton while both helped with the French Revolution sequences for the Selznick–MGM epic, *A Tale of Two Cities* (1935). By 1942, Tourneur's career had run into a *cul–de–sac*; he was only too happy to sign on with Lewton. The next appointed member was film editor Mark Robson. Though a top-of-the-line artisan, Robson had found himself demoted to the B–pictures as a result of guilt–by–association.

"I was one of Orson Welles' editors on *Citizen Kane*," Robson told us, "and that picture cost a lot of time and money that it didn't recoup. Management tended to blame all of RKO's financial troubles on Orson, and those of us who'd worked with him in 1941 had to share the blame. So Val Lewton's B–unit proved a sort of safe haven for me, but more than just a holding pattern."

The exile proved an unanticipated break for Robson, who made significant contributions to Lewton's preproduction and story-planning sessions. Robson's experience as a second-unit director also figured. As *Cat People* neared completion, Lewton wrote to Koerner: "If I were asked to name one single factor, beyond the director's work, which helped me most ..., I would name Mark's work. Jacques says of him that he cuts like a director, which, from a director, is praise indeed."

Jacques Tourneur.

Lewton absorbed valuable lessons from a veteran B–unit producer, Herman Schlom, who had become one of RKO's leading talents at delivering slick, economical melodramas. Schlom explained to Lewton the many ways of cutting costs in preproduction, especially in the planning of sets to accommodate blocking and camera placements, and to serve multiple functions.

The wartime government's imposed limit of $10,000 per picture on set construction made it necessary to use existing sets almost entirely. RKO had stored away a great many sets from which to choose. In addition to its Hollywood studio, the company had access to the 40-acre backlot and sound stages at RKO–Pathé in Culver City and the RKO Ranch at Encino. From Schlom, Lewton learned how to lavish elaborate décor upon one or two major sets and scrimp elsewhere with lighting and camera placements. In this respect, *Cat People* concentrates its main action upon the cat–girl's studio apartment, whose imposing exterior is a brownstone front along Pathé's famous New York street expanse. A marvelous staircase on a Pathé sound stage, used just a few months earlier for Orson Welles' *The Magnificent Ambersons*, was altered with the addition of an adjoining elevator cage brought in from the scenery dock. The Central Park settings were already familiar to admirers of the song-and-dance exploits of Fred Astaire and Ginger Rogers. Offices and stairwells had served the 1941 comedy *The Devil and Miss Jones*.

Here, a standing café set was re–dressed as a coffee shop, and there it was reinvented as the pet store—and yet elsewhere, as an ethnically accurate Serbian–American bistro. Wild (*i.e.*, mobile) walls set up with scene-dock props were fashioned into other sets. Art director Walter Keller disguised these mock–locales so artfully as to hide any suggestion of second-hand origins. Set decorator Al Fields smothered the settings in appropriate furnishings and filigree, combing the prop-

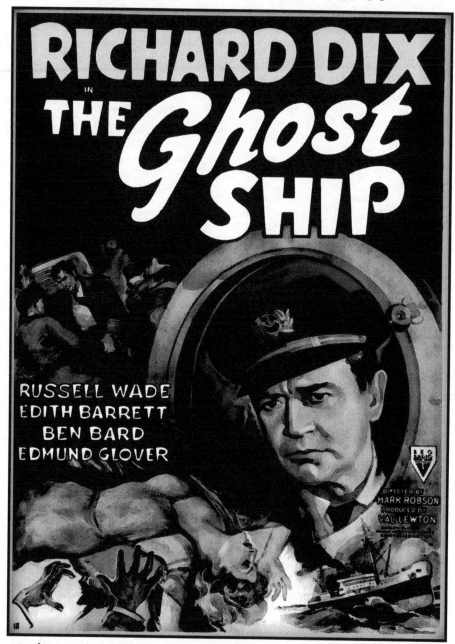

erty department and the prop-rental houses for items that would mark and reflect the troubled progress of the characters.

Casting was essential to the campaign to avoid horror-film conventions. Lewton insisted to Ostrow: "I'd like to have a girl with a little kitten–face like Simone Simon, cute and soft and cuddly and seemingly not at all dangerous." He added: "I took a look at the Paramount picture *Island of Lost Souls* [1932], and after seeing their much-publicized 'panther woman' [a reference to Kathleen Burke], I feel that any attempt to secure a catlike quality in our girl's physical appearance would be absolutely disastrous."

Bodeen in 1982 amplified upon this memo: "Val told me from the first to write the part of Irena around Simone Simon. He seemed confident that he would be able to get her." A leading star in her native France, Miss Simon had made a number of films in the United States but never achieved the popularity her sponsors at 20TH Century–Fox had anticipated. Lewton sent the actress a copy of the first draft while she was appearing on stage in Chicago, and she promptly accepted on terms that would accommodate the fixed budget.

The ambiguous character of the rationalizing would-be debunker, a doctor named Louis Judd, evolved from a sinister European named Mueller. Lewton at first wanted the German actor Fritz Kortner, who would "add a great deal of menace and a certain conceited Continental quality that would make audiences dislike him," according to one memorandum. As the script found its truer level, however, Lewton re-envisioned the character as a youngish and dashing but world-weary Britisher. Likable Tom Conway, a contract player who had recently succeeded his brother, George Sanders, as the star player in RKO's *Falcon* line of mysteries, proved an apt choice.

Kent Smith, a successful leading man from Broadway, had signed an RKO contract in 1941 but then spent nine months without appearing in anything beyond a run of Army training films. Lewton saw Smith as the actor commuted to the studio on his bicycle and decided that Smith might make an ideal Oliver, the rock-steady but bewildered protagonist of *Cat People*. Smith's sympathetic portrayal would launch a lengthy film career.

Jane Randolph, also a contract player, was chosen for the second female lead because she was anything but the ingénue type usually favored for such roles. Tall and efficient of manner, Miss Randolph epitomized the modern career woman who had emerged as a social force since the start of World War II. The other actors, down to the bit players, were selected by Lewton and Tourneur from the list of contract talents and the *Standard Casting Directory*. The most striking small role is that of a catlike woman who appears in one scene—an unforgettable cameo from the statuesque Elizabeth Russell.

Cinematographer Nick Musuraca had long been typed as a photographer of Westerns and other high-adventure pictures before he was assigned to *Cat People*. Musuraca's five films for Lewton would establish him as a master of brooding, dramatic lighting. His distinctive technique is now celebrated as a basis of the *film noir* style. After graduating to a string of similarly atmospheric films, including *The Spiral Staircase*, *The Locket*, and *Out of the Past* (1945–1947), Musuraca complained that he had typed himself anew, this time as a mystery expert, and would appreciate a chance to shoot "more normal pictures."

Despite Lewton's determination to eschew the conventions of horror films, the examples of the masters were hardly lost upon him. Greater innovations in sound-recording technique, for example, had been introduced in the spookers and the mysteries than in the more readily accepted mainstream works. Lewton held that dialogue should be used only when the story could not be advanced through a combination of visual imagery and natural sound.

When the studio's Accounting Department demanded to know why John Cass' recording crew spent an extra three days on *Cat People*, Lewton explained that the engineers worked one day at Gay's Lion Farm, recording growls and roars; and two days at the echo-laden indoor swimming pool of the Royal Palms Hotel, capturing reverberation effects. A vocal-effects actress, Dorothy Lloyd, was hired to create an array of catlike noises. The bean–counters, ready to do the treacherous bidding of Lou Ostrow, regarded such activities unusual for a B–unit project, and thus suspect.

Val Lewton.

Lewton rejected the studio's tactic of assembling patchwork musical scores for its lower-budget pictures. He conferred with musical director Constantin Bakaleinikoff and composer Roy Webb before the screenplay could find its shape. Webb was brought into the story sessions to contribute ideas for linking scenic values and visual cues with music. Like most film composers, Webb was accustomed to being consulted only after principal photography had wrapped. His involvement in the planning, enabled him to deliver a more evocative score.

"We were searching for a lullaby theme suited to a story about cats," wrote Lewton, "something with a haunting, memorable quality somewhat like the short bit from 'Anitra's Dance,' which was used so memorably in the German picture *M*. And we wanted a little strain of music to be sung or hummed by the heroine, to have a catlike feeling and a sinister note of menace." None of the many compositions thus considered embodied the qualities that Lewton wanted. Then one day on the set, Simone Simon sang for Lewton a traditional French lullaby she remembered from childhood, the cooing "Do, Do, Baby, Do." Lewton seized upon the melody, and Webb agreed that it would make the ideal *leitmotif*. A Russian writer, Andrei Tolstoi, was hired to translate the lyrics into Russian and to coach the actress in pronunciation and delivery.

Although the budget permitted little visual-effects work, Vernon Walker's excellent camera-trickery unit made important contributions. Veteran technical artist Al Simpson, after receiving a request from Lewton for alterations to a matte painting, scrawled out a contemptuous note to his boss: "Getting damned hard to please these 'B' producers."

Linwood Dunn, chief of the optical department, composited a beautifully crafted, dreamlike montage of gracefully animated Art Deco panthers and diffused images of Tom Conway, wearing ancient armor and brandishing a sword—a crucial subtext. Dunn also supplied special transitional wipes with deliberately softened, uneven edges, the better to suggest shapeless shadows. The most memorable optical effect shows Simone Simon beginning to change into a cat after receiving an unwelcome kiss from Conway. Lewton had decided against showing a metamorphosis, but after viewing the sequence as filmed Tourneur and Lewton agreed that the close–up of the baby-faced actress, recoiling, failed to convey sufficient menace to justify the subsequent cut to Conway's terrified reaction.

"There was no preparation of any kind for the effect," Dunn said in 1978. "Otherwise, it would have been easy. I made her appear to darken by a complicated application of density manipulation and masking

within the optical printer. There was no retake involved—we just ran with what we had and made it work."

Principal photography was completed in 24 days on an intended budget of $118,948. The Accounting Department inflated the budget to $141,659 after shooting had begun. The final tab was actually $134,959. Ostrow had attempted to fire Tourneur after a look at the first three days' rushes, but Koerner intervened and the production progressed smoothly. Some of the department heads grumped about Lewton's attention to detail, which extended even to the credit titles. He insisted that the writing credit be changed to "Written by..." from "Original Screenplay by..." because it would make "a smoother and more tasteful title card." Having negotiated this alteration with the Writers' Guild, Lewton then had the writer's card moved from its customary position—preceding the technical credits—to appear between the credits for producer and director. Lewton believed that the writer should receive recognition on a higher par.

Lewton also insisted upon opening and closing the film with pretentious literary quotations—an uncommon delicacy, even among the more highfalutin' films. *Cat People* is prefaced by a passage from a fabricated work supposedly written by Tom Conway's Dr. Judd, *The Atavism of Fear.* "Even as fog continues to lie in the valleys, so does ancient sin cling

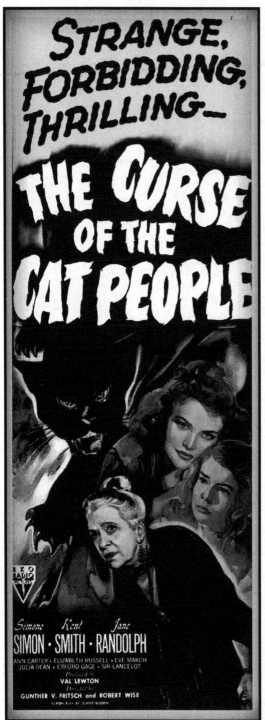

to the low places, the depressions in the world's consciousness." And in lieu of the traditional end title, a quotation from John Donne's "Holy Sonnet V" appears: "But black sin had condemn'd to endless night / My world, both parts, and both parts must die."

The preview was a resounding success—to the astonishment of most of the brass. It was decided, however, that the panther (represented in the preview version only by indistinct shadows) must be seen in the sequence where it threatens Oliver and Alice in his offices. Trainer Mel Koontz and a panther were brought in for one day of fiming. Tourneur's clever staging, compounded by Robson's cutting, make the three obligatory visions of the cat seem almost unreal, yet sufficiently palpable to satisfy the more literal-minded souls.

Cat People's $4 million–plus in paid admissions outgrossed many more self-important pictures in key cities. The film received critical acclaim and provoked enthusiasm within the industry. In a letter to Koerner, David Selznick said: "I wish that other studios were turning out small-budget pictures ... comparable in intelligence and taste..."

Cat People is hardly without flaws, of course. There are scattered awkward moments, and the Lewton–Tourneur team is a bit too archly Continental in manner to convey with thorough conviction the ordinariness of working folk. The film sets a classic standard, nonetheless, both in intrinsic storytelling value and as a turning–point in the genre—especially in the ability to establish a monster without thrusting the creature into the glare of daylight.

THE BLACK MENACE CREEPS AGAIN!

THE CURSE OF THE CAT PEOPLE

The basis is good–vs.–evil, but the telling is never so simplistic. Simone Simon's Irena is driven by forces beyond her control—as are most of the central characters in Lewton's pictures. A character in Lewton's *The Leopard Man* states the condition to perfection as he watches a bauble gyrating in the jet of a fountain: "We know as little of the forces that move us and move the world around us..."

Miss Simon captures Irena's ambivalence very well, building upon a naturally childlike charm. She conveys the fears that drive her, but only gradually does she betray any whiff of the sinister. Kent Smith and Jane Randolph seem sufficiently normal that the fantasy becomes all the more persuasive. Tom Conway makes a convincing Dr. Judd, bringing a sense of self-possessed crackpot authority to a role that could have been inexplicable if less forcefully played.

Both Nick Musuraca's photography and Walter Keller's sets are perfectly keyed. The interiors have the delicate shadings of a fine etching, with rich shadows and striking highlights. The exteriors convey a clear sense of the changing seasons crucial to the story, from a placid Indian summer through the rains, snows, and mists of winter.

The attention to sound engineering proves a worthwhile extravagance: The distant noises from the everpresent zoo animals; the foreboding echoes around the swimming pool; the urgent clacking of high-heeled shoes during a chase, then the sudden hush as that pursuit falls silent; the hiss of air–brakes on a bus at the instant one expects a panther to pounce—these are sounds married to the visuals to inspire unease, fear, anticipation, and shock. The bus effect proved so successful that Lewton would use variations over the longer haul. Whether the jarring intrusion came from a train, a horse, a tumbleweed, or an Apache warrior, Lewton called the effect "a Bus."

Roy Webb's music advances the sense of menace without calling attention to itself, adding immeasurably to the gathering atmosphere of dread. The scoring meshes with Musuraca's photographic style—and their teaming would be repeated. Particularly ingenious is the placement of Irena's delicate lullaby as a counterpoint to a heavily dramatic theme. The subtleties are too numerous to attempt to catalogue. There are, for example, the feline images that permeate the backdrops. The most prominent prop in Irena's apartment is a folding screen upon which an Art Deco panther slinks through a jungle, a motif introduced as a title background. A Goya print depicting a cat hangs in the apartment, and a florist's shop displays tiger lilies in its show–window. Alice, shuddering as she senses someone watching her, explains, "A cat just walked over my grave." Lewton himself professed "an atavistic fear of cats" and doubtless worked some of this phobia into the proceedings.

Lewton would deliver 10 additional pictures for RKO, all but two of them in this reinvented form of a genre that could only prove confining, his stylistic latitude adide. Among RKO's productions prior to Lewton, only two seem particularly to anticipate his arrival in terms of attitude or dreamlike style: These are Boris Ingster's little-known fantasia on serial murder, *Stranger on the Third Floor* (1940), with Nick Musuraca's camerawork, Roy Webb's music, and the surrealistic contributions of Vernon Walker's camera-

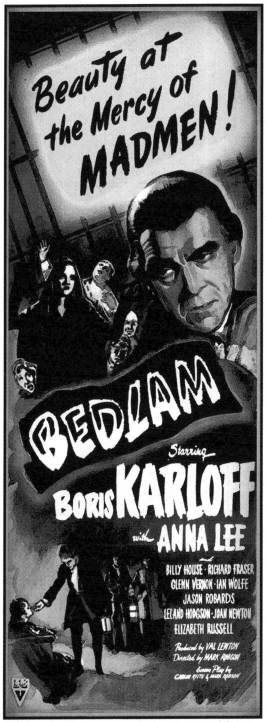

effects department and Linwood Dunn's optical inventions; and Orson Welles' heralded *Citizen Kane* (1941), with its collaborative mastery of the film-cutting art by Lewton's associates-to-be, Robert Wise and Mark Robson, as well as Walker's crew and Dunn's embellishments.

Lewton's style—never as a director, but consistently as a director of directors, and as a scenarist who seldom assigned himself a writing credit—is inimitable. The matter is self-evident in a comparative lack of imitators. Columbia Pictures' B–unit would approach the Lewton manner with Will Jason's *Faust*-themed *The Soul of a Monster* (1944). Likewise for Republic Pictures (a self-contained companywide B–unit, and proud of it), with Walter Colmes' witch-craft melodrama *Woman Who Came Back* (1945). Each such example recaptures the trappings of Lewton, with the literary pretensions and outbursts of philosophical, often stilted, dialogue, but neither possesses the guiding vision or the audacious confidence. (Robert Wise once told us his theory of Lewton-style distinctiveness: "It was all in the collaboration in pursuit of a single vision. All in the service of mustering the talents to make the best picture possible.")

Lewton's follow-through productions are, from 1943: *I Walked with a Zombie, The Leopard Man, The Seventh Victim,* and *The Ghost Ship*; from 1944: *The*

Curse of the Cat People, Youth Runs Wild, and *Mademoiselle Fifi;* from 1945: *Isle of the Dead* and *The Body Snatcher;* and from 1946: *Bedlam.* All were predicated, like *Cat People,* upon tasteful restraint (with welcome literalized exceptions, as in *The Leopard Man* and *The Body Snatcher*) and an assumption of intelligence among the paying customers. And as the titles suggest, most were exploited with the gaudiest of promotional hyperbole.

By the middle 1940s, Lewton had enjoyed as much as he could stand of RKO, its intrigues and ham-fisted marketing ploys. After Koerner died of leukæemia, Lewton gave up on the studio as a place to realize any larger ambitions. Never again would Lewton come so near to achieving creative fulfillment.

Lewton produced what he considered his least pictures (1948's *My Own True Love* [Page No. 28] and 1950's *Please Believe Me*) during stints with Paramount and MGM. His attempt to organize an independent production company collapsed in a series of disagreements. Only for his last production, a Technicolor Western called *Apache Drums* (1951; facing page), would Lewton return to the standards he had established at RKO. This gripping Frontier Gothic uses suspense, outbursts of terror, psychological insights, and technical artistry to tremendous effect. Lewton died of a heart attack in March of 1951 while handling a preproduction assignment with the Stanley Kramer Co.

Other key members of Lewton's RKO unit went on to illustrious careers. Jacques Tourneur (also of *I Walked with a Zombie* and *The Leopard Man*) became an acclaimed director of the *film noir* school and in 1957 delivered the English-made *Night of the Demon* (A.K.A. *Curse of the Demon*) in homage to Lewton. Mark Robson and Robert Wise, who started as film editors, eventually directed films for Lewton. Wise made his establishing mark as a replacement director amidships on *The Curse of the Cat People,* whose originally assigned director, the documentarian Gunther VON Fritsch, proved ill attuned to the speed required of a B–unit production. *The Body Snatcher* affirmed Wise's standing as a director, which was bolstered in turn by such exemplary assignments as *The Day the Earth Stood Still* (1951), *West Side Story* (1961), and *The Andromeda Strain* (1971), among an extensive rèsumé into the 21ST Century.

DEWitt Bodeen was promoted after writing *The Seventh Victim* and *The Curse of the Cat People.* He contributed scripts for many bigger pictures, including *I Remember Mama* (1947) and *Billy Budd* (1962). (Despite its title and the return of Kent Smith and Simone Simon, *Curse of the Cat People* is more a fugue than a sequel, centering upon a poetic fantasy about a child who conjures a ghostly Irena as a playmate.)

Bodeen termed *The Curse of the Cat People* overrated, adding: "Val and I had a dispute... [He rewrote] the ending I'd done. I think his ending [suggesting an imaginary basis for Irena's appearances] ruined it. I wanted it to be more supernatural, more of a horror story. Lewton resented being considered a horror specialist, I think, and he had even pressured the studio to change the title to *Amy and Her Friend.* No such luck, of course. This was a highly personal project for him, involving some emotional baggage between Val and his daughter. But horror was what he did best."

Lewton in 1944 summed up his approach for the newspapers. He was speaking of *The Seventh Victim*—a conspicuous flop, with the critics and the customers alike—but the description applies to *Cat People*:

"This picture's appeal, like that of its predecessors, is based on three fundamental theories. First is that audiences will people any patch of prepared darkness with more horror, suspense and frightfulness than the most imaginative writer could dream up. Second, and most important, is the fact that extraordinary things can happen to very ordinary people. And the third is to use the beauty of the setting and camerawork to ward off [an audience's] laughter at situations which, when less beautifully photographed, might seem ludicrous."

By such means did Lewton dramatize humankind's inborn Fear of the Unknown, of things imagined so intensely as to become perceptibly real. Through the resources of the cinema, Lewton expressed the primitive anxieties that abide in the most civilized souls amongst us.

(First composed as a chapter intended for the Price & Turner book Human Monsters: The Bizarre Psychology of Movie Villains *[1995]. The original draft dates from 1978, and after its removal in 1980 from the* Human Monsters *manuscript the piece was shortened—though padded with excerpts from other commentaries by Price & Turner—for a 1982 presentation in* Cinefantastique *magazine, timed to coincide with the release of Paul Schreoder's revisionist remake of* Cat People. *A successive version appeared with incomplete attribution as to sources and authorship in the 1989 anthology* The Cinema of Adventure, Romance, & Terror, *from A.S.C. Press. This appearance marks the text's first publication in an authentic form, as restored, revised, and expanded following the death of George Turner in 1999.)*

WALKING WITH ZOMBIES ON CAT FEET: AN ON-THE-SPOT MASS–MEDIA EXAMINATION OF THE FILMS OF VAL LEWTON

One doesn't ordinarily look to the mass-market slick magazines as a source of enlightenment on a specialized genre. Even a marginally smarter package like *Entertainment Weekly*, with all the resources of *Time* magazine at its disposal, will turn snarky and superficial at the drop of an assignment to consider anything remotely fantastic or chilling, especially if the topic happens to be a rediscovery from times past.

From times past, for that matter, might mean anything that was a Boy–Howdy Big–Deal New Release six months ago, as far as the shallow 'n' trendy sector of entertainment journalism is concerned. The lazy adjective *campy* often comes into play—a facile attempt to camouflage a writer's contemptuous failure to grasp any deeper qualities in the subject at hand. Such pernicious columnists of this hipper-than-thou bent will often label their work with a headline reading "Buzz," thereby proclaiming their gossipy intentions in a single irritating word.

Time was, as a schoolboy movie buff, when I used to feel a sense of vindication every time that *Life* or *Look* or *The Saturday Evening Posthole* would devote an article to the spookers. Karloff on a booshwah mainstream magazine cover? It happened, and it was some thrill. But I soon learned that such coverage served a maddeningly narrow range of purposes: There was the one extreme of gee-whiz journalism ("Hey! Wow! Holy Cow! Monsters Are Back in Style Again!"), which trivialized the topic with condescension. And then there was the other extreme of cautionary concern, which asked: "Are horror movies turning our young people into antisocial maniacs?" when it really meant: "Horror movies *are* turning our young people into antisocial maniacs!" Or words to that effect. You get the drift.

Now, granted, *Famous Monsters of Filmland* and its kind—ghettoized genre fare, like *True Detective* or *True West* or *True Confessions*, that nonetheless achieved massed newsstand distribution—were just

as superficial and prone to pandering, but at least they pandered in the right directions and a kid could ignore the fatuous captions, so often irrelevant and/or inaccurate, that befouled all those fascinating photographs. So barring the occasional dead-earnest scare-show piece in *Films in Review* or *Sight & Sound*, there was always a periodic(al) refuge from the slicker magazines' fashionably condescending disdain for Our Kind of Movies.

Lately [*during 2002*, I.E.] I've been cleaning out a wall's worth of file cabinets whose contents cover a 35-year collaboration that I conducted in partnership with the late film historian George E. Turner. Most of these files have gone into the completion of our final shared projects, an expanded edition of *Spawn of Skull Island*; and into new sequels, both completed and forthcoming, in the *Forgotten Horrors* series.

The file-sorting experience is a mixed bag of nostalgia, fresh insights, and occasional infuriated over–reactions. The latter is usually occasioned by a fresh reminder of George's entrenched habit of scissoring the film studios' pressbooks into scrapbook-style clippings but usually getting distracted before he could paste the pieces into any coherent order. Many of my own files, handed down from a theatre-manager uncle, suffered this well-intentioned process after George and I had pooled our resources. Tip the folder labeled *Tower of London*, and 500 slips of paper come sailing out like oversized confetti. Then multiply that experience by 24–someodd filing drawers, and here I've been, nostril-deep in paper, since George shuffled off this Mortal Coil in 1999.

Nice work if you can get it, though, and it is particularly pleasant to run across the random revelation where least expected. George had consolidated most of our *Human Monsters* files—that being the title of our 1995 book—into a dedicated staging area, containing even the selections that,

though considered and often acted upon, did not make the cut. Which is where Val Lewton's general output of WWII Era pictures comes in.

I hadn't re–examined our chapters on *I Walked with a Zombie* and *Cat People*—composed for *Human Monsters*, but removed early on from the playbill—since I had typed and proofed the final drafts during 1977–1978. And I had never seen this one particular file folder dealing with Lewton's groundbreaking productions of 1942–1946. It contains a photo-illustrated spread from a 1944 issue of *Collier's* magazine, and so I started to pass on reading through it.

But then the photographs (above) caught my attention: Here was Darby Jones as Carrefour, most prominent among the soulless stalkers of *I Walked with a Zombie*, but posed with an out-of-character expression of astonishment. (Jones' accompanying prop is a slave-ship figurehead from the film.) And here was Christine Gordon, as another of the death-in-life characters, but posed with a model, Gino Maxeur, who does not figure in the movie. These photos were unique to that publication, staged and shot by George DE Zayas. The *Collier's* article could only prove as lacking in depth as any other such slick-magazine article I had ever bothered to read—or so I thought—but even so, there seemed something extraordinary about it.

Which there was. The author is Barbara Berch, and for every too-clever quip she inflicts, she manages to say something substantial, if unwittingly so, about the way the earlier Lewton productions were perceived in their day among a theatregoing audience. In the main, this article called "Gold in Them Chills" articulates a popular view that took shape long before the Lewton films could become fodder for over-intellectualization among the Film Snob tribe.

And yes, it is as annoying to catch Robin Wood calling Lewton's films "at once a demonstration of the limitations of the *auteur* theory and its vindication" (say *what?*), as it is to find Barbara Berch, here, speculating with snide vapor–headedness on the potential for an *Andy Hardy*-like franchise in a sequel to *Cat People*. But so why take my word for it? If George Turner had a good reason for preserving the arti-

cle, then there must be a case for reconsidering it. The piece follows, with corrections and amplifications in brackets:

GOLD IN THEM CHILLS
WHAT HAPPENED WHEN HOLLYWOOD
DISCOVERED THAT PEOPLE WILL PAY
GOOD MONEY TO SCARE THEMSELVES SILLY

There's a new kind of horror picture nowadays [in 1944]— *snappy little spook shows full of beautiful girls and sharp dialogue, good food, and French lullabies* [a reference to a musical theme in CAT PEOPLE]. *They hide under fireside-chat titles like* Cat People, I Walked with a Zombie, [THE] Leopard Man, [THE] Seventh Victim, [THE] Ghost Ship, *and* [THE] Curse of the Cat People; *they're emancipating the tired spook-show formula by chucking the monsters and going in for class; and while they cost a niggardly (for Hollywood) $80,000 to make they gross over a million apiece.* [The Lewton budgets ran more toward the $100,000-$150,000 range, and the grosses as a rule were nearer the $3 million–$4 million bracket.] *We're packing the theatres to hair-raising capacity to see this new-type phenomenon that scares the living daylights out of us—quietly, gently, psychologically!*

They show us pretty girls changing into man-killing cats [CAT PEOPLE], *registered nurses who believe in zombies* [I WALKED WITH A ZOMBIE], *and gorgeous lady executives joining screwball societies dedicated to satanic pursuits* [THE SEVENTH VICTIM]. *At least we think they do—which is how these high-class horrors operate. They provide the overturned chair, the muffled footstep, the creaking door, the wild eye—then let our imaginations take over and do the real work.*

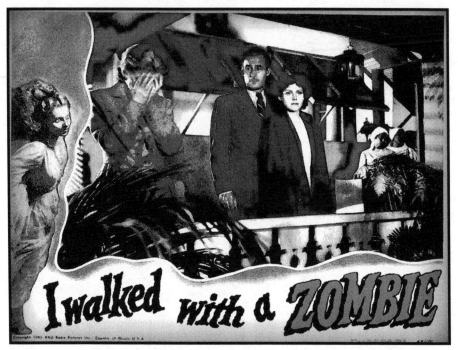

The psychological terror boys sneer at test-tube bloodsuck-ers, scrambled innards, and two-headed men. They use the old theory of mind–over–matter, remembering that an ounce of imag-ination is worth a ton of bleeding, biting, and scratching. The psychological horror show comes to life to make the rest of the industry admit that maybe there is something to this business of being subtle, after all.

The first of these brand-new scare shows [CAT PEOPLE] is about a beautiful lady dress designer [Simone Simon, yet unnamed at this point in the article] who picks up a guy [Kent Smith] in a park, invites him to her apartment for tea, falls in love with him, and marries him. Grisly? Not yet. It really gets grim on their wedding night when she tells hubby not to be mad if she doesn't let him kiss her. If he does, she's sure to turn into a cat and kill him.

TAKING A CHANCE ON LOVE

So he turns her over to a psychiatrist [Tom Conway] with an appreciative eye, who's willing to take a chance on being clawed to death. Comes the big love scene—then a strange little tinkle of music on dark film [the image darkens, but the screen does not actually go dark], a few discords—the psychiatrist is lying on the floor, good and dead, and the lady, who is now a cat [the film leaves this perception largely to the imagination], is making for the leopard cage at the zoo to commune with her relatives. Gay? [The author can only have used the term with its soon-to-be-archaic definition in mind.]

The latest, [THE] Curse of the Cat People, carries on where the starter in this collection of creeps left off and promises to *become another family affair, in chapters, like the* [Andy] Hardy *business.* [The author appears to be writing from no basis of familiarity with THE CURSE OF THE CAT PEOPLE beyond its title; the kinship is tenuous, despite recurring characters. The attempt at drawing a parallel with MGM's HARDY FAMILY series is an inspired moment of fatuous drivel.]

Under any other kind of treatment, these scripts would only be funny. In their present form, however, they're actually masterpieces of suspense and horror, because we're only allowed to see half of what we think we're seeing.

Val Lewton is the man responsible—for horror pictures with no horror to speak of. He's a nice fat fellow with kind eyes, a gentle voice, and a profitable feeling that audiences in wartime are essentially dotty, anyway. He also says we all have war jitters, "but you come to my movies, have a fine time killing people for me, then go home, worn out, tired and relaxed."

It started in a small office at RKO [RKO–Radio Pictures] *last year* [actually, early in 1942, two years before this article saw print] *when Charles Koerner, the boss* [newly appointed vice president for production], *cast about for a hypo to liven up the studio's dying product.* [In fact, RKO's B-as-in-budget movies were faring well enough to counterbalance the expensive flops, typified by Orson Welles' CITIZEN KANE of 1941—but the company needed more of the B–unit productions. CAT PEOPLE and a non-Lewton entry, HITLER'S CHILDREN, would tip the ledger decisively into the black.] *Koerner remembered a title he'd kicked around for years—*Cat People*—and presented it by memo to Val Lewton, a new producer on the lot. "Naturally, I was appalled,"* *Lewton admits.* [Another lapse of factuality: Koerner had come up with the title only recently, as a result of hearing a suggestion during a round of cocktail-party chatter that "nobody has done much of anything about cats." And Lewton kept his "appalled" opinion to himself for the time being, setting out to find or fabricate a story to suit the proposed title.]

He [Lewton] *called in DeWitt Bodeen, a writer, and Jacques Tourneur, a director, and the three of them worked out the story of Irina Barovna* [Irena Dubrovna, that is], *descended from the Mamelukes of Egypt, which, they chuckled, would mean cat blood in her veins. They cast Simone Simon as* [Irena], *peopled the rest of the film with good-looking Americans who spoke snappy language, and found a hollow-cheeked sylph named Elizabeth Russell to be Simone's sister cat.* [This "sister cat" role amounts merely to an unnerving cameo.]

PROVOKING THE IMAGINATION

They continued by throwing in the three fundamental fears: darkness, sudden sound, and wild animals. They pampered a tame leopard they'd hired from the Los Angeles Zoo by spilling perfume on his raw meat to provoke growling at the proper time. [Pure fabrication: The leopards used in various scenes were trained beasts hired along with trainer Mel Koontz, and Koontz was of course too much the professional to resort to provoking any desired reactions from his animals.]

Stage 8 was the noisiest on the lot, but 10 weeks later Mr. Koerner had his Cat People, *Mr. Lewton had a sizeable hike in*

pay, and the RKO investors were running their fingers through the cash and murmuring, "Gold!" [Extreme visualizations of this sort are typical of hacks pondering wealth and cultural significance such as they will never possess.]

The second brain–gnashing resulted in I Walked with a Zombie, and another gold rush to the box office—not only in theatres specializing in "Triple Horror Show Tonight," but in neighborhood houses where the whole family gathers. So the Lewton unit has been booming since then, turning out more like it. [The "boom" was not so pronounced with THE SEVENTH VICTIM, a conspicuous misfire with the critics and the customers alike.]

Lewton, himself, was born in Russia, lived there the first seven years of his life, then changed his address to West 10TH Street, New York City. At 17 he was writing poetry, at 18 he sold his first short story, at 22 he was writing four novels a year and came out with a book on Russian Cossacks. Then [producer] David [O.] Selznick, fingering Gogol's Taras Bulba with an eye to its filmability, sent out a call for writers who knew Russia. Up came Lewton, the least expensive of the two or three writers heard from, and forthwith drew a free ticket to Hollywood, with a one-day stopover in Chicago to see the World's Fair.

Selznick never made Taras Bulba, but Lewton stayed on in his keep for nine years—until RKO beckoned with a producer's berth. [Lewton, of course, had earned his way as a researcher, publicist and story editor, during which period he also established crucial connections with Tourneur and Bodeen.]

Lewton lives in a house at the beach with a wife, two children, two donkeys, a dozen chickens, five dogs, eight or nine *rabbits, a slew of canaries, and other miscellaneous livestock. Recently the neighbors gave Lewton 24 hours to dispose of his animal kingdom.*

"But I'll have to kill the chickens," he wept. "I can't do it..."

"I'll wring their ugly little necks myself," volunteered the lady who lived next door. And as she readied herself to invade the barnyard, she stood on tiptoe, pulled bogeyman Lewton's ear down to her size and came through with a blood-curdling "Boo!"

And here ends Barbara Berch's bold and incisive analysis, having written itself into a *cul-de-sac* of incoherent digression during those last few paragraphs. The fixed-in-time fascination of the piece, however, outweighs its essential silliness: It is a rare preserved reaction to Lewton at the very time when his radical reinvention of horror, Hollywood–style, was gathering momentum and identifying its strengths and limitations by provocative example. The distinction is that Lewton was concerned not so much with violence, as with the emotional consequences of violence.

DeWitt Bodeen told George Turner and me during the early 1980s about an early meeting with Lewton: "Val said there were only two kinds of horror picture. One is where they dispense the thrills so early in the film that the rest of it is all downhill. The other, the kind *we* made, is where you build your mood so carefully that the viewers begin to see, or to *think* they see, things that may or may not actually be there. The audience becomes involved in the telling of the story, at a personal level. Everyone is obsessed with one fear or another, and we helped them tap into those very personal obsessions in a communal experience of moviegoing."

The box-office failure of *The Seventh Victim* notwithstanding, Lewton remained a mainstay at RKO for a respectably lengthy stretch. He ascribed the chilly reception granted *Victim* to the film's uncompromisingly suicidal bleakness at a time when Homefront America preferred cathartic escapism, and he maintained a fondness toward the picture. *The Seventh Victim*'s Greenwich Village setting, he told Bodeen, reminded him of his carefree days as a young newspaperman at large in bohemian New York.

Lewton's persistent desire to work outside the genre yielded *Youth Runs Wild* (1944), a wartime tale of juvenile delinquency; and *Madamoiselle Fifi* (1944), based upon a pair of class-struggle stories by Guy DE Maupassant. And yes, Lewton had rendered *The Curse of the Cat People* more a poetic fantasy than a thriller, with its emphasis upon a lonely child's communion with the (real or imagined) spirit of Simone Simon's *Cat People* character.

Early during preproduction for *Curse*, Lewton wrote this memorandum to RKO's Charles Koerner: "What you will see will be, I hope, a rather tight-knit story about a child's friendship with a benign ghost, three horror episodes engendered by old legends (only one is now in the script; the 'Headless Horseman' episode), and finally a scene of great violence in which the ghost rescues the child."

Popular acceptance notwithstanding, Lewton found most of the show-business tradepapers hostile to his approach. To one early champion among the critics, James Agee of *The Nation*, Lewton wrote: "...you understand our problems and our shortcomings as well as our small triumphs over the type of material with which we had to deal."

DeWitt Bodeen said that much of Lewton's attempt to distance himself from horror pictures came as a reaction to scorn heaped upon

the genre from within Lewton's family: "His mother, who was a writer herself and a script appraiser at MGM, couldn't understand what Val was doing, making all those 'awful' pictures," said Bodeen. "And his aunt, a very important actress named Alla Nazimova, who was still active in films during Val's first few years as a producer—well, she seems to have found Val's work an embarrassment. So guess which member of the family is better remembered today."

With the generalized commercial success of his pictures, Lewton came ever more under the scrutiny of the RKO Suits: He had the blessing of the brass' full attention, and he had the curse of the brass' full attention. The death in 1944 of Charles Koerner, Lewton's unwavering ally, left Lewton feeling unprotected and (*per* DeWitt Bodeen) increasingly paranoid, especially as Lewton's own health began to falter. Lewton suffered a heart attack during the autumn of 1944. RKO accommodated his recovery by assigning him a ground-floor office, but his feelings of persecution increased to such a point that "he was just eager to get away from that studio—never mind where to," as Bodeen put it.

One of the earlier head-office impositions—in Lewton's opinion, according to Bodeen—was an assignment to work with Boris Karloff on three contracted pictures. "Val believed that Karloff was too solidly aligned with the more conventional type of horror film," said Bodeen, "but together they came up with some strikingly good work.

"Val was not happy with the Karloff assignment at first," Bodeen continued, "because of course Karloff's reputation with the more conventional types of horror had preceded him. RKO also had hired Bela Lugosi for work yet to be determined, and Bela's presence only compounded Val's unease. This one involved that R.L. Stevenson yarn, *The Body Snatcher*, which Val was to rewrite ... with Philip MacDonald.

But Val [found Karloff] just as eager as Val had been in 1942 to bring a new dimension to the spookers. Karloff was very keen on the assignment, and he recommended that Val add a role that [Bela] Lugosi could fill, as well.

"Karloff was having some very severe problems with his back at the time, but he never complained—relished the entire experience, so Val told me. Lugosi was not at all well, either, but he was very grateful for the assignment, and he and Karloff clearly enjoyed working together again," said Bodeen.

The Body Snatcher (1945), a vaguely fictionalized account of Scotland's notorious Burke & Hare case, turned out so well as to vie for supremacy among the Lewtons with *Cat People* and *I Walked with a Zombie* in a consensus of history. Lewton's second project with Karloff, *Isle of the Dead* (1945), concerns a small group of individuals stranded in uncomfortably close quarters during an outbreak of plague. The third, *Bedlam* (1946), takes place in an 18TH Century lunatic asylum where Karloff is the sadistic overseer. *Bedlam* also would mark Lewton's impatient exit from RKO.

Without Koerner's protective guidance and encouragement, Lewton had given up on the studio as a place to fulfill any larger ambitions. Never again would Lewton come so near to meeting his personal standards.

• • •

And a sidelight about Darby Jones (pictured at Page No. 40), from a provincial black-community newspaper of 1944, *The California Eagle*:

Twenty years is a long time for anyone to be engaged in a profession, but when the person is a young man in his early 30s, the record is all the more unusual.

Darby Jones, a native Californian who graduated from grammar and high school in Los Angeles, has been acting in motion pictures for over 20 years...

Recently Collier's Weekly, *widely circulated throughout most of the civilized world, featured a full-page spread on Jones as a sidelight on a type of picture that had been done experimentally and had caught on to the extent of several million dollars. Darby was featured in this picture, and his portrayal stood out and contributed more than any other factor in making the picture the great success it is...*

Yes, and how odd that the anonymous Afrocentric journalist neglects to mention the picture by either its title or its genre. The reference is to *I Walked with a Zombie*, of course, and damned if I know why the paper wouldn't just come right out and say, "horror movie." A "type of picture that had been done experimentally," indeed...

BOOLOO: A SACRIFICE UPON THE ALTAR OF SHOWMANSHIP

A popular fascination with the Third World—excepting, perhaps, the prospect of dirtying one's hands on poverty, disease, tribal unrest, and squalor—afflicts enough citified Westerners that there always has been a thriving market for trinkets, artifacts, and entertainment from the planet's more distant reaches. Hence such entrenched successes as *The National Geographic*, Pier 1 Imports, Inc., the global tour-package racket, and such rough-and-ready off-Hollywood filmmaking teams as those of Cooper & Schoedsack and Martin & Osa Johnson. Frank Buck brought 'em back alive, but most civilized consumers pre-

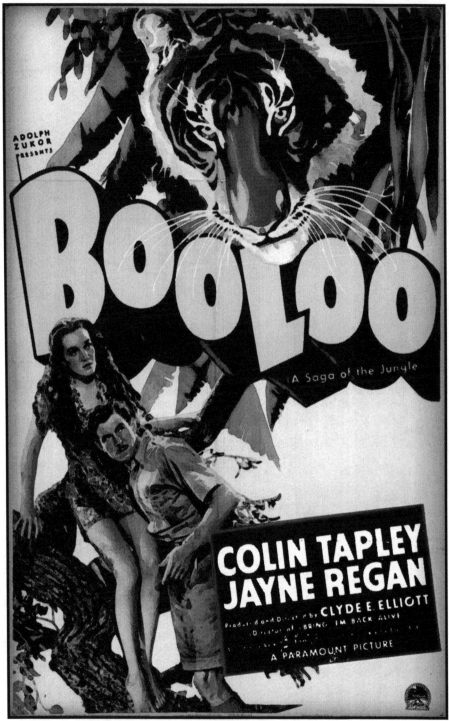

fer 'em brought back stuffed and mounted, acquired for pennies on the dollar, or captured on movie film. You may not be able to find jodhpurs, mosquito netting, and pith helmets any longer at your local Banana Republic Fashion Pit, but that refined state hardly alters the trendy company's origins as a glorified Army–Navy Store hawking surplus Equatorial gear. Pier 1 Imports, too, has gone the way of the dehydrated-fern centerpiece and the matched throw-pillow combination—Dust-Catchers "R" Us, now, that's more like it—while its picture-show counterpart, the big-screen safari into places barely touched by the Imperialist Colonizing Imperative, has evolved from menacing sensationalism to a sterile educational function.

It is not so much that interest has waned, as it is that gawking has become less fashionable. Much as the evocative term *jungle* has given way to the more polite and environmentally sensitive *rainforest* in the massed consciousness, so entire industries built upon the notion of plunder from forbidden lands have retooled themselves to offer bland travelogues and sanitized merchandise that *suggests* the Third World more so than it actually brings the Third World into your home. Harry Carey's rough-and-ready signature character, Trader Horn, would be appalled at the vapid antics of Steve Irwin's *Crocodile Hunter*—all due memorial respect.

Clyde E. Elliott's *Booloo* (Paramount; 1938) is consistent with the Sterner Stuff of Old Hollywood's safari-film tradition. Based upon ancient legends of tigers under demonic influence, Elliott's story (with screenwriter Robert E. Welsh) tracks the troubled progress of Capt. Robert Rogers of the British Army (Colin Tapley), whose book about an expedition conducted by his father meets with ridicule by the Imperial Exploration Society. Rogers sets out for Malaysia to vindicate his father's reputation by finding a white tiger known as Booloo.

A violent tribe, known to sacrifice virgins as appeasement for Booloo, decimates and scatters Rogers' troupe and disables his radio after a guide has sighted the elusive tiger. Rogers persists, having summoned a rescue squadron, and interrupts a sacrificial ritual—only to face a mauling from the tiger. Taken prisoner, Rogers faces peril anew from the tiger but is rescued by the hair's-breadth arrival of the Army. Firepower drives away the savages. The Official Account validates the extravagant claims of Rogers' book.

Surviving prints clock in at 61 minutes—a fraction of camera chief Carl Berger's 14 months of toil in the Malayan jungles north of Singapore. An early plot summary, published in *The Motion Picture Herald* in May of 1938, suggests a larger story (involving the sacrificial virgin, played by Mamo Clark) than that which made the final cut. Producer–director Elliott assembled the picture during March and April of 1938 at Paramount Pictures.

Thrills abound, barring some tedious establishing sequences that fail to match the tensions described in the spoken word. A purportedly ferocious water buffalo reacts indifferently to a lassoing by leading man Colin Tapley. The payoff comes from the fierce, indignant natives and an array of bone-crushing snakes. A contrived dramatic resolution, in which Tapley (no less indignant) confronts the stuffed-shirt members of the Explorers Society, plays out to satisfying effect.

HAL ROACH: THE MAN WHO MADE COMEDY SAFE FOR HORROR

Among the several artists who invented the way we look at movies, few survived to observe the consequences of their legacies with first-hand immediacy. Nat Levine, who boosted the star-driven action-adventure genre with a little-known player named John Wayne in 1932, lived to 89 in 1989—long enough to see that, for better or worse, there would have been no *Die Hard* without that influence.

Paramount Pictures' co–founder, Adolph Zukor, had passed a 103RD milepost at the time of his death in 1976. The Los Angeles *Times*' Charles Champlin tells of a friend's encounter with Zukor and another man over lunch: "'You know my kid,' Zukor said, by way of introducing his companion. His son was 75."

Closing in diligently, now [*in 1992, that is*], on Zukor's record for longevity is Hollywood producer Hal Roach, who turned 100 in January. As a guest at sessions of the USA Film Festival in Dallas, Roach devoted as much enthusiasm to constructive criticism of current moviemaking practices as to reminiscing about his own history.

"We were one of the biggest horror-movie factories in Hollywood," averred Roach, "right up there with Universal and Paramount and their ilk, 'cept Roach Studios is the outfit that made comedy safe for horror, back even before Universal set the bandwagon rolling with *Dracula* and *Frankenstein* [in 1931]. Always liked the creepy business, myself, because a terrified reaction by the right comedian can be as funny as a punchline or a pratfall. Like the times we turned Harold Lloyd or the *Roach's Rascals* kids loose in those creepy houses. [The allusion is to "Haunted Spooks" [1922] and an early-talkie *Our Gang* short, "Moan & Groan, Inc."] Or Thelma Todd and Patsy Kelly in 'The Tin Man,' which was our riposte to *Frankenstein*. Or Stan [Laurel] and Ollie [Hardy] in 'The Laurel–Hardy Murder Case' and 'Oliver the Eighth,' which traded on the creepy old-house tradition with a serial killer at large."

HAL ROACH *presents* HAROLD LLOYD

"if that isn't a spook it's a good imitation"

in HAUNTED SPOOKS (REISSUE) Pathépicture

Roach also detailed the surprisingly simple process by which he created the kid-comedy trademark known, variously, as *Our Gang, Roach's Rascals,* and the *Little Rascals.* And he removed a veil of mystery from his 1939–1940 collaboration with the pioneering screen director D.W. Griffith on a prehistorical fantasy called *One Million B.C.*—which history has long misinterpreted as a failed attempt at a comeback by Griffith.

In his productive prime from 1915 into the dawning mass-market television era of the 1950s, Roach's chief concern lay with making people laugh. Finding fault with the more purely physical comedy of his silent-screen rival Mack Sennett, Roach undertook early on to base his own pictures in storytelling values with empathetically identifiable characters. These many years later, Roach still analyzes the work of others—all heirs to his influence—with a critical eye.

"Comedy all boils down to how effectively you can tell a joke," said the man who discovered Harold Lloyd's comic potential and who harnessed the energies of two solo players, Stanley Laurel and Oliver Norvell "Babe" Hardy, into a team whose films are better known today than during their Depression Era heyday.

"You take two guys, each of them trying to tell the same joke," Roach said. "The first guy makes it short and to the point—timing being crucial—and gets such a good laugh that you're anxious to hear another one from him. The second guy, now, he's got the same joke, but he pads it out to where he loses the point... And before he reaches the punchline, even though it's a good joke, you're worn out from listening to this long-winded version."

Roach's allegory crystallizes a compelling theory of narrative comedy: "With the movies, you can't expect to make people laugh for longer than half an hour. Anything more is a filmmaker's conceit.

Murder afoot in the Dream State in Oliver the Eighth.

Now, I don't keep up with many of the films that are being made today—my hearing's not what it used to be," he paused to gesture to a hearing aid attached to each ear, "but I talk to the people who go to the movies, and the commonest complaint I hear is that practically all the films being made today—even the best ones—run 'way too long.

"And for a comedy, 'specially, two hours is too long. The two-reeler format was just right for most of our pictures, and when we made feature-length films we took pains to keep 'em short and direct." (A two-reeler runs under half an hour. Among the Roach studios' feature films, the Laurel & Hardy starrer *Way Out West* [1937] runs only 65 minutes; Roach's *Topper* entries [speaking of spookers] range in length from 85 to 97 minutes; and his production of *Of Mice and Men* [1939], a rare foray into sobering drama, clocks in at 107 minutes.)

"The advent of the dualer [double feature, *i.e.*], in the 1940s, is what knocked us out of the two-reeler business," Roach said. "Where we were stupid, was in our failure to move more promptly and aggressively into the development of the 40-minute short-feature comedy, which would have been natural because we had made the occasional three-reeler, almost that length, all along. This continues to interest me personally, because I believe the extreme standard length of a feature today is exhausting for the audience. An ideal presentation would be a 90-minute feature film, paired with a half-hour comedy. And so many of the comedy features they're turning out today have just about enough in the idea department to fill a two–reeler."

Harold Lloyd (1893–1971) had registered early on as an imitator of Charles Chaplin's Little Tramp character, but neither Lloyd nor Roach was satisfied with the portrayal. Discarding the customary toothbrush moustache and clownish wardrobe, Roach redefined Lloyd as an ordinary-looking sort whose trademark would be an oversized pair of spectacles. This notion of throwing an Everyman into outlandish situations—such as the famous clock-tower sequence in 1923's *Safety Last*—made Lloyd one of the more conspicuous originals of American comedy.

"The real difference about Harold Lloyd, you know, was that he was not a comedian," Roach said. "He was an actor *playing* a comedian. Harold would never ask us, 'Okay, now, what do I do next?' He

would ask, 'What does *he*, meaning his character, do?' And he made his character one of the great storytellers: If a script called for Harold to be in one room, here, and then in another room in the next scene, he wouldn't move on it until I had given him a transition, some bit of funny business, to move his character from one place to the other."

Roach cites no particular inspiration beyond logic for his formal teaming of Laurel with Hardy on a 1927 short called "Putting Pants on Philip." Said Roach: "The idea of playing a skinny guy and a fat guy off one another made sense on the surface of it. No one realized until it began happening what great geniuses these men were."

Roach attributes his development of the *Our Gang* ensemble to a reaction against a procession of prettified child players through his casting office: "There were all these Kid Star types and their stage–mothers coming through, early in the '20s, there," Roach said. "I became fed up with 'em—perfect makeup, eyelashes out to here, hair slicked back. They disgusted me, even though I knew there had to be a market for kid comedy.

"I had retreated to my office and was looking out the window into the alley below, behind a neighboring lumberyard. There, this band of neighborhood children was playing with these strips of lumber the company had trimmed off and thrown away. It was as though these sticks were swords, and the kids were having this life-or-death argument as to who was the owner of the longest of the sticks.

"So I was eavesdropping on this important occasion, as they took sides to decide what it was that had to be done to resolve the issue. By the time I tore myself away, 15 minutes had passed.

"Now, *there* was an inspiration. I had my idea for making kid comedy—just pay kids, not necessarily Kid Actors, to do what they do naturally, and you've got a fascinating movie." Roach's *Our Gang* prototype was the *Sunshine Sammy* series (1921–1922), starring Sammy Morrison, who became the anchor of a *Gang* ensemble recruited more for physical appearance and natural appeal than for proven talent. The series lasted more than 20 years, growing to include such household names as Matthew "Stymie" Beard and George "Spanky" McFarland, and retaining its unaffected charm until Roach sold the trademark to MGM Pictures in 1938.

Roach told an amusing story about his awkward transition from silent-film technology to the making of talking pictures during the late 1920s: "We were doing our first talkie, 'Hurdy Gurdy,' with Edgar Kennedy and Thelma Todd—our first talkie, and the first talkie I directed. We were viewing the first day's takes, and the projection room was absolutely packed. From the screen, from the loudspeaker, I heard a voice that wasn't supposed to be in the picture: 'That's good,' it said. Happened again on the second take: 'That's good!' I was getting annoyed. Happened again, third take: 'That's good!' Finally, I yelled to the projectionist, 'Stop! Who's that fool who keeps saying, "That's good'?" He yelled back, "Why Mr. Roach, that's *you*!' Which is how I learned to keep my big mouth shut when shooting the talking pictures."

The story of D.W. Griffith's late affiliation with Roach has provoked speculation since *One Million B.C.* arrived in 1940. The film, which stars Victor Mature, Lon Chaney, JR., and the tragic Carole Landis as tribal adventurers in conflict with nature and one another, holds up well despite its outlandish contradictions of natural history. The Conventional Wisdom holds that Griffith (1875–1948), whose monu-

LIFE WAS LIKE THAT IN ONE MILLION B.C!

Men Were Men-and Beasts Were Beasts-in Prehistoric Days when Giant Monsters Roamed the Earth

mental career had run aground with a disastrous picture called *The Struggle* in 1931, was meant to be the director of *One Million B.C.* and supposedly supervised portions of the film without acknowledgment.

"There's a very sad story about *One Million B.C.*," Roach said. Prefacing to his reply to a question about Griffith, the remark proved to be an illustration of Roach's playful theory of comedy timing.

"And the sad story is that we ran out of money to do the picture right," he continued. "It's a good enough picture, as far as that goes, but *so much of it* just doesn't look *real*.

"But, no," Roach continued, "a lot of people have insisted that I hired Griffith to direct *One Million B.C.* The story got out that I had hired him to direct and that he didn't work out and walked the assignment after handling a few scenes. And unfortunately, that story has persisted, with nobody ever bothering to ask me what really happened.

"I'd been friends with Griffith since the days when he was a Big Shot, and by the time we ended up working together I had got the impression that he was broke. I'd've liked to hand him some work, but Griffith was not a comedy director, and practically all we did was comedy."

Roach said *One Million B.C.* originated as a co-director assignment for himself and his son and partner, Hal Roach, JR. (1921–1972). Roach had long admired Griffith's genesis-of-man film, *In Prehistoric Days* (1913), to which Roach had paid spoofing tribute with a Laurel & Hardy comedy called "Flying Elephants" (1928).

"Because this *One Million B.C.* was a *dramatic* picture, I asked Griffith if he'd like to help out and got him put on the payroll. He was a consultant to us—helped design the rocks and cliffs, the sets that figure as a backdrop. Griffith was a tremendous influence, but he added nothing in any possible, any practical, way to *One Million B.C.* except helping me," Roach said. "And when the job was done, we parted ways cordially—because Griffith had no feel for the kinds of comedy we were doing."

Roach's appearances at that 1992 installment of the USA Film Festival included screenings featuring vividly remembered players—Harold Lloyd, Laurel & Hardy, Our Gang—as well as the since-obscure comedian Charley Chase. Roach's studio delivered vastly more films than are widely known today; his peak output of perhaps 50 comedies a year also included series that teamed Ben Blue with Billy Gilbert and

Thelma Todd with, by turns, ZaSu Pitts and Patsy Kelly. While practically every Roach production plays agreeably before a present-day audience, the transcendent pieces are the *Laurel & Hardy*s and the earlier *Our Gang*s.

"Why *is* that?" asked Roach, repeating a question posed to him while formulating its answer. "Well, the *Gang* kids were natural kids, for one thing. And Stan and Ollie—they were simply better than anybody before, or during, or after their time. Of *course* their pictures're going to hold up, after all of us are long gone."

He was correct, of course. Roach died later on that year, and even his more obscure comedies, including the *Taxi Boys* series (with Ben Blue and Bily Gilbert) and the Thelma Todd–Zasu Pitts–Patsy Kelly shorts, have persisted in cable-network and DVD presentations.

A highlight of that film-festival appearance was a reunion with George "Spanky" McFarland, one of the leading *Our Gang* personalities. Spanky told me, "Here I am, 64 years old, sitting across from a man who's 100 years old who probably still thinks I'm a little fat kid wearing knickers." McFarland hailed Roach's defiant insistence on having an integrated *Our Gang*, noting that the equally popular black players "were kids in the neighborhood. You didn't see a bus bringing them in. He didn't hire *actors*, he hired *kids*."

McFarland said he found Roach "a wonderful conversationalist. I'm glad I had those two hours."

(Originally published in a briefer version in the Fort Worth Star–Telegam, *1992. Additional conversations with Spanky McFarland can be found in our companion volume,* Thick Lights, Loud Smoke, and Dim, Dim Music: The Honky–Tonk Badlands of Texas.*)*

So Who Was This Kay Kyser, Anyhow? You'll Find Out

The Amazonian giant kept watch over the State Fairgrounds of Texas for generations—attracting, in turn, throngs of admirers during her heyday as a new work of monumental sculpture, but fading back into the fixtures as the times passed her by and her mighty Art Deco temple fell into neglect and near–ruin. Even when she was fresh from the unveiling, no one among the masses seemed particularly to wonder who her human model might have been. The mighty lady was just that imposing a figure, so ideally suited to the name Dallas had given her to commemorate a milestone in Texas' history: *Spirit of the Centennial*.

Friends and kin of the model, of course, knew the origins of the 16-foot work of statuary: Her inspiration was a local schoolgirl named Georgia Carroll, an ambitious beauty with an even more ambitious aunt who had pushed her into a competition to select a guide for Eleanor Roosevelt's visit to the Centenary State Fair of 1936. That honor eluded Miss Carroll, but an artist among the judges asked her to sit for a portrait.

The painter's attentions proved lasting, and when a larger project was undertaken to refurbish a 1910 Fairgrounds building in tribute to pioneering women, Miss Carroll was invited to pose for the pavilion's guardian monument. And so what has all this provincial history to do with James Kern "Kay" Kyser?

Well, meanwhile, the North Carolina-born Kyser was riding high as a Big Band impresario, approaching a mass-audience radio breakthrough with a mock-classroom quiz-show gimmick and edging toward the movies. Georgia Carroll was seeking a break on the fashion-model scene in New York. Conquer Madison Avenue and the Garment District, Miss Carroll's stage-motherly Aunt Edna reasoned, and

Hollywood can only be next. The paths of Kay Kyser and Georgia Carroll had yet to cross—although she certainly knew the music that would make him a household name—but their ambitions would turn the eventual connection into more than a mere crossing.

Kay Kyser (1905–1985) was a professorial Deep Southerner—serious of demeanor but frenzied of manner when struck by the spotlight—who made a dead-earnest living by acting the fool. His truer arena lay in the realms of the concert hall, the society-dance pavilion, network radio, and the 78-R.P.M. phonograph record. The tour bus was as much his home as the mansion he would build with a fortune in hit-song royalties, box-office revenues, and corporate sponsorships.

From the waning 1930s into the post-WWII years, Kyser charted with 11 No. 1 hit records (including "Praise the Lord and Pass the Ammunition" and "The Woody Woodpecker Song") among 35 Top Ten releases. His seven feature films landed him among the heavy-duty likes of Boris Karloff, Bela Lugosi, Peter Lorre, Lucille Ball, and John Barrymore. A radio program, *Kay Kyser's Kollege of Musical Knowledge*, lasted 11 years (beginning in 1938) as an NBC–Radio moneymaker, then made a tentative leap to television—only to lapse permanently when confronted with a sponsor's wife who fancied Kyser too much the goof for her own snooty tastes. And popular appeal be damned.

Whereupon Kyser quit the unappreciative racket. He retired at age 45 in 1950 with no formal announcement—went home to North Carolina, there to immerse himself in family life, church leadership, and public service. He died in 1985, right around the start of a swing-music revival that found such bands as Big Bad Voodoo Daddy and Red Young & the Red Hots invoking much of the spirit and manner of Kyser's music, though with scant popular acknowledgment of the source.

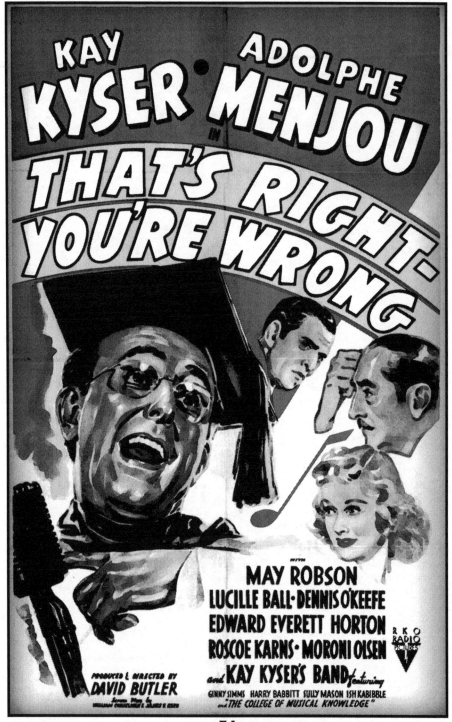

KAY KYSER • ADOLPHE MENJOU

in

THAT'S RIGHT- YOU'RE WRONG

with

MAY ROBSON
LUCILLE BALL • DENNIS O'KEEFE
EDWARD EVERETT HORTON
ROSCOE KARNS • MORONI OLSEN
and KAY KYSER'S BAND featuring

GINNY SIMMS HARRY BABBITT SULLY MASON ISH KABIBBLE
and "THE COLLEGE OF MUSICAL KNOWLEDGE"

RKO RADIO PICTURES

PRODUCED & DIRECTED BY
DAVID BUTLER

Screen Play by
WILLIAM CONSELMAN & JAMES V. KERN

Though hardly a post-retirement recluse, Kyser made it plain that he preferred to speak of his projects on behalf of Christian Science and the Public Broadcasting Service rather than lunch out on Show Business Nostalgia. His antic wit remained intact. When named president of the Worldwide Church of Christian Science in 1983, Kyser jokingly cautioned the press not to make too big a deal of the story: "It's an honorary title. I haven't been elected Pope or anything."

That refusal to take himself too seriously served Kyser well as a Hollywood personality. Like fellow bandleaders Spike Jones, Cab Calloway, and Phil Harris, Kyser was so secure in his managerial skills and his mastery of jazz-inspired pop music—and so confident in the artistry of his featured players—that he could trade upon a cornball crowd-pleasing stage presence. Swingmasters Benny Goodman and Glenn Miller seemed dour by comparison. Come to think of it, Goodman was a grouch and proud of it.

Kyser's début film, the Hollywood-on-Hollywood spoof *That's Right— You're Wrong* (1939), originated as a response by RKO–Radio Pictures' David Butler to the popularity of Kyser's NBC–Radio broadcasts. (The title is one of Kyser's catch–phrases from his quiz-contest segments; Kyser tended to play himself, more or less, in the movies—although "himself," in the popular view, was alien to the serious nature that drove Kyser's backstage dealings and his private life.) Kyser shares top billing in *That's Right* with Adolphe Menjou, who plays a conniving producer intent on casting the folksy Kyser against type as a Latinate romancer. Kyser calls Menjou's bluff and tackles the preposterous role, humiliating the producer and then abandoning Hollywood for his home turf in Rocky Mount, North Carolina. Lucille Ball co–stars.

Although Kyser never lost touch with his rural origins and would continue to exploit the rustic image of Rocky Mount (his actual birthplace), he also had better sense than to quit the Major Leagues amidst such high promise. His second film, the RKO production of *You'll Find Out* (1940), is a more assured effort, with Kyser at his most rambunctious, a classic-manner Old Dark House setting, and an agreeably sinister backup cast including Boris Karloff, Peter Lorre, and Bela Lugosi. Kyser bandsman Ish Kabibble, with his pudding-bowl haircut and his air of childlike indignation, supplies a generous measure of slapstick comedy.

"The word that fits Kyser to a *K* is *corn*...," reads a fan-magazine article from 1940, touting *You'll Find Out*. (And pity the theatre manager who, when obliged to field questions of what was playing, had to answer, "*You'll Find Out*," and try to keep a straight face in the bargain.) Adds the publication: "*Hokum* was a good enough word for Grandpa but would never adequately describe Kay, Ginny Simms, Ish Kabibble, Harry Babbitt, and the rest of Mr. Kyser's remarkable cross between a dance orchestra, an amateur hour, a spelling bee, and the grammar-school boys back in Rocky Mount, North Carolina, cutting up on Halloween with stolen corsets and kazoos...

"*You'll Find Out* gains no little of its charm from the presence of Bela Lugosi, Peter Lorre, and Boris Karloff, who are almost as cute as Mr. Kyser's makes-you-want-to-dance music...," this piece of fatuous hype continues. "[T]he audience is one minute scared out of its pants by Lorre, Lugosi and Karloff, and the next is soothed by Kyser's rippling Dixie drawl..." History tends to lump together *You'll Find Out* and Columbia Pictures' *The Boogie Man Will Get You* (1942) as a waggish summit meetings of Hollywood's more famous horror-movie actors. The pictures are, however, distinct and unrelated products save for their shared teamings of

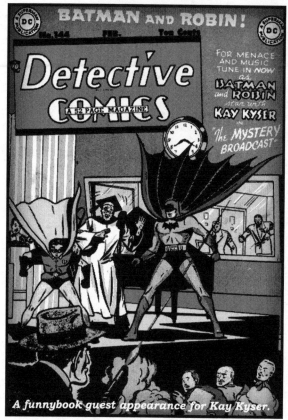

A funnybook guest appearance for Kay Kyser.

Boris Karloff and Peter Lorre. Bela Lugosi further distinguishes *You'll Find Out*, completing the triumvirate of the talking-picture era's pioneering bogeymen.

The larger point of *You'll Find Out* is to showcase Kyser's ersatz-jazz shenanigans. The critic–historian Phil Hardy goes so far as to declare Kyser the most horrifying thing about *You'll Find Out*. Kyser is an acquired taste, all right, but a natural for the cameras—and a delight for those who have acquired the taste. The Lorre–Lugosi–Karloff teaming is a marvel, of course, holding forth in a gloomy mansion—where the Kyser orchestra has conveniently been engaged to perform— and plotting the murder of an heiress (Helen Parrish) for the customary reasons. Kyser even gets to play the hero, ordering a séance to smoke out the menace(s) and finally tackling Karloff when the badman resorts to gunplay.

The sprightly musical selections issue from the team of Jimmy McHugh and Johnny Mercer. Art director Van Nest Polglase, orchestral composer Roy Webb (also of the Val Lewton unit at RKO), and camera artists Frank Redman and Vernon Walker provide as unnerving a labyrinth, as foreboding a strings-and-horns backdrop, and as dark and stormy a night as ever graced any more straightforward chiller. Karloff, Lugosi, and Lorre guest–starred on Kyser's radio show in support of the picture.

The third Kyser feature, *Playmates* (RKO; 1941), pitches Kyser and a self-mocking John Barrymore as the stars, with featured billing for vocalist Ginny Simms. The screenplay rather cheekily portrays Barrymore as a has–been, and indeed the Great Actor and notorious wastrel had by now found himself reduced to a caricature. The motivating gimmick requires an impatient Barrymore to coach Kyser in the finer points of Shakespearean delivery. Kyser responds in his customary Dixieland twang. *Playmates* boasts perhaps the most bizarre romantic triangle ever captured on film, with Lupé Veléz as a passionate bullfighter torn between Barrymore and Kyser. All ends agreeably for all concerned, and Kyser manages a musical mangling of Shakespeare with a song called "Romeo Smith & Juliet Jones." (Earlier in 1941, Kyser's band took an extended showcase sequence in an installment of the *Hedda Hopper's Hollywood* short-film series.)

The fourth, and the silliest, of the Kyser films is *My Favorite Spy* (RKO; 1942), not to be confused with a like-titled Bob Hope starrer of

1951. Here, Kyser finds himself drafted—and not merely into the Army. The conscription proves to be a case of mistaken identity, but Kyser is invited to become a Military Intelligence agent, with orders to crack a spy ring operating out of the very ballroom where the Kyser orchestra is performing. In the Real World, Kyser was a bit long in the tooth for the draft; he had begun a regimen of wartime service, at any rate, by becoming one of the first celebrities to donate entertainment as a morale–booster for enlisted personnel. By 1943, Kyser had sworn off accepting new commercial engagements, using his radio program, his military-base appearances, and his movie contract to promote the Hollywood Cavalcade War Bonds Drive.

Georgia Carroll had become a familiar advertising image and cover girl for the slick magazines, and at length a Hollywood starlet and aspiring singer. Miss Carroll joined the Kyser War Bonds troupe early in 1943, in time to take a featured turn in Kyser's fifth feature–lengther, *Around the World* (RKO; 1943–1944). Kyser had lost several years' worth of orchestral arrangements in a touring-bus fire in 1942, and several of his musicians had gone into uniformed service. Kyser used these crunches to reshape his style along harder-edged swing-band lines; the fresh approach shows in *Around the World.* The title describes a slapstick travelogue that draws tension from a battle of wits between Kyser and the droll comedian Mischa Auer. Miss Carroll has a memorable duet with Harry Babbitt on the Jimmy McHugh–Harold Adamson tune "Candlelight and Wine." (Guest appearances by the Kyser ensemble grace two other pictures from 1943: *A Rookie & His Rhythm* and *Thousands Cheer.*)

MGM Pictures lured Kyser away for 1944's *Swing Fever*—a grand title for an ineptly mounted spoof of prizefighting and pop music. Kyser plays a small-town maestro who possesses some strange hypnotic power and fancies himself a serious classical composer. The entertainer musters an adequate heroical/romantical/comical presence but seems ill at ease with the requirement that he subdue his familiar stage-and-radio personality. The assignment would have better suited a Danny Kaye or a Joe E. Brown.

MGM let the option lapse to Columbia Pictures for a final Kyser feature, *Carolina Blues* (1944). Kyser returns to portraying himself. Georgia Carroll's self–portrayal is more of a fiction: Where she and Kyser had married in June of 1944, the movie finds her contemplating retirement from Kyser's orchestra in order to marry an Army officer. The finale imagines Kyser's return to North Carolina—more prophetically, this time, than the ending of *That's Right—You're Wrong.*

"Kay always said that, if it all should cease to be fun, why then, he'd go right back to where he'd come from," Georgia Carroll Kyser said during the late 1990s. "The end of the war, I think, left him feeling that his work in show business was pretty much over and done with, but he had old-time band members returning from the service overseas and ready to get back in harness, and he had long-term contracts in need of honoring."

During the immediate postwar years, Kyser began curtailing his participation; his name–recognition was enough to buoy the radio show and the recording deals. He took up philanthropic activities in earnest. Before his long involvement with the Christian Science movement—which he had joined in the hope of finding relief from a back ailment that had defied conventional medicine—Kyser helped to finance an expansion of St. John's Hospital in Santa Monica. Kyser traveled widely as a lecturer on Christian Science during the 1970s.

He remained fond of discussing the Big Band days as a sidelight but showed no interest in reviving that career.

"The times were magical for all of us," as vocalist Harry Babbitt has recalled in times more recent. "As such, they were simply too fine to last." Babbitt, who doubled as a romantic crooner and a falsetto-voiced novelty singer, took his act solo after Kyser's retirement and became a mainstay of Steve Allen's groundbreaking television programs. Babbitt remained active as a performer into advanced age.

Featured vocalist Ginny Simms, who died in 1994, fared well as a solo act after the boss' retirement but eventually became a real-estate investor. Original Kyser bandsman Sully Mason, a saxophonist and eccentric vocalist, found the going more difficult in the post-Kyser days; he died during the 1970s. Ish Kabibble, né Merwyn Bogue, became a busy Las Vegas entertainer with his Dixieland ensemble, the Shy Guys. His autobiography, published in 1989, explains the mystery of his nonsensical-sounding stage name: *Ish Kabibble* derives from the Yiddish expression *ische ga bibble?*—meaning, essentially, "What? Me worry?" This attitude was appropriated during the 1950s by *MAD* magazine as a motto for its Ish Kabibble-like fictitious mascot, Alfred E. Newman. The genuine Ish died in 1994.

The restoration in 1999 of Dallas' long-neglected *Spirit of the Centennial* statue (and an adjoining exposition hall) led to the rediscovery of Georgia Carroll Kyser. Her connection with Kay Kyser, though essential to the resulting news stories, provoked somewhat less of a thrill of rediscovery among the trend-gawking Mass Media. One vapid mock–journalist from Dallas' hip-'n'-with-it *D Magazine*, assigned to cover the development from a historical vantage, was heard to respond: "Kay Kyser? Never heard of her."

Mrs. Kyser proved philosophically aware of the anti-celebrity bug that had transformed Kay Kyser from fame to obscurity during his lifetime: Lose the spotlight, and the spotlight might never again find you.

"I really did find it admirable," Mrs. Kyser said, "that Kay took that never-look-back stance when he broke ranks with show business. But that hasn't kept me from looking back, and in looking back I can see that he really deprived the culture of a lot of the fun of the Kyser orchestra's music—and deprived himself, in the bargain. It was vital, that music, and I only wish now that Kay had kept himself more visible, retirement or no retirement."

SHERLOCK HOLMES & THE AFFAIR OF THE APOPLECTIC ADAPTATIONS

No sooner had Sherlock Holmes proved himself a viable dramatic property, than the movie versions began cropping up. "Sherlock Holmes Baffled," a vignette photographed during April of 1900 and released the following month, holds pride of place, but the film scarcely does the character justice: A burglar rifles Holmes' household and vanishes into nothingness, then reappears for an impudent getaway.

The next known Holmes effort, "Adventures of Sherlock Holmes," is—or *was*, given its status as a lost film—a one-reeler bearing a 1905 copyright. An Italian series dates from 1907–1913. Others, better attuned to the Holmes mystique and blessed with more generous running times, would crop up soon enough. "Sherlock Holmes in the Great Mystery" (Crescent Film Co.) and the Danish-made "Sherlock Holmes" (Nordisk Films Co.) arrived late in 1908 and yielded two sequels dur-

From the Viggo Larsen series.

James Bragington.

ing the first quarter of 1909: "Sherlock Holmes II: Raffles Escapes from Prison" and the apostrophe-deficient "Sherlock Holmes III: The Detectives Adventure in the Gas Cellar."

Star player and writer–director Viggo Larsen would take this Nordisk series through six entries by the year's end, capping his tenure as Holmes with a takeoff on *The Hound of the Baskervilles* called "The Grey Lady"—which substitutes a ghostly woman for the familiar devilish dog. Nordisk carried on capably enough with Alwin Neuss in lieu of Larsen, but Larsen's departure left Holmes less well represented on screen until 1914, when Neuss would come into his own as Holmes.

Harry Benham.

William Gillette's screen début, reprising a stage role (Page No. 62), occurred in the Essanay Company's *Sherlock Holmes* of 1916, by which time other talents had delivered many varying impressions of Holmes. Harry Benham starred in "Sherlock Holmes Solves the Sign of the Four" (1913), a two–reeler described in one review as "intensely fascinating." Two distinct versions of *A Study in Scarlet* (one English, the other American) date from 1914. To say nothing of adaptations of *The Hound of the Baskervilles*.

The U.K. *Scarlet*, from the Samuelson Company, gave Great Britain its first feature-length indigenous production. G.B. Samuelson drafted his Birmingham-based comptroller–of–accounts, James Bragington, to impersonate Sherlock Holmes. Holmes figures but marginally in the free-handed appropriation of Doyle. (A second

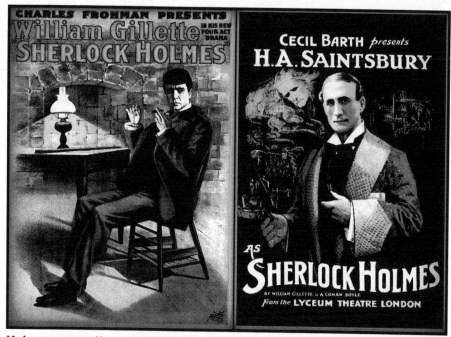

Holmes-according-to-Samuelson film, 1916's *The Valley of Fear*, would star H.A. Saintsbury, a stage-based Holmes of less prominence than the signature player Gillette.)

The American "A Study in Scarlet" (Gold Seal–Universal) came about almost simultaneously as a self-starring director assignment for Francis Ford, elder brother of John Ford and in his own day quite as prolific and formidable a filmmaker. The Ford version runs a brisk 20 minutes.

We should skip over a great deal of the rest, for the point here is more of a preamble and less of a laundry–list, with the main idea of getting at the most peculiar of the Holmes films from the early-talkie era, Edwin L. Marin's *A Study in Scarlet*, from 1933. But context is crucial—and what *aficionado* of detective movies can resist a reminder of the epic-calibre tangle that is Germany's *Hound of the Baskervilles* saga?

Der Hund von Baskerville (1914) is a two-part serial from the Vitascope Company (together clocking in at two hours), whose first installment accounts for a reasonably true-to-Doyle adaptation—as though fidelity to the source would make up for a failure to secure the author's permission. Holmes' colleague, Dr. John Watson, is written out altogether, but Richard Oswald's screenplay compensates with a solid emphasis upon Holmes (played by the stocky but vigorous Alwin Neuss, from the final Nordisk pictures) and a fiery depiction of the gigantic dog whose presence portends doom. Karl Freund, a mainstay–to–be at Universal Pictures, photographed the opening 65-minute installment.

Der Hund von Baskerville's Part No. 2, *Des Einsame Haus*, catches up with the culprit (Friedrich Kuehne) upon his escape from prison. The schemer builds an elaborate trap, only to succumb as a consequence of Holmes' intervention. Director Rudolph Meinert became chief of production for Germany's Decla Film combine, where he helped to develop Robert Weine's *The Cabinet of Dr. Caligari* (1919).

John
Barrymore
in
SHERLOCK
HOLMES

Directed by Albert Parker. Adapted from
William Gillette's stage play founded on
Sir Conan Doyle's stories

A Goldwyn Picture

Producer Josef Greenbaum knew a good thing when he stole it. Having dodged Conan Doyle's copyright lawyers through two successful *Baskervilles* features, Greenbaum now snatched the purloined property away from the influential Vitascope Company and formed his own production outfit—taking along star player Neuss and others from the ensemble cast, along with scenarist Oswald. At the doubly crooked new Greenbaum Film Company, Oswald was promoted to writer–director for a third *Der Hund von Baskerville* (*Das Unheimliche Zimmer;* 1915), in which the villainous Friedrich Kuehne proves to have survived. A Part No. 4, *Die Sage von Hund*, serves as what nowadays would be called a prequel, an explanation of the origins of the ghostly hound.

Vitascope, which had changed its named to PAGU, was not to be hoodwinked: The company, suddenly in unwanted competition with the defectors Greenbaum and Oswald, countered in 1915 with *Der Hund von Baskerville: Das Dunkle Schloss*, installing Eugen Burg as Holmes and re-enlisting Kuehne. PAGU lodged criminal and civil complaints against Greenbaum, whose maverick *Baskervilles* pictures were as a result banished from distribution until after the end of World War I. Vitascope/PAGU remained unapologetic as to its own piracy of Conan Doyle.

Josef Greenbaum, however, was patient, and relentless. In 1920, he re-launched a *Baskervilles* series, with a Part No. 5 (*Doktor MacDonald's Sanatorium*) and a Part No. 6 (*Das Haus Ohne Fenster*). When released the following year, these final installments were met with renewed competition from PAGU, which took a line of lesser resistance by recutting its two-parter of 1914 into a self-contained feature.

During 1921–1923, Eille Norwood played Holmes in an ambitious slate of 47 films, cinching a distinctive vision of the detective ("My idea of Holmes

CONAN DOYLE'S Master Detective **SHERLOCK HOLMES** with **CLIVE BROOK** Miriam Jordan Ernest Torrence
FOX PICTURE

is that he is absolutely quiet. Nothing ruffles him.") and learning such finer characterizing points as the correct handling of a violin. John Barrymore brought a better-established star power to the Goldwyn Company's *Sherlock Holmes* in 1922 (preceding page); the same year saw a superficial spoofing in Metro's *Sherlock Brown*, and in 1924 Buster Keaton delivered a more focused parody in his Metro production of *Sherlock, Jr.*

The numerous Holmes portrayals of Clive Brook and Arthur Wontner during the Depression years are of course stories for another day—and they receive a satisfying attention on the Web at www.mycrofts.net— while the Basil Rathbone series gets a fair say in the accompanying chapter (Page No. 67). Which brings us to that most anomalous of the talkie-era Holmes pictures, the 1933 *A Study in Scarlet.*

The KBS/World Wide production of *Scarlet* stands apart, barely touching upon the Doyle novel though made with authorization. Holmes and Watson bear no resemblance to the popular image, with Reginald Owen cutting a portly figure as Holmes and Warburton Gamble cutting a leaner, almost severe, figure as Watson. Just the previous year, Owen had played Watson to Clive Brook's Holmes in a Fox production of *Sherlock Holmes*. Somebody forgot to remind this *Scarlet*'s screenwriters—Owen and intended director Robert Florey— that Holmes resides at 221B Baker Street, for the reference here is to 221A. And when Holmes refers to his unwelcome colleague from Scotland Yard, Inspector Lestrade (Alan Mowbray), the name is pronounced with an unaccustomed long *A.*

Such discrepancies aside, this *Scarlet* is a satisfying twist, with enough touchstones to Doyle to qualify as a Holmes adventure and capital performances all 'round. The larger departures are easily explained: The studio had obtained the rights to only the title, then paid Florey and

Owen $1,000 to deliver an original screenplay. The story has to do with an exclusive club, the Scarlet Ring, whose dwinding ranks benefit from each new death of a fellow member. Eileen Forrester (June Clyde), whose father is among the deceased, senses foul play and finds herself requiring a rescue. The ringleader is one Thaddeus Merrydew (Allan Dinehart)—in Holmes' words, a "gliding, slimy, venomous snake."

The idea of serial murder in close quarters has been mistakenly cited elsewhere as a crib from Agatha Christie's *Ten Little Indians*, A.K.A. *And Then There Were None*, but Florey and Owen were far ahead

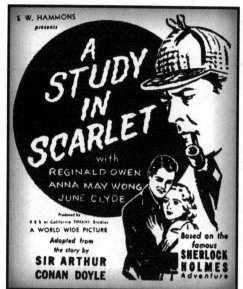

E. W. HAMMONS
presents

A STUDY IN SCARLET

with
REGINALD OWEN
ANNA MAY WONG
JUNE CLYDE

Produced by
K B S at California TIFFANY Studios
A WORLD WIDE PICTURE

Adapted from
the story by
SIR ARTHUR
CONAN DOYLE

Based on the
famous
SHERLOCK
HOLMES
Adventure

of the overrated Dame Agatha: Her novel was six years away, and its stage adaptation would not come for another decade, then finally reach the screen for the first of many times in 1945.

Florey had estranged himself from Universal Pictures with an angry reaction to his removal from *Frankenstein* (1931), compounded by a rudeness toward the big-boss Laemmle family during his consolation assignment, *Murders in the Rue Morgue* (1932). The *Scarlet* job was a descent from the major leagues—even though the modest production would wind up as a Fox release—and Florey was grateful to have it. Not so grateful, however, that he could resist a conflicting offer from Warners, which led Florey instead to the 1933 productions of *Girl Missing*, *Ex–Lady*, and *The House on 56TH Street*. This departure opened an opportunity for Edwin L. Marin, who had scored in 1932 with *The Death Kiss* for KBS/World Wide. Marin tackled *A Study in Scarlet* with a ferocious momentum and a taste for idiosyncratic characterizations and foreboding atmosphere.

Scarlet also benefits from the evocative cinematography of Arthur Edeson. Edeson had distinguished *Frankenstein* and *The Old Dark House*, among many others. London's fogbound Limehouse district has seldom looked so grotesque, or so picturesque, and the interior studies of a menacing countryside mansion, with its hidden rooms and dizzying angles, are ideal. Likewise of major-studio calibre are Ralph DeLacy's settings. These are used to best collaborative effect when Edeson places a subjective camera in the role of the killer as he calls upon an accomplice. "The setting of a mystery story," Edeson said at the time, "is obviously the most perfect medium for experimentation with strange camera angles and tricky lighting effects."

Though far removed from Doyle, the complex story is rich in details from the canon: "Quick, Watson—the game is afoot!" is uttered at precisely the correct moment. Holmes is properly nasty toward his usual foil, Lestrade, played as a well-meaning, self-important bumbler by Alan Mowbray. Warburton Gamble nails Watson's level-headed manner with an efficient brusqueness. Anna May Wong, radiant with the æthereal qualities of her Chinese ancestry, is a perfect *femme fatale*. And the stage veteran and playwright Allan Dinehart makes a fine stand–in for Prof. Moriarty, smoking the correct Doyle-calibre Trichinopoli cigars and warning his intended victim (June Clyde) that "this is a very wicked world we're living in," even as he maneuvers her toward a taste of that very wickedness. The verbal sparring between Owen and Dinehart is right up to snuff, and Owen is perfectly shrewd and analytical, even in the tightest of scrapes.

(Originally composed for Mad about Movies *magazine [2001], this account amplifies a chapter in* Forgotten Horrors: The Original Volume—Except More So.*)*

IN WHICH UNIVERSAL PICTURES REINVENTS SHERLOCK HOLMES, AND VICE VERSA

...But still the game's afoot for those with ears
Attuned to catch the distant "View–Haloo!"
England is England yet, for all our fears—
Only those things the heart believes are true...
Here, though the world explode, these two survive,
And it is always 1895.
—FROM VINCENT STARRETT'S "221B"

One of the most meaningful declarations in the canon of lore surrounding Sherlock Holmes occurs not in the writings of Conan Doyle, nor even in a massive body of dramatizations dating from the turn of the 19TH Century into the 20TH. The poet, author, and Holmes scholar Vincent Starrett distilled that fascination to an essence in just half a couplet: "It is always 1895." Starrett would have a great deal more to say about Holmes over the longer haul, but this one line resonates over all else.

Yes, and never mind that the year of 1895 is entirely arbitrary as a linchpin of the era of Holmes & Watson—who require no further introduction—though quite within the characters' range of aggressive sleuthery. The year not only enables a rhyme within Starrett's context; it also establishes a state of mind crucial to the popular acceptance of Doyle's Victorian mythology as relevant beyond its day. Thus frozen in time, the creation proves timeless.

It is but a coincidence that Starrett's sonnet, "221B," first saw print during the same year that Universal Pictures appropriated the *Sherlock Holmes* franchise for a series that would swell to contain a dozen movies. If Universal's point in 1942 was to modernize Holmes and his circle as agents in conflict and/or cahoots with the Axis Powers, then the abiding spirit of Holmes assured that—superficial modernism be damned—an 1895 attitude would prevail.

Arthur Conan Doyle cannot have reckoned with the power of cinema to impose its own peculiar values: Filmmaking at his turn of the century was still a medium of vignettes, with a fully fledged novelistic storytelling function yet to develop. And of course the resourceful innocence of Doyle's Great Detective still plays out most impressively upon the printed page. Holmes' dramatic possibilities had proved a temptation to Doyle during the 1890s: The author's attempt to draft a play in five acts dovetailed with a show of interest from a more seasoned hand, the American playwright–actor William Gillette.

Doyle's participatory interest lapsed after an agreement had been struck, and by the time the breakthrough production of *Sherlock Holmes* premiered in 1899 at Buffalo, New York, its script had been thoroughly revised. Gillette's interpretation would define the balance of a distinguished career, including a seven-reel *Sherlock Holmes* feature–film of 1916, a touring revival of the play in 1928, and radio dramatizations during the 1930s. At his death in 1937, Gillette was still the preeminent Holmes—other striking impersonations notwithstanding. The identification would shift in 1938, when 20TH Century–Fox settled on Basil Rathbone as Holmes for an adaptation of Doyle's often-filmed novel of 1902, *The Hound of the Baskervilles*.

Though not properly a starring picture for Rathbone—this *Baskervilles* fancies itself more a vehicle for Richard Greene, as a menaced aristocrat—the spring-of-1939 release caused such a popular

sensation that Fox put Rathbone back in character that summer for *The Adventures of Sherlock Holmes*. Principal billing, this time, was a foregone conclusion not only for Rathbone, but also for his returning Dr. Watson, Nigel Bruce.

Comparisons with William Gillette were unavoidable. Rathbone weathered such appraisals with authority and an incisive understanding of the character. Rathbone also invested in Holmes a practical respect for Victorian protocols and mannerisms, along with a thorough knowledge of the legendary basis of Conan Doyle's benighted House of Baskerville. Nigel Bruce provided the finishing touch, a Watson who combines a patient intelligence with a (seemingly) muddled, grandfatherly air. Bruce had come well prepared to the role, his sheer Englishness anticipating just such a Watson with any number of Lovable Duffer roles through the 1930s.

"Nigel merely did what came to him naturally," Rathbone told me during the middle 1960s. "He despised finding himself required to present Watson as a bumbler—which was, of course, what a Hollywood version of Holmes & Watson required, a sidekick who points up the shrewdness of the detective—but he feigned the bumbling so well that he became a prisoner of his own artistry. But any good actor brings more to the role than is written, no matter how well written, and it was Nigel's subversive masterstroke, I believe, to invest Dr. Watson with a great indignation underneath it all, and a ferocious, heroic loyalty to the side of the good. Nigel could always take reassurance that our dear old friend from Australia, Dennis Hoey, had yet a greater bumbler to play, as our recurring Inspector Lestrade.

"I had my own concerns over typecasting, as it developed," Rathbone continued, "and it's scarcely a secret that it was Holmes who drove me back to the stage, at length, to re–establish myself as being capable of some greater range. Only with the greatest of caution did I return, then, to Hollywood. But what saved Holmes for me, over those 14-and-then-some pictures and God alone knows how many radio programs, was that I was always in the good company of Nigel Bruce—who was just as thoroughly well trapped within Watson as I had come to feel I was trapped within Holmes."

Rathbone's reference to "14-and-then-some" such assignments is accurate enough, covering the two Fox entries of 1939, the 12 Universal escapades of 1942–1946, and a self-spoofing cameo along-side Bruce in Edward Cline's *Crazy House*, a slapstick farce from 1943. (The official count of radio broadcasts is 275, spanning 1939–1943 on the NBC Network and 1943–1946 on the Mutual Network.) Given the strategic placement of Rathbone & Bruce in *Crazy House*, a starring picture for the fading comedy team of Ole Olsen & Chic Johnson, it seems almost surprising that Universal never arranged to have Holmes & Watson meet up with Bud Abbott & Lou Costello. Stranger things *nearly* happened.

It is scarcely a revelation to note that Universal Pictures during the 1940s also was home to the most popular horror-movie franchises. Rathbone had contributed to this Gothic legacy with Grand Manner star turns in 1939's *Son of Frankenstein* and the more nearly Shakespearean *Tower of London*. By the early 1940s, Universal had added a lucrative trademark with a substantially original *Wolf Man* character. The acquisition of the Holmes identity, via an agreement with the Conan Doyle Estate, was consistent with this heritage of chill–mongering.

A brief correspondence between the film historian George E. Turner and the publicity department of Universal Pictures indicates that Holmes & Watson might once have squared off against Universal's monster populace, if not for reconsiderations among the studio brass and the urgency of moving ahead with the formal *Sherlock Holmes* series. During my college-years apprenticeship to George in the 1960s, he opened this file on one memorable occasion, starting with a carbon–copy of a letter he had written while a movie-struck schoolboy in 1943.

In the opening letter, George had complimented the studio on its launching of the *Holmes* series, and on its confrontation between monsters in Roy William Neill's *Frankenstein Meets the Wolf Man* (1943). Then George had dropped a suggestion—the term *high concept* had yet to be admitted into the language—for a picture in which Holmes & Watson would encounter a Who's Who of the Universal monsters: Count Dracula, the Frankenstein Monster, the Wolf Man, the Invisible Man, the Mummy, and so forth. A publicity-desk functionary wrote back, assuring George that his idea had been anticipated—and that he could look forward to a production called *The Devil's Brood*, which as conceived would feature such a combination.

The premature announcement proved too good to be true, for by the winter of 1943 *The Devil's Brood* had become a troubled project—shunt-ed back and forth among writers and producers and finally going before the cameras in April of 1944 with Holmes & Watson nowhere to be found, nor any Mummy or Invisible Man. The picture, of course, would wind up bearing the title *House of Frankenstein* (1944–1945), which promptly yielded a sequel, *House of Dracula* (1945), and at length the coda of *Abbott & Costello Meet Frankenstein* in 1948.

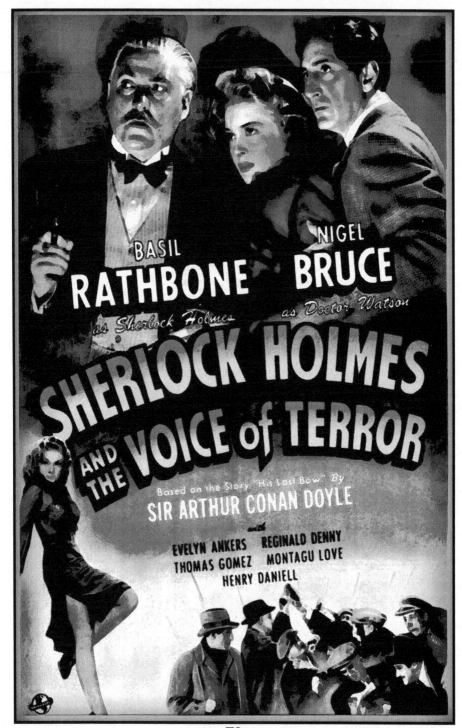

Holmes & Watson had bigger business to transact. Their agenda would broaden beyond the immediate Axis-buster concerns to take in the launching of two of Universal Pictures' lesser horror-movie franchises.

It comes as rather a jarring experience, the leap from the period-piece adventures of the two Fox *Holmes*es to the contemporary setting of *Sherlock Holmes and the Voice of Terror* (1942), but Rathbone and Bruce stabilize the transition as ably as they inhabit their characters. First of the Universals and the only entry directed by action–adventure specialist John Rawlins, *Voice of Terror* is a free-handed reworking of Doyle's story "His Last Bow: The War Service of Sherlock Holmes," from 1917. The screenplay requires Holmes to save London from a German invading force, and in the process to unmask a titled nobleman as an impostor lurking about since World War I.

Roy William Neill took over as director–for–life with *Sherlock Holmes and the Secret Weapon* (1943). Universal's $300,000, seven-year lease of story rights called for alternating original screenplays with adaptations, but this second project took its cue, as well, from a Doyle tale: 1903's "The Adventure of the Dancing Men." Holmes infiltrates the ranks of Nazi espionage, the better to smoke out an enemy of long standing, Prof. James Moriarty (played by Lionel Atwill). Moriarty's defection to the aristocracy of the Axis is trial enough, but his reasons for doing so are all the more disturbing: The master criminal intends to manipulate the resources of the Third Reich to defeat Holmes. Moriarty's fiendishness is such by now that he attempts to dispose of the detective with a blood-letting procedure. Foregone conclusion or not, Holmes' rescue comes suspensefully late, allowing Dr. Watson a welcome show of heroism.

By now, the sight of Holmes & Watson in mid-20TH Century attire will have become acceptably familiar, although their use of modern-day technology and motorized transportation still seems a stretch. To the studio's credit, much time is spent at 221B Baker Street, with the investigations taking Holmes to criminally infested slum districts and waterfronts. These are crucially timeless settings, as if a perpetual 1895; the timelessness is reinforced with Scots-born Mary Gordon's recurring portrayal of Holmes' housekeeper, Mrs. Hudson.

Sherlock Holmes in Washington (1943), the third entry, extends the modernization to American soil, with Holmes & Watson tracking the German abductors of an English diplomat. Screenwriters Bertram Millhauser and Lynn Riggs might even have picked up on the tone of Vincent Starrett's poetastery, for a Foreword assures the audience that "Holmes ... is ageless, invincible and unchanging. In solving problems of the present day he remains—as ever—the master of deductive reasoning." Henry Daniell plays a key enemy agent, and George Zucco, the letter-perfect Moriarty of 1939's *The Adventures of Sherlock Holmes*, is a German operative–turned–spymaster.

Northumberland, England, is the remote setting for the fourth film, *Sherlock Holmes Faces Death* (1943), adapted by Millhauser from Doyle's 1893 novella, *The Musgrave Ritual*. A Baskerville-styled setting reinforces the Victorian attitude, with a foreboding ancestral estate and its crypt harboring the remains of a slain resident, and a gigantic chessboard (with human pawns) holding the promise of a solution.

If *Sherlock Holmes Faces Death* had tipped the scales from war propaganda toward the patented Universal horror-movie style, then 1944's *The Spider Woman* dropped a persuasive hint of how Holmes &

Watson might have served that never-to-happen conceptual spring-board to *House of Frankenstein*. The menace is a female Moriarty (played by the severe Gale Sondergaard), who runs an insurance racket fueled by (apparent) suicides. The implement of murder is a poisonous spider, planted by a dwarf accomplice (Angelo Rossitto). The Homes & Watson cameo in *Crazy House* was made as a pick-up shot on a set from *The Spider Woman*, whose production during May–June of 1943 had wrapped shortly before the start of *Crazy House*.

Miss Sondergaard's title character gave the *Holmes* series its first horror-picture spin-off, 1946's *The Spider Woman Strikes Back*—a loose sequel, if only in name and outlook. Her character's name would change from picture to picture, but Miss Sondergaard's presence provides continuity. Her henchman in *The Spider Woman Strikes Back* is no dwarf, but instead an actor afflicted with glandular gigantism, Rondo Hatton—who also would figure prominently in another *Holmes* entry, *The Pearl of Death*, and two overtly horripilating spin–offs.

While *The Devil's Brood*–become–*House of Frankenstein* lurched toward its place within the Universal program, the *Sherlock Holmes* series wallowed ever deeper in a gathering horrific nature. *The Scarlet Claw* (1944) takes its cue from a Canadian village called Le Mort Rouge (in English: the Red Death), where a murderous, luminescent phantom stalks the marshes while church bells toll at a disturbing hour. Holmes' function is chiefly to debunk any ghostly trappings in the name of deductive reasoning, but the all-too-human menace proves no less a monster.

The Pearl of Death (1944) is hardly the first film to exploit the deformities of Rondo Hatton, who had come gradually to an acting career since the Depression years. *Pearl* is, however, the picture that

would define Hatton most prominently as a character called the Creeper—the Hoxton Creeper, in the Holmesian context—a brute-force murderer in the service of a gentlemanly criminal (Miles Mander). Doyle's "The Adventure of the Six Napoleons" (1904) is the source, and Holmes' task is to tie together a rampage by the Creeper with a stolen gem and a set of plaster busts of the Emperor Napoleon. Hatton's Creeper takes a fatal bullet at the finale, but Hatton would present a variation on the character in two Universal productions, *House of Horrors* and *The Brute Man* (both from 1946, the latter divested by Universal), before his death as a result of the disfiguring ailment.

The House of Fear (1945) hinges upon the loyalties between Holmes and Watson, whose rescue from an insurance-scam mob prompts Holmes to turn over a reward to the townsman responsible for saving Watson. The film also works on a darkening atmospheric level, with a gloomy seaside mansion in Scotland housing a club whose seven members seem marked for death. The source is Doyle's "The Adventure of the Five Orange Pips," from 1891.

The Woman in Green (1945) marks the return of Prof. Moriarty, played now by Henry Daniell and as death-defiant and elusive as Holmes is deathless and outgoing. A trail of evidence involving the severed fingers of murder victims leads to Moriarty by way of a lethal-lady accomplice, played by Hillary Brooke.

Pursuit to Algiers (1945) marks a significant postwar return to political intrigues, with a seafaring setting involving a jewel theft and the threatened overthrow of a postage-stamp nation. Rex Evans serves as a stand–in for Moriarty, the plotter of a royal abduction.

Terror by Night (1946) sets an eerie tone with a visit to a casket–builder's shop and progresses to a campaign of poison-dart murder. Alan Mowbray takes the Moriarty-equivalent role of Col. Sebastian Moran. Holmes stages a vanishing act with a priceless diamond.

Dressed To Kill (1946) ends the series with a plot device similar to that of *The Pearl of Death*, using music boxes instead of plaster effigies. A cryptic code of musical notes leads to a cache of £5 currency plates stolen from the Bank of England. Popular wisdom holds that Rathbone refused to continue as Holmes beyond this point, but he did sustain the impersonation on radio, stage, and even television as the occasion suited him. Likelier, Roy William Neill had more to do with the series' discontinuation, whether through broadening ambitions or in death.

Apart from *Frankenstein Meets the Wolf Man* and scattered incidental assignments, Neill had devoted his greater energies to the *Holmes* series since its second installment. After wrapping *Dressed To Kill*, Neill made a drastic and successful departure to a more cynical and timelier style of crime melodrama with a watershed *film noir*, *Black Angel* (1946). This promising new beginning was cut short by Neill's death of a heart attack at 59 in December of 1946.

Although the Universal *Holmes*es are more uniform in quality of enactments and writing than, say, Universal's *Inner Sanctum* series of this same period, the Committed Viewer will notice a budgetary pinch as the postwar economy tightens—and as postwar tastes shift to a more cynical manner, epitomized by Neill's *Black Angel*. The mannered Victorianisms of Holmes & Watson, which had proved so right for confrontations with the thuggishness of Naziism, seemed ever quainter as a general disillusionment asserted itself.

But the Holmes & Watson of Rathbone & Bruce proved a ready attraction for syndicated television. Their sustained portrayal of determination and friendship helped to assure the persistence of civility. The Universal *Holmes* pictures remain popular, and Rathbone still defines the Great Detective in the face of latecomer competition. Perhaps as much Conan Doyle himself, the Rathbone–Bruce *series* has cinched Vincent Starrett's longing assertion: "It is always 1895"— as long as we have these stirring tales of rationalism and courage.

A Universal Cast Is Worth Deleting: A Lost and/or Languishing Legacy

The name of Universal Pictures, its implicit universality notwithstanding, has become synonymous with one narrow realm: the most famous horror movies ever to splash across the screen. The devotée may be lured away by the subtler terrors of Val Lewton (Page Nos. 13 *et Seq.*); awed by the tragic fantasy and inspired artifice of Cooper & Schoedsack's *King Kong*; lulled by the fershlugginer crackpot weirdness of Monogram and PRC; or thunderstruck by the opulent ferocity of Hammer Films' revisionist Gothics. But one always seems to come home to Universal and its two-decade span of pageantry centering upon *Frankenstein*, *Dracula*, *The Wolf Man*, and embellishments thereupon.

Universal made historical epics and mysteries and high-adventure yarns and middlebrow literary adaptations in a class with the better–and–best of Old Hollywood. Some of these, such as *Tower of London* and *The Man Who Reclaimed His Head* and *The Love Captive* and *The Crimson Trail*, would embrace horrific elements to such an extent that they could be marketed on multiple fronts. But the deciding identity fell into place long after the studio's Depression-into-wartime heyday, when in 1957 Universal's groundbreaking chillers— the more overtly hair-raising ones, at any rate, plus scattered mystery-and-suspense items—were deployed to television (via Columbia's Screen Gems syndication branch) under the inclusive identity of *Shock! Theater.* The intended audience was of a youthful demographic, the same adolescent-to-teenage schoolkids who had been queuing up and shelling out since the postwar 1940s–into–1950s to see such big-screen rampages as *Unknown Island, The Beast from 20,000 Fathoms, Them!,* and *Creature from the Black Lagoon.*

I was that audience, distilled to a single digit, and my grade-school classmates of 1957–1958 established their worthiness according to whether they could speak knowingly on a Monday morning about the prior weekend's installment of *Shock! Theater.* The program cropped up as a wild-card maverick entry from an upstart third channel, the ABC–TV affiliate, in my hometown of Amarillo, Texas. Three whole entire teevee channels among which to choose: What a concept.

I had found my way to the program somewhat later than I would have liked. Three neighborhood chums and I secured parental permissions to Stay Up Late and rallied 'round the receiver at my house for

Gatefold pop-up from the Shock! Theater promotional book. Note Cerlox binding ring at center.

FRANKENSTEIN DRACULA
THE MUMMY THE MAD GHOUL
THE WOLF MAN THE INVISIBLE MAN
THEY'RE ALL IN

SHOCK!

52 of Universal's most **spine-tingling**, full-length feature films for **first-run** television

presented by

SCREEN GEMS

what we thought would be our introduction to the notorious *Shock! Theater*. The show that was just starting, whatever it might have been, looked pretty ordinary—something about an elusive foreigner crook—and we'd have tuned it out if not for the other characters' repeated references to the badman by the name of "Shock." Or so it sounded to us. Half an hour into the thing, with nothing particularly shocking yet transpired, my father ambled into the living-room.

"So how's your *Shock! Theater*?"

"Pretty punk-ola so far, Dad. This Shock guy hasn't even croaked anybody yet."

Dad watched for a moment, then burst out laughing.

"Why, this isn't *Shock! Theater*—that character's name is *Jacques*! You boys've got the wrong channel!" By the time we had corrected the oversight and switched to the correct spot on the dial, we had missed a goodly portion of *Son of Frankenstein*.

Grown-ups might as well not have applied unless drawn in by the nostalgic impulse, which in most cities was kept at bay by the wise-cracking *Shock! Theater* hosts, those Little Theatre-calibre buffoons of the various local stations that bought the package. Indeed, keenly though my father admired Claude Rains—and he had seen to it that I would possess every last one of that fine actor's Bible-story phonograph records—Dad raised such a noise about the "morbid cackling idiocy" of the costumed announcer who kept interrupting *The Invisible Man*, while I was trying to lose myself in that film one autumn night in 1958, that I gave the attempt up as a Lost Cause and switched off the television set. I didn't get a crack at viewing *The Invisible Man* undisturbed (except by that inane local host, whose yapping came with the territory) until some months later.

Our local host in Northwest Texas called himself Mr. Shock. He was an all-'round studio talent named Fred Salmon, who also handled kid-show hosting chores on after-school weekdays and Saturdays and specialized in phoney Irish, Yiddish, and Scandahoovian dialects. The strain of coming up with the imaginative name of Mr. Shock would seem to have exhausted Mr. Salmon's supply of wit otherwise, for his one–liners had all the subtle wit of an *Archie* comic book.

Mr. Shock's chronic-to-acute gimmick, apart from a ghoulish makeup modeled after that of the more prominent John Zacherly, was a done-to-death exclamation of annoying frequency, and I *do* mean frequency—as in *piercing*. This high-pitched *"Yeeowww!"* sounded unnervingly like a baggy-pants comedian, Sam "Banana Man" Levine, one of the more eccentric characters ever to appear on the *Captain Kangaroo* show. Fred Salmon's Mr. Shock got his comeuppance when he nearly electrocuted himself with a short-circuited microphone cable while staging a live-remote broadcast from alongside a pond at Llano Cemetery, at the edge of town. *"Yeeowww,"* indeed. This stunt–gone–haywire lent a new and untoward meaning to the concept of *Shock! Theater*. (While learning the Spanish language at around this same time, I discovered that *llano*, or *flatlands*, is pronounced exactly like *ya no*, which translates into English as "no longer." Our Mr. Shock had almost become *ya no* at *Llano*.)

But for all its excesses, *Shock! Theater* also proved wrong any nay–sayers in our local market. It lasted into the 1960s, when a new Mr. Shock, impersonated by Bob Hendricks, took charge.

"We all thought KVII/Channel 7 was crazy for investing in this crack-pot upstart movie package—like they were trying to make Halloween a year-'round occasion," recalled Allen Shifrin, a veteran announcer and broadcasting executive in Amarillo, in a 2002 conversation. "But with that *Shock! Theater* thing, they tapped into something bigger than anything that the local syndie [syndication, *i.e.*] television field had ever seen, and they showed our established bigger stations [the CBS and NBC affiliates] a thing or two about crowd-pleasing showmanship."

Yes, and I digress, as usual. Anyhow, we were talking about the parental attitude toward *Shock! Theater* and its genre in, well, general. I learned, during the heyday of that program, that my mother was more sharply attuned than I had suspected: While browsing through one of her Depression Era schoolgirl scrapbooks (a clipping is reproduced at right), I found newspaper advertisements for *The Raven*, *The Mummy*, *Dracula*, and the like—yellowed touchstones to a Bygone Day, pasted in place adjoining box-camera snapshots and pressed flowers and notes from neighborhood chums.

Now, I had known these films were no original-for-television programs, having studied up on them in a collection of studio kits and movie-business tradepapers kept by my theatre-manager uncle, but now it developed that my mother must be a lapsed fan who had enjoyed the pictures as new arrivals on the big screen. She voiced no enthusiasm for the newer likes of *I Was a Teenage Werewolf* and *Macabre*, but the chillers of her younger days seemed worth remembering.

Mother's scrapbooks contained other titles, as well: Among just the Universals were such tantalizing titles as *East of Java*, *The Love Captive*, *The Secret of the Blue Room*, and *The Great Impersonation*—all of which sounded as forbidding and inviting as anything *Shock! Theater* had unveiled—along with a cowboy picture called *Smoking Guns*, whose advertising promised a massed attack by alligators. *Cross Country Cruise* sounded somehow less appealing in that light, but one learns,

soon or late, not to judge a movie by its title. (*The Great Impersonation*, like *The Secret of the Blue Room*, was part of the original *Shock!* package, but our local channel deployed some titles in other slots. Oftentimes, a lesser official *Shock!* selection would be announced in the newspaper's listings, only to wind up pre–empted at the last moment by a repetition of one of the established favorites, usually one of the *Frankenstein* or *Dracula* pictures.)

My mother offered helpful perspective: "Oh, you don't automatically need a Frankenstein or a Dracula to make it a horror movie," she explained, cryptically at first but then amplifying the point. "Sometimes, a forbidden romance or a wild exotic adventure can be as terrifying as anything supernatural. My goodness, but some of those were more thrilling than the monster pictures."

And thus does a broader appreciation develop: Since that home-front revelation, right in the midst of *Shock! Theater*'s remarkable wave of retroactive enlightenment, I have maintained a Short List of the Universals that my hometown version of *Shock! Theater* neglected to exploit, whether to the fullest or even at all. Some are marginal and some are full-blooded hair–raisers, and all are of interest to the aficionado of Universal's better-known spookers. The list has grown lengthier in times more recent, as Universal's video sub-

sidiary—a postmodern *Shock! Theater* for the program-it-yourself Information Age—has piled horror upon horror but nevertheless has declined to place many a title within that appropriate context. Videocassettes and digital video discs, of course, are more of a challenge to sell than syndicated television programming was during those midcentury years of televison as an enticing novelty. And MCA/Universal Home Video took such a bath in its mid-1990s attempt to create a Five-Foot Shelf of Buck Jones' Depression Era Westerns that any renewed attempt to expand its classic-horror line beyond the Known Quantities must seem a fool's errand.

My list of the mislaid, waylaid, and delayed Universals gets an airing every few years as I go about expanding the province of a book that the late George E. Turner and I wrote some years ago called *Forgotten Horrors*. Now, the point of *Forgotten Horrors* and its sequels has been to bring to light a wealth of, *uhm*, forgotten motion pictures from the low-budget independent studios. But colleagues and Constant Readers have insisted that the major studios delivered their share and then some of horrors since forgotten. As though I needed any persuading. My recent unearthings of Warners/Vitaphone's "The Attic of Terror" (as covered in *Midnight Marquee Monsters* magazine) and two short-subject *Frankenstein* spoofs ("The Tin Man" and "Third Dimensional Murder," in *Monsters from the Vault* magazine) point decisively in this direction, as does the Turner & Price book *Human Monsters: The Bizarre Psychology of Movie Villains* (1995–2004).

It all harks backward to that list that I had begun as a schoolboy, under the heading: *What's Missing from Shock! Theater?* Most conspicuously missing, at least in the television packages that my hometown received, are many of the Depression-period titles following, which in many cases remain among the missing—or at least among the officially unavailable. (*The Man Who Reclaimed His Head* and *Secret of the Blue Room* appeared as one-shots in my town's *Shock!* lineup, but they never took the customary encores except in other time-slots, minus the *Shock!* escutcheon. James Whale's *The Old Dark House*, long among the missing as a consequence of tangled proprietary claims, found its way at length to video-shop prominence—though not from any Universal sources.)

To know of these films is, for the adventurous cineaste, to seek them out. To relish them, once found, or even to accept them as worth mentioning in the same breath with the familiar benchmarks of Universal's terrors, is strictly a matter of individual taste. For which there is No Accounting.

The Last Warning (1929; German one–sheet at facing page)

Issued in both silent and part-talking versions, *The Last Warning* is a gem in either form, an assertion of director Paul Leni's comfort with an established medium, and of his adaptability: The added dimension of sound figures chiefly in jarring sound effects and menacing voices.

Leni had come to America from Germany at the behest of Universal's Carl Laemmle. The artist weighed in Stateside with *The Cat and the Canary* (1927), a precursor of the Universal horror style. Leni followed through with *The Chinese Parrot* (1927) and *The Man Who Laughs* (1928), then proved ready for the talkers with *The Last Warning*. A siege of blood poisoning killed Leni in 1929.

The Last Warning tells of a jinxed stage play that is revived five years after the murder of its leading actor, Woodford (D'Arcy Corrigan).

The fresh start finds itself plagued by threats and plunges into darkness, during which the new leading man goes missing. A haunting by the ghost of Woodford appears responsible, but the guilty parties prove entirely human. This self-debunking formula, a holdover from Broadway's Mystery Farce tradition, would lapse from popularity over the long haul; it endures, however, as a chronic plotting device in the Hanna–Barbera cartoon factory's *Scooby–Doo* franchise.

The Last Warning was remade in 1939 as *The House of Fear*. That same year, Universal delivered a detective thriller called *The Last Warning*, which found its way into the *Shock!* package.

Various niche-market video editions of the silent-only version have come to light in recent years. Elements necessary to a legitimate reconstruction of the talkie version have proved elusive.

The Charlatan (1929)

"The old hocus–pocus about crystal gazers, swamis with midget assistants, cabinets in which women alternately disappear or are murdered..." So grumbled the New York *Times* in a passive so–what? response to a strategic use of newfangled talking-picture technology, more elaborately deployed than in *The Last Warning*.

Holmes Herbert.

"[F]urther complicated by a dialogue sequence," complained the critic. *The Charlatan* was presented in both silent and part-talking, fully scored versions. The products veered far from the plans of studio chief Carl Laemmle, but the necessary replacement of the intended leading man, Conrad Veidt, with the distinguished English actor Holmes Herbert proved an inspired touch.

Though announced as Veidt's next picture, *The Charlatan* was postponed in favor of *The Last Performance* (1927), a hypnotist-as-madman melodrama with talking sequences and sound effects. But then, Veidt returned to Europe—suffering from microphone anxiety. In February of 1929, *The Charlatan* went into production with Herbert. (In Germany, Veidt would reassert himself as an important talent for the talkies.)

Herbert serves *The Charlatan* as circus clown Peter Dwight. Dwight's wife, Florence (Margaret Livingston), quits him for the wealthy Richard Talbot (Rockcliffe Fellows) and takes Dwight's daughter. Dwight swears vengeance. Years later, disguised as a Hindu seer, Dwight arrives as a hired entertainer at the Talbot mansion. Unrecognized, Dwight learns that Florence plans to leave Talbot. As a thunderstorm rages, Florence takes part in a vanishing trick—only to turn up slain. Dwight impersonates a detective and pursues a solution. Exonerated, his revenge exacted by proxy, Dwight takes his daughter (Dorothy Gould) away from the murder house.

Herbert makes a convincing transformation from bland entertainer to saturnine mystic. Veidt might have provided a demonic emotional core, but Herbert offers a welcome hint of such shadings.

The part-talking edition was issued a week after the silent film. The closing reel was re–shot with dialogue, and an elaborate orchestral score

CARL LAEMMLE *presents*
The most
EXCITING
Picture
ever filmed!
"EAST
of BORNEO
• A UNIVERSAL PICTURE •

was assembled. Sound effects also were employed, notably so during a storm. Herbert was a veteran of the stage, of silent films, and of the second all-talking Vitaphone picture, *The Terror* (1928). It was his tough luck that English accents seldom sat well with American audiences—a fact that would exile Herbert to the realm of supporting character roles.

A strictly silent edition of *The Charlatan* cropped up during the late 1990s from Grapevine Video.

East of Borneo (1931)

A likelier prospect for the *Shock! Theater* package, though neglected as such, is this compact study of madness and superstition in a lost jungle kingdom. Charles Bickford and Rose Hobart are an estranged married couple—he, a self–exile from civilization; she, an intruder hoping to recapture her husband from the Third World madman whom he serves. Dr. Allan Randolph (Bickford) has become physician–in–residence, a chronically drunkard, to the court of Hashin (Georges Renevant). Hashin is a Sorbonne-educated tyrant, descended from Aryan stock, who believes that the existence of his kingdom hinges upon his keeping a distant volcano dormant. The ruler's response to dissent is to throw nay–sayers into a pit of crocodiles. Hashin takes a fancy to Linda Randolph (Miss Hobart).

Dr. Randolph, who had mistakenly believed Linda unfaithful, warms to her as he begins to comprehend the menace. Hashin thwarts their escape, planning to turn Randolph over to the crocs. Linda opens fire on Hashin. The volcano erupts. The reunited Randolphs make a dash for higher ground as Hashin waits to die with his empire.

Director George Melford and Bickford, Old Hollywood's ablest snarling tough guy, would work together to greater advantage on 1935's *East of Java* (Page No. 98). This warm–up to that masterwork of Green Hell horrors is, all the same, a satisfying exercise that tempers the embittered desperation with a hard-earned safe-and-sound resolution. Setpiece horrors along the way include the sacrifice of a native to a roiling mass of crocodiles. The volcanic eruption is a wonder, spewing torrents of lava and stone onto the outpost of savage mock–civilization.

Georges Renavent, a versatile and prolific character man whose career would continue for another decade, is properly vile and arrogant as the cultured but superstitious dictator. Many a viewer has mistaken Renavent here for Bela Lugosi, with whom he shares a Grand Manner affinity for arch and overripe oratory. A bonus is the presence in the supporting cast of Lupita Tovar, leading lady of Universal's Spanish-language *Dracula* (1931).

A 66-minute television print, under the proxy title of *White Captive*, was the last version to come to our attention until Sinister Cinema came through with a satisfactory edition.

King of the Arena (1933)

In which championship frontiersman Ken Maynard, as a Rangers operative, is commissioned to dispose of a murderous gang known as the Black Death. The mob has targeted a circus, which Maynard infiltrates as a performer. He earns a mortal enemy early on by stealing the thunder of an egotistical trouper named Bargoff (Bob Kortman), who puts out a contract on Ken's life but then must take vengeance into his own hands. Incidental mayhem points to the Black Death, of which Bargoff proves to be an agent. Ken trails Bargoff into Mexico, where the brains behind the racket proves to be another conspicuously Russian type (a scowling Michael Visaroff), traveling under the name of Smith. The Bargoff identity can only signify an attempt to coin a name evocative of Boris Karloff, point–man among Universal's chiller stars.

King of the Arena is scarcely a patch on Maynard's later *Smoking Guns* (Page No. 89) in terms of weirdness, but Bob Kortman's show of rabid villainy belongs more to the cinema of horror than to the cinema of adventure. The film indulges Maynard's prevailing taste for bizarre touches, serving as a bridge between his non-Universal horseback horror, *Tombstone Canyon* (1932), and Universal's *Smoking Guns*.

Surviving prints of *King of the Arena*, assuming survival in hidden locations, long eluded even the American Film Institute's comprehensive *Catalog of Feature Films* project. Various Web-vendor catalogues have offered DVD–R copies (bootlegs, that is) in times more recent.

Secret of the Blue Room (1933)

A sealed-chamber murder case of surpassing excellence with a residue of mystery, Kurt Neumann's *Secret of the Blue Room* would figure as a property worth remaking on into the 1940s. It is itself a remake, of the 1932 German film *Geheimnis des Blauen Zimmers*. The next American version would be 1938's *The Missing Guest* (Page No. 106).

Three people have been slain in the Blue Room, a guest suite of Castle VON Helldorf, where Irene VON Helldorf (Gloria Stuart) is celebrating her 21ST birthday in the company of patriarch Robert (Lionel Atwill) and three suitors, Capt. Brink (Paul Lukas), Frank Faber (Onslow Stevens), and Thomas Brandt (William Janney). Brandt challenges Faber and Brink to stay a night in the room—a grandstand play to demonstrate his courage.

Brandt takes the first night and turns up missing. Robert declines to summon the police. A would-be

strangler attacks Irene. Faber, next to take the dare, turns up dead. The customary forbidden disclosures follow, mouldy secrets suggesting that the shadowy attacker can only be a disgraced and banished relative. Capt. Brink sets a trap that leads to the unveiling of an altogether more ordinary killer. The immediate case is cracked, but the earlier three murders remain tantalizingly unexplained.

No primary-source archival print has been satisfactorily traced.

Cross Country Cruise (1934)

The viewer is lulled into modest expectations as a model named Sue (June Knight) waits at a bus station in New York for her lover, Steve (Alan Dinehart). Steve arrives in the company of his possessive wife, Nita (Minna Gombell). Sue, who had been unaware of any wife, rebuffs Steve's attempt to explain. The bus pulls out with all aboard. Norman (Lew Ayres), traveling on business to California, finds himself fascinated by Sue.

From such soap-operatic narrative cloth, director Eddie Buzzell and writers Elmer Harris and Stanley Rauh fashion one of the more cold-blooded murder thrillers. The story begins deceptively as a lightweight romantic clash, and yet its development into a freakish crime yarn proves only too logical. Extensive location work in transit lends momentum and a sense of frenzied disorientation.

During a stopover in Denver, Steve trails Sue to a department store. Nita arrives unexpectedly. Sue tries vainly to explain, then absents herself while Nita berates Steve. Alone with his wife, Steve skewers her with an arrow from a sporting-goods display.

Remaining hidden past closing time, Steve substitutes the corpse for a shop-window mannequin. He returns to the bus, explaining that Nita will remain in Denver with relatives. A window-dresser discovers the body. The police trace the bus from Nita's ticket. Steve tries to frame Sue, then kidnaps her and makes a getaway in the bus. A police plane lands just ahead. Steve swerves, and the bus tumbles over a cliff and into a stream. Sue's rescue is a foregone conclusion; no such luck for Steve.

REDISCOVERIES • UNIVERSAL

Lew Ayres—Universal's top draw at the time—is as great a heroic asset here as his leading lady, June Knight, a *Ziegfeld Follies* standout who had doubled Greta Garbo for the celebrated dance sequence in *Mata Hari* (1931). The strongest performances, however, belong to Alan Dinehart as the cad–turned–killer and Minna Gombell as his hated and hateful better half. Dinehart—a cultured intellectual who pursued parallel careers as a theatrical producer and a zoologist—gives the role the right conniving charm and plays the Mad Scene business for seething contrast. Miss Gombell, also of the stage, followed through with many similarly bitchy studies.

Although the picture plays a bit choppily because of its overabundance of bus-passenger characters, it finds its focus in the impulsive murder. Most gripping is the scene in which Dinehart plants his victim as a window-display prop—an early exploration of the terrifying possibilities of a big retail space after hours. Elsewhere, John P. Fulton's composites, process photography, and miniature work seem unnervingly real.

Buzzell's usual realm lay in musicals and romantic comedies. Here, the festering intrigues, the ghastly slaying, and the desperate chase are handled with the same skill that Buzzell applied to his more characteristic work. His one return to the crime-thriller genre came with *Song of the Thin Man* (1947), last of the William Powell–Myrna Loy series.

A 35-millimeter archival print and a backup print of *Cross Country Cruise* are documented in the Universal vaults but have proved unavailable, eluding even repertory or film-festival purposes. Known 16MM television prints had been formally retired as of 2001. Bootleg video editions have surfaced in a few Web catalogues.

One More River (1934)

James Whale's study in sadistic erotica (from the novel by James Galsworthy) attracted as great an eruption of censorship as Edgar G. Ulmer's more widely known Universal picture, *The Black Cat*—likewise from 1934, the year the Roman Catholic Church's Legion of Decency imposed a parasitic control over the Motion Picture Association. The respective jobs of butchery were unalike: Universal held a grudge against Ulmer for an indiscretion with an executive's wife (see our companion volume, *Human Monsters*); the Laemmle family was eager to subject Ulmer to a sacrificial mutilation. The studio's mangling of *One More River* was more a cowed response to the bullying tactics of the Legion and its Production Code puppet, Joseph I. Breen.

Colin Clive.

One More River concerns the stalking of Lady Clare Corven (Diana Wynyard) by her estranged husband, Sir Gerald Corven (Colin Clive). Any horrific element is in the eye of the beholder, for the villain's comeuppance has more to do with Lady Corven's survival of a divorce-court ordeal than with any spectacular undoing. Filthy-minded Joe Breen rejected the first script out–of–hand: "[N]o objection to your developing the character of … a brutal man who has beaten his wife and thus compelled her to leave him, but we cannot allow any suggestion, directly or indirectly, referring to sadism." Among Breen's pusillanimous complaints in an April 1934 memorandum: "Clare's line, 'He's a sadist...,' Clare's line, 'I see. I'm fruit—not blossom,' Corven's line, 'I won't stand for another man having you!' Clare's line, 'Then. if I want him to divorce me. I have got to commit adultery.'" Director Whale sent a revision of R.C. Sherriff's script to Breen, with this memo: "I have taken out not only the subject of sadism but all references to it, so that now any dialogue ... can quite easily be taken as meaning extreme cruelty and ill temper. The end of the picture, I have completely remodeled..."

Breen responded in May: "[T]he changes suggested seem to us to cover pretty well the dangerous elements in this story... [O]ur final judgment will depend pretty much on the manner in which the picture is shot. Sadism or any possible inference of it is a dangerous subject from a Code standpoint, and we urge you again to exercise great care to keep it absolutely free from any possibility of offense."

The completed film drew further Puritanical petulance from Breen: "Delete line, 'You see, my husband's attentions are without witnesses—they're *that* kind...'" Change ... 'He seems to be quite a beast' to either 'cad,' 'rotter,' or 'bounder...' Delete line, 'Some women like rough handling...' [Delete] Clare's line, 'Did he tell you that he used his riding whip on me?'" And so forth, *ad infinitum, ad nauseam, al fresco.*

The film received a Purity Seal in July of 1934 from the Motion Picture Association, but the Legion of Decency issued a C–for–Condemned rating. Wrote Breen, "This is the first picture passed under the recently set-up machinery to be so condemned... [W]e are helpless under the circumstances." Breen neglected to mention that he had been planted in that office as a Trojan Horse by the Legion of Decency—a self-evident truth, even though he pretended to represent the better interests of the filmmaking industry.

The Love Captive (1934)

While the Purity Zealots were sniping over *One More River* and *The Black Cat*, Max Marcin's *The Love Captive* sneaked through intact. It is as provocative a film, though less frank in the use of censor-bait terminology. This variation upon *Svengali* (as filmed at Warners in 1931) also deals effectively in weirdness, without the expected dark shadings. Even as a fresh release, the picture attracted little attention. Which is the moviegoers' loss, for *The Love Captive* is a tense perfect-crime yarn with a loathsome fiend and a satisfying surprise ending.

Dr. Alexis Collender (Nils Asther), an unscrupulous hypnotist, influences his nurse, Alice Trask (*The Old Dark House*'s Gloria Stuart), to set up housekeeping with him and break her engagement to Dr. Norman Ware (Paul Kelly). The quack becomes ever more popular and influential. Lawyer Roger Loft (Alan Dinehart) dissuades Ware from killing Collender. Ware does, however, bring down ethics charges from the Society of Physicians. Mary Williams (Virginia Kami), a former victim, promises to testify, but Collender brings her once more under his power.

Collender seeks to demonstrate his powers before the Medical Society, proposing an experiment in which a person under his influence cannot fire a pistol. Collender encounters Loft's wife, Valerie (Renée Gadd), and entrances her. Valerie becomes restless when kept away from Collender. At last, Collender is granted a hearing. Loft volunteers as a subject. Collender orders: "You will try to shoot me but will be unable to do so." The hypnotist is gunned down, and the lawyer is exonerated.

Journalist–turned–playwright Marcin came to Hollywood during the early-talkie period after a string of Broadway productions that were purchased in turn by various movie studios. After a hitch at Paramount, Marcin was brought to Universal to tackle his play *The Humbug*, basis of *The Love Captive*.

Marcin avoided Gothic trappings and frightful makeups, preferring a sophisticated, up-to-date approach with a glamorous villain, lavish settings, clever dialogue, and characters straight out of the Social Register. The climactic scenes occur in a medical observatory where hundreds of scientists have gathered. Gil Warrenton, former cinematographer to Paul Leni, deploys a sparkling style usually reserved for the top-shelf romantic dramas.

Nils Asther.

Marcin even had Nils Asther, a darkly handsome Swede who specialized in romantic portrayals, shave off his well-known moustache so he would have none of the distinguishing affectations of a typical movie villain. The actor's almost Oriental eyes, shown in close–up, are Marcin's lone concession to a horror-movie style. Marcin, needless to say, was appalled when Universal's New York office, at the last moment, rechristened *The Humbug* as *Dangerous to Women*—and then changed that to the even more lurid *The Love Captive*.

No archival print is documented within the Universal vaults—not to say that master elements are known not to exist—and known television-syndicate prints appear to have been retired from active duty. Anyone is welcome to disprove that information.

Smoking Guns (1934)

Recipe for an exercise in mind-boggling cockamamie horrifical lunacy: Take a cowboy shoot–'em–up, then stage most of its action on a Hallowe'en night in an Old Dark House. Add a graveyard, a lost mine, a jungle manhunt, malaria and murder, gangrene and alligators, parenticide and suicide and the Slumber of Reason that breeds monsters, amnesia, and abundant leading-lady cleavage and mistaken identity and Southern-fried backwater superstition. A volatile combination.

The result of this genre-splicing experiment would be *Smoking Guns*, the weirdest horse opera in a century–and–change of the film-making art. The film stars Ken Maynard, in a story concocted by Ken Maynard, produced by Ken Maynard Productions, Inc., with second-unit location photography by Ken Maynard. Maynard did not direct—his close associate, Alan James (alias Alvin J. Neitz), handled that chore—but *Smoking Guns* is as intensely personal a film as anything by Chaplin or VON Stroheim, and every bit as eccentric.

This wild Texas Gothic also supplies the traditional slam-bang action. If ever there were a sagebrusher capable of elbowing its way into the *Shock! Theater* lineup, this is the one. (Its generic title kept *Smoking Guns* stranded in the cowboy ghetto; Maynard had shot it under the title *Doomed To Die*, which derives from a line of dialogue.) Outright horrific are the ravings of a crazed law enforcer (Walter Miller) when he realizes he has contracted gangrene: "Rotting like carrion in the sun! Eating its way up, *up, UP!...* To lay here and die by inches, to rot away like something un*clean...* !"

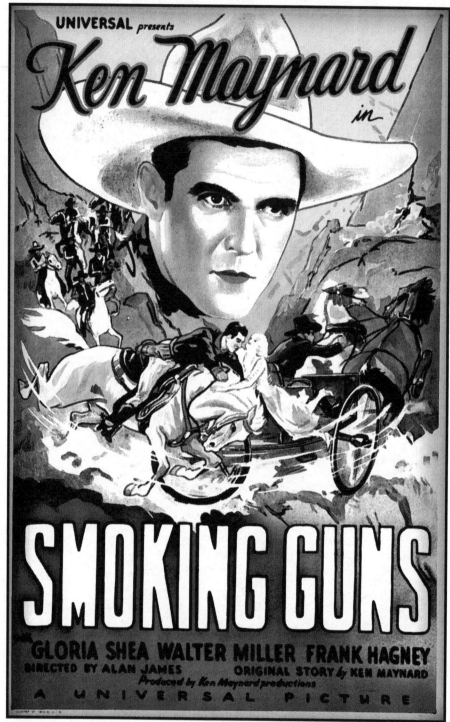

Ranger Dick Logan (Miller) tracks Ken Masters (Maynard), on the lam from a frame–up for murder, to a desolate swamp. Logan collapses with malaria and suffers a mauling by an alligator. Ken prepares to perform an amputation, but Logan commits suicide rather than submit. Ken returns to town, impersonating Logan. A graveyard tryst between servants (Martin Turner and Etta McDaniel) is interrupted by a purported ghost. Other make-believe spooks prove to be local thugs, but the apparition of Ken's presumed-dead father (Ed Coxen) is the man himself, tormented into madness by a crooked gang. Ken pursues the chief heavy, whose wagon plunges over a cliff.

This 16TH and last of Maynard's Universals ran well overdue, exceeding a $125,000 budget. Carl Laemmle, JR., production chief and son of the president, called for retakes along more conventional lines. Maynard, a famously ill-tempered sort, gave Junior a royal cussing–out and left for Europe without altering so much as a frame. Laemmle could not axe the film because it had been pre–sold. The strange opus was previewed during April of 1934 as *Doomed To Die*, but then it was recalled and released two months later under the generically upbeat name of *Smoking Guns*. Maynard was *kaput* at Universal, and the most popular Western series of the early 1930s came to an end. It can only have infuriated Junior Laemmle that *Smoking Guns* proved immensely popular.

Maynard's location footage of real alligators in the Yucatan is interspersed with backlot action involving several scary but patently bogus saurians left over from *East of Borneo* (Page No. 83). Interiors and scenes in the swamp, the town, the graveyard, and the creaky old house were made at the studio. The climactic chase was photographed on Dark Canyon Road, running through the mountains southeast of the backlot.

Smoking Guns resurfaced during the 1980s as a telecine transfer from sources outside the Universal machinery, utilizing a surviving 16MM print in private hands.

Life Returns (1934–1938)

A lapsed and defrocked Universal production: In May of 1934, in Berkeley, California, Dr. Robert Cornish and a team of researchers announced that they had restored life to a dog whose death Cornish had caused by clinical means. This canine *Frankenstein* episode, a supposed breakthrough that seems to have led no further, was bolstered in turn by motion-picture footage, presented as a document of the experiment.

From Life Returns.

True or false? No one seems capable of saying, beyond Cornish's self-interested account. Cornish later was denied access to the bodies of executed criminals, and he seems to have abandoned the cause. (A replica of Dr. Cornish's laboratory apparatus can be seen in Warners' 1936 production of *The Walking Dead*.)

In any event, the early declaration of success inspired an ambitious dilettante filmmaker, Dr. Eugen Frenke, to develop for Universal a heart-tugging science-fictional Soap Opera around the remarkable but dry clinical case. *Life Returns* is a poorly made but nonetheless fascinating relic. Though by no means a horror film, it pertains to the genre because of the very topic—to say nothing of the presence of Valerie Hobson, of 1935's *Bride of Frankenstein*, and Onslow Stevens, who only several years later would play a Frankenstein-styled physician–turned–vampire in *House of Dracula* (1945).

Cornish himself, Stevens, and Lois Wilson play medical students seeking to conquer death. A subplot involving Stevens' rebellious son (George Breakston) and his pet dog brings the radical theories into play: The pooch runs afoul of the local dogcatcher (Stanley Fields) and is gassed. This is the melodramatic setup for the insertion of the Cornish lab footage, which leads to a hopeful ending.

Universal had bankrolled *Life Returns* but then pronounced it "not suitable for the regular Universal Program" following ill-received preview showings during 1934, according to one trade-publication account. Threatening legal action, Frenke managed by 1935 to remount *Life Returns* for release under the ScienArt Pictures banner. The copyright notice contains no mention of Universal—but surviving prints still bear the Universal end-scroll under the famous heading, "A Good Cast Is Worth Repeating." Nothing happened in the way of distribution until a limited release in 1938. Seldom has such fuss been made over so insignificant a picture.

The obvious flaws aside, *Life Returns* has met unfairly, nonetheless, with a measure of wrongheaded *kvetching*. We've witnessed some harrowing rants from the more single-minded souls among horror-movie buffs about the film's utter (deliberate) lack of Shock Value and overt megalomania—as though the cinema hadn't enough of those qualities in innumerable other pictures. Plain insipidity is the greater problem. The truer value lies in an inadvertent suggestion that all those Mad Doctors of popular fiction and the movies might have something on the ball, after all.

Great Expectations (1934)

Henry Hull's first star turn at Universal is in fact a Boris Karloff portrayal–by–proxy. The assignment, even the makeup, had been tailored to Karloff, and Hull carried on in the expected manner after casting priorities had changed. Modern-day viewers routinely mistake Hull for Karloff in the pivotal role of Magwitch, a jailbreaker who proves influential upon the fortunes of an orphan named Pip (played by George Breakston as a child and Phillips Holmes as a young man).

Great Expectations fared poorly at the box office—prompting insiders to joke that the elder Carl Laemmle had decided not to pick up Charles Dickens' option—but even so, director Stuart Walker was given a substantial budget for another Dickens entry, the *Shock!*-worthy *Mystery of Edwin Drood* (1935), starring Claude Rains. Although *Drood* has become identified with the Universal horror canon, *Great Expectations* has remained obscure and unattached to the popular perception of any such celebrated bodies of work, even though Walker and Hull would prove essential to Universal's *Werewolf of London* (1935).

Expectations' tale of torments and salvation from unlikely quarters hinges upon an act of kindness done for Magwitch by the child Pip, who will grow up in the strange company of a vain young woman (Jane Wyatt); an embittered benefactor (Florence Reed) who despises men; and a strange legacy. The tale runs *Drood* a close second for oppressive weirdness, and the opening scene—Pip's encounter with the fugitive in a graveyard—is played for full wrenching impact.

CARL LAEMMLE presents

Charles

DICKENS'

IMMORTAL CLASSIC

GREAT EXPECTATIONS

The movie treat of the season!

with HENRY HULL, PHILLIPS HOLMES, JANE WYATT, FLORENCE REED, ALAN HALE, VALERIE HOBSON

Screenplay by GLADYS UNGER   Directed by STUART WALKER
A STANLEY BERGERMAN PRODUCTION

A UNIVERSAL PICTURE

Secret of the Chateau (1934)

This one was issued to television as a *Shock! Theater* installment, but then it was denied the customary encore in my local-viewing experience. Circumstances of repetition varied, of course, from city to city.

The tolling of a tower bell in the dead of night foretells doom. There lies the redeeming grace–note of eeriness in this sealed-room mystery involving a plot to lure a killer into the open with an auction of a victim's collection of rare books.

Claire Dodd stars as a thief lured into complicity in a scam to steal a Gutenberg Bible. The least of the borderline Universal chillers, *Secret of the Chateau* has been caught sporadically in small-market television syndication since the 1980s.

The Man Who Reclaimed His Head (1934)

Having completed his first film, *The Invisible Man* (1933), Claude Rains returned to New York for Paramount's *Crime Without Passion* (1934). Rains was summoned back to Universal in September of 1934 for *The Man Who Reclaimed His Head* and *The Return of Frankenstein* (which became *Bride of Frankenstein*, without Rains). Rains and Jean Arthur had starred on Broadway in 1932 in *The Man Who Reclaimed His Head*, an antiwar play by Jean Bart (A.K.A. Marie Antoinette Sarlabous), produced in 1932.

The Man Who Reclaimed His Head was filmed during September–October under director Edward Ludwig, who more commonly specialized in lighter fare. Direction and photography are unusual for their avoidance of the trappings of both horror and war cinema. Even such Grand Manner performers as Rains and Lionel Atwill apply restraint in a mortal struggle that ends—not to give away too much—with the pacifist author Rains taking back symbolically that which the plagiarist warmonger Atwill has stolen from him.

"I wanted back what was *me*, what was *mine*...," Rains says, by way of confession and explanation.

Universal tried two advertising angles—one, emphasizing the antiwar stance; the other, touting a horror picture. The exhibitors preferred the Shock Value campaign. The horror fans were disappointed. When Realart Pictures mounted a reissue in 1949, an all-out horror campaign alienated a new generation. The property was remade in 1945 as the apolitical *Strange Confession*, part of Universal's six-picture *Inner Sanctum* series, with Lon Chaney, JR., wielding a machete to reclaim his head from J. Carrol Naish. This, too, was reissued by Realart with a blood-and-horror campaign and a new title: *The Missing Head*. They never learn.

The Man Who Reclaimed His Head remains formally unissued as a video-market title. George Turner identified archival elements at Universal as late as 1990. Bootleg-market copies abound, assuming one knows where to look.

Rendezvous at Midnight (1935)

Rendezvous at Midnight had been the pre-release title of 1934's *The Secret of the Chateau*. No point in allowing a perfectly okay title to go to waste, and so the identity was reapplied to this slight but atmospheric murder yarn.

Ralph Bellamy plays Police Commissioner Robert Edmonds, whose high-toned sweetheart, Sandra Rogers (Valerie Hobson), stands accused in the slaying of a disgraced lawman (Arthur

Vinton) who had attempted to blackmail her. The film is chiefly of interest in the present context because of the presence of Valerie Hobson (of *Bride of Frankenstein*, *Werewolf of London*, *Mystery of Edwin Drood*, &c.); and of *The Raven*'s Irene Ware, in a role crucial to the mistaken-identity murder case. The title of the source–play, *The Silver Fox*, refers to a fur-trimmed garment that figures in the mystery.

The Crimson Trail (1935)

Buck Jones was Junior Laemmle's choice to replace rough-riding Ken Maynard as Universal's top cowboy star. Laemmle's backstabbing gesture had been in the works before the debacle of *Smoking Guns* (Page No. 89), which provided Junior with a convenient finishing stroke. Though more easygoing than Maynard, Jones shared the affinity for the horrors-on-horseback business. This quality predominates in *The Crimson Trail* in the person of a murderous halfwit—played to the malicious giggling-idiot hilt by John Bleifer.

The traditional goods of the genre are delivered in a cattle-rustling racket and a range feud between ranchers Charles French and Carl Stockdale. Jones plays the nephew of one rancher, who comes to the rescue of his uncle's rival following an attack. Indignant at finding himself under suspicion, Jones smokes out the ringleader, a trusted foreman played by Ward Bond. Bond is in cahoots with the madman, who captures Jones and makes ready to do away with him. It all wraps with a showdown, mutually lethal, between Bond and Bleifer.

Such eccentric menaces figured generously in Hollywood's wealth of Germanic Westerns during the Depression years. These also would include the likes of *Under Texas Skies*, *The Rawhide Terror*, *Big Calibre*, *Tombstone Canyon*, and *Randy Rides Alone*. All capture the requisite spirit of adventure, but they also nail that cruel sense of life-out-of-balance that prevails in a society where treachery and brute force are allowed to pass for Law & Order.

The Crimson Trail resurfaced during the early 1990s as a grainy videocassette offering from Foothill Video. MCA/Universal Home Video axed its overambitious Jones series in 1996 before it could get around to a classier edition of *The Crimson Trail*.

CARL LAEMMLE *Presents*

NIGHT LIFE OF THE GODS

For the Love *of* Mique!

MYTHOLOGY opens up and spills all the Greek gods and goddesses on Modern Broadway. Imagine Neptune, Venus, Mercury, Adonis, Apollo, Diana, Bacchus, Hercules swarming into a fashionable night club and stampeding the high-hats and low necks of today. That's the picture.

It is a hilarious novelty comedy [from the book by Thorne Smith] fantastic and odd—so unusual and so well directed by LOWELL SHERMAN that the whole world will love it.

Produced by Carl Laemmle, Jr.

IT'S A UNIVERSAL

Night Life of the Gods (1935; trade-press advertisement, Page No. 97)
The estate of source–author Thorne Smith (springboard of Hal Roach's *Topper* films) has seen to it that this absurdist fantasy has gone unseen for generations. Universal appears not to have preserved usable master elements, although inventory documents indicate at least a dead-storage reference print. The comedy fits squarely in among the Known Realm of Universal terrors, what with its establishing story of a Mad Scientist named Hunter Hawk (Alan Mowbray), who torments the parasitic members of his household with noisy experimentation and, at length, perfects an alchemical device that can transform flesh to stone. This ray serves first to paralyze Hawk's more grasping relatives.

Another such gizmo brings statues to life. Accompanied by a sweetheart (Florine McKinney) who claims to be an ancient sprite, Hawk sets out to bring to life the statues of Græco–Roman gods at New York's Metropolitan Museum of Art. Civilization grates upon the nerves of these reanimated ancients, however, and they return willingly to stone. A just-a-dream finale seems the only reasonable exit; this facile resolution was in the shooting script all along, although the scene may not have been added until after previews.

The laugh-a-minute pace seems poised throughout to lapse into outright horror, which is the conjoined opposite of humor, in any event. Alan Mowbray exhibits sufficient contempt for the social norms as to seem a menacing figure. A barroom siege, with patrons fleeing the sweep of the transforming ray, tips the scales decisively.

Night Life of the Gods proved to be the last film for director Lowell Sherman. A chronic respiratory ailment sidelined him. Sherman died of pneumonia while at work on the first three-color Technicolor feature, *Becky Sharp* (1935). Two 35MM prints are known to exist outside Universal—one, at the UCLA Archive; the other, in private hands.

Remember Last Night? (1935)
James Whale delivered this high-society murder–comedy as a follow-through to *Bride of Frankenstein* (1935). The spirited dialogue contains a pointed reference to *Bride*. A drinking binge among friends, led by Tony Milburn (Robert Young) and his wife, Carlotta (Constance Cummings), would seem a jolly affair—if not for a domestic problem that leaves wealthy Vic Huling (George Meeker) in danger of a kidnapping.

The next morning finds the revelers afflicted with blackout hangovers. No one can remember much about the previous night. Huling turns up slain. The mayhem escalates, complicated by an embezzlement scam and extramarital intrigues. Edward Arnold toplines the cast as an impatient district attorney who assumes that the ordeal must have taught the Milburns the greater virtues of sobriety; they raise a toast to his suggestion.

East of Java (1935)
Here we have the most relentlessly terrifying jungle thriller short of RKO–Radio's back-to-back combo of *The Most Dangerous Game* and *King Kong* (1932–1933)—and one of Universal's most tensely wrought productions, with a massed, lurking menace drawing ever nearer a diminishing encampment of warring civilians.

The demanding star–player role nearly killed Charles Bickford: He was mauled by a lion, well along into the filming, but recovered in time to return for additional scenes following the wrapping of principal photography. Footage of the spontaneous attack found its way into an installment of the weekly *Universal Newsreel* short-subject series.

The Picture of a Thousand Surprises!

CARL LAEMMLE

HOWARD CONSTANCE
ARNOLD · CUMMINGS

SALLY ROBERT
EILERS · YOUNG

*Remember
Last Night?*

ROBERT LOUISE
ARMSTRONG · HENRY

GREGORY REGINALD
RATOFF · DENNY

DIRECTED BY
JAMES WHALE

A CARL LAEMMLE JR PRODUCTION
A UNIVERSAL PICTURE

You'll Never Forget It!

Charles **BICKFORD**
EAST OF JAVA

Bickford is Red Bowers, a fugitive, who bribes his way onto a steamer. The treacherous captain (Leslie Fenton) forces Bowers to tip his hand: He demands to be put ashore. A typhoon forces the ship aground upon a deserted island. The crash would be an ordinary shipwreck, except for a freed cargo of predatory animals that had been captured by passenger Muller (Siegfried Rumann), a circus trainer.

Bowers becomes the survivors' protector. He puts down a rebellion by Wong Bo and a more nearly sympathetic passenger named Larry (Frank Albertson), but then finds himself forced to kill the captain. Muller's lions and tigers pick off most of the others, one–by–one. Muller, maddened, confronts the beasts under the delusion that he is back in his circus arena. Larry and Ann Martin (Elizabeth Young) develop an uneasy truce with Bowers. As a rescue 'plane approaches, Bowers torches the underbrush to distract the cats from Larry and Ann—only to draw the creatures toward himself as a consequence.

Undocumented as a Universal archival property, *East of Java* was last seen in 1999 as a 16MM print among the effects of the George Turner estate—eBayed into oblivion by surviving kin.

The Great Impersonation (1935)

A *Shock!* entry, of course, and shown as such in most metropolitan markets, though not necessarily in all. Edmund Lowe—the movies' original Chandu the Magician—stars as an aristocrat pursuing a dangerous double life in this odd narrative fusion of political treachery and inflicted madness, framed within the tale of a rascal's struggle for redemption. Dwight Frye, that fine secondary-menace bogeyman of *Dracula* and the first two *Frankenstein*s, accounts for a measure of the prevailing tensions, appearing briefly as a lunatic–at–large.

Anachronism runs rampant. Though set in 1914, the film keeps its characters "dressed throughout in 1935 modishness ..., driving about in streamlined automobiles." So noted *Variety*, that influential movie-biz tradepaper, which allowed further: "Probably doesn't matter." More problematical, as the *Variety* critic mentioned, was the laughter of an opening-week audience at a bit of incongruity in which Edmund Lowe "went up to bed with candles [and later was seen] pushing an electric light switch." Such gaffes scarcely compromise the greater effectiveness of a smart adaptation of Phillips Oppenheim's famous novel.

Edmund Lowe and Valerie Hobson.

Lowe plays a banished war-mongering Austrian, VON Ragostein, who rescues a disgraced English lord, Dominey (Lowe, likewise), from an African jungle, only to plot the Englishman's murder as a means of assuming a new identity. Dominey turns the tables on Ragostein, however, and returns to seek a new lease on his own life and quash Ragostein's schemes against the Crown.

Dominey's long-abandoned wife, Eleanor (Valerie Hobson) has gone half–crazy from worry over a murder that she may only have imagined. A forbidding locale known as the Black Bog is a source of unease. A vanished servant (Frye), presumed slain, becomes Eleanor's insane tormentor. Amidst such complications, Dominey regains his title, and his household in the bargain.

A Paramount production of *The Great Impersonation*, directed by George Melford, dates from 1921. John Rawlins' remake (likewise at Universal) dates from 1942.

Night Key (1937)

Shock! Theater used this one, too. It scored low marks among my neighborhood circle of devotees—what with kids being more keenly attuned to thrills more blatant. Even his one wholly benevolent star turn at Universal finds Boris Karloff in an unseemly situation: He is a betrayed and justifiably circumspect genius of an inventor in *Night Key*. The role dovetails with the greater body of Karloff's Mad Doctor pictures, with less a stretch than one might expect.

Universal was no longer its old familiar self by now. The Laemmle regime had ended. A New Universal, whose chief distinguishing mark was a bottom-line obsession in the Accounting Department, retained the impressive production values with none of the adventurous creative attitude that had flourished under Carl Laemmle.

Dave Mallory (Karloff) has been nosed out of the rights to a sophisticated burglar-alarm system by his former partner, Steven Ranger (Samuel S. Hinds), a predatory capitalist. Mallory renders the earlier invention obsolete. Ranger buys into a refined system—only to keep it off the market. Enraged, Mallory informs Ranger: "What I create, I can destroy." (The situation is very like that which would drive Bela Lugosi to a fugue of murderous invention in 1940's *The Devil Bat*.)

Mallory neutralizes the Ranger system. He and a small-time yegg, Petty Louie (a scene-stealing Hobart Cavanaugh), enter protected

establishments, leaving humiliating evidence. There arises a greater threat from a mob boss (Alan Baxter), who kidnaps Mallory's daughter (Jean Rogers) and forces Mallory to help with an outbreak of burglaries. The case seals itself with a car crash that disables the mob. Ranger, in a seemingly generous turnabout (watch out for these backstabbing Chamber of Commerce glad–handers), declines to press charges against Mallory and welcomes him as a partner.

If Karloff had longed for a change of pace, he found it in *Night Key*, which of course was a case of Universal's marking time for the duration of an embargo on American horror films by the British and European censorship machines. Karloff's furious indignation is as intense as ever, however, and his displays of malicious mischief suggest such a subversive guerrilla intellect that it is a wonder the Status Quo enforcers of the Motion Picture Association's Production Code Administration did not object.

The Black Doll (1938)

Here is a remarkable crossover: *The Black Doll* is a key series entry for Universal, delivered by a bare-bones independent producer, Walter A. Futter, whose truer province lay amongst the stepchild-of-Hollywood Poverty Row studios. Futter soon relinquished his involvement with Crime Club Productions, Inc., a franchise tied to a series of popular novels, the better to concentrate on lurid fare that a big outfit like Universal would not remotely consider. The *Crime Club* series would grow to contain 11 titles.

The Black Doll hangs on C. Henry Gordon's seething portrayal of wealthy Nelson Rood, a hateful grouch harboring ugly secrets. The sudden appearance of *la muñeca negra*—the black doll, symbolic of a

THE New UNIVERSAL Presents

"The BLACK DOLL"

WITH

NAN GREY
DONALD WOODS
EDGAR KENNEDY

A Crime Club production

WILLIAM LUNDIGAN · DORIS LLOYD
SID SAYLOR · C. HENRY GORDON
From the novel "The Black Doll" by William Edward Harris

A New UNIVERSAL Picture

Screen play by
HAROLD BUCKLEY
Story by
O. GARRETT
Produced by
IRVING STARR

curse born of rural Mexican superstitions—in his study leads Rood to summon his former partners (John Wray and Addison Richards). They suspect the hideous token is connected with a fourth partner, Barrows, whom Rood had murdered.

Rood is stabbed to death. His daughter, Marian (Nan Grey), summons Nick Halstead (Donald Woods), a detective who happens to be passing through. Halstead takes up the case alongside an incompetent sheriff (Edgar Kennedy). Corpses accumulate. Nick learns that Rood has claimed Marian, Barrows' daughter, as his own offspring. A family friend, harboring a festering old resentment, is revealed as the murderer.

The accurséd household yields a measure of shivers, all right, but it is the irascible comic Edgar Kennedy who carries the yarn along on a crest of ham-fisted humor. The Universal identity sits unsteadily upon *The Black Doll*, which—despite some striking work by that great cinematographer, Stanley Cortez—unspools more like a production of Monogram Pictures or a lesser entry from Republic Pictures. The *Crime Club* series, which occasionally leaned toward the horrific, had started out more auspiciously in 1937 with *The Westland Case* and would continue on bolder notes with such titles as *Danger on the Air, Gambling Ship, The Lady in the Morgue* and *The Last Express* (all from 1938) and *The House of Fear* (Page No. 107), *Inside Information, The Last Warning, Mystery of the White Room* and *The Witness Vanishes* (all from 1939). By comparison with the *Crime Clubs*, however, Universal's uneven *Inner Sanctum* series of the 1940s looks positively top–of–the–line.

The "Crime" of Dr. Hallet (1938)

Big Science and Bad Medicine, in mortal conflict with one another in a Sumatran jungle, drive this marginally science-fictional entry. The motivating quest involves a cure for an epidemic, which claims a colleague of Dr. Paul Hallet (Ralph Bellamy) and pharmacist Jack Murray (William Gargan) in the midst of their research.

An upstart recruit, society physician Phil Saunders (John King), reaches a maverick solution, which he tests upon himself—only to die from a miscalculation on Hallet's part. Hallett swaps identities with Saunders, intending to credit Saunders with the breakthrough but also to enjoy the resulting acclaim on his own terms. The masquerade veers toward Soap Opera when Saunders' estranged wife (Barbara Read) reconsiders upon learning of Saunders' shot at a Nobel Prize. Hallett faces prosecution until the widow decides to publish her husband's findings to spite Hallet. Hallet, back in touch with his more nearly altruistic nature, resumes the vital research.

Ralph Bellamy seems sympathetic throughout, the scam notwithstanding. The role is more a misguided healer than a Mad Doctor–type, but Bellamy's intense manner pushes things in that more genrefied direction. The search for a remedy, with appropriate tensions, forces a premature peak, after which the clash between the deceitful doctor and the vengeful social-climber wife proves a letdown.

Sinners in Paradise (A.K.A.: Secrets of a Sinner; 1938)

A conflicted production on several fronts, this desert-island melodrama is the first of two B–unit assignments imposed upon James Whale as a condition of his completing a contract with Universal; Whale was given the additional duties of producer, and a featured billing as such, without additional compensation. Such ploys only bespoke the New Universal's contempt for the Laemmle period, of which Whale had been a leading figure. Whale spoke of *Sinners in Paradise* and *Wives under Suspicion* as "my punishment pictures." The telling is nonetheless vivid, with a proletarian/antiwar skew amidst a respectable measure of mayhem.

Frankenstein's John Boles plays a reclusive islander who shows more resentment than compassion toward the survivors of an airplane crash that has interrupted his solitude. The castaways include a cold-hearted industrial heiress (Charlotte Wynters); an underworld figure (Bruce

TEMPTRESS! VIXEN! FIREBRAND!
A GIRL WHOSE SINFUL PAST REACHES OUT TO DESTROY MEN!

SECRETS OF A SINNER

Starring
MADGE EVANS
JOHN BOLES
BRUCE CABOT
GENE LOCKHART

Cabot), on the lam from a Mafia hit squad and in possession of a fortune in cash; and warmongering munitions manufacturers (Milburn Stone and Morgan Conway), rivals in a bid to influence a congressman (Gene Lockhart)—who also is among the unwelcome arrivals.

The inevitable outbreaks of violence and ugly revelations lead to the recognition of Boles' Jim Taylor as a surgeon who had fled a murder conviction. A more nearly sympathetic survivor (Madge Evans) convinces Taylor that he must return to civilization. With the more problematical castaways now defunct, there is now room in a boat for an escape.

Sinners in Paradise became a battleground for its scripters' screen credits, with Lester Cole and Harold Buckley attempting to have Louis Stevens' name removed and Stevens filing a counter–complaint with the Writers Guild. All three names finally secured billing via arbitration, although a fourth contributing writer, Robert Lee Johnson, found himself left without formal recognition.

Wives under Suspicion (1938; French poster at facing page)

Practically anything of James Whale's will command the attention of the thriller enthusiasts, except perhaps for the 1936 musical sudser *Show Boat*. This second outcropping of the director's exile rewards renewed interest with a particularly macabre gimmick. The film is a remake of Whale's own *The Kiss before the Mirror* (1933), a soapier and less overtly thrilling study of near–madness provoked by jealousy.

Warren William stars as District Attorney Jim Stowell, who keeps track of his coups the way a gunslinger enumerates his kills. Except that instead of notching a six–shooter, Stowell uses a Chinese-style abacus with beads shaped to resemble miniature skulls. A newly convicted miscreant threatens Stowell with retribution.

Ralph Morgan contributes a fine turn in support as a professor who stands accused of slaying his unfaithful wife. Stowell, who has no patience with the crime-of-passion defense, soon finds himself in a situation similar to that of the professor. Sobered by this realization, Stowell reduces the charge and reunites with his wayward wife (Gail Patrick). Stowell's closing gesture is to order his assistant (Cecil Cunningham) to smash the ominous abacus.

As with *Sinners in Paradise* (above), a tolerable print of this one has surfaced at Alpha Video. Not to say a restored print. Just a down-and-dirty telecine transfer from a shopworn 16MM print that never got shipped back to the distributor after it had done its duty on teevee. Universal did not curate its films uniformly well, and a good many master elements were destroyed outright in a cost-efficient silver-reclamation chemical procedure. So who says recycling is a Boon to Civilization?

The Missing Guest (1938; pictured at Page No. 108)

Rehashed from 1933's *Secret of the Blue Room*, *The Missing Guest* indulges in too much gratuitous comedy to capture the necessary air of gathering menace. The revised shooting script does, however, raise the ante on the creepy business by throwing in a hinted incestuous attraction. Paul Kelly stars as reporter Scoop Hamilton, who scams his way into a private party at a supposedly haunted mansion. William Lundigan is a daring romantic sort who volunteers to disprove the legend of an accursed sealed room—only to turn up missing, and later to engage Kelly in a climactic showdown. An array of ghastly noises is explained away as the work of a treacherous butler. Not to give away too much, y'know; as if foreknowledge would spoil the pleasure of feeling smarter than the movie one happens to be watching.

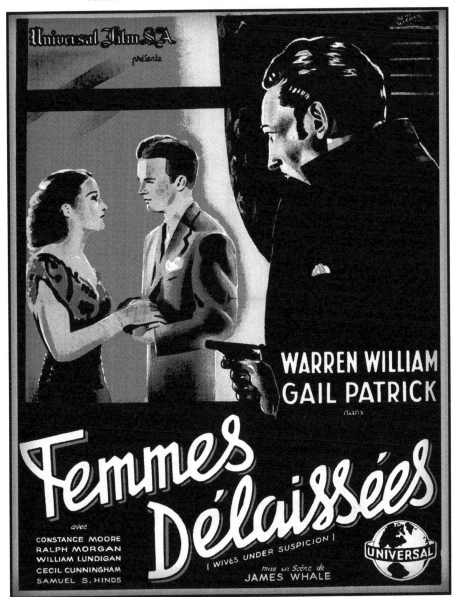

Universal Film S.A présente

WARREN WILLIAM
GAIL PATRICK
(alias)

Femmes Délaissées

avec
CONSTANCE MOORE
RALPH MORGAN
WILLIAM LUNDIGAN
CECIL CUNNINGHAM
SAMUEL S. HINDS

(WIVES UNDER SUSPICION)
mise en Scène de
JAMES WHALE

UNIVERSAL

***The House of Fear* (1939; pictured at Page No. 109)**

A *Crime Club* series entry from the stepchild-of-Universal Crime Club Productions, Inc., *The House of Fear* is in fact a remake of Paul Leni's historic *The Last Warning* (1929), with police-procedural embellishments. John Woodford, a slain actor, appears to have returned as a ghost, prowling the very precincts where he was murdered in mid–performance. Detective Arthur McHugh (William Gargan), posing as a producer, reopens the theatre and re–stages the fatal production, assuming that the murderer will make a comeback in the bargain. The

actor (Walter Woolf King) who has assumed Woodford's role falls victim, and ghostly threats assail the troupe. The investigation leads to a poisoned needle hidden in a microphone. It boils down to a real-estate scam, calculated to diminish the value of the theatre. A money-hungry actress (Dorothy Arnold) gets in the last word with a surprising revelation.

Neither this one nor the 1929 source-film is to be confused with 1938's *The Last Warning*, a conventional sleuthing piece that served as both a *Crime Club* installment and a continuation of the adventures of detective Bill Crane, as played by Preston Foster. Nor does this *House of Fear* bear any kinship, beyond the Universal pedigree, to a like-titled *Sherlock Holmes* series picture (Page No. 74).

• • •

For many years, the availability of such films as these remained a matter of luck-of-the-draw television-syndicate play. Which was really more a matter of riding herd on the fine print in *TV Guide*—itself a helpful tool in the film-archaeology game. Used to be, anyhow, until Rubert Murdoch's sleazemongering publishing empire transformed *TV Guide* into just another celebrity-gossip rag. Much of that thrill-of-the-hunt vibe has been diminished by the greater likelihood of finding this title or that in rotation on the Turner Classic Movies channel. Diminished in a *good* way, I mean to say.

AMERICAN CINEMA: A CURATED EXHIBITION

How to Make a Monster: I had trained for a career in Museum Administration under the tutelage of Dr. H.D. Bugbee, a Working Artist who also (during the midcentury) ran Texas' Panhandle–Plains Historical Museum. The lure of the newsroom took prior claim, however, while I was in high school, and by college I had taken the Journalistic Vows of Poverty and never looked back. Still, the museum racket beckons, and on several occasions I've slipped back into the Curatorial Uniform to handle film exhibitions for such institutions as the Amon Carter Museum of American Art, the Modern Art Museum of Fort Worth, the Fort Worth Museum of Science & History, and lesser egghead venues. This section documents the development of such an exhibition, the Carter's *American Cinema* (2003–2004), in conjunction with a seasonal exhibition of paintings and sculptural works from the permanent collection. Accompanying essays were published as collaterals distributed amongst the audience.

AMERICAN CINEMA SERIES: AMON CARTER MUSEUM

The series offers a concise and accessible survey of American cinema from the Studio System period of Old Hollywood, concentrating upon American regional cultures as seen through the (sometimes skewed) perceptions of the studios and their resident artists. One authentically provincial production (of North Texas origins) is included for the sake of a more striking context, and for a heightened localized interest.

In a sequence of showings and discussions covering six weeks, the selections will provide a kaleidoscopic view of familiar American locales, each rendered with a mixture of attempted accuracy and that larger-than-life glamour that is a hallmark of the motion-picture industry. Genres will vary, as well, and enlightening program notes will accompany each selection.

1. The Depression Era South: Charles Laughton's *The Night of the Hunter* (1955). Hard times breed extraordinary perils and resourceful survivors in Davis Grubb's tale of a predatory holy-roller confidence man and his attempts to claim loot from a robbery. Charles Laughton's only turn as a director and (uncredited) screenwriter; Robert Mitchum's finest performance of a distinguished career; and Lillian Gish's finest performance as a survivor of the silent-picture era.

2. The Urban Crime Drama: Roland West's *Alibi* (1929). Defining example of the evolution of a resilient genre, with a remarkably progressive reconciliation of sound with pictorial qualities for a picture so early in the talking-picture revolution. Long considered a lost film, and still seldom seen outside the archival realm.

3. The Civilized West: Erich VON Stroheim's *Greed* (1925). The epic tale of a San Francisco community turn asunder by a thirst for wealth. Stroheim's career as a director effectively ended with the extravagances of *Greed*, although the artist would reinvent himself as a busy actor later on during the 1920s.

4. Small-Town America of the 19TH Century: Sam Wood's *Kings Row* (1942). A bracing examination of small-town life in terms of thwarted romance, abuse of economic power, and misguided loyalties.

5. The Borderlands: William Wellman's *The Ox-Bow Incident* **(1943)** or Lewis Milestone's *Of Mice and Men* (1939). Each film has a distinguished literary pedigree, and each is acknowledged as a classic.

6. American Ethnic Cinema: Spencer Williams' *The Blood of Jesus* (1941). A departure from the generalized concentration upon major-studio productions with *The Blood of Jesus*, a production from Sack Amusements of Dallas, which was affiliated with a number of Los Angeles' smaller studios but shot its own films on North Texas locations. Filmed around Waxahachie with a largely nonprofessional cast, this film was designed specifically for African–American neighborhood theatres of its day and went largely unseen otherwise. I served on the team responsible for its preservation, which came about following the accidental discovery in 1983 of a wealth of abandoned motion pictures in a long-neglected warehouse at Tyler, Texas. Hence the Tyler, Texas, Black Film Collection, at Southern Methodist University.

Incidental Notes and Items for Consideration:

1. One of the more appealing aspects of my *Classics* series for the Modern Art Museum is the inclusion of short comedies and cartoons as a prelude to the featured selections. This amenity can be provided on video, as well, with a large selection of one- and two-reel titles (five to 20 minutes each) amongst which to choose.

2. If the series should coincide with the week of Halloween, a classic film from the horror genre would serve a genuinely crowd-pleasing function and perhaps even broaden the audience. A natural choice in this respect would be 1943's *Son of Dracula*, which is distinctive as the first in Universal Pictures' famous series of Gothics to be set upon American soil, as opposed to the traditional English or Mittel European setting.

• • •

An additional curatorial project for the Carter Museum, *American Film Noir* (2003), involved these preparatory notes:

AMERICAN FILM NOIR SERIES: AMON CARTER MUSEUM

The series proposes a representative survey of the American *film noir* style through three prominent examples dating from (1) its post-WWII heyday; (2) the near–end of the original cycle during the latter 1950s; and (3) a resurgence during the distinctly different social climate of the middle 1960s.

Film noir (literally, "black film") is more accurately considered a figurative concept, in the sense of reflecting a turbulent *zeitgeist*. With the Western film, as the cultural historian Alain Silver has pointed out, *noir* shares the distinction of being an indigenous American film style, with few precise literary or social antecedents.

The selections are predicated upon the presence (and the lasting popular appeal) of such seminal *noir*-manner directors as Nicholas Ray, Jacques Tourneur, and Edward Dmytryk, and of such ideally suited star players as Humphrey Bogart, Aldo Ray, Anne Bancroft, and Gregory Peck.

1. Nicholas Ray's *In a Lonely Place* **(1950).** Humphrey Bogart's first independent production away from his longtime home base at Warner Bros. is a haunting study of the killing urge latent in a WWII combat veteran and struggling Hollywood screenwriter who finds himself under suspicion of murder. The pictorial design is crucial to a gathering mood of unease and desolation, drawing upon such eccentric landmarks as the meandering Mulholland Drive and a police station modeled after the Taj Mahal.

2. Jacques Tourneur's *Nightfall* (1957). A victim of random misfortunes, Aldo Ray looks every bit the type who should be able to overcome such obstacles—if only his responses were not compromised by a mounting paranoia. The circumstances, and Ray's responses, are classic ingredients of the *noir* style. Jacques Tourneur had proved himself an ideal director for the emerging idiom during the 1940s at RKO–Radio Pictures, a studio crucial to the movement. With the late-in-the-game *Nightfall* and another picture of the same year, the supernaturally motivated *Night of the Demon*, Tourneur paid efficient homage to the producer who had given him an early break, Val Lewton. [See also: Page Nos. 13 *et Seq.* in the present volume.]

3. Edward Dmytryk's *Mirage* (1965). Dmytryk had become an important *film noir* stylist during the 1940s with *The Devil Commands* and, especially, *Murder, My Sweet.* The idiom practically had run its course by the end of the 1950s, but Dmytryk returned with renewed purpose in *Mirage*, substituting corporate and Cold War intrigues for the wartime and postwar social ills that had fueled the original cycle. Gregory Peck plays a sufferer of amnesia, struggling to recollect experiences that might be better left forgotten. Walter Matthau provides an element of nervous comic relief that serves at length to darken the mood.

KARL BODMER SERIES: AMON CARTER MUSEUM

And herewith, a set of examples of film-exhibition essays, reproduced from yet another curated festival for the Amon Carter Museum, *Karl Bodmer's Influence on Hollywood* (2003). This show was presented in conjunction with the special exhibition *A Faithful and Vivid Picture: Karl Bodmer's North American Prints.*

Elliott Silverstein's *A Man Called Horse* (1970)

In such grueling Real World experiences as the ordeals of the frontiersmen Simon Girty and John Eli Colter, and in such factually inspired fiction as Richard Connell's often-filmed "The Most Dangerous Game" (1924), lie the origins of Elliott Silverstein's *A Man Called Horse* (1970) as a persuasive account of the clash of Cultural Imperatives between the new settlers of North America and the native tribes. The resolution of this remarkable film points more hopefully toward integration and mutual assimilation than did either Colter's adventure of the early 1800s or a Depression Era film that was based more directly upon the explorer's fight for survival—but *A Man Called Horse* packs a wealth of truth more accurate than any mere recitation of history.

Much of this accuracy has to do with the Maximilian–Bodmer Expedition, whose wealth of images (drawn from life) proves to have exerted an influence upon the attitude of *A Man Called Horse*. Karl Bodmer's art, in turn, would inspire such 20TH Century historians as Clyde Dollar, who not only demanded greater truthfulness from the Hollywood establishment but also became a consultant to this film's production company. The tribulations of Colter—an early visitor to what is now Yellowstone Park, and discoverer of a hot-springs area known as Colter's Hell—provides a springboard from which *Horse*'s source–author, Dorothy M. Johnson, and screenwriter Jack DeWitt lend a sense of desperate adventure to the true-to-life settings.

In 1825, Lord John Morgan (Richard Harris), a British aristocrat (a Bostonian in the novel), sets out through America's Western frontier. His guides are slain by a Sioux war party. Morgan is taken prisoner. His captors name him "Horse" and treat him as a beast of burden. Morgan learns the way of life from another captive, Batise (Jean Gascon).

The Sioux gave him a choice, live like an animal or die like one.

RICHARD HARRIS as "A MAN CALLED HORSE"
Also Starring DAME JUDITH ANDERSON Co-Starring JEAN GASCON
MANU TUPOU Introducing CORINNA TSOPEI
Produced by SANDY HOWARD Screenplay by JACK DE WITT Directed by ELLIOT SILVERSTEIN A SANDY HOWARD Production
Music by LEONARD ROSENMAN PANAVISION® TECHNICOLOR® A NATIONAL GENERAL PICTURES RELEASE OF
A CINEMA CENTER FILMS PRESENTATION

Upon comprehending that he can regain freedom only by assimilating, Morgan struggles for acceptance upon tribal terms. He wins the affections of the chief's sister, Running Deer (Corinna Tsopei); he gains the respect of Chief Yellow Hand (Manu Tupou) by undergoing an agonizing ritual by which the Sioux test and sometimes even acknowledge the bravery of their most ferocious warriors. And at length, Morgan fights alongside his Sioux brothers against the rival Shoshones and then leaves with an armed escort to assure his return to civilization. Civilization, of course, will never look quite the same.

Apart from a very Hollywood-styled immersion in violence and a melodramatically induced battle sequence—qualities that earned *Horse* an M-as-in-*mature* rating, ancestor of the R Certificate, from the Motion Picture Association—and its facile conceit that only an infusion of Euro–British strategy can enable a Sioux victory, the film is a splendid example of historical and cultural accuracy and anthropological observation in the service of commercial storytelling.

As the result of a combination of the so-called New Freedom in Hollywood (allowing an unaccustomed harshness and frankness under the R ratings), and a gathering interest in cultures apart, the late 1960s and early 1970s became an era of revisionism in American cinema—not so much a revision of history, as a return to the historical record in defiance of the stereotypes and clichés of 20TH Century Popular Culture. Building upon such breakthroughs of the post-WWII years as Delmer Daves' *Broken Arrow* and *Drum Beat* (1950–1954) and William Wellman's *Across the Wide Missouri* (1951), the new revisionist filmmakers dissected the conventions of the genre and replaced or merged them with sterner attitudes. Ralph Nelson's *Soldier Blue* and Arthur

Penn's *Little Big Man* (1970–1971) looked beyond the simplistic divisions of Cavalry-vs.-Indians campaigns to find the more daunting issue of conspiratorial treachery. Sam Peckinpah's *The Wild Bunch* (1969) pronounced honorable heroism a Lost Cause in a wilderness suffocated by predatory capitalism. *A Man Called Horse* declares tribal life superior (with qualifications) to Polite Society.

The excruciating centerpiece is the ritual that Richard Harris undergoes. The ordeal involves his suspension by blades embedded in his pectoral muscles. The makeup and camera-and-stagecraft effects remain unnerving.

If *Horse*'s insights are compromised by the central presence of an outsider—a point of identification for the Mass Audience—then at least DeWitt's screenplay seldom condescends. The general avoidance of spoken English among the Sioux conveys meaning without the artifice of subtitling, and it becomes patent that Richard Harris' Morgan will owe his greater freedom (from stifling civilization) to tribal captivity. (Harris would reprise the role in 1976's *Return of a Man Called Horse* and in 1982's *Triumphs of a Man Called Horse*.) The character arc of Morgan, however, goes unmatched by any of the Sioux characters.

The most direct cinematic ancestor of *A Man Called Horse*, incidentally, would be Mack V. Wright's *Riders of the Whistling Skull* (Republic Pictures; 1937), which contains virtually a re–enactment of the pursuit of John Colter and his frantic strategy to outlast his stalkers.

William Wellman's *Across the Wide Missouri* (1951)

The chief trouble with high-adventure movies of the present day is that few of their makers are adventurers in their own right. Granted that all movies are make–believe to one extent or another, still the essence of make–believe lies in a sense of truth underlying the fantasy thus deployed. With their roots in Hollywood deal–making more so than in bold exploration or wartime heroism, such latter-day stalwarts of the action picture as Joel Silver and Jerry Bruckheimer bring considerably less credibility to their pictures than such authentically adventurous forebears as William Wellman, W.S. Van Dyke, or the partnership of Merian C. Cooper and Ernest B. Schoedsack.

William A. "Wild Bill" Wellman, the director of the present selection, earned his nickname the hard way. He joined the French Foreign Legion upon the outbreak of World War I, and when America entered the conflict three years later he flew with the Lafayette Escadrille. Mustered out of service on account of combat injuries, Wellman became a stunt flyer and barnstormer in the United States. He broke into movies after a chance meeting with Douglas Fairbanks, when Wellman's 'plane made a forced landing on the actor's estate. Wellman tried acting, in Fairbanks' production of *Knickerbocker Buckaroo* (1919), but learned early on that he preferred to be in charge. He worked his way from prop–handler to assistant director to fully fledged director, and in 1927 his personally motivated *Wings*, a drama of camaraderie among WWI aviators and the first Academy Award winner for Best Picture, propelled Wellman to the front ranks.

Known as an uncompromising maverick who occasionally settled disagreements amidships with fistfights, Wellman closed out his career in 1958 with a return to a WWI aviation setting in *Lafayette Escadrille*, to which he contributed a narration that seems almost a memoir. Many of his pictures are considered classics today—1931's *The Public Enemy*, 1943's *The Ox–Bow Incident*, and 1945's *The Story*

of G.I. Joe, to name a few—while many others, such as 1954's proto-typical disaster melodrama *The High and the Mighty* and 1933's Chinatown crime–thriller *The Hatchet Man,* remain ripe for popular rediscovery. Likewise for *Across the Wide Missouri.*

Wellman was particularly adept within the Western genre; he had polished the skills during the 1920s as a favorite director of the cowboy star Buck Jones. Wellman's affinity for an authentically conceived American frontier had drawn him particularly to the paintings and field sketches of such adventurer–artists as Karl Bodmer and George Catlin.

Across the Wide Missouri is particularly in the debt of Bodmer—not merely in the scenic authenticity that Wellman demanded of art directors James Basevi and Cedric Gibbons, but also for the approximation of Social Authenticity. The source is Bernard DeVoto's Pulitzer-bait novel *Across the Wide Missouri,* published in 1947 as part of a monumental shelf of frontier history and containing images from the Bodmer catalogue. DeVoto had christened his book after a phrase from the traditional folksong, "Shenandoah," and the movie version takes its narrative cue from that same song's lyric involving "a white man [who] loved an Indian maiden."

The film draws its thrust from the culture–clash between Native Americans and white settlers during the early 19TH Century. In 1829, trapper Flint Mitchell (Clark Gable) forges into the wilderness in search of pelts. Mitchell approaches the hostile Blackfoot Indian territory with a strategy to marry a tribeswoman whose family controls prime territory. Mitchell's bride, Kamiah, is played memorably by the Mexican film star Maria Elena Marqués. Kamiah gradually brings out a hidden tenderness in Mitchell. Their small expedition moves deep into an untamed land, where the threat of aggression is portrayed more in terms of mood than via the easier route of thrilling violence.

The danger is less that which is faced by Clark Gable and his *compadres,* as it is the implicit threat that Gable's brand of civilization poses to an idyllic way of life. In this light, the film "alternates between lyricism and bitterness," as the cultural historian Phil Hardy has interpreted it. Underscoring this mixed attitude is an off-screen narration by Howard Keel, whose otherwise un-introduced character proves to be the son of Mitchell and Kamiah. Beyond the vivid character portrayals and a gripping story, *Across the Wide Missouri* proves just as valuable as an exceptional scenic study, with camera chief William C. Mellor's compositions often seeming to recapture Bodmer's vision of the settings.

Clocking in at a brisk 78 minutes, *Across the Wide Missouri* was originally shown in a lengthier cut that the studio trimmed prior to general release. The resulting pace is reminiscent of the headlong rush of Wellman's *The Ox–Bow Incident,* but Wellman is less concerned with indicting the meaner aspects of civilization than he is with lamenting the demise of a more nearly natural way of life—and with honoring Bodmer, in the process.

Delmer Daves' *Drum Beat* (1954)

A finer understanding of *Drum Beat,* an obscure film by Delmer Daves, requires an acquaintance with the director's better-known *Broken Arrow,* from only four years earlier. In 1950, a courageous move by director Anthony Mann—more active at the time as a *film noir* stylist—had caused the development of a maverick picture at MGM called *Devil's Doorway,* in which one heroic Native American character would become not only the focus of the story but also an emblem of sympathetic concentration upon the social problems of Indians as a class.

WARNER BROS. present

ALAN LADD

in DELMER DAVES'

"DRUM BEAT"

They called him
the Wanderer
because a horse
was his home...

they called him
'Injun Lover'
but never
to his face...

BUT THEY
CALLED ON HIM
WHEN EVERYONE
ELSE HAD RUN
AWAY !

CinemaScope

WARNERCOLOR

AUDREY DALTON · MARISA PAVAN ROBERT KEITH · RODOLFO ACOSTA A JAGUAR PRODUCTION

WRITTEN AND DIRECTED BY DELMER DAVES PRESENTED BY WARNER BROS.

Devil's Doorway served, however, merely to pave the way for Daves' *Broken Arrow* at 20TH Century–Fox. So concerned was MGM about the perceived radical sensibilities of *Devil's Doorway* that the big studio delayed the opening, allowing Fox abundant time to charge into production on the similarly concerned *Broken Arrow*—which wound up beating *Doorway* into release. Only after *Broken Arrow* had caused a popular sensation and, in turn, touched off a trend without precedent, did MGM proceed with distribution of *Devil's Doorway*. (The progressive nature of these films is tempered by the fact that each used a non–Indian in its leading role: Robert Taylor as a factually based fictional character in *Doorway*, and Jeff Chandler as the warrior Cochise in *Arrow*. Such were the realities of casting for star–value in Old Hollywood.)

As the trendsetter by default—and a less tough-minded film than *Devil's Doorway—Broken Arrow* not only gave Jeff Chandler his first of quite a few American Indian roles but also teamed him with James Stewart, as a Cavalry scout who settles in among Cochise's Apaches and helps to prevent an outbreak of hostilities. Where Hollywood eventually would muster the gumption to blame the mistreatment of the Indians upon governmental and Big Business interests, here Daves and screenwriter Michael Blankfort confine the element of villainy to small-time crooks and renegade settlers. Nevertheless, Chandler's Cochise is the courageous essence of the tale, and tribal life is seen—as witnessed during the 19TH Century by Karl Bodmer in field sketches, paintings, and polished engravings—as cultured and ordered, rather than savage and transient. More daring (for its time) is the element of romance between Stewart and Debra Paget, as a tribeswoman, even though the resolution requires her death and his return to white society.

Daves had started out behind the cameras in the Western genre, as a propmaster on James Cruze's acknowledged classic of 1923, *The Covered Wagon*. A gift for writing cinched Daves' career toward the close of the 1920s, and by 1943 he had become a busy director, adept in a variety of genres. His passion for Western history caused Daves to mount *Drum Beat* as a project more personally motivated than many other assignments. Where he had examined the culture–clashes of Westward expansion from an Apache vantage in *Broken Arrow*, now he would assume the viewpoint of the settlers.

Alan Ladd stars as Johnny Mackay, who is commissioned by President Grant (Hayden Rorke) to establish a treaty in the Pacific Northwest with the warlike Modoc nation. The chieftain Kintpuash (Charles Bronson, in his first prominent role) uses territorial claims as a pretext for sustaining a campaign of terrorism. All attempts at a settlement prove futile when Kintpuash stages a massacre during a peace summit. Mackay's allies among the Modocs include Manok (Anthony Caruso) and a prospective romantic interest, Toby (Marisa Pavan). Complicating matters is the arrival of Nancy Meek (Audrey Dalton), who also has an interest in the peace commissioner. Mackay and Kintpuash settle matters with a bracing riverside showdown.

Ladd is in his heroic element, but Charles Bronson comes close to stealing the show as the indignant tribal agitator—handily as memorable a performance as Chandler's in *Broken Arrow*, and only slightly less central. Anthony Caruso and Marisa Pavan do well with the more sympathetic Indian roles, and Warner Anderson is outstanding as a doomed commander. Robert Keith is particularly memorable as a settler bearing a grudge, with ample reason, against Kintpuash.

As significant as the portrayals and the historically smart screenplay are the majestic scenic values achieved by camera chief J. Peverell Marley. These compositions are modeled after the Bodmer plates, particularly in the re–creations of tribal life. The shooting locations are in the vicinity of Slide Rock State Park near Sedona, Arizona, south of Flagstaff. The strategically well-irrigated Slide Rock region provided a principal shooting site for both *Broken Arrow* and *Drum Beat.*

John Ford's *My Darling Clementine* (1946)

Nothing in the history of the Hollywood-style Western movie is so complex that an understanding of John Ford cannot clarify it. Ford, a linchpin of a genre, redefined a Code of the West in crystalline terms even while he helped to bolster the frontier-adventure picture against its own escalating simple–mindedness as the Depression Era of the 1930s gave way to the wartime 1940s.

Escapism is not such a bad thing in itself, but in practically a stroke the Western had broken the faith with its hard-bitten origins— an acknowledgment of the cruelty of life on the unsettled fringes, filtered through the harsh Germanic Expressionism of early-day Hollywood—and become fatuous as a consequence.

From the bold dignity of James Cruze's *The Covered Wagon* (1923) and Raoul Walsh's *The Big Trail* (1930), on through the shabbier naturalism of Robert North Bradbury's low-budgeted but dead-earnest matinée Westerns of the early 1930s (many of which served to cushion John Wayne's fall from the premature prominence of *The Big Trail*), the Western as a class captured certain homely truths about the times and the places it attempted to revisit. Things took a turn for the sillier in 1935, when a radio singer and small-roles actor named Gene Autry found sudden movie stardom with an unlikely musical/science–fiction/Western serial called *The Phantom Empire*—triggering a cowboy-crooner sensation that would all but marginalize the sterner qualities of the traditional Western. Not all Westerns are created equal, but John Ford can only raise one's expectations of all Westerns.

Ford's masterstroke, with *Stagecoach* in 1939, had been simply to refit the Western with a stately and intelligent appeal to customers who might enjoy a rip-snorting frontier adventure built along the same lines of dramatic substance that would figure in a *Grand Hotel* or a *Mutiny on the Bounty.* Ford had been practicing the screen-directing craft since 1917, often as a persuasive voice for the Western genre, and *Stagecoach* made for a profound reassertion.

Hardly one to typecast himself, though, Ford would tell other stories about other times and other places—including an array of War Department productions for captive audiences of enlisted men during WWII—until he found the occasion right for another bravura Western. Hence 1946's *My Darling Clementine* and its vivid account of a pivotal showdown in the history of how formalized justice, if not necessarily civilization, came to the borderlands of the 19TH Century .

The singing-cowboy movies had persisted, of course—but the arrival of a John Ford Western lent hope. Ford represented his own brand of escapism, a reappraisal of history in terms of a longing for a vanished near–wilderness, a historical perspective, and a patina of romanticized sentiment glazing the tough-as-leather imagery. An ultimate admiring remark would be to hail Ford for "painting a Remington," figuratively speaking, on moving-picture film. Frederic Remington, that is—not the firearms of that name.

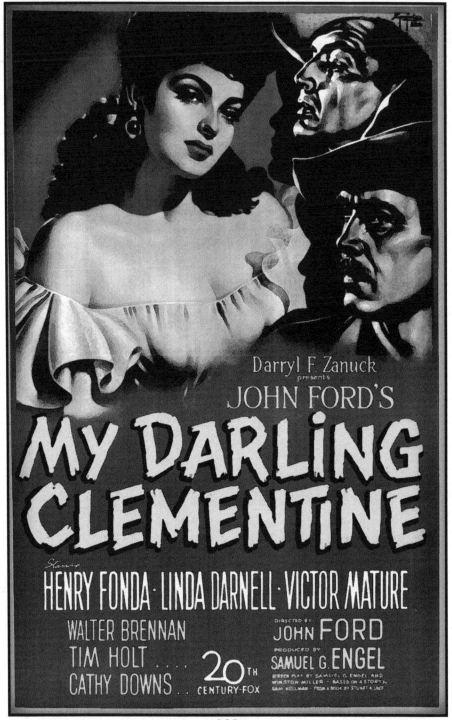

For *Clementine*, Ford tackled an often-filmed combination of history and legend—specifically, as told in Stuart N. Lake's book, *Wyatt Earp: Frontier Marshal*, published in 1931 and filmed twice as *Frontier Marshal* during its own decade. Where those prior versions had derived more-or-less strictly from the book, Ford's approach held the advantage of a direct encounter with Wyatt Earp (1848–1929): Earp had taken up residence in Los Angeles, and Ford arranged a meeting in which Earp offered a detailed description of the gunfight at the O.K. Corral.

The tale is that of the Earp Brothers—Henry Fonda as Wyatt, Tim Holt as Virgil, Ward Bond as Morgan, and Don Garner as James—and their campaign to rout an entrenched mob from the region surrounding Tombstone, Arizona. Of fundamental weight is the all-but-antiheroic presence of Doc Holliday, a doomed and deadly catalyst in the range war, as played by Victor Mature. The title role of Clementine Carter, whose arrival triggers a chain–reaction of intrigues and romantic tensions, is played by Cathy Downs, but the prevailing female presence belongs to Linda Darnell, as a saloon dancer torn by conflicting loyalties.

With *Clementine*, Ford and his collaborative screenwriters were helping to invent a subgenre that would come to be called the Adult Western as the postwar 1940s gave way to the 1950s, blazing a trail for not only his own regathering interest but also for such since-acknowledged classics as Fred Zinnemann's *High Noon* (1952), George Stevens' *Shane* (1953), and Nicholas Ray's *Johnny Guitar* (1954). An emphasis upon romantic anguish allowed "consequently less time for six–shooting and hoof–beating ... a bit tame for the average outdoor fan," as the show-business tradepaper *Variety* said in a review published a week before *Clementine*'s premiere on Oct. 16, 1946, in San Francisco. *Variety* continued: "[A]dded appeal for the *femme* trade will more than compensate."

Nothing tame here about Ford's eccentric visualization, which risks achieving style for style's sake at the sacrifice of a relationship with the story itself. If the picture occasionally halts in its tracks to allow Ford and camera boss Joe MacDonald to achieve an artistic effect, then the film vindicates such choices with a panoramic quality that achieves in black–and–white what many a Technicolor shoot would fail to accomplish.

Henry Fonda anchors the tale—a bereaved and vengeful brother, moved to accept a Law & Order job on personal grounds but gradually assuming a more selfless stance. Doc Holliday, an embodiment of John Donne's famous verse about "run[ning] to meet death," emerges as the most extravagant presence, establishing Victor Mature as an actor of depth and nuance where he had managed previous roles largely on looks. Dallas-born Linda Darnell turns in a passionate portrayal (though outside her ethnicity) of a tempestuous dancer from Mexico, vying with Cathy Downs' cultured Bostonian, Clementine Carter, for control of the affections of the uncontrollable Doc Holliday. (The musical *leitmotif* for Cathy Downs' character, the traditional melody "My Darling Clementine," inspires an astonishing range of variations from composers Alfred Newman and Cyril Mockridge.)

The necessary menace is represented by Walter Brennan, as the vile patriarch of a clan that escalates from cattle–rustling to murder. Brennan's comeuppance, following the satisfying payoff of a harrowing showdown, is one of the more rewarding such moments in cinema.

The ensemble cast is a Who's Who of Old Hollywood dependables, with such standouts as Grant Withers—a producer and stock-company actor, usually as a lawman, with such low-budget studios as Monogram and Republic—in the role of badman Ike Clanton; and old-timer J. Farrell MacDonald, a heroic and sympathetic presence from the 1920s and 1930s, as a bartender. Seen as a troublemaker whose drunken rampage inspires an early act of heroism is gaunt Charles Stevens, a grandson of the Apache warrior Geronimo. The director's brother, Francis Ford, seen as a town character, had been a prominent director. Though personally estranged from John Ford, Francis would continue to serve John's films as a memorable backup player.

Fox President Darryl F. Zanuck could not resist tampering: He ordered approximately half an hour trimmed to achieve a 97-minute running time. Zanuck claimed a more coherent exposition as a consequence, but likelier the recutting was aimed at allowing the theatres to squeeze in an extra showing each day. Some of the scissored footage survived, however, and a partial restoration from 1995 by the U.C.L.A. Film Archive clocks in at 102 minutes. (The version on view here is announced as the original Zanuck cut.)

John Ford can scarcely be said to have created single–handedly the more timeless and mature-minded approach to the Western—indeed, even the rip-snorting 1930s had seen the occasional foreshadowing of *Stagecoach* and its kind, from studios large and small—but Ford exerts the most emphatic influence at filtering the harshness of frontier life through that crucial lens of historical perspective. A Ford hallmark is the use of speculative, analytical dialogue, as opposed to the more typical Western in which (as the historian Wheeler Dixon has put it) "everything is immediate, vicious, do–or–die, [and] all dialogue is reduced to motivation." Where a Western by, for example, Robert N. Bradbury or Joe Kane is a work *of its moment*, operating on an immediate antagonistic level, a Ford Western is a work *of our moment*, an extended glance backward in search of an understanding of the Human Condition.

In a follow–through to *My Darling Clementine*, Henry Fonda and Cathy Downs starred in a 1947 dramatization for *Lux Radio Theatre*. Stuart Lake's *Wyatt Earp: Frontier Marshal* also would provide the basis of the 1953 film *Powder River*. Wyatt Earp has figured in any number of other motion pictures; more recent filmings have been 1993's *Tombstone* and 1994's *Wyatt Earp,* starring Kevin Costner.

John Ford's *Wagon Master* (1950)

In an earlier session involving John Ford and his 1946 film, *My Darling Clementine*, we had touched on the Code of the West that Ford managed to crystallize in his recurring commitment to elevating the frontier adventure picture beyond tuneful Saturday-matinée melodrama. This system of values—a reconsideration of times past in search of enlightenment, more so than reactionary nostalgic indulgence—may be most vividly defined in Ford's lesser-known *Wagon Master*.

Now, *Wagon Master* is almost a forgotten film today, at least by comparison with such star-driven entries as 1939's *Stagecoach*, 1948's *Fort Apache*, and of course Ford's finest hour (*two* hours, actually), 1956's *The Searchers*. Many people who hear the title of *Wagon Master* tend to identify it with a network teleseries that occurred later on during the 1950s as a loose spinoff of *Wagon Master*—a weekly portmanteau Western called *Wagon Train*, which elevated the movie's key backup player, Ward Bond, to the starring role and even involved John Ford's participation at one point in 1957.

Nowadays, it is more common to see a teleseries spin off into a big-screen movie—a phenomenon that has occurred with teevee programs as diverse as *Twin Peaks* and *Scooby-Doo*. The movies had a greater confidence in John Ford's day, however, and whether a picture generated a sequel or a television takeoff was immaterial. Ford made self-contained stories for the screen, and beyond this constancy of purpose he preferred never to dwell on any one favorite film lest it interrupt his progress at finding ever-stronger ways to tell each new story.

Wagon Master found Ford in the continuing good company of producer Merian C. Cooper, a World War I aviator–turned–moviemaker whose documentary ventures of the 1920s had drawn him and his original partner in business and artistry, Ernest B. Schoedsack, into Corporate Hollywood early on in the Great Depression. Cooper and Ford had worked together as early as 1934, when Ford's tale of war in the Mideast, *The Lost Patrol*, fell under Cooper's administration at RKO–Radio Pictures. Cooper was a believer in virile, larger-than-life narrative values (his ultimate statement to that effect is the 1933 *King Kong*, with Schoedsack), and Cooper's eventual partnership with Ford had seemed a foregone conclusion.

Their Argosy Studio was a godsend for RKO, yielding such successes as *The Fugitive* (1947), *3 Godfathers* (1948), *Fort Apache* (1948), *She Wore a Yellow Ribbon* (1949), and *Rio Grande* (1950). Their less commercially successful collaborations for RKO were *Mighty Joe Young* (1949), a sentimentalized semi–remake of *King Kong* with director Schoedsack at near-constant odds with producer Ford; and Ford's own *Wagon Master*, which became the final RKO release of an Argosy production.

Ford nevertheless held *Wagon Master* among his favorites, relating to several late-in-life interviewers his belief that "*Wagon Master* came closest to what I had hoped to achieve." The film is an optimistic account of a Mormon wagon train's journey over a treacherous path into Utah. More an all-star production (which is to say *no* stars, in terms of marquée names) than the customary Ford picture, *Wagon Master* builds itself around the robust ensemble playing of Ward Bond, Ben Johnson, and Harry Carey, Jr.—each of whom has his showier solo moments. Emphasizing interaction and character development over gunplay or fisticuffs, the film delivers a fascinating mixture of archetypal Western presences including devout pilgrims, hard-working cowboys and trailhands, deranged badmen, and hard-drinking show-business hams. An encounter with a Navajo party might result in a fireside communion rather than in mayhem. A villainous bunch of saddle-tramp hoodlums must lay siege to the peaceable Mormon group, but the villains' rout can only prove efficient and exhilarating.

With camera chief Bert Glennon capturing the most sparkling footage ever shot of Utah's Monument Valley, Ford marks his pilgrims' progress with scenic grandeur, a soundtrack punctuated by rustic tunes that sound *almost* authentically folkloric, and a romanticized, sentimentalized finale that plays out with honesty and vigor. The film might even be Ford's most virtuous picture in its direct simplicity and clarity of vision. And the opportunity to see Bond, Johnson, and Carey cut loose as star players—far removed from the long shadows of John Wayne and Henry Fonda—is not to be missed.

The popular impression of TV's *Wagon Train* notwithstanding, Ward Bond is not the star player of *Wagon Master*, but instead an irreverent Mormon named Jonathan Wiggs. Wiggs persuades two horse-trading drifters, Travis Blue and Sandy Owens (top-billed

Johnson and Carey), to take charge of the wagon train headed by Wiggs and the more pious Adam Perkins (Russell Simpson). Johnson's Travis Blue becomes smitten with a traveling entertainer (Joanne Dru), whose troupe has hooked up with the Mormons for safety's sake—only to find that Bond's unusually worldly preacher–man also has eyes for the lady. Even such points of contention play out with a picaresque spirit, reserving the element of mortal danger, a showdown with the malicious Uncle Shiloh Clegg (Charles Kemper) and his family-like mob, for an exhilarating climax.

Ben Johnson was en route here to becoming a Defining Figure, what with his being a genuine Working Cowboy who also proved a natural at addressing the cameras. Johnson had drifted into the movies, driving a herd of horses destined for the Howard Hughes–Howard Hawks production of *The Outlaw* (1943). Hawks hired Johnson as a wrangler and stunt player. John Ford was equally impressed when he saw Johnson come charging to the rescue during a stunt-action accident on the shooting of *Fort Apache*. Johnson's big promotion came with the leading role in *Mighty Joe Young*—essentially, a cowboys-in-Africa adventure—and he went on to grace half–a–dozen Ford movies, plus Peter Bogdanovich's *The Last Picture Show* (1971), which Johnson grudgingly accepted at Ford's behest.

Carey had come just as naturally to the movies, though through birthright more so than discovery. The son of the prominent leading man Harry Carey and the actress Olive Carey, Junior grew up on the family's ranch, largely among Navajo tribespeople who worked for his father. (Carey learned the tribal language before he began using English.) During World War II, Junior joined the Navy as a medical corpsman in the Pacific Theatre of Operations, then was transferred to Commanding Officer John Ford's O.S.S. unit. Carey's attraction to show business landed him in a handful of small acting parts that led to a backup role alongside his father in Howard Hawks' *Red River* (1948). After the death of Harry Carey, Sr., Ford assigned Junior a key role in 1948's *3 Godfathers*—a film that Ford dedicated to the memory of Harry, Sr.

Wardell "Ward" Bond was a veteran of the Western cinema, scoring initially as a Bad Guy player but embracing a wider variety of character and lead assignments in many genres with a brusque intensity and considerable versatility. Bond owed his early momentum to Ford, who had promoted the actor from an extra part to supporting status on 1929's *Salute*. Known as well for his right-wing politics as for his boisterous nature, Bond served hundreds of pictures with a broadly conceived yet nuanced interpretive skill, a rich and resonant voice, and an air of brusque authority. Bond's *Wagon Train* series was still in production when the actor died of a heart attack in 1960 at Dallas.

Among the supporting cast of *Wagon Master*, former child star Dickie Moore (formerly of the *Our Gang* comedies) has a small role worth noticing. The belovéd Jane Darwell (of Ford's *The Grapes of Wrath*, from 1940) and the director's estranged but collaborative brother, Francis Ford, contribute their usual memorable characterizations. Likewise for the renowned Indian athlete, Jim Thorpe, whose life would be dramatized just a year later in *The Jim Thorpe Story*, starring Burt Lancaster. A memorable show of villainy comes from James Arness, still several years away from stardom with network television's *Gunsmoke*. Seen in a small role as a tribeswoman is the lovely Movita Castañeda, a star in her own right within Mexico's film industry. And was there ever a keener name for a movie star than *Movita*?

FANEX FILM–FESTIVAL SERIES: BALTIMORE 2001
Alfred Hitchcock's *Rope* (1948)

Rope, as in enough with which to hang oneself, is the now-figurative, now-literal, title of Alfred Hitchcock's most taxing experiment. His most taxing, and possibly his most artistically successful. To accomplish the objective, Hitchcock tapped his memories of the most primitive age of talking-picture technology, *ca.* 1927–1930, when the intimidating new dimension of sound had temporarily reduced picturemaking to a state resembling photographed stage–plays. Hitchcock knew these limitations well, having strained against them on the first made-in-England talking picture, 1930's *Blackmail.*

But with *Rope*, Hitchcock also reimagined that historical reality in terms of a heightened mobility for the camera. Where lengthy takes of exposition had gone unrelieved by camera motion or intercutting in the earliest talkies, Hitchcock devised a means of imparting relentless motion *to* the camera, which captured the action of *Rope* in uniformly long takes of 10 minutes each, the length of a reel of film.

Source–author Patrick Hamilton had based his London stage–play of 1929, *The Rope*, upon the Leopold–Loeb thrill-killer case, in which two sociopaths had committed murder in a bid to demonstrate their supremacy over humankind–at–large. Hitchcock's version only superficially tones down the culprits' homosexual relationship, making plain via suggestion what the censors of the day would not have permitted in words or deeds. (Richard Fleischer's retelling of Leopold–Loeb, the 1959 *Compulsion*, is of similar restraint; Tom Kalin's 1991 rendition, *Swoon*, feigns a documentarylike realism while imposing an anachronistic gay agenda upon the 1920s case.)

Hitchcock had wanted Cary Grant for the role of the culprits' former prep-school mentor, but he settled for James Stewart, who rewarded the opportunity with a determined performance that cinched a long-term working relationship with the director. Hitchcock had wanted Montgomery Clift for the more aggressive of the perpetrators, but he settled for John Dall, who fails to lose himself entirely in the role. Farley Granger is similarly tentative as the more skittish killer. Stewart refuses to play down to their inexperience as he sets Dall and Granger ill–at–ease with the theoretical argument that murder should be an art practiced by a superior few. This approach elevates the ensemble work.

The confined space and the confining situation—a dinner party in the very room where Dall and Granger have hidden their conspicuously absent victim, with the events clocked in real time—challenge Hitchcock throughout to keep things clicking along. Much of the interest derives from the participatory mobility of the camera, enabled by the use of wheeled walls and an extraordinarily graceful tracking dolly. But the greater charm lies in the genially seething intensity with which Stewart places Dall and Granger at the end of their rope.

Hitchcock dealt further in lengthy takes in *Under Capricorn* (1950), a less successful venture into psychological torment. At length, Hitchcock abandoned the interest, declaring, after all, that "films must be cut"—that is, *edited* after the shooting.

This injunction, however, is emphatically *not* the case with *Rope*, whose editing-in-camera techniques not only transcend gimmickry but also stand as the inspiration that moved Orson Welles (10 years later) to open his 1958 masterpiece, *Touch of Evil*, with an astonishingly lengthy job of camera acrobatics.

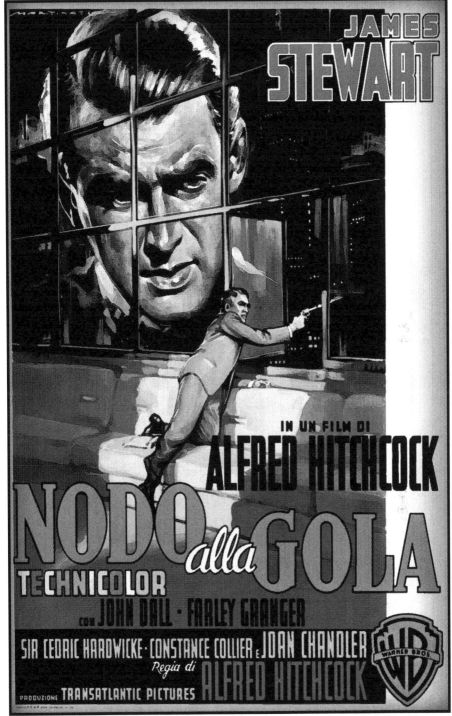

Even on her wedding night
she must share the man she
loved with the "Female Thing"
that lived in the Tomb of the Cat!
AMERICAN INTERNATIONAL
VINCENT PRICE
ELIZABETH SHEPHERD
EDGAR ALLAN POE'S
TOMB of LIGEIA
COLORSCOPE
Screenplay by ROBERT TOWNE · From the Story by EDGAR ALLAN POE · Produced and Directed by ROGER CORMAN

Roger Corman's *The Tomb of Ligeia* (1964)

Usually, when some expressly popular artist borrows a page from some higher literary idiom, it becomes questionable whether the idiom uplifts the artist or the artist degrades the idiom. Gordon "Sting" Sumner's occasional dabblings in jazz come to mind. A significant exception is Roger Corman's succession of Edgar Allan Poe movies: Corman does as much for Poe as Poe does for Corman.

The last of the Corman Poes, 1964's *The Tomb of Ligeia*, is also the most riveting and emotionally affecting of the lot, and an ultimate validation of Corman as an earnest filmmaker. No perception of Corman can be complete without an awareness of his greater body of purely exploitational pictures. But his Poes, and *Ligeia* in particular, place the director more solidly in line with the likes of Paul Leni, Tod Browning, James Whale, Edgar G. Ulmer, and Terence Fisher.

Vincent Price serves *Ligeia* as Verden Fell, a squire of Old Norfolk, who lives in the mingled hope and fear that his deceased wife, Ligeia (Elizabeth Shepherd), is due for a resurrection. Her spirit is poised for precisely that, awaiting only the triggering effect of Fell's taking a next wife. That innocent usurper would be the Lady Rowena (Miss Shepherd, again), whose overt perils maneuver Fell into Ligeia's metaphysical grabbing range.

Price affects a pair of smoked horse-blinder eyeglasses, obscuring even his peripheral vision in a symbolic sightlessness that can only point toward a genuine blinding. Thus denying himself the use of his most expressive asset, his soulful gaze, Price still registers a finer intensity than many another actor could if mugging the camera or playing to the balcony's cheap seats. Lord Fell simultaneously rejects and confronts the truth: "She will not die, because she willed *not* to die." His attraction to a look-alike new bride is a troubling reminder of his inability to shake the obsession.

Corman literalizes Fell's preoccupation via deceptively conventional touches—the yowling and prowling of a black cat, the sudden animation of the face of an entombed corpse, the climactic fire scene—but the director views the ordeal primarily through Fell's figurative blindness. This astonishingly coherent indulgence in subjective surrealism anchors itself in the unusual (for Corman) use of a rock-solid authentic manor house in lieu of *ad hoc* studio sets. The approach combines with the austerity of Robert Towne's exquisitely dialogued and psychologically provocative screenplay to make *The Tomb of Ligeia* the screen's most rewarding attempt to reconcile the spirit and the letter of Poe with the box-office imperative.

(More on *The Tomb of Ligeia* can be found in our companion volume, *Forgotten Horrors Vol. 8: The Resurrection of Edgar Allan Poe*.)

THE COMICMIX COLUMNS

I spent 2007–2008 in the service of an ambitious comic-book publisher known as ComicMix, a Web-based venture of veteran editor Mike Gold. ComicMix licensed two of my collaborative funnybook projects, the crime-and-horror series *Prowler* (with Timothy Truman and John K. Snyder III) and the Southern Gothic *Fishhead* (with Mark Evan Walker, Lawrence Adam Shell, Guillermo DEL Toro, and Joe R. Lansdale). The timing was off, and the *Prowler* and *Fishhead* anthologies wound up issuing from my own imprint, Cremo Studios, while an additional *Prowler* script has sat idle as a casualty of more commercially viable distractions. Such as the *Forgotten Horrors* books, y'know. Not to put too fine a point on the matter.

Where ComicMix did deliver the goods, however, was in an array of weekly columns by such prominent figures as Denny O'Neil and John Ostrander. Gold commissioned one such column from Yrs. Trly., and we called that feature *Forgotten Horrors*. The better to hyperbolize the series of books, of course, even though my range of topics often veered from the movies and that one genre.

But why go about rebuilding the clock when all you've asked is the time of day? Herewith, the complete run of ComicMix columns, with a little something along the way for everybody and then some:

SPIDER–MAN 3: SPECTACULAR OVERKILL

May 6, 2007: It helps to remember, now that a third *Spider–Man* epic has arrived to herald the school's-out season at the box office, that the title character had started out as the comic-book industry's least likely recruit to the ranks of superheroism. The idea of a human being with the proportionate strength of a spider had been kicking around since the 1950s. Comic-book pioneers Joe Simon and Jack Kirby seem to have arrived there first, with an undeveloped concept known as *The Silver Spider*. The inspiration ran afoul of a publishers' bias against spiders and other such crawly creatures, the bankable success of *Batman* notwithstanding. But Simon and Kirby steered the basic notion into print in 1959 with a change-of-species Archie Comics series called *The Fly*—capitalizing upon an unrelated but like-titled hit movie of 1958.

By the early 1960s, Kirby was slumming at a low-rent publishing company that was soon to become the influential Marvel Comics. Kirby and writer–promoter Stan Lee had found competitive leverage with a band-of-heroes comic called *The Fantastic Four*—grimmer and edgier than the fare offered by big-time DC Comics. DC's *Superman* and *Batman* franchises anchored a line of costumed heroes who got along well enough to have formed a superheroes' club.

Lee and Kirby's retort to DC Comics' *Justice League* magazine had been a *Fantastic Four* whose members quarreled and exchanged threats and insults. After Kirby had raised the Silver Spider as a prospect, Lee and Steve Ditko envisioned Spider–Man as a teenage nebbish, afflicted with superhuman abilities by a bite from a radioactive spider. Artists Kirby and Ditko combined qualities of strength and neurosis in the char-

acter design: Superman's alter–ego, Clark Kent, wore eyeglasses and feigned social withdrawal as a disguise; Spider–Man's alter–ego, Peter Parker, wore eyeglasses because he was a nearsighted dweeb.

The embryonic Marvel Comics, having little to lose and plenty to prove, launched Spider–Man in a failing magazine and hoped that somebody might notice. Sales figures spiked against expectations. Lee's unsophisticated attempts at philosophical depth struck comic-book readers of the day as comparatively profound. Spider–Man's début in his own title involved a violent misunderstanding with the members of the Fantastic Four.

Sam Raimi's *Spider–Man* movies date from times more recent (2002–and–counting), but they recapture well that early stage of 45 years ago in which Peter B. Parker, alias Spider–Man, marks time between altercations by wondering whether he deserves to be saddled with such responsibility. Raimi's *Spider–Man 2* (2004) is one of the more mature-minded comic-book films, reconciling sensationalism with provocative ideas. *Spider–Man 3* finds Parker (Tobey Maguire) developing a swaggering presence, consistent with later issues of the Stan Lee–Steve Ditko books. Parker no longer feels compelled to guard his dual identity from romantic interest Mary Jane Watson (Kirsten Dunst), and as Spider–Man he is experiencing an unaccustomed surge of favorable crime-buster publicity. Chalk it all up to pride before a fall, for soon enough Parker will encounter a cosmic force that can only unleash in him a grimmer personality, complete with redesigned costume.

As though the split-personality problem were insufficient, director Raimi's collaborative screenplay raises the ante with a recurrent menace known as the Green Goblin (James Franco)—Green Goblin, Jr., is more like it—and a new arrival called the Sandman (Thomas Haden Church). Neither villain comes near the finer dramatic resonance that

Alfred Molina achieved as the rampaging Dr. Octopus in *Spider–Man 2*, but the Sandman's strange abilities to alter his shape account for some jaw-dropping visual effects. The script balances things out with an entirely human professional rival for photojournalist Peter Parker, until aggressive photographer Eddie Brock (Topher Grace) finds himself changed into a supervillain known as Venom. Enough, already.

The larger idea of having Parker explore his darker nature proves an ill-developed plotting device, lost in the shuffle of too many bad guys and a fitfully interesting subplot of jealousy involving Kirsten Dunst's Mary Jane Watson and Bryce Dallas Howard's Gwen Stacy, an endangered innocent in need of a rescue by Spider–Man. Amidst the noise, Thomas Haden Church stands out with his portrayal of the Sandman as a figure of sorrow as well as menace. Topher Grace, who might as well be auditioning for the title role in some eventual *Spider–Man 4*, lends a current of ferocity that is lacking in the script. Although the present film does a fair job of tying things into a coherent trilogy, it also drops hints of yet another installment.

Dunst is uncharacteristically lethargic and petulant this time out, and her scenes with Tobey Maguire's Parker lack the vitality of their earlier pairings. Maguire fares better at conveying Parker's impatience with his own boyish naïveté, attempting to counter his mild-mannered nature with clumsy attempts at appearing confident and even arrogant. None of which will matter to the fans who come to witness the more spectacular outbursts. In gee-whiz technical terms, the picture is right up there with the earlier efforts.

MOVIES IS COMICS AND COMICS IS MOVIES

May 13, 2007: I've gone into detail elsewhere about how my *Forgotten Horrors* series of movie encyclopedias (1979 and onward) dovetails with my collaborative comic-book efforts with Timothy Truman and John K. Snyder III and Todd Camp, amongst others. The present batch of *Forgotten Horrors* commentaries will have more to do with the overall relationship between movies and the comics and, off–and–on, with the self-contained appeal of motion pictures. I have yet to meet the comics enthusiast who lacks an appreciation of film.

Although it is especially plain nowadays that comics exert a significant bearing upon the moviemaking business—with fresh evidence in marquée-value outcroppings for the *Spider–Man* and *Teenage Mutant Ninja Turtles* franchises and suchlike—the greater historical perspective finds the relationship to be quite the other way around.

It helps to remember: Both movies and comics, pretty much as we know them today, began developing late in the 19TH century. And an outmoded term for *comics* is *movies*; its popular usage as such dates from comparatively recent times. The notion of movies–on–paper took a decisive shape during the 1910s, when a newspaper illustrator named Ed Wheelan began spoofing the moving pictures (also known among the shirtsleeves audience as "moom pitchers" and "fillums"), with cinema-like visual grammar, in a loose-knit series for William Randolph Hearst's New York *American*.

Christened *Midget Movies* in 1918, Wheelan's series evolved from quick-sketch parodies of cinematic topics to sustained narratives, running for days at a stretch and combining melodramatic plot-and-character developments with cartoonish exaggerations. Wheelan's move to the Adams Syndicate in 1921 prompted a change of title, to *Minute Movies*. (Don Markstein's Web-based *Toonopedia* points out

that the term is "mine-*yute*," as in *tiny*, rather than "minnit," as in a measure of time. No doubt an intended sense of connection with the Hearst trademark *Midget Movies*.) Chester Gould showed up in 1924 with a Wheelan takeoff called *Fillum Fables*—seven years before Gould's breakthrough with *Dick Tracy*.

The larger staying power of *movies* as a synonym for comics rests not with Ed Wheelan—although his newspaper concoction continued into 1935 then reappeared in various comic books of the 1940s—but rather with the provincial team of writer John Rosenfeld, JR., and cartoonist Jack Patton. Their feature, *Texas History Movies*, began in 1926 in the Dallas *News*, which also published Patton's editorial-opinion 'toons and advertising art. *Texas History Movies* outlasted by a long stretch its original purpose, thanks in part to a hardcover schoolbook collection of 1927–1928—Texas' teachers found the cartoons to be a practical, attention-grabbing tool—and, then, to a lengthy run of classroom paperbacks subsidized by Magnolia Petroleum (later, Mobil Oil and still later, Exxon/Mobil).

The persistence persists in a version called *New Texas History Movies*, recently issued by the Texas State Historical Association. The thorough reworking (supplanting the Patton–Rosenfeld material, with its quaint ethnic caricatures and its narrower window of history) is among the final projects of Jack "Jaxon" Jackson (1941–2006). Jaxon is unusual among comics artists as both a seminal figure in the rebellious Underground Comics scene of the 1960s and a writer–artist dedicated to a naturalistic view of Texas' turbulent history. He often traced his interest to his discovery as a schoolboy of the Patton–Rosenfeld comics. Jack also claimed the films of Federico Fellini and Akira Kurosawa, by turns dreamlike and naturalistic, among influences.

Probably the most self-evident historic link between the movie industry and the comic-book industry is the influence exerted by Roland West's second filming of the Avery Hopwood–Mary Roberts Rinehart play, *The Bat*, upon a groundbreaking comics series, *Batman*. Co–creator Bob Kane often acknowledged West's 1930 production, *The Bat Whispers* (actually, a dual remake, with wide-screen and conventional-screen versions shot separately) among key inspirations for *Batman*—not merely in terms of a nocturnal stalker, but also in the film's angular design and sharply defined shadowplay.

And *Batman*, in turn—and its companion feature, *Superman*, among other examples—would exercise an influence upon the movies, beginning with the *Superman* cartoons of 1941–1943 and *The Batman*, a 1943 cliffhanger. Such reciprocity between Art and Commerce will supply plenty to discuss as we move forward, here; in fields so rich in the cycles of tradition and innovation and stagnation, there always is a story for another day.

ALLEY OOP'S STAGEBOUND TEXAS HOMECOMING

May 20, 2007: The formidable dinosaur–replica standing guard at the entrance to the Museum of Science & History in Fort Worth, Texas, is a native Southwesterner in more ways than one. The creature goes by the academic name of *Acrocanthosaurus atokensis*, and as such it was not discovered until around 1950.

But a Fort Worth-based cartoonist named Vincent T. Hamlin had in fact discovered that unknown monster in the fertile substrata of his imagination—almost a generation's span before the first Real World unearthing of any such fossil remains. Hamlin called the creature by less of a mouthful of a name, and he made Dinny the Dinosaur a prominent player in a rip-snorting comic strip called *Alley Oop*, about a prehistoric Everyman. Dinny's resemblance to the *Acrocanthosaurus*, or high-spined lizard, is uncannily prophetic.

This tidbit of provincial history took on a manifold relevance a couple of years ago with a smart accident of timing. No sooner had the Museum of Science & History opened its epic-calibre *Lone Star Dinosaurs* gallery, than Fort Worth's Hip Pocket Theatre launched a stage adaptation of *Alley Oop*, in August of 2005. The bold juxtaposition of provocative science–fact with adventurous science–fantasy is one of those nowhere-but-Texas coincidences that would leave Vince Hamlin beaming with pride. If he were still around to do any beaming, that is.

In the interest of B.F.D. (Belated Full Disclosure), I should mention that I hold a stake in all these developments. I composed the musical score for Hip Pocket's *Alley Oop*. My own book of prehistorical lore, a restoration of the late George E. Turner's 1950s dinosaur comic strip *The Ancient Southwest* (TCU Press), had its rollout at the Science & History Museum. And V.T. Hamlin (1900–1993) was my first major-league mentor in the cartooning profession. Sooner or later, everything comes full-circle.

After all, it was the West Texas landscape, with its outcroppings of prehistoric remains and its air of primeval antiquity, that had given the Iowa-born Hamlin an inspiration for *Alley Oop*, 'way back during the 1920s. He was working as a newsroom cartoonist for the Fort Worth *Star-Telegram* at the time, producing a comics-panel series called *The Panther Kitten*, a chronicle of the ups and downs of a tenacious baseball team called the Fort Worth Cats. And Hamlin's nearness to the natural history of West Texas became a springboard to *Alley Oop*. (And more about *The Panther Kitten* in our companion volume, *Alley Oop's Ancestors: The Newspaper Cartoons of V.T. Hamlin*.)

"Y'know, I really created the blueprint for *Alley Oop* there at the Fort Worth *Star–Telegram*," Hamlin told me in 1990. The occasion involved Frank Stack's and my efforts to compile and annotate a set of *Alley Oop* reprints at Kitchen Sink Press. Hamlin added: "Well, I suppose I had been drawing the guy who would become Oop ever since I was a kid.

"But the one I called the Panther Kitten—he was my proving ground ... for the real Oop character. Y'might say I took this baseball cat and transformed him into this big caveman I called Oop. I was more interested in prehistory, anyhow, than I was in baseball—not that my tendencies to mix cavemen up with dinosaurs could be considered accurate prehistory!"

The *Telegram* also provided Hamlin with the forced leverage he had needed to break through to a bigger sphere.

"Fort Worth, I recall with a certain pleasurable fondness," Hamlin said, "even though they canned me there at the *Star–Telegram*. It was at the *Telegram* where I had the freedom to get frisky with my drawing—polish it up to the level it needed to be at—and where I had the responsibility placed on me to crank out the stuff on a routine basis..."

Hamlin also ranged Texas as a news photographer. He shot the zeppelin *Shenandoah* from atop Fort Worth's 24-story F&M Bank Building—one such photo appeared in *The National Geographic*—and he showed up with camera in hand at a watershed moment in Texas' oil-boom history, when the No. 2 well of Ira and Ann Yates (hence the townsite's exotic-sounding name of Iraan) came in a gusher in 1928, signaling a land rush.

That wild and desolate landscape, Hamlin recalled, "got me to thinking about the dinosaurs that must've been all over the place back in prehistory ... I had a dinosaur cartoon in mind before I got up the sense to throw in a caveman and call him Oop." He christened Alley Oop after the French expression *allez–oop!*—a sporting exclamation, betokening strenuous activity.

But how about that sacking from the *Telegram*?

"Like I said: They canned me," Hamlin explained, describing a freelance venture that he and an engraving-department colleague conducted, using the newspaper's equipment.

"No big deal to the brass," Hamlin continued, "'cause we made no secret of it, and they had more or less given us a nod and a wink to do so. But what soured the deal was the nature of some of the work we were getting on the side. This was during Prohibition, remember, and one of [our] lines was making these counterfeit labels for—well, for bootleg whiskey bottles.

"Well, the boss ... called me on the carpet, in a friendly but stern way. I was kind of lippy as a youngster, so 'stead of going, 'Yes, sir, I was wrong, sir. I won't do it again, sir,' like I was s'posed to do, I just went mouthy. And he fired me... So here I was, scrambling again. New wife, baby on the way, and we ended up having to pawn [her] wedding ring..."

After a few years' frustrations and false starts, Hamlin moved to Florida, put *Alley Oop* into production, and landed a newspaper-syndication deal. After his first syndicate went bust, Newspaper Enterprise Association stepped in to rescue *Oop* and had made the feature a popular success by the end of 1933. The strip remains in production all these years later, now in the hands of the Tulsa-based artist–writer team of Jack and Carole Bender. (The Benders attended *Oop*'s opening weekend in 2005 at Fort Worth and pronounced the time well-spent.)

Hamlin again, from 1990: "I came back to visit Fort Worth after Oop got to going pretty good," Hamlin told me. "Looked up the *Star-Telegram* people for old times' sake..." Hamlin said the editor who had sacked him offered this greeting: "Well, I sure as hell kicked your ass upstairs, didn't I?" To which Hamlin replied: "Well, it sure was a roundabout way of gettin' upstairs!"

Although Hamlin never presented himself as an authority on prehistory, he weaved something near a purer-science background into *Oop*'s Sunday-funnies installments, with sidebar–features called *Dinny's Family Album* and *Fragments of Man's Early History*. Dinny was strictly a concoction of the artist's imagination—or so even Hamlin himself believed until the discovery of *Acrocanthosaurus* remains in Oklahoma and Texas proved him predictive as well as productive.

Upon announcing his retirement during the early 1970s, Hamlin had complained among friends: "Nobody's interested in dinosaurs or prehistory anymore." This sad insight may have seemed accurate enough to an artist who had weathered the pop-cultural trends of more than two generations and by now found his eyesight failing.

But Hamlin also maintained ties to *Oop* and lived long enough to take part in the preparation of that ambitious series of books, reprinting many of the series' transitional episodes of the 1940s. (The Kitchen Sink Press editions yielded the "Black Dinosaur" continuity that became the basis of the Hip Pocket Theatre play.) Hamlin also lived long enough to witness practically everybody become interested all over again in that area of his greatest fascination: Hamlin died not long after Steven Spielberg's movie version of *Jurassic Park* (1993) had reawakened that interest in a big way.

And as to whether anybody's "interested in dinosaurs and prehistory" all these years beyond that surge—well, the Fort Worth Museum of Science & History has made a sustained success of its *Lone Star Dinosaurs* exhibit, with plans for an expansion of that gallery. There's even a hint of a V.T. Hamlin exhibit, remarking the predictive power of the artist's imagination. The cumulative effect suggests something of a posthumous homecoming.

DICK TRACY, FROM STRIP TO SCREEN

May 27, 2007: Much as the crime melodrama had helped to define the course of cinema—especially so, from the start of the talking-picture era during the late 1920s—so Chester Gould's *Dick Tracy* proved a huge influence upon the comic-strip industry, beginning in 1931. It was a foregone conclusion that the paths of Tracy and the movies should intersect, and none too soon.

It took some time for both the talking screen and *Dick Tracy* to find their truer momentum. Bryan Foy's *Lights of New York* (1928), as the first all-talking picture, marked a huge, awkward leap from the part-talking extravagances of 1927's *The Jazz Singer*. And *Lights of New York* proved impressive enough (despite its clunky staging and the artists' discomfort with the primitive sound-recording technology) to snag a million-dollar box-office take and demonstrate a popular demand for underworld yarns with plenty of snarling dialogue and violent sound effects. Gould launched *Tracy* with a passionate contempt for the criminal element but made do with fairly commonplace miscreants until his weird-menace muse began asserting itself decisively during 1932–1933.

Chet Gould's fascination with such subject matter, as seen from a crime-busting vantage as opposed to the viewpoint of outlawry, appears to have influenced Hollywood as early as 1935—when William Keighley's "G" Men and Sam Wood's *Let 'Em Have It* arrived as trailblazing heroic procedurals. These watershed titles posed a stark contrast against such antiheroic sensations as Roland West's *Alibi* and *The Bat Whispers* (1929–1930), William Wellman's *The Public Enemy* (1931), and Mervin LeRoy's *Little Caesar* (1931). It bears wondering whether Edward Small, producer of *Let 'Em Have It*, may have taken a cue from *Tracy*, for the film pits an FBI contingent against a disfigured human monster (played by *King Kong*'s Bruce Cabot) whose scarred face and vile disposition seem of a piece with the grotesques whom Gould would array as foes for Dick Tracy.

I've been on a renewed *Tracy* kick since the arrival last year [2006, *i.e.*] of IDW Publishing's *The Complete Chester Gould's Dick Tracy*, a debut volume covering 1931–1933 (a second volume, going up to 1935, was released earlier this month). The interest extends to a re–watching

of the *Tracy* movies that began in 1937 with Republic Pictures' *Dick Tracy* serial. Cable–teevee's Turner Classic Movies has staged recent revivals of the (considerably later) *Tracy* feature–films from RKO–Radio Pictures, and various off-brand DVD labels have issued dollar-a-disc samplers of the (still later) live-action *Tracy* teleseries. An audio-streaming Website has come through with two *Tracy*-spinoff record albums from the post-WWII years; one, *The Case of the Midnight Marauder*, involves a ferocious encounter with Gould's most memorable bad guy, the Peter Lorre-like Flattop. (The less said, the better, about UPA Studios' animated *Tracy* series of 1961. And likewise for Warren Beatty's 1990 *Dick Tracy*, which commits the sin of "cartooning the cartoon," as the saying goes, its live-action basis notwithstanding.)

Comics-to-movies adaptations had registered particularly well in 1936 with Universal Pictures' serialized *Flash Gordon*. Upstart Republic Pictures had fared nicely with the *Flash*-like *Undersea Kingdom* (1936, likewise), when the studio paid $10,000 to the Chicago Tribune Syndicate for the rights to develop a *Tracy* cliffhanger. (The term has to do with the chapter-a-week serials' custom of leaving the audience in suspense at the end of each episode en route to the finale.) Republic reconceived Tracy as an FBI agent as part of a plan to star Melvin Purvis, the famous Real World G–man.

The screenwriters dispensed with the other Gould characters except Junior Tracy, the enforcer's schoolboy ward, concocting back-up roles from Whole Cloth. After the deal with Purvis fell through, a bit player named Ralph Byrd was selected to portray Tracy at $150 a week during a 25-day shoot. (The casting proved ideal: Byrd starred as Tracy in three additional Republic serials, two entries in the RKO feature series, and a 1950–1951 run of teevee episodes. Byrd died of a heart attack in 1952. As usual with serial favorites, his broader run of feature-film assignments proved unworthy of Byrd's talents.)

Republic's *Dick Tracy* (1937) is one of the epic serials—a $128,000 production that, in striving merely to convey a generous entertainment value, fell together without conscious effort as a genuinely great film of its kind. The fundamental charm is a pervading air of horror (more the spirit than the letter of Gould), a rancorous view of gangland that has figured in the acknowledged classics of crime melodrama from Charles Brabin's *The Beast of the City* (1932) to Martin Scorsese's *GoodFellas* (1991). High adventure is a given with *Tracy*, but the overriding tone is set in an opening sequence in which a shadowy mob boss stalks and slays a rebellious underling, played by surly Byron K. Foulger.

The criminal mastermind, known variously as the Spider and the Lame One, is handily as strange as Gould's comic-strip villains. His face hidden throughout by shadows and angular compositions, the ganglord is discovered only in the last chapter to be another character, a purported philanthropist, in disguise. This elusive approach to characterization is a business-as-usual technique of the serial-thriller impresario Nat Levine (1899–1989), who had joined Republic following its absorption of his Mascot Pictures in a leveraged buyout. The Lame One's hunchbacked Mad Scientist assistant (John Picorri) is equally weird. Weirder yet is the portrayal of Dick Tracy's brother as, first, a mild-mannered lawyer (Richard Beach) and, then, a brainwashed villain (hard-faced Carleton Young).

Narrative construction differs from prior serials in that it is built upon several distinct plots within the framework of the major premise of general-purpose underworld terrorism; each internal yarn is resolved in a few reels' running time. The overriding story involves the various strategies of the Lame One as he moves from scheme to scheme, each of which is frustrated by Tracy's escalating manhunt. This formula became a standard at Republic and often was imitated by the serial-making units of Universal and Columbia Pictures. Some of the 15 episodes defy logic, but all are exciting and imaginative.

And just as Gould's *Dick Tracy* proved visionary in its technological fantasies—and what is the audio-video cellphone, if not a realization of Tracy's two-way wrist-radio-teevee?—Republic's *Dick Tracy* dispensed a practical prophecy of its own: A futuristic craft called the Flying Wing anticipates the development of the Northrop B–35, a four-engine, 172-foot wonder that went through a dozen prototypes beginning in 1942 and had its first test flight in 1946. (And more about all this in *Forgotten Horrors: The Original Volume* and my Foreword to the IDW Publishing edition of *The Complete Dick Tracy: 1936–1938*.)

THE LONG SHADOW OF BOODY ROGERS

June 3, 2007: People and events of consequence cast their shadows before them, never behind. Oklahoma-born and Texas-reared Gordon "Boody" Rogers (1904–1996) owns one of those forward-lurching shadows—an unlikely mass-market cartoonist whose oddball creations anticipated the rise of underground comics, or comix, and whose command of dream-state narrative logic and language-mangling dialogue remains unnerving and uproarious in about equal measure.

I had discovered the artist's more unsettling work as a schoolboy during the 1960s, via the used-funnybook bin of a neighborhood shop called the Magazine Exchange. One such title, *Babe*, amounted to such an exaggerated lampoon of Al Capp's *Li'l Abner* as to transcend parody. (One lengthy sequence subjects a voluptuous rustic named Babe Boone [!!] to a gender-switch ordeal that finds her spending much of the adventure as Abe Boone—almost as though Capp's Daisy Mae Scragg had become Abner Yokum.) Such discoveries drew me back gradually to Rogers' comic-strip and funnybook serial *Sparky Watts* (eyes right), a partly spoofing, partly straightforward, heroic feature about a high-voltage superman. Rogers resurfaced in my consciousness quite a few years later. A college-administration colleague showed up one day around 1980, sporting a canvasback jacket adorned with cartoons bearing an array of famous signatures—Al Capp and Zack Mosely and Milton Caniff among them. The garment proved to be one-of-a-kind.

"Oh, it's my Uncle Gordon's," my associate explained. "Kind of a family heirloom, I guess—something his cartoonist pals fixed up for him on the occasion of his retirement. He lends it out to me, now and then."

Okay, then. And who is this "Uncle Gordon," to have been keeping company amongst the comic-strip elite?

"Oh, you've probably never heard of him," she said. "He was a cartoonist, his ownself. Went by the name of 'Boody.'"

Not Boody Rogers?(Yes, and how many guys named Boody can there *be*, anyhow?)

"None other. So maybe you *have* heard of him?"

Well, sure. Used to collect his work, to the extent that it could be had for collecting in those days of catch-as-can trolling for out-of-print comic books and newspaper-archive strips.

So, *uhm*, then, he's, like, a *local* guy?!?"

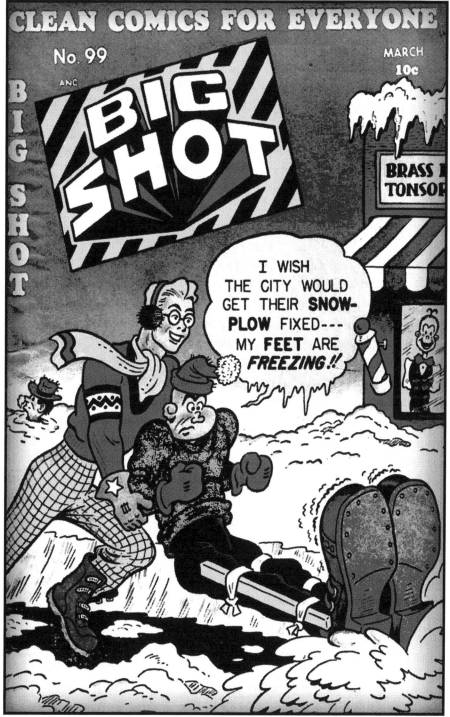

"Well, not exactly right here in town," answered my colleague. "But he lives not far from here"—*here* being Amarillo, Texas, in the northwestern corner of the state—"over to the east. Do you ever get over to Childress? You ought to drop out there and meet him."

No sooner said than did, as Boody Rogers might have phrased it. I had frequent business in Childress, in any event, what with my regional-newspaper connections and a responsibility to range the Texas Panhandle provinces as a student-recruitment representative for Amarillo Junior College. I mentioned Boody Rogers to Childress' newspaper publisher, Morris Higley, who recognized the name right off.

"Yeah. Something of a local character, ol' Boody," said Higley. "Kind of famous, too, although he mostly keeps to himself anymore. Used to do some newspaper cartoons. Approached our paper once, about getting some print-shop quotes to publish a memoir. Colorful ol' guy."

By this time, of course, Rogers was among the last survivors of a vanishing tribe of first- and second-generation comics talent—long since strayed from his funnies-racket territory in New York and Chicago, long since retired not only from cartooning but also from a second career in the art-supplies retailing market. But still a natch'l-born storyteller, and still in charge of his memories if no longer of his dreams and ambitions.

Rogers proved to be as garrulous as the narrative voice of his comics yarns had suggested—youthful in outlook though "pushin' 80 with a bulldozer," as he put it, and intent upon chronicling his eventful life in a book that he intended to call *Homeless Bound.*

"That's on account of anywhere I hang my hat is home," as Rogers explained the cryptic title. "And if I ever had me a home to call my own—well, I loved New York, but the Southwest, the Texas Plains, has always been the place I wanted to be.

"Can't be a working cartoonist and base yourself out in the boondocks. Gotta be smack–dab in th' middle of where the syndicates and the publishers are. But when I quit the business [during the early 1950s], I homed right in on the South–by–Southwest. And I was raised on the Texas Plains, movin' from town to town, whichever way the wind blowed, and Childress is as good an excuse for a hometown as I ever had to call my own. Went to high school here, anyhow."

Midway through the 1980s, Rogers published *Homeless Bound* through Pioneer Books, Inc., and laid in an inventory of the hardcover edition for mail-order sale. The book proved to contain frustratingly little information about Rogers' cartooning career but compensated with a rambunctious, bawdy, and often poignant account of a nomadic childhood, a freewheeling young adulthood in New York of the 1920s, and a hell-raising tour of uniformed duty during World War II. The book had rather a low profile until the early 1990s, when Art Spiegelman's comics-as-art journal *RAW* devoted a hefty space to a reprint from the fever-dream *Babe* series and took pains to call attention to *Homeless Bound.*

Today, 11 years after Rogers' death, *Homeless Bound* is more generally available from this Web catalogue or that—as close within reach as a Google search, though somewhat pricier than Rogers' $10-postpaid going rate. The book reads more like Woody Guthrie's *Bound for Glory* (1942) or Billy Porterfield's *Diddy Waw Diddy: The Passage of an American Son* (1994) in its obsessive, reflective homesickness for a Southwest untouched by the nicer civilizing influences.

Homeless Bound takes wildly digressive leaps, from a rootless and adventurous childhood to some preposterous wartime incident and back again, but Rogers' conversational tone and overriding enthusiasm keep the book anchored. If, by the time of its writing, memories had outstripped ambition, Rogers nonetheless remained determined to transform those memories into New Art.

"My early ambition in life was double–barrelled," writes Rogers. "First, to be a football quarterback and win the girls, and second, to be a cartoonist and make people laugh." A wisenheimer from childhood, he revels in such episodes as the early triumph of antagonizing a school principal with this suggestion for a class slogan: "When in doubt, eat ham and eggs."

Rogers earned the nickname of *Boody* via schoolboy football, in recognition of his place-kicking ability. The odd spelling, he explained, "is how us kids pernounced *boot*." (As in "*boot* that thaing," no doubt.)

The book glosses over Rogers' academic preparations, which included studies at the Art Institute of Chicago. And although Rogers lived as a high-roller among name-brand cartoonists—apprenticing under *Smilin' Jack*'s Zack Mosely, appearing as a featured artist in more than 200 newspapers, and hobnobbing with the titanic likes of Capp and Caniff—the book avoids name–dropping.

Homeless Bound excels at recalling a vanished Southwest, from the viewpoint of an observant and prankish son of a household (Rogers' father was a small-town storefront restaurateur) that moved about routinely. He tells uproariously of how he became "the only four–year–old to cause a large restaurant to be totally evacuated twice in one month"— an account that the book itself should be allowed to deliver in its own sweet time. And he describes a circle of roughhousing schoolboy friends bearing such Redneck Dickensian names as Dirty Shyrock and Fine Comb Shit (*sic*) and Bill Somethin'–or–'Nother.

Only in such out-of-the-way archival sources as Woody Guthrie's Library of Congress recordings, or the Institute of Texan Culture's series of Dust Bowl survivor interviews, can one find more intimate accounts of growing up in an American Southwest that still belonged more to the rip-snorting frontier than to polite civilization. And only in the cartooning of such kindred souls as Gene Ahern (*The Nut Bros.*) and Bill Holman (*Smokey Stover*) and Basil Wolverton (*Powerhouse Pepper*) can one find as outlandish a combination of Big Ideas and gratuitous absurdity as Boody Rogers' work conveys.

"Being nutty wasn't necessarily a prerequisite for being a cartoonist," as Rogers tells it, "but it surely helped."

RISE OF THE SILVER SURFER

June 4, 2007: Long before an emerging Marvel Comics Group dared to hope its upstart superhero funnybooks might attract the attention of Corporate Hollywood, the comics fans had started speculating about how *The Fantastic Four*—the colorful exploits of a circle of powerful misfits, united by reciprocal affections and resentments— might weather a transplant to film.

Dream-casting fantasies abounded during the early 1960s: How about Neville Brand or Jack Elam—popular favorites at portraying plug-ugly tough guys—as the misshapen Thing, test pilot–turned–musclebound rockpile? Or Peter Lorre, as a recurring villain known as the Puppet Master? (Something of an easy call, there, inasmuch as lead artist Jack Kirby had modeled the bug-eyed Puppet Master after Lorre, in the first place.)

It took a while for such wonders to develop—well past the mortal spans of Lorre and Brand and Elam and a good many other wish-list players. And in the long interim, the Marvel line of costumed world-beaters made lesser leaps from page to screen in a variety of teevee spinoffs, both animated and live–action, that never quite seized the cinema-like intensity of the comic books. A live-action *Fantastic Four* feature of 1994 fared unexpectedly well on a pinch-penny budget, although this version has gone largely unseen outside the bootleg-video circuit.

The Marvel-gone-Hollywood phenomenon escalated around the turn of the century (beyond all early-day fannish expectations) with a big-studio *X–Men* feature, concerning another team of misfits in cosmic conflict. Success on this front brought an onrush of adaptations.

Prominent among these, Sam Raimi's *Spider–Man* series launched in 2002. *X–Men* has sequelized itself repeatedly. Ang Lee's take on *The Hulk* proved as indebted to Nietzsche and Freud as to the *Jekyll & Hyde* bearings of the earlier comic books. A 2005 *Fantastic Four* feature won over the paying customers but irked a majority of the published critics: Bellwether reviewer Roger Ebert called that one no match for *Spider–Man 2* or the DC Comics-licensed *Batman Begins*. No accounting for taste.

Now comes *Fantastic Four: Rise of the Silver Surfer*, which raises the cosmic-menace stakes while keeping the continuity anchored with director Tim Story and a familiar cast. The story derives from the comics' episodes about a planet-destroying being whose scout, the Silver Surfer, arrives to determine whether this particular planet is ripe for plunder. Now, if the notion of a surfboard-jockey space traveler sounds intolerably silly on first blush, consider that the character proved persuasively earnest from his first appearance—thanks to Jack Kirby's vigorous drawings and Stan Lee's dumb-luck ability to make arch, contrived dialogue seem right for the circumstances. As impersonated by Doug Jones (of *Pan's Labyrinth* and the 1994 *Hellboy*) and voiced by Laurence Fishburne, the movie's Silver Surver nails the spirit of the funnybooks. The Surfer's attraction to the Fantastic Four's Invisible Woman (Jessica Alba), who owes her greater loyalties to team boss Mr. Fantastic, lends a jolt of intimate conflict to the larger crisis.

The collaborative screenplay allows sharper exposure for Ben "the Thing" Grimm (Michael Chiklis) and Ioan Gruffud's Mr. Fantastic, along with a more richly conceived characterization for chronic villain Victor VON Doom (Julian McMahon). Gruffud develops confidence and wisdom on a level with his character's essential intelligence. Chris Evans remains fittingly temperamental as the Human Torch.

Improved visual effects stem from a refined job of make-up prosthetics for the Thing—Michael Chiklis' tragicomic emoting comes across more effectively—and from the polished work of the Weta Digital CGI crew. The Silver Surfer tends to upstage the central characters in terms of spectacle, but the key performances are uniformly well matched.

The deeper history of such pop–literature as moving-picture fodder has suggested that comics heroism belongs in the B–movie ghetto, more so than comic-book movies should entertain epic pretensions. Prominent reinforcement of that stereotype can be found in such examples as Sam Katzman's endearingly shabby *Superman* serials of the post-WWII years, not to mention any number of teevee-'toon comics adaptations.

But then, Max Fleischer's *Superman* cartoons of the earlier 1940s had served to literalize the grand struggles that the comics' stories had suggested. A handful of the *Batman* adaptations since 1989 have done likewise. And in trying somewhat too hard to intellectualize its funny-book inspiration, Ang Lee's *Hulk* (2003) suggests that Stan Lee and Jack Kirby were summoning ideas bigger than their sector of the comic-book industry had come prepared to convey during the early 1960s.

The new *Fantastic Four* movie occupies a more tenable middle ground between epic pretensions and gee-whiz sensationalism. The film recaptures primarily the spectacle that has belonged to the comic books all along—becoming, in the process, the movie that a good many fans have been seeing in their heads for a couple of generations, now.

SPY SMASHER SMASHES SPIES

June 10, 2007: In a bygone age of self-defeating fair-play isolationism, comparatively few outposts of the U.S. entertainment industry saw fit to take issue with the congealing Axis powers. Timely Comics' *Captain America* books tackled a larger agenda of wish-fulfillment Nazi–busting in 1941 at a moment when popular sentiment and much of the mass communications media, stateside, were still holding out for an anti-inflammatory approach. Just two years earlier, the lower-berth Hollywood producers Ben Judell and Sigmund Neufeld had run afoul of their industry's attempts to repress a film called *Hitler—Beast of Berlin*, starting with a Production Code Administration complaint that the very title might pose an affront. It is always an awkward choice, even in the realm of heroic fiction, between pre-emptive action and a wait-and-watch attitude.

And between this difficult patch for the Judell–Neufeld movie and the ferocious début of Captain America, the Third Reich began insinuating such self-glorifying motion pictures as *Campaign in Poland* and *Victory in the West* into American theaters. Said the show-biz tradepaper *Variety,* bucking the mollifying influence of the Production Code: "Instead of making Americans frightened of the terrible power of the Reich's Army, [*Victory in the West*] inflames them."

The *Captain America* stories may have been thusly inflamed, but likelier Joe Simon and Jack Kirby, the talents responsible, were springing from an intuitive sense of developments more appalling than any ostentatious display of aggression. (Superman had tackled fictional, allegorical aggressors and, then, squared off against Adolf Hitler and Josef Stalin as early as 1940—though far outside his own formal continuity, in an isolated gimmick story for *Look* magazine.)

As emphatic a stand belonged to the comics series known as *Spy Smasher*, from Fawcett Publications. The property's retooling as a movie serial began taking shape in 1941 at Republic Pictures—which recently had adapted Fawcett's *Captain Marvel*, with a tone markedly grimmer than that of the funnybooks—and a shooting script was completed shortly before the Japanese invasion of Pearl Harbor. It was with a newfound sense of propagandistic ferocity that the *Spy Smasher* serial went into production on Dec. 22. The attraction began arriving in weekly big-screen installments on April 4, 1942.

The serial takes smart liberties, providing the lead character—Alan Armstrong, alias Spy Smasher—with a civilian twin named Jack, whose presence obliges star player Kane Richmond to handle three roles. A recurring villain called the Mask is *un*–masked for the screen, allowing Hans Schumm a richer opportunity for characterization.

The story starts off in bravura fashion, with Spy Smasher captured in occupied France while uncovering a Nazi plot to undermine the American economy. Over the course of a dozen chapters, Spy Smasher faces (seemingly) certain doom from a gasoline explosion; machine-gun and torpedo volleys; an engineered flood; the crash of a futuristic flying machine; a descending elevator car; a brick-cutting blade and a blast of steam; a collapsing tower; a comparatively mundane automobile crash; an industrial-strength pottery kiln; and a headlong fall from a rooftop amidst a hail of bullets. Needless to say, the hero survives to receive a medal for valor—although the story takes on a strong tragic resonance, typical of Republic's interest in the darker shadings, in the death of Spy Smasher's brother.

Richmond (1906–1973), more generally seen as a supporting player, makes not only an impressive costumed presence but a winning pair of guys in street clothes, as well. A sophisticated combination of split-screen shots and body-double casting leaves no question but what there are two Kane Richmonds on the scene. A strong romantic interest is provided by Marguerite Chapman, who usually graced the B–unit productions of Columbia Pictures. Sam Flint makes a classy Naval Intelligence honcho.

Veteran director William Witney pulls a curious departure from serial-shooting tradition, handling the assignment solo rather than the customary team-directing approach. Over the course of 17 prior chapter–plays, Witney had co–directed with John English. The tactic of attaching two directors to one serial had become S.O.P. as early as 1932's *The Shadow of the Eagle*, enabling one party to prepare for the next day's shooting while his colleague was on the set. Witney wrapped *Spy Smasher* in a brisk 38 days.

Scenic locations include a factory in the L.A. area's Temecula Canyon, where Spy Smasher comes close to being sliced into building–blocks. Designers Russell Kimball and John McCarthy provided magnificent interiors that would have been right at home in some top-of-the-line picture from MGM or Fox. Brothers Howard and Theodore Lydecker delivered their usual astonishingly realistic miniatures and life-sized mechanical props. Mort Glickman's imposing musical accompaniment incorporates Beethoven's *Fifth Symphony*.

How Doooo You Do!!!

June 17, 2007: The Rubber Reality phenomenon that one takes for granted in the animated cartoons and a good many comics seldom crosses over into live-action cinema—CGI and/or the influence of David Lynch notwithstanding. A low-rent music-and-slapstick comedy from 1945 called *How Doooo You Do!!!* makes for a striking exception and bears recalling here, in the context of a series devoted to stalking the pop-cultural borderlands in search of—well, of whatever oddities might turn up. No shortage of those, if one knows where to go prowling.

No entertainer seems to have more fun and less sustained success in appearing before the cameras than the radio gimmick–comic Bert Gordon (1895–1974). Gordon's presence lay primarily in a persuasive and memorable voice (rather like the once-ubiquitous Paul Frees, of a somewhat later day). Gordon's big-screen starring career consisted largely of false starts and commercial misfires. He had become so successful, however, as a supporting-act broadcast player—a regular with Eddie Cantor, from 1930 on through the 1940s—that the movies seemed a logical next step for a decade–and-change, progressing from supporting parts to attempted stardom.

Ralph Murphy's *How Doooo You Do!!!* takes its title from Gordon's signature–phrase. Nobody, but nobody, could intone that commonplace platitude, "How do you do?" with the style or the passion of Bert Gordon. In his radio-program guise of the Mad Russian (sometimes known as Boris Rascalnikoff), Gordon transformed the offhand question into the most emphatic of exclamations, a sustained marvel of escalating dou-

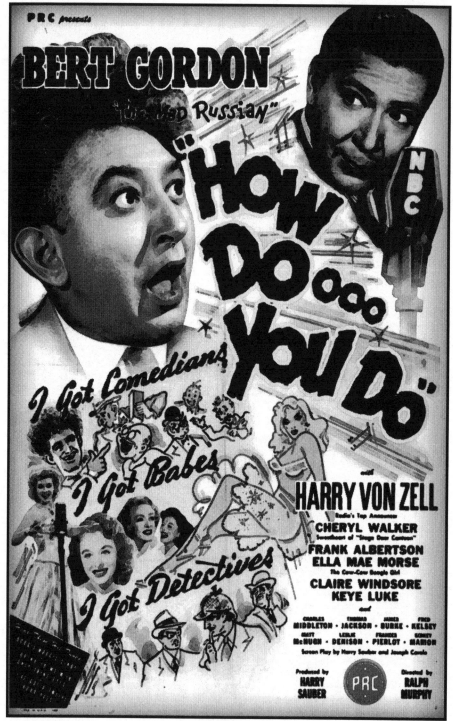

COMICMIX • HOW DOOOO YOU DO!!!

ble–O's that would move a studio audience to applause before he could complete the phrase. Sometimes, he would worry the first *do* into submission; on other occasions, the second *do*, like a jazz musician milking the improvisational possibilities from some nursery-rhyme melody.

This indelible signature–line was the most logical of titles, then, for a Gordon-starring picture—and in fact, the less imaginatively transcribed *How Do You Do?* had been the work-in-progress title of a 1942 Columbia comedy that got released as *Laugh Your Blues Away*, with Gordon and Jinx Falkenberg. If any studio was attuned to Gordon's more eccentric tastes, it had to be Producers Releasing Corp.—better known by its initials, which a less charitable cineaste might hold to stand for "Pretty Rotten Crap." Anyhow, PRC Pictures (better known for its horse–operas, rudimentary *noirs*, and Mad Doctor chillers) seems precisely the right studio to have given Gordon and his radio accomplices free rein. And precisely the wrong studio to be taken earnestly by the critics or the paying customers.

The film plants Gordon and radio cohort Harry VON Zell amidst their own broadcasting culture. Exhausted by the grind, Gordon and VON Zell (playing themselves, in broad strokes) retreat to a desert resort. Two other associates, Cheryl Walker and Claire Windsor, arrive on their own in a similar quest for serenity. Neither party is aware of the other's presence until VON Zell spots the women and panics: VON Zell's wife suspects an adulterous affair between VON Zell and Walker. Meanwhile, Gordon's over-amorous co–star, Ella Mae Morse, has trailed him to the retreat.

One night, Morse overhears a ruckus from some other suite. Next morning, the troupers find themselves under house arrest by a grouchy sheriff (Charles "Ming The Merciless" Middleton, Old Hollywood's most nearly perfect hand at droll intimidation). Mayhem is afoot: The victim appears to have been a well-despised show-biz agent named Thornton.

The corpse goes missing, only to be rediscovered, lost again, found again, and so forth. Walker stands accused. VON Zell supplies her with an alibi that can only mean trouble, if–and–when his wife learns of it. Gordon cables several actor chums—guys who have played detectives in various moving pictures—to come solve the case; they only confuse the issue. Finally, the sheriff pegs the hotel manager as the culprit, even as Claire Windsor comes forth with a confession. The resort's manager (Francis Perliot) proves by the oddest damned irrelevant coincidence to be Windsor's father.

The deliberately dingbat story peaks—*or does it?*—when the purported victim turns up, alive and well, accompanied by a physician (Sidney Marion) who attributes the seeming demise to an experimental drug. The doctor has been moving the comatose patient from place to place in an attempt to keep the treatment a secret.

Whereupon the picture ends—or does it? The camera draws back to reveal that the entire misadventure has been a movie, being viewed by Bert Gordon, Harry VON Zell, and their producers. One of the studio chiefs declares that this film does not bear releasing, arguing that the victim should have proved genuinely croaked. Gordon orders that the closing moments of the picture be re–screened. When the image of the revived "victim" reappears, Gordon produces a gun and opens fire upon the on-screen character, thus rendering the film fit for distribution. Or not.

Strange is too bland a descriptive term for *How Doooo You Do!!!* even though the picture's engagingly bizarre awareness–of–self is hardly an innovation—and even though director Ralph Murphy and screenwriters Harry Sauber and Joseph Carole play things matter–of–factly, allowing the genial strangeness of Gordon's presence to steer the course. (Gordon's *shtik* had been caricatured beyond its built-in extremes on screen just a year earlier in Bob Clampett's "Hare Ribbin'," a Warner–Toons short subject pitting Bugs Bunny against a Mad Russian sound–alike, voiced by Sammy Wolfe.)

The similarly offbeat comedy team of Ole Olsen and Chick Johnson had long since covered similar film-within-film turf in 1941's *Hellzapoppin'*, a drastically cinematic reworking of their like-titled Broadway revue. And even *How Doooo*'s aggressively romantic portrayal by the comedian–singer Ella Mae Morse derives patently from a role played by Martha Raye in *Hellzapoppin'*.

But then, *How Doooo You Do!!!* allows vastly more time to elapse before it reveals itself as a movie that (per the crackpot logic of the script) has yet to be released. At 81 minutes in length, the picture is a good third of an hour longer than the typical PRC entry. A lengthy out-of-character prologue serves to acquaint the viewer with the radio-broadcasting milieu. Gordon's summoning of a handful of movie-detective actor chums (including Keye Luke, of Fox's *Charlie Chan* series and Monogram Pictures' final *Mr. Wong* picture) provides an eventful detour that functions more as movie-buff pandering than as ordinary padding.

PRC's confidence in this *How Doooo* (as seen in the overgenerous running time, which cranked not only the budget but also the per-reel rate of taxation) seems to have been in vain. The picture never caught on as anything more than a double-bill programmer, and even a surprisingly favorable review from the tradepaper *Variety* came five months too late to lend much momentum.

Variety, incidentally, noted that the film "isn't Gordon's first *[far from it]* but gives him one of his better efforts." This "better effort" proved to be the Mad Russian's last turn as a movie player. Gordon resurfaced before the cameras 19 years later with a one-shot appearance on network teevee's *The Dick Van Dyke Show*.

CONAN THE OILPATCH ROUGHNECK

June 24, 2007: Devotees of comics and the high-adventure pulp magazines know the story almost by heart: Before he had turned 30, Robert E. Howard, of Cross Plains, Texas, had staked out several prominent stations in American literature. He was a poet of Homeric promise, for example, and a contributor to the H.P. Lovecraft school of cosmic terrors—and a prolific South-by-Southwestern regionalist and steward of cowboy lore. And then some.

Had Howard lived past 30, he likely would have outgrown the shirtsleeves-fiction arena to find formal acceptance as a major literary figure. But the pulps—those cheaply produced mass-market publications that thrived during the first half of the 20TH Century—made an ideal proving ground, and a lasting monument to a talent too big to confine to a category.

A constant element is a sense of Howard's nomadic upbringing in rural Texas, during a time when the first oil-and-gas booms were transforming much of the state into a barbaric land of violence and mercenary opportunism. In a recent book called *Blood & Thunder: The Life & Art of Robert E. Howard*, Austin-based scholar Mark Finn makes plain the influence that the boom-town phenomenon, with its brawling new breed of citizenry known as roughnecks, worked upon Bob Howard.

Had he lived to become a more seasoned artist, Howard

MHPRICE • after ED EMSHWILLER

(1906–1936) probably would not have outgrown his appetite for rambunctious adventure, whether or not he might have left behind the characters who had earned for him an eager and widespread readership. Such recurring characters include a trouble-prone Westerner named Jeopardy Grimes and the Puritan avenger Solomon Kane. To say nothing of Conan the Cimmerian, the barbaric warrior whose exploits have overshadowed the greater range of Howard's work.

The *Conan* trademark remains especially bankable, 71 years after the author's death. Dark Horse Comics offers a mounting series of new exploits, written nowadays by my old-time chum and blues-and-comics collaborator Timothy Truman. And many people still picture Gov. Arnold Schwarzenegger with perhaps a smidgen of accuracy in terms of his *Conan* movies of a generation ago. But Howard's restless spirit is gaining ground on his fictional creation.

Finn's *Blood & Thunder* (Monkey Brain Books) represents more than a perceptive portrait. Taken together, separate biographical studies of Howard by Rusty Burke and Mark Finn prove persuasive and probably definitive. To a Southwestern region that has reawakened during the past several years to the mixed blessings of oil-and-gas exploration—a consequence of destructive but lucrative natural-gas play within the Barnett Shale geological formation—Finn's book is particularly valuable as an examination of an earlier Texas in the throes of boom-town mania.

"Howard remains to most an Oedipal figure who created [Conan] as a wish-fulfillment fantasy," as *Publisher's Weekly* has appraised Blood and Thunder. "Finn quietly and expertly demolishes these and other misconceptions [and] discusses Howard in the context of a populist writer whose dyspeptic view of civilization was forged in the corrupt Texas oil-boom towns in which he grew up."

Every fictional character must have some basis in Real World observation or experience. Finn's persuasive argument, interpreted from Howard's published and private writings, holds that Conan, with his air of defiance, his appetites for mayhem and his "gigantic melancholies and gigantic mirths" (in Howard's terminology) owes much to the oilfield social dynamics of the early 20TH Century—the upshot of abrupt industrialization and its social and environmental corruption.

From Finn's book: "Even a cursory examination of Robert E. Howard's body of work reveals several recurring themes. The rise and fall of civilizations..., and a singular, moral man against a horde of immoral adversaries can be found in the stories of Conan the Cimmerian, Bran Mak Morn, Solomon Kane, King Kull, and even in lesser characters... It's a philosophy cobbled together from a precocious and voluminous amount of reading and from shrewd first-hand observation of the tension between the old Texans of the frontier and the new Texans with oil, and sometimes blood, on their hands."

A distinction bears mentioning between the earliest boom days and the renewed activity centered upon the Barnett Shale: The temptations of sudden prosperity remain constant, but the civilizing influences of Law & Order and environmental responsibility were less readily enforced in bygone times. Not to suggest that the forces of Law & Order cannot be bought, y'know.

Finn quotes Howard at length, such as these words from 1928: "[T]he town was deluged with oil workers and magnates ... roughnecks who swaggered and jostled their way through life ... loud-mouthed, steely-eyed promoters..." Explains Finn: "Howard had good reason to hate the oil boom. His father ... had chased prosperity... Every year or two, the Howards would ... start over again."

Howard wrote in 1930 to H.P. Lovecraft, 'way off in Rhode Island: "I've seen towns leap into being overnight and become deserted almost as quick. I've seen old farmers ... become millionaires in a week, by the way of oil gushers ... and die paupers. I've seen whole towns debauched by an oil boom..."

His parents' eventual settlement in Cross Plains gave Howard the anchorage he had needed to begin maturing as a writer—one of the first, as the *Conan* series' artist-turned-writer Timothy Truman points out, to develop tales of virile heroism and fantastic adventure from a laboring-class narrative setting. The nature of Howard's profession, pounding a typewriter in solitude, made him something of an outcast in a town where the menfolk were expected to toil conventionally for their bread. Howard's suicide, in 1936, left a bewildering void. Finn's thoughtful and provocative biography helps to explain the complex influences that drove Howard to such surges of creativity and destruction.

"[H]e built a career ... as a professional writer in an intellectual vacuum, surrounded by a town's indifference...," writes Finn. "Despite Robert's wish to avoid the oil boom, it was a part of his identity... [I]n the midst of Texas' greatest time of change, his thoughts and opinions became the building–blocks for one of the most significant bodies of work in contemporary literature.

"The story of Robert E. Howard is the story of 20TH Century Texas."

CARTOONING OVERRIDES POLITE PORTRAITURE

July 1, 2007: My home-base city of Fort Worth, Texas, has (since the 1950s) complicated its countrified essence with a set of class-and-culture conceits that range from the Van Cliburn International Piano Competition—America's "So, there!" riposte to Khruschev and/or Tchaikowsky, dating from a peak period of the Cold War—to four heavy-duty art museums of international appeal and influence. The local-boosterism flacks babble about "Cowboys 'n' Culture!" at every opportunity, with or without provocation.

Oscar Wilde.

But apart from the self-evident truths that Old Money (oil 'n' cattle) fuels the High Cultural Impulse and that the cow-honker sector finds chronic solace in the Amon Carter and Sid Richardson museums' arrays of works by Frederic Remington and Charles M. Russell, these communities seldom cross paths with one another.

The *détente* was tested beyond reasonable limits in 2001, when a yee-haw country-music promoter moved a mob-scene outdoor festival from the Fort Worth Stockyards to the fashionable downtown area—at precisely the moment the Cliburn Competition was settling into nearby Bass Performance Hall, itself an ostentatious assertion of an Old World civilizing stimulus for the New Linoleum. I mean, Millennium.

Yes, and the juxtaposition of clashing tribal imperatives scarcely could have been more emphatically pronounced. I should add that it wasn't the Cliburn audience that went about mooning and boob–flashing the C&W entertainers in mid–performance, nor was it the Cliburn audience left that mound of shattered beer bottles in the City Center Parking Garage. Never the twang shall meet.

Despite the persistence of "Cowboys 'n' Culture! Yee–Haw!" as a rallying cry for the tourism racket, either element fares very well, thank you, without the other's interference. The North Side's Stockyards area has Billy Bob's Texas and the restless ghosts of the meat-packing industry. The West Side's Cultural District has, well, its notions of Culture. And so who gets to call it "Art," anyhow? I'm homing in, here, upon a newly opened *[as of 2007]* exhibition at Fort

Worth's Kimbell Art Museum. The title is *The Mirror and the Mask: Portraiture in the Age of Picasso* (through Sept. 16). This one is the most promisingly commercialized show the Kimbell has mounted in recent memory. (The lame-duck director, Dr. Timothy Potts, has long indulged a preference for antiquities grounded as much in anthropology as in artistry, and popular appeal be damned. More power to him.) The exhibit also recaptures a historic Fine Art Crisis that might as well belong to the shirtsleeves realm of cartooning.

Cartooning is, after all, as much a prehistoric wellspring of Fine Art as it is a self-sufficient Modern Age Phenomenon. (Ted Richards and Justin Green's "Two Fools in a Cave," a *Comix Book* story from 1974, suggests persuasively the rowdier origins of formal portraiture.)

Rude origins notwithstanding, portraiture had long since set itself apart from cartooning by the waning 19TH Century. But cartooning had crept back in, repeatedly and all along, as a function of propaganda. Take Richard III, f'rinstance: Neither the Shakespearean version nor the historical personage of Richard III is anywhere to be found in this provocative *Mirror and Mask* show at the Kimbell. The objective here is Modernism, after all—in the 20TH Century sense, that is—and such antiquity as the thoroughly demonized Richard represents has no place in a proclaimed Age of Picasso.

One can only wonder, all the same, how the 15TH Century English ruler might have fared as the subject of a sitting before such a painter as Pablo Picasso or David Hockney or Frida Kahlo. Official portraiture of Richard's era depicts a pleasant-looking figure—although famous variants (a form of editorial cartooning, safely outside the subject's mortal span) since the reign of Henry VIII suggest increasingly a hunched back and a withered arm, more in keeping with the vilifications associated with Sir Thomas More and Shakespeare: "An envious mountain 'pon my back," indeed!

Of many painted Richards, one in particular (*ca.* 1550, some 65 years after his death–in–combat) captures such a thoroughly twisted figure as Shakespeare describes. And one other, a normal-looking figure of grace and dignity likely from the 1480s, seems drawn from life. Yes, and what Royal Portraitist ever had the guff to deliver an unflattering likeness of his ruler?

That question figures persistently in the Kimbell's unique display: Should portraiture affect an idealized view of humankind? Or seek some perceived truth at the sacrifice of prettification? The working cartoonist knows the answer, without prompting. Just ask Drew Friedman, who has worked both sides of that street to striking effect over the long haul—and who has lately resumed the warts-and-all approach to portraiture/caricature with an affectionately warty book called *Old Jewish Comedians*. (See also: Page No. 284)

The arrival of *Mirror and Mask* coincides with Timothy Potts' announced departure from the Kimbell, to join the Fitzwilliam Museum at the University of Cambridge. The deployment here of many popular-favorite artists (including Van Gogh, Matisse, Picasso of course, and Hockney and Kahlo) bespeaks as keen a marketing-department influence as a curatorial relevance. (I could stand to see the context deepened with a Basil Wolverton panel or two—or a Boris Artzybasheff, or a selection from the ranks of the recognized Great Editorial Cartoonists, for whom a mastery of portraiture is a necessary function of caricature.)

This *Mirror and Mask* show is a benchmark, nonetheless. The absorbed viewer will respond naturally to the implicit influence of cartooning. The exhibit might find a telling summation in Oscar Wilde's Faustian yarn of 1890, *The Picture of Dorian Gray.* "Every portrait that is painted with feeling," wrote Wilde, "is a portrait of the artist, not the sitter." *Mirror and Mask* captures seemingly the very moment upon which the more influential Artists–with–a–Capital–A of the 19TH–into–20TH Centuries decided, as if by subconscious vote, to cease currying favor and patronage with flattering portraiture and start delivering exaggerations, even distortions, of the fellow human beans who sat before them as models. Where once the development of photography might have sidelined portrait-painting altogether, the portraitists retrenched as cartoonists—whether or not consciously so.

Once an idea has weasled its way into the communal dream–stream, its spread is assured. Oftentimes, such artists found it expedient to pose for themselves—hence an upwelling of self–portraiture, famously associated with Vincent Van Gogh—whether because they feared insulting some Ruling Class client with newfangled radical notions of anatomy, or because they were too impoverished to engage hired models.

The Kimbell's masterstroke is to catch this vast society of artists (also among them: Paul Cezanne, Joan Miró, and Max Beckmann) in the act of turning away from conventional portrait–painting while looking to such alien influences as Third World tribal sculpture and their own skewed inner-cartoonist perceptions. And might a deliberate distortion mirror the soul more accurately than a literal, photo-realistic act of portraiture?

Portraiture had flourished historically as a matter of fidelity to nature, or to Conventional Wisdom: The popular notion of a Good Likeness is largely a matter of what a subject wishes to see staring back from the canvas. And yet the portrait–form found new momentum in the tempestuous experimentalism accumulated here. Abstraction of the human form became the newer norm.

In a shift amounting to a Sea Change in the practice of portraiture, the modern artists broke ranks with the custom of the made-to-order commissioned painting, which had been the meat–and–potatoes of the Working Artist. The sitters now became the artists themselves, or friends or relatives, rather than paying clients. As often as not, the paintings became gifts—not merchandise for the peddling. The notion of portraiture as a sharply defined genre helped to engage the expectations of the viewer, and then to defy such expectations with mask-like imagery rather than a recognizably lifelike vision.

Hence the *Mask* in the title of the exhibit. The *Mirror* part addresses, of course, a principal tool of self-portraiture. In a more figurative sense, such an artist might envision him– or herself in some other model entirely and paint the perception more so than the model. And hence Oscar Wilde's assertion: "... the artist, not the sitter."

AMAZING COLOSSAL SCULPTURES

July 8, 2007: Last week's dispatch from this quarter drew some parallels between cartooning and Fine Artsy facial studies, as provoked by an exhibition called *The Mirror and the Mask: Portraiture in the Age of Picasso*, at the Kimbell Art Museum of Fort Worth, Texas. A companion opener at the Modern Art Museum of Fort Worth has less of an academic mouthful of a title—*Ron Mueck*, plain and simple—but digs comparably deep into the function of portraiture during Times of Anxiety (which is to say, damned near *all times*) by concentrating upon the assembled work of one present-day artist. Namely, Ron Mueck, Muppeteer–turned–monumental sculptor.

So I'll be expecting my Hearty Handshake any day now from the Greater (than what?) Fort Worth Chamber of Commerce, on account of doing my bit for Provincial Tourism and the hometown arts-and-farces scene. These exhibitions, of course, are anything but provinciable.

Mueck: Untitled (Seated Woman).

Mueck will require little introduction, although some of his now-cryptic, now-blatant clay-into-silicone signature–pieces are more widely recognized than his name. The *Untitled (Seated Woman)*, a smaller-than-real piece of unnervingly lifelike resonance, has been an object of worldwide fascination since its début in 2002 as a fixture of the Modern Art Museum of Fort Worth. Send this one out on institutional loan or place it in temporary storage, and the North Texas enthusiasts will mount a massed protest. Mueck's namesake exhibit has previously graced the Brooklyn Museum and the National Gallery of Canada.

I find that Mueck's works, though engaging if approached cold and without preamble, make a great deal more sense when regarded in a pop-literary context—all due respect to the stodgier curatorial realm. The tinier human figures might leave the absorbed viewer feeling a great deal like Mr. Swift's Lem Gulliver, awakening to find himself confronted with motionless Lilliputians. Mueck's larger-than-life figures reduce the observer, conversely, to the state of the awestruck expeditioners of 1933's *King Kong*, edging warily past a fallen Stegosaurus. Mueck sums up his approach with a simple manifesto: "Life–size is ordinary." Which recalls this echo from Old Hollywood: "It's not big enough!" raged the filmmaking artist Merian C. Cooper (1893–1973), on so many occasions that his Hollywood crews learned to anticipate his demands—by thinking in unreal proportions and translating such impressions to the movie screen.

How big? Well, that 1933 accept-no-substitutes original *King Kong* is Cooper's chief surviving brainchild. Cooper has many creative descendants, as well. And from the Whole Cloth of one big-thinking motion picture, about a titanic ape's indignant response to an intrusion from normal-sized humanity, the variously gifted heirs of Cooper have crafted immense accomplishments around the adventurous, challenging and often unsettling notion that—putting it into practice long before Ron Mueck could find the words—"life–size is ordinary."

Merian Cooper's legatées need not confine themselves to motion pictures, of course. Popular fiction has long since nailed a grasp of gigantism and miniaturization—and how better to explain Richard Matheson's *The Shrinking Man*? Or Marvel Comics' *Ant–Man/Giant–Man* dichotomy? Or *Superman*'s Titano the Super–Ape or that Ozarka–bottleful of shrunken Kryptozoonians? Not to mention Ron Mueck.

Mueck seems to be channeling and modifying the cinematic soul of Cooper, thinking by turns in massive and miniaturized terms. Anyhow, a visit to the exhibition can leave one with the impression of having stumbled into a freeze–frame of some special-effects fantasy film. The imaginative thrall is that persuasive.

The aforementioned *Untitled (Seated Woman)* depicts a tiny geezer–lady of advanced age, clothed in attire too drably genuine to be dismissed as doll–costuming. So lifelike is she in every detail that some museum–goers will stand staring for minutes at a stretch, as if anticipating some sign of respiration.

Seated Woman triggers the same popular-response vibe that a second-generation protégé of Merian Cooper's company, the sculptural animator Ray Harryhausen, struck when he began testing and inverting the bigger-is-better rule—as early as 1957. With a movie assignment called *20 Million Miles to Earth*, Harryhausen challenged himself to come up with a creature sufficiently huge and expressive to give King Kong pause. But first, Harryhausen made the beast small enough to occupy a lab-specimen cage, none too happy to be there and all too ready to swell to outlandish proportions.

Harryhausen found a more telling variation in a cowboys-and-dinosaurs escapade called *The Valley of Gwangi* (1969). The truer show–stopper there is a tiny prehistoric horse, a prelude to the more extravagant thrills. Those who have seen that meticulously crafted horse, on display out of context, speak of it with the same hushed wonder that one hears from admirers of Ron Mueck's *Seated Woman*.

So influential is the Cooper legacy than even some less gifted successors—the low-budget filmmaker Bert I. "Mr. B.I.G." Gordon, for example—have thrived on the practice of confronting everyday reality with gigantic and/or miniaturized presences. Gordon's cheaply constructed trilogy of *The Cyclops*, *The Amazing Colossal Man*, and *War of the Colossal Beast* (1957–1958) would be preposterous to contemplate if not for his instinctive ability (unconvincing camera–trickery aside) to personalize his monstrosities on a pained emotional level. *Colossal Man*, in particular, suggests such an unsettling study of a tormented soul— the condition of gigantism can only prove fatal—that one loses sight of the shortcomings in the special-effects department. (Between *Colossal Man* and *Colossal Beast*, Gordon delivered a miniaturized-humans movie called *Attack of the Puppet People*. This one is a takeoff on a 1940 picture called *Dr. Cyclops*, from Merian Cooper's colleague Ernest B. Schoedsack. Small world, indeed, you should pardon the expression.)

Ron Mueck no doubt owes less than I might be suggesting, here, to the screen-thrills influence—which as a linchpin of the Popular Culture is nonetheless impossible to ignore and decidedly essential to a sharper understanding of the exhibition. The artist is a thoroughgoing original who has absorbed the historic influences of Monumental Sculpture and cinematic fantasy and shaped them into a body of work whose individual pieces (like Merian Cooper's put-upon Kong and Bert I. Gordon's maddened Colossal Man) connect with the observer on what feels like a personal level.

It scarcely comes as a surprise to learn that Mueck, 49, spent his childhood as an amateur toymaker and began working in earnest as a puppet–builder for such television programs as *Sesame Street* and *The Muppets*. His current endeavors take the human form to a remarkable state of heightened realism, picturing individuals who look as though they might spring to unhealthy life at any second.

Better motionless. *Big Man*, the chief attention–getter in the museum display, is a sullen colossus, "barefooted all over" (as Stymie Beard might put it), and slumped in a state of perpetual disgust. Where the celebrated *Seated Woman* seems lost in a reverie, *Big Man* appears determined to convey unhappiness to anyone who walks past: The illusion of eye–contact is jarring beyond all good sense.

By an opposing token, Mueck's *Wild Man* seems the object of some ghastly ritual of torture, if not a psychotic episode. He, too, sits naked and vulnerable though larger-than-life, frozen in time and space and yet galvanized by some Unimaginable Terror.

The effect is as startling as it is fascinating. Australian-born and London-based, Mueck has tapped in the realm of the Finer Arts that same impulse that has enthralled and haunted humankind, with its appetite for extremes, since prehistory. That obsession with size sloshes relentlessly between the inseparable vessels of Art and Commerce.

Mueck's mastery stems from an understanding that, no matter how huge or how small, a figure must engage its observer on a level of intimate communion. Mission accomplished, and then some.

MOE LESTER: ROMÁN NOIR, OR ROAMIN' NOSE?

July 15, 2007: The ungainly fellow pictured alongside is a concoction of my grammar-school days, modeled originally after an authoritarian physical-education teacher who took immense delight in reminding us younger kids that soon we would matriculate to the intermediate grades where he held sway. Talk about your incentives for under-achievement!

Because one must ridicule that which one cannot combat outright, I proceeded to reduce this intimidating presence to a cartoon character—exaggerating his pronounced nose and chin, as well as his intense Texas Redneck Honyock dialect—and set about subjecting him to sundry humiliations within the pages of a Big Chief composition tablet. These pages in turn were duly, if guardedly, circulated for the amusement of sympathetic classmates. The confiscation of these prototypical Underground Comics (*ca.* 1955) was long in coming, but inevitable: I was having too much fun in plain view of a cheerless society.

The agent of my character's simultaneous popular discovery and christening was one Mrs. M.E. Jenkins, Third Grade homeroom teacher and Tireless Champion of the Status Quo. Inquiring as to the contents of my sketch–pad, Mrs. Jenkins noticed its star player straightaway— and invited me to explain his *raison d'etre* to the assembled class. I improvised: "Aw, he's just this goofy ol' guy who gets in trouble a whole lot." Then she asked: "And what is his name, Michael?"

Gulp! Well, now, *no way* was I going to identify my dreaded life–model—and so I made up an alias on the spot: "His name is *Moe Lester*, Missus Jenkins." (Pre-emptive crisis-control tip: Never speak in puns to people who neither Get It nor want to do so.)

"A MOLESTER!?!" bellowed Mrs. Jenkins, grabbing me by one ear and leaving the classroom to its own snickering devices as she hupped me down the cavernous hallway to the Principal's Office.

Not quite nine, and already the author of a Banned Book. Over Mrs. Jenkins' bellowing, Principal Howard Amick prevailed with somewhatly a saner voice: He found the pages worth a chuckle but, even so, pronounced them a Waste of Talent. Damnation by faint praise, in other words, within a public-school system whose elementary art curriculum consisted of finger–painting and construction-paper cut–outs.

The menacing teacher who had served as an unwitting life–model for Moe Lester found himself transferred before I could reach Fourth Grade. So *whew*, already. But others like him have cropped up ever since and all along, in the form of schoolyard bullies, college deans, petty bureaucrats, dimwitted newspaper editors, police officers of a thuggish bent, and so forth. *[Flash forward to 2016 and witness the Confederacy of Malicious Knuckleheads seeking the Republican nomination for President.]* Abuse of authority is rampant, as if you didn't know, and those who can't bring themselves to buy in are well advised to find what humor they can in its ridiculous essence.

A recurrent, if not entirely current, incarnation of Moe Lester dates from 1969–1970, when as a college undergraduate I based a revamped version upon such influences as (1) a uniformly lunkheaded and ill-intentioned campus-cop department at West Texas Suitcase University, (2) Lyndon "Beans" Johnson, and (3) a big-shot rancher–turned–political agitator named J. Evetts Haley. Haley at the time was holding forth as the Phantom President of W.T.S.U.—my *alma mater*, such as it was and is—in hopes of marginalizing the on-campus outcroppings (yes, even in the provinces) of such influences as the Panthers and S.D.S. A primary æstheti-cable influence would involve the likes of Basil Wolverton, Walt Kelly, Gene Ahern, Al Capp, and Boody Rogers (Page No. 140)—masters of convoluted wordplay and cartoonish exaggeration. Many of the more recent *Moe Lester* pages, including a 1993 appearance in *Heavy Metal* and a couple of stories–in–progress with fellow Texas-bred cartoonist Frank Stack, date from times more recent. But the template was struck long beforehand.

Portrait of Moe Lester by Mark Evan Walker.

Not to suggest that Moe's misadventures are political cartoons in any sense of social betterment or constructive protest. They are ridicule, at best—and mere silliness, oftener than not—a *reductio ad absurdam* of the hostility and intolerance that are part and parcel of the Human Condition. A spot of sarcasm helps somehow to keep the irritants at bay.

In a monumental treatise called *What's Funny—and Why* (1939), the humorist and educator Milton Wright cited an ancient story about "the time the family played a game to see who could screw their features up to look the funniest."

"It was Grandma ... who was declared unanimously to be the winner," wrote Wright. "But Grandma wasn't playing."

Thus did Prof. Wright nail what might be the funniest brand of humor, and probably the oldest, in a laugh-provoking heritage that is older, even, than humankind. A fellow funnyman, Fred Schwed, Jr., argued to the contrary in a 1951 memoir, *The Pleasure Was All Mine* (illustrated, incidentally, by *Pogo Possum*'s Walt Kelly). Schwed maintained that spontaneous witticisms, such as "'cute' sayings of small children ... are not true humor, of course; they are charming misconceptions..."

But Funny Is Funny, whatever the trigger. In the opinion of Milton Wright, the first guffaw ever guffawed must have belonged to some primeval simian—and the provocation must have been some dead-earnest fellow creature that wasn't trying at all to amuse.

It became my good fortune to discover that Wright volume during 1956–1957 in the library of the West Texas grammar school where, as a Third Grader of rebellious leanings, I had begun drawing up the adventures of Moe Lester in parody of that bullying phys–ed teacher. I recognized instinctively that my despotic inspiration was not attempting to be funny—no, he fancied it his mission to intimidate—but his very attitude rendered him laughable, if in a scary way. It took Milton Wright's *What's Funny—and Why* to explain.

Fortunately for my immediate age–group, this teacher did not toil at the primary levels and indeed would be reassigned to some other school altogether before my own class could advance to the Fourth Grade. But the gent also doubled as a recess supervisor—in which capacity he made the playground feel more like a Boot Camp Obstacle Course than any jolly refuge from the drudgery of the classroom.

I grew to welcome his intrusions, in a sense, for often he would wax philosophical—commandingly so, of course—in an attempt to impart to us "childeren" (his terminology) the wisdom born of a career devoted to the molding of pre-adolescent citizens.

"Now, y'all boys, yew're comin' up to 'roundbout th' age where yew might be tempted tuh try a–smokin' some of these here cig'rettes," he would tell us, even as he tapped a Lucky Strike (unfiltered) from its deck and fired it up. "But I mean t' tell yuh *whut*: Don'tcha *do* it!

"B'cause if'n yew 'uz tuh start a–smokin' 'fore yew're *old enough*, it'll *stump your growth*, an' I ain't a–jokin'!" (*Sic, sic,* and *sic*.)

A pure-dee Moe Lester moment if I ever witnessed one.

And with such an abunderance of raw material polluting the very air, I seldom found it necessary to contrive any jokes to go along with my childish stabs at cartooning.

Right around this time, I discovered that book of Milton Wright's—and through it, the traditions of the Irish Bull, of the Rev. W.A. Spooner and his tongue-tangled monologues, of Sheridan's Mrs. Malaprop, and of such wordplay-laden institutions as Deep Southern Minstrelsy, with its reciprocal class-and-color yawps, and Vaudeville and Burlesque. To say nothing of *MAD* magazine. None of these Grand Insights, however, came close matching to the uncalculated comic tension engendered by Moe Lester's original model, who was at once terrifying (because he wielded authority, along with a spanking–paddle) and hilarious (because he was a self-important nincompoop with a drawl as thick as sorghum molasses).

Moe Lester has found many supplementary inspirations: An aunt who wanted her garden walkway paved with "gobblestones," and who took up hobbies "to break the monopoly." A highfalutin' neighbor–lady who had outfitted her house with "lavalier" (read: *louvered*) doors; a college professor who lectured about the origins of "the Angelican Church." A local steel-buildings contractor who announced his "speciality" to be the construction of "quonsick huts" and "jeeze–o–delic domes" and reported that his company was experiencing "unpresidented growth." And so on and so forth, *ad infinitum, ad nauseam, al fresco*.

But it is that dedicated P.E. instructor of my careworn schoolboy days who looms largest in the monument to nincompoopery that Moe

Lester has built, blunder by blunder. The published account should bear a grateful dedication to the life–model, but for my inability to recall the old honyock's name.

Continued stubsequently, if not immidiotly...

MOE LESTER AND THE
PERSISTENENCE OF ABSURDITUDE

July 22, 2007: Only on occasion, nowadays, do I revisit at any length the bizarre Southwestern region whose Dominant Culture gave rise to the chronic-to-acute exploits of Konstable Moe Lester. I use the word *character* facetiously, for in all his years of published misadventures (whether small-press or nearer some nebulous mainstream) and privately circulated gag strips, Moe has never been anything more than a facile caricature, a "type" embodying and exaggerating traits, mannerisms, and attitudes that prevail amongst the denizens of West Texas' so-called Panhandle region.

Portrait of Moe Lester by Meatwood Flack.

Now, I feel a profound and abiding nostalgia for that territory, having grown up there and having spent the first decade–and–a–half of my career touring those Panhandle backroads as both a rock-band musician and a reporter for a centrally located daily newspaper. But nostalgia must be acknowledged as an ailment before it can be dealt with on any practical level: When its pangs of home-sickness intrude upon my mostly idyllic self–exile to a more nearly metropolitan base of operations, Moe Lester simply rears his ugly proboscis as a reminder of why I had put that sprawling Panhandle country behind me, in the first place.

Once a lusty land, the Texas Panhandle slouches into the 21st century as a scattering of dying hamlets—Larry McMurtry's *The Last Picture Show*, writ large. The long-gone corporate land-grab barons, whose minions (bureaucratic, military, religious) subdued the native tribal culture, left behind an empire of once-vast ranches, once-thriving railroads, and once-monumental oil-and-gas production outfits that in scarcely the span of five generations have given way to an economy driven by speed traps, Dairy Queen cuisine, prison-system boondoggles and bureaucracies-within-bureaucracies, and the occasional Swill–Mart—bane of the independent small merchant. New methods of fossil-fuel reclamation (drilling at a slant to tap the resources beyond the reach of old-school vertical methods and cracking the very Caprock) yield wealth and environmental hazards galore; the citified corporate interests get the wealth, and the towns-people get the hazards. You get the picture.

This is Moe Lester Country, and welcome to it. "The land of the living dead," as Bob Dylan and Sam Shepard characterized the region in an all-but-epic narrative poem of 1986 called "Brownsville Girl." Where the more progressive restaurants divide themselves into two sections: one for smoking, one for chain–smoking. Where reciprocal bigotries endure despite superficial desegregation, and where law enforcement practices a policy of intimidation as a stop–gap against (or a prelude to) harsher measures. Moe Lester is the emblematic intolerant Hillbilly with a Badge.

But of course the Texas backwaters are scarcely the sole domain of rampant Yahooism, and I don't mean the Other Google. I've heard readers and colleagues from Maine to Alabama to Orange County (thank you, Barry Goldberg) remark that they've met a Moe Lester or two in their own localized ramblings. And yes, Moe's patently shallow characterization manages to ignore the benevolence and common decency that remain to be found in such provinces. If one looks, anyhow.

Portrait of Moe Lester by Effingwell Wright.

Because benevolence and common decency aren't particularly funny. And self-important ignorance is the very stuff of lowbrow, big-nose/big-foot humor. Besides, we all Talk Funny down yonder in the boondocks.

Yes, well, and many's the time I've dismissed the Moe Lester comics as "those stupid 'cop' cartoons," but all the same they have been a constant in a career whose more artistically earnest endeavors have proved fleeting or erratic. I've been putting this character—I mean, *facile caricature*—through his paces for long enough to know that there must be some reason greater than the mere urge or economic need to see one's words and pictures in cold print.

Moe didn't even see generalized publication until my senior year in college—1969–1970—when as new editor of the campus newspaper at West Texas State University I drafted him into the service of lampooning an oppressive administration and its bullying uniformed security force. What with the paper's being an Official Publication, I took discretionary pains to couch Moe's adventures in a context of ridiculosity. For this quality, I found it practical to draw upon such Real World absurdities as rampant half-baked surveillance tactics and the Kampus Kops' entrenched redneck intolerance.

Bill Lee, a good and decent man who was in charge of our Journalism Department, Got the Joke right away when I pitched the first few weeks' worth of comic strips. "You *do* know," Bill cautioned, "that we'll have to run this feature by Administration."

Which we did, expecting some outcry. Which we received, from no less a personage than Dr. James P. Cornette, the college's Figurehead President. (The rancher and divide-and-conquer gadfly J. Evetts Haley, author of a caustic and befuddling tract called *A Texan Looks at Lyndon*, was the school's truer chief though not on payroll, with Dr. Cornette as a lackey and cat's–paw.)

"Seems awfully silly to me, lad," the Great Administrator told me as he pored over a stack of *Moe Lester* pages. I was expecting to hear an objection over the christening. But no. Dr. Cornette droned on:

"I suppose these will pass muster—but one thing I really *do* find objectionable..." Bracing for a confrontation, I leaned in closer for the Officiable Pronouncement.

"You seem to be doing this in each little cartoon," said Dr. C. "You have this officer—what was his name, again?"

"Lester, sir. *Moe Lester.*"

"Yes, well. You seem to have this Officer Lester drinking beer at the end of each episode, as though that is to be his reward for a job well done. Now, I do not believe that this is the image we wish to be fostering for our campus policemen, now, *do* we, Mr.—*uh...*"

"Price, sir. *Mike Price.*"

"Yes, of course. Mr. Price. Now, *do we*, Mr. Price?"

"Do we *what*, sir?" I asked.

"Do we want our Security Police portrayed as drunkards, Mr. Price?"

Knowing better than to overplay my hand, I allowed the concession by retaining the bottle-of-beer drawings but removing the verbal references. (Moe's "I need a beer!" references were a flat-out swiperoo from a character in Robert Crumb's stable, the Old Pooperoo.) I neither knew nor gave much of a hang how applicable the image of a beer-swilling Kampus Konstable might be. If Moe's greater irreverences had gone zinging over the head of Dr. J.P. Cornette, then let the old sycophant pride himself on a victorious act of Institutionalized Censorship.

"I shall look forward to reading your little cartoons in our newspaper, son," said he, offering a congratulatory dead-fish handshake.

As it turned out, none of Moe's more immediate life-models ever seemed to Get the Joke, although enough stoodents and faculty-types took the character sufficiently to heart that Moe's escapades continued as a weekly feature for a year after I had wrested my diploma from the clammy grasp of Dr. James P. Cornette. The range of contributors to the gag-writing chores grew to include Bill Lee his ownself, along with fellow students-turned-colleagues Dennis Spies and Ken Brodnax and such senior-grade newspaper editors as Fred and Mary Kate Tripp and George E. Turner, later on my co–author on the original *Forgotten Horrors* movie-history book.

Most of those 1970–1972 strips do not bear reprinting—being too topical and too provincially esoteric to stand without annotation, and appearing in general as scarcely a patch upon such finer influences as Robert Crumb, Jay Lynch, Skip Williamson, Jack "Jaxon" Jackson, Frank Stack, and Gilbert Shelton. Technically speaking, the early entries tend to prove indistinguishable from most of the later stuff, inasmuch as my big-nose/big-foot style has seen few refinements over the longer term. Hence the involvement on various Moe Lester stories since the 1990s of such more polished illustrators as the seminal underground artist Frank Stack (a crucial early influence, owing to my school-days discovery of his college-magazine and proto-Underground material) and comparative newcomers Todd Camp, Dale Taylor, and Don Mangus.

One gag panel that appears somewhere amidst this chronicle (Page No. 166) appears through the courtesy of the artist Mark David Dietz, a savvy and otherwise tasteful collector of comics art. Mark shelled out cash–money at a 1994 Dallas Fantasy Fair charity auction in exchange for ownership of the original drawing. This moronic half–pager saw publication in 1988, in a newsletter produced by 4Winds Studios, where I had begun working with such formidable players as Timothy Truman, John K. Snyder III, Chuck Dixon, and Graham Nolan.

It should go without saying that I wasn't working on any *Moe Lester* foolishments at 4Winds. No, our bunch meant to ennoble the art–form, what with such titles as *Scout, Prowler, Sgt. Strike, Airboy,* and *The*

Spider and, later, with provocative graphic novels from such masterful talents as Sam Glanzman and Quiqué Alcaténa. But this 4Winds newsletter cartoon proved transitional in its half-baked way.

For once resurrected from the Wolvertonian Limbo to which I had banished him, Moe Lester proved unwilling to resume that suspension. Moe has since made his cloddish presence felt in a newspaper gag–strip called *What Next?!*; in such magazines as *Heavy Metal* (via Mark Martin's *Strip Tease* department within that title) and *Crime & Passion* and *Krime Duzzin't Pay!*; and in earlier incarnations of the *Southern-Fried Homicide* series of postmodern Undergrounders. The newer *Moe* stories–in–the–works with Frank Stack include a crossover with Frank's long-running *New Adventures of Jesus* series and a bit of Satan-cult absurdity called "Hellbent for Lester." Moe about all this as things develop. (A *Moe Lester* omnibus, *Felimonious Krimes*, arrived in 2014 from Cremo Studios.)

JIGGS & MAGGIE AT THE MOVIES

July 29, 2007: George McManus (1884–1954), once a household name via his long-running domestic-shenanigans comic strip *Bringing Up Father*, stands as a practical embodiment of the comics' cinematic possibilities. The last of his comics-into-movies adaptations, *Jiggs and Maggie Out West* (Monogram Pictures; 1950), came to hand recently during the excavation process for a fifth volume of John Wooley's and my *Forgotten Horrors* film-encyclopedia series.

What? Bringing Up Father's Jiggs and Maggie in a horror and/or Western movie? Well, not precisely so—but close enough to fit the *Forgotten Horrors* agenda. The books' greater point all along has been

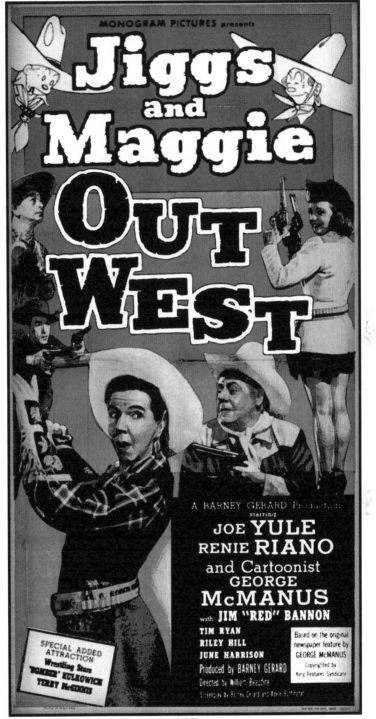

that of isolating the weirdness in a range of motion pictures beyond the narrowly defined genres of horror and SF. And more peculiar than William Beaudine's *Jiggs and Maggie Out West*, they don't hardly come.

Born in St. Louis to Irish parents, McManus registered early on in the last century as a newspaper cartoonist capable of finding a resonant absurdity in everyday domestic life, and of veering into dreamlike fantasy in the manner of Winsor McCay's *Little Nemo in Slumberland*. With McCay, during the 1910s, McManus began exploring the finer possibilities of cartoon-movie animation: It is McManus, in a live-action prologue to the 1914 animation-charged "Gertie the Dinosaur," who stakes a wager with McCay about the challenges of bringing a prehistoric beast to a semblance of lifelike motion. McManus' larger filmography dates from 1913, as source–author, animator, and occasional actor.

Monogram Pictures' formal *Jiggs and Maggie* series spans only 1946–1950, but the funnypapers' *Bringing Up Father*—a broadly parodic but subtly satiric study of an Irish-immigrant workingman, Jiggs, and his social-climbing wife, Maggie—had become fodder for the movie business many years beforehand. The Monogram series stars Scots-born Joe Yule (surname streamlined from Ewell) as Jiggs. Yule had been a headliner in burlesque and vaudeville but found his career eclipsed by the success of his son, Mickey Rooney, as a kid star. Rooney's career found traction in 1927 with the *Mickey McGuire* slapstick series, derived from the comics of Kentuckian Fontaine Fox.

Yule retrenched in Hollywood during the waning 1930s and made fresher marks of his own as a character man and bit-parts player—specializing in Irish-immigrant types. Toward the end, Yule settled in as the crowd-pleasing star of Monogram's *Jiggs and Maggie* series, with the kindred-soul participation of George McManus.

The earlier Monogrammers, starting with *Bringing Up Father* in 1946, are scarcely more than situation-comedy prototypes, though hardly without their rough-hewn charms. Yule is most winning in the born-to-play role of Jiggs, a striving sort who longs for the company of his old-time gang of hard-drinking laborers and lollygaggers. Renie Riano likewise fits the role of the temperamental Maggie. Modest production values and uninspired pacing (here, by the prolific Beaudine, of the traffic-cop school of screen directing) merely come with the Monogram turf.

Jiggs and Maggie Out West pulls a doubled-up genre–switch with a ghost-story premise in a frontier setting. (The *Forgotten Horrors* Rule for artificial resuscitation of a flagging franchise: Just Add Monsters.) Maggie, determined to prove herself the rightful heir to a fortune, finally gets a break with word of a legacy awaiting in a ramshackle settlement. In a swell touch of in-joke self–consciousness, the town is called Gower Gulch—after the Hollywood locale most commonly identified with Monogram's Poverty Row class of independent studios.

The ghost of her grandfather urges Maggie to move the household to Gower Gulch, where all concerned run afoul of a feud perpetrated by Snake Bite Carter (Jim Bannon) and his half–brother, Bob Carter (Riley Hill). At stake is the MacGillicuddy Gold Mine, which Maggie stands to inherit. Following another ghostly apparition, the absurdities peak with Maggie's abduction by Snake Bite, who takes her to a meeting with George McManus—playing himself, more or less, in a detour into Rubber Reality narrative sense.

The awareness *of* the film, *by* the film, was a commonplace at such nothing-to-lose studios as Monogram and Producers Releasing Corp. The June 17 installment of this column (Page No. 147) covers one such picture, PRC's *How Doooo You Do!!!* (1945). Monogram producer Sam Katzman indulged in such self-referential nonsense with the likes of *Voodoo Man* (1944) and *The Ape Man* (1943)—both credited by Stan Lee as an inspiration for a recurring gimmick at the midcentury's proto-Marvel Comics: the comic-book story about a comic-book writer whose outlandish ideas spring to waking life.

Anyhow, McManus assures *Jiggs and Maggie Out West* of an irreversible tangent into the bizarre: McManus (as the Real World artist responsible for the situation), explains to Maggie (as his indignant brainchild) that he had transplanted her and Jiggs to this desolate locale merely to see how they might react. Maggie reacts, all right—with one of her customary tantrums.

Whereupon the picture ends. And so does the series. Joe Yule died at 65 in March of 1950. *Jiggs and Maggie Out West* was released the following month. The Monogram series contains these pictures in addition to *Out West*: *Bringing Up Father* (1946), *Jiggs and Maggie in Society* (1947), *Jiggs and Maggie in Court* (1948), and *Jiggs and Maggie in Jackpot Jitters* (1949). The directors, by turns, are Bill Beaudine and Edward F. Cline.

FROM BAREFOOT GEN TO WHITE LIGHT

August 5, 2007: Steven Okazaki's documentary feature *White Light/Black Rain: The Destruction of Hiroshima and Nagasaki* marks the 62ND anniversary of the arrival of thermonuclear warfare. The film's harrowing impact has been a matter of record since 2007's Sundance Film Festival in Utah. Though hardly the first of its kind, *White Light/Black Rain* proves a timely and emphatic reminder. It possesses a sharp consistency with the pioneering *Barefoot Gen* manga-turned-anime tales of Keiji Nakazawa, and with Masuji Ibuse's novel *Black Rain*, as filmed in 1989 by Shohei Imamura. Okazaki's film brings full–circle, East–meets–West, a persistent question raised by one history-in-the-making Hollywood epic of 1947, *The Beginning or the End*, which traces the Manhattan Project to a climax at Hiroshima and Nagasaki. (In its very title, *The Beginning or the End* had declared thermonuclear weaponry a topic of perpetual relevance. Further outcroppings include 1982's *The Atomic Café*, a pageant of A–Bomb boosterism propaganda; and 1995's *The Plutonium Circus*, concerning the Texas town [namely, Amarillo] most thoroughly identified with Nuclear Preparedness [term used advisedly] as a Tax Base.)

White Light/Black Rain finds its more persuasive voice in interviews with survivors of the bombings, illuminated by a gauntlet of harrowing archival footage. Appreciation requires context, lest *White Light/Black Rain* be mistaken for an unprecedented re–examination. Nearer origins lie in the graphic novels of Nakazawa, whose first-hand account of Hiroshima—he professes to have noticed the approach, followed by "a million flashbulbs going off at once"—yielded two *Barefoot Gen* animated movies of the 1980s. Nakazawa has aligned himself with Steven Okazaki since the 2005 documentary "The Mushroom Club," a short-film stage–setter for *White Light/Black Rain*.

The bombings have amounted to fodder, both imaginative and factual, for the American motion-picture industry since well before that turning-point of World War II. In a time of reciprocal hostilities, the U.S. entertainment industry felt a duty to commit propaganda as a function of advocating an any-means-necessary end to the war. WWII, of course, no more ended with the bombings than it can be said to

BAREFOOT GEN

A Cartoon Story of Hiroshima

KEIJI NAKAZAWA

VOLUME TWO

have begun at any absolute moment. One war bleeds into another, like the ocean ignoring its explorers' charted boundaries, over the greater sweep of history. It is a simpler matter to cinch the moment at which Hollywood—itself an occupied territory at the time, given the imposed presence of the armed forces' motion-picture bureaucracy at studios large and small—began anticipating a bombing run over Japan as a matter of meeting the Axis Powers in decisive terms.

That moment occurs in a since-obscure film called *China's Little Devils* (1945), which peaks with an airborne raid upon Tokyo. Its date of release, not quite three months before Hiroshima, lends the picture a harrowing resonance that its author, the Old Left playwright and agitator Samuel Ornitz, probably had not intended. The point was, rather, to suggest an outraged response, triggered by the depiction of a Japanese assault upon a Chinese orphanage. *China's Little Devils* stops short of nuclear devastation, although it suggests an instinctive awareness of the Manhattan Project on Ornitz' part. The movie came from an upstart low-budget studio, representing a corporate-Hollywood underclass that has blazed trails all along for the larger, more cautious, companies to commandeer as their own.

The first film to acknowledge Hiroshima and Nagasaki came, likewise, from Hollywood's low-rent sector. *Shadow of Terror* (1945) had started out as a generic Axis-buster adventure, with a top-secret explosive device as the maguffin at risk of falling into enemy hands. The Real World deployment of the A–Bomb took place while *Shadow of Terror* was approaching completion, and the studio responded by ordering a rewrite to climax the tale with Hiroshima, incorporating U.S. government footage of a bombing test in New Mexico. Your Tax Dollars and Mine, at work in the special-effects department.

Not until 1947 would the Manhattan Project become the essence of a commercial motion picture, with big-time MGM Pictures' *The Beginning or the End*—a film that addresses both the immediate patriotic Good War impulse and the broader implications, complete with a High Mass Blessing of the hellfire mission. The Japanese film industry rallied in 1954 to explore nuclear warfare in allegorical terms: Ishiro Honda's *Gojira* (better known as *Godzilla*, and grimmer by far than most people will assume) imagines a legendary monster as the embodiment of the Atomic Bomb.

Such back-story elements are crucial to an understanding of *White Light/Black Rain: The Destruction of Hiroshima and Nagasaki*, which offers concise and nightmarish coverage as a cautionary reminiscence. Okazaki traces the history of the bomb's development, then speaks with representatives of the American military and scientific establishments. The film concentrates upon Japanese survivors. They relate their circumstances with a jarring immediacy, many leaving the impression that survival might not have been preferable to oblivion. A closing segment draws upon footage that many viewers may find unbearably intense—"powerfully unpleasant," as the show-business tradepaper *Variety* summed up the Sundance showing.

Perhaps most troubling is the state of vapid unawareness exhibited by a number of modern-day Japanese youngsters when Okazaki inquires as to the implications of August 6, 1945. Their blank stares convey a Tribal Amnesia as terrifying as the deployment of the bomb itself. The film, in turn, proceeds to propose—even to administer—a remedy in the form of a cathartic reminder, undiluted by equivocation or political theorizing.

CAN'T GET ENOUGH OF OL' B.T.K.

August 12, 2007: You just can't live in Texas if you don't have a lot of soul, as Doug Sahm would have it. No, and you can't live in Arizona if you don't have a sense of Yuma.

But we were talking about Texas, where you also just can't live without an immersion in the lore of Billy the Kid. Folklore and pop–fiction, that is, as opposed to factual knowledge or even Perceived Truth. By the time of the post-middle 20TH Century, such mis–familiarity had so thoroughly outstripped the facts in the case of this most notorious badman that most of the B.T.K. legendry bombarding the youth of America—and not merely the Texas/New Mexico Plains region—came not from Texas, but rather from Texas as filtered through movies and pulp-magazine prose and comic books.

For years on end, my most vivid images of Billy the Kid came from Toby Press' *Billy the Kid Adventure Magazine* (29 issues, spanning 1950–1955 and boasting artwork by the likes of Al Williamson, Frank Frazetta, and Harvey Kurtzman), and from the after-school telecasts of an extensive run of low-budget movies starring, by turns, Bob Steele and Buster Crabbe. At a turning-point for such awareness, while visiting Northwest Texas' Panhandle–Plains Historical Museum with the folks, I noticed a display containing this document:

Tascosa, Texas
Thursday Oct 26TH
1878

    Know all persons by these presents that I do hereby sell and diliver [sic] *to Henry F. Hoyt one Sorrel Horse Branded BB on left hip and other indistinct Branded on Shoulders, for the Sum of Seventy five $ dollars, in hand received.*

                    [Signed] *W.H. Bonney*
                        Witness
                  Jos. E. Masters
                  Geo. J. Howard

"You know who wrote that, don't you?" asked my Dad. "Your teevee-cowboy hero, Billy the Kid—that's who. Billy Bonney.

"Except he wasn't any teevee hero," Dad continued. "More of a juvenile-delinquent punk, if you ask me."

"They had juvenile delinquents in 1878?" I asked in reply, missing the point altogether. I was sufficiently flabbergasted by the revelation that Billy the Kid had been a Real Guy—or that the movies and the comic-book series (both loosely conceived and dense with internal contradictions) could claim a basis in fact—to find myself at a loss for words as to this larger concern.

The right words would occur to me later. My father had heard at first hand some harsh accounts of Billy's dealings, via a Depression Era acquaintance with Elizabeth "Frenchy" McCormick (*ca.* 1852–1941), last survivor of the long-abandoned frontier settlement known as Tascosa. So Dad and I had plenty to discuss—my Hollywood-and-funnybooks perception, *vs.* Dad's owlhoot-punk opinions.

I've spent a great long stretch of a career in attempting to reconcile folklore with fiction with historical documentation—whether dealing with the motion-picture industry, or music, or the comics—and to this day Billy the Kid remains one Great Enigma of a persistent interest in the Western frontier as represented and misrepresented in history and popular literature.

Yes, and I've returned time and again to that Panhandle–Plains Museum, drawn chiefly by such relics as the W.H. Bonney letter—one of the rarest of autographs. Most eminences–become–legend will leave a trail of many signatures. But Billy the Kid was a man of few words, written or uttered.

The horse mentioned in the bill–of–sale was a gift from William H. Bonney, alias Billy the Kid—going through the motions of a paid transaction, for the official record—to Dr. Henry Hoyt, the first civilian physician in the Texas Panhandle. The witnesses were the proprietors of a general store. Dr. Hoyt eventually became Surgeon General of These United States. The bill–of–sale found its way into the museum early in the last century.

Many historians consider Billy a moronic thug. There are facts to support such a view. And yet a visit to New Mexico's Lincoln County Courthouse, where some of Billy's correspondence is preserved, prompts second thoughts. Written in a flowing hand with only occasional misspellings, the letters suggest a fairly erudite chap despite a lack of formal education.

An opposing camp pictures Billy as an avenging angel—a Hamlet on horseback, as suggested in Bob Steele's movie portrayals of the 1940s—bringing relentless justice to murderers beyond the reach of the law. There is some justification for this romanticized view, as well, for most of the men against whom Billy set his hand were among the instigators of a terrible range war in which innocents were slain while the elected authorities looked the other way or even participated.

Billy was feared and despised and adored and revered. The one tintype–photograph generally accepted as an authentic likeness reveals an ungainly and repellent youth. This tintype, being a metallic mirror–image, also has given rise to the legend that Billy the Kid was a left-handed gunslinger. (Hence Gore Vidal's *The Left Handed Gun*, as filmed by Arthur Penn in 1958.)

Other photos, identified as genuine by associates who survived Billy, show a much better-looking cowboy—closer to the descriptions provided by friends. Sallie Chisum, an Eastern-educated niece of the cattle baron John Chisum, called Billy "as courteous a little gentleman as I ever met." And George Coe, a fellow ranchhand, stated: "Billy, with his humorous and pleasing personality, got to be a community favorite ... so popular that there wasn't enough of him to go around."

An arrest-warrant poster, issued when Billy was 18, describes him as blond, standing five–foot–three, weighing 125 pounds and possessed of "regular" features. The poster describes him as being the leader of "the worst gang of desperadoes the Territory has had to contend with." Then there are those 21 men he is supposed to have killed before his 21st birthday.

Only one thing is certain: The true story of Billy the Kid will forever be obscured by a tangled mythology.

Apart from a likely birthdate of November 23, 1859, in New York, the first fact known (or generally accepted) about Billy is that his widowed mother, Catherine McCarty, married a drifter named William H. Antrim in 1873 at Santa Fe, New Mexico. The younger of Mrs. Antrim's sons, Henry, is the individual later known as Kid Antrim, who rechristened himself William H. Bonney and, from that, Billy the Kid. The first killing formally ascribed to Bonney is that of a blacksmith named E.P. Cahill, on August 17, 1877.

But only after Billy's arrival that same year in Lincoln, New Mexico, does he come into a crisper focus. Lincoln County was the site of the range war, with ranchers John Chisum, Alexander McSween, and John H. Tunstall allied against a banking-and-mercantile syndicate run by Maj. L.G. Murphy and J.J. Dolan. Although Bonney had first gone to work for the Murphy–Dolan gang, Tunstall saw in the youngster the makings of a leader and hired him away. Tunstall became the nearest thing to a father the Kid had known.

Tunstall's murder in 1878 on orders from the Murphy–Dolan interests—a scenario re-enacted most vividly in a motion picture of 1988 called *Young Guns*—triggered a vengeful impulse in Billy. Within months, Billy had begun making good on an oath to kill everyone involved in the ambush–slaying. The act that made Billy a fugitive–for–life was his attack on four lawmen in the employ of Murphy and Dolan.

Billy migrated during the fall of 1878 to Tascosa, in the Central Panhandle of Texas. Though a known fugitive, Billy Bonney had many friends in Tascosa. The warfare had escalated; President R.B. Hayes intervened to installed a governor, Gen. Lew Wallace, who offered amnesty to all concerned—all except Billy the Kid, that is.

In a letter to Wallace, Bonney offered to testify against the Murphy–Dolan thugs in exchange for exemption. The outlaw and the governor reached an agreement, which of course ended in betrayal for one of them, and I don't mean the governor. After escaping a death–cell in April of 1879 and eluding capture for months, Billy finally met his end in an ambush by Sheriff Pat Garrett.

Billy the Kid had been long in the grave when Dr. Henry Hoyt learned the truth about the horse Billy had given him in 1878. In 1921, a detective named Charles Siringo showed a copy of that bill of sale to James Brady of Carrizozo, New Mexico.

"That was my father's horse!" Brady shouted. "He was riding it when he was killed by the Kid!" Brady's father, William Brady, was the corrupt sheriff who had arranged for the ambush of John Tunstall, and who in turn fell prey to Billy's campaign of vengeance.

Historian George E. Turner and I have related this yarn in print on several occasions since we first pieced it together from original research during the 1960s. A 2004 version in my home-base newspaper received an immense popular response—including a letter-to-the-editor rebuttal sufficiently audacious to bear mentioning. Always something new that bears learning, even by those of us who make a profession of inflicting our opinions upon a massed audience.

I have tended, or pre–tended, to ignore the past several years' ruckus over a campaign to order the exhumation of the mortal remains of Billy the Kid—and those of his purported and/or actual mother—for newfangled DNA sampling. My preference is to stick with the story as researched and codified by Turner and Yrs. Trly., in league with Texas' Panhandle–Plains Historical Society.

Genealogist Emily C. Smith, of Idaho, wrote in cordial disagreement: "Billy was born December 31, 1859, in Buffalo Gap, Texas (not New York!), and he died December 27, 1950, in Hico, Texas. His mother was Mary Adeline Dunn–Roberts, a half-sister to Catherine Bonney-McCarty... Billy's mother died when Billy was about three years old, and he went to live with Catherine, her husband, William H. Antrim, and Catherine's son, Joseph, by her first marriage to Michael McCarty..."

Smith's response seems in accord with our qualified perception of Billy the Kid as something of an avenger. But Smith insists: "Billy did not meet his death at the hands of Sheriff Pat Garrett; that is a lie historians have handed down over the years after reading Pat Garrett's own accounting..."

The notion of the Kid's long-term survival—into an age of his golly–gee–whiz portrayals in the movies and the comics—is fascinating, if only because it grates so strikingly against the romanticized notion (accepted in lieu of any thesis more authoritative) of a volatile career and an early crash–and–burn. Such sweeping revisionism parallels that which has been applied to Billy's Southern contemporary Jesse James, who might seem nowadays to have survived a 19TH Century ambush and lived to an advanced age in Louisiana and Texas.

Further, from Emily Smith: "[O]n November 29, 1950, Billy [traveled] to meet with the governor of New Mexico [to renew a] petition for [a] pardon... [T]he two men met with such opposition and confusion that Billy, now known as Brushy Bill Roberts, age 90, became so ill that [his lawyer] had to take Billy to a local doctor... Billy returned home to Hico... [Then,] on December 27, 1950,... [while] walking to the post office, Billy fell to the ground... dying from a heart attack... Billy's heart was literally broken because his pardon was never granted... I realize, with great distress, [that this] information is not popular thought, nor does it follow what historians ... believe to be true."

New Mexico's 21ST Century re–investigators—talk about a Cold Case Unit!—resent seeing the likeness of Pat Garrett emblazoned upon official insignia, having grown to believe that Garrett was a murderer, or a liar, or some combination thereof whom. Outcries both for and against an exhumation have surfaced in Texas. ("Part of the interesting problem," per Emily Smith, "is that you have several Billy the Kids in graves in the South." All of which, one might add, make for a greater boon to the tourism racket than to historical integrity.)

And yes, folklore and history are inseparable, here, in any event. My favorite Kid stories, and history be damned, occur in producer Sigmund Neufeld's entirely fraudulent series of WWII-era movies starring Bob Steele and, later, Buster Crabbe. (Neufeld and his brother, director Shmuel "Sam" Neufeld/Newfield, fared well over the long haul with borderlands world-beaters named Billy, from a *Lightnin' Bill Carson* series of the 1930s, through the *Billy the Kid* pictures and an interrelated *Billy Carson* franchise.) Other *Kid* movies, from name-brand studios and grindhouse factories alike, date from Old Hollywood to times very recent. Even Roy Rogers tackled a *Kid* picture, in 1938.

The original version of George Turner's and my account, incidentally, had appeared under the title "They Couldn't Get Enough of Billy." Seems they still can't get enough of Billy. Whoever *they* are.

A CANINE FRANKENSTEIN

August 19, 2007: The kinship between science and fantasy runs deep into antiquity—deeper, yet, than the well-aged but comparatively modern notion of science fiction. The filmmaker Ray Harryhausen, in his foreword to my revised edition of the late George E. Turner's *Spawn of Skull Island: The Making of King Kong* (2002), invokes the spirit of the alchemist Paraceleus (1494 –1541) in describing the imaginative zeal necessary to bring (seemingly) to life the impossible creatures of cinema. Paraceleus, of course, believed that the power of imagination also was necessary to the development of Real World scientific breakthroughs. His speculations about the creation of life in a laboratory setting prefigured nothing so much as that most influential novel of science fiction, Mary W. Shelley's 19TH Century morality play, *Frankenstein, or a Modern Prometheus*. (Prometheus, of course, had beaten both Ms. Shelley and Paraceleus to the punch, if only in the realm of ancient mythology.)

History and science have long since validated *Frankenstein* as a plausible argument. Real Science absorbs the most extravagant science-fictional influences and wonders, "Why the hell *not?*"—and then maneuvers fiction into plausible fact. Hence the experimentation that has long since led to the transplanting of limbs and organs in workable, life-saving terms, if not to the creation of Life Its Ownself. The relationship will continue apace as long as Big Science holds humankind in a thrall of mingled hope and unease.

One of the odder collisions between science–fantasy and credentialed research took place during the spring of 1934, in a University of California research laboratory at Berkeley. Here, Dr. Robert E. Cornish announced that his team had restored life to a dog, Lazarus by name, that had been put to death by clinical means. Cornish bolstered his claim—a purported breakthrough that seems to have led no further—

Second Dog Is Restored to Life

ROBERT E. CORNISH, California biologist, who amazed the scientific world last spring by reviving a dog clinically put to death (MODERN MECHANIX AND INVENTIONS, July, 1934) recently repeated the success of his original experiment with even more encouraging results.

Lazarus IV, subject of the first successful experiment, has learned to crawl, bark, sit up on its haunches and consume nearly a pound of meat a day. The dog is blind and cannot stand alone, but results encouraged Dr. Cornish to launch a new series of experiments.

Recently Lazarus V was put to death with an overdose of ether. Half an hour after its breathing had stopped and five minutes after its heart was stilled, the animal was revived by means of chemicals and artificial respiration. Dr. Cornish, enthusiastic, has been reported as saying that Lazarus V returned nearer normalcy in four days than the other Lazarus in thirteen days.

Dr. Robert E. Cornish, California biologist, is holding Lazarus IV and looking at Lazarus V. Both dogs were restored to life after they were clinically put to death.

Scientist to Make Bold Attempt to Revive Human Dead

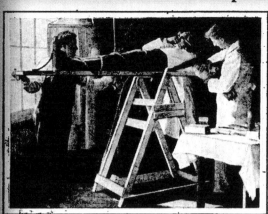

Dr. Cornish, rear, demonstrates method of reviving dead. The subject is placed on a teetering board to promote circulation as stimulant is injected.

D R. ROBERT E. CORNISH, young California scientist who astounded the nation by bringing the dead dog, Lazarus, back to life, is now preparing to repeat his experiment using human subjects.

He has petitioned the governors of the three states, Colorado, Arizona and Nevada to furnish him with the bodies of criminals after they are pronounced dead in the lethal gas chambers — but his petitions have been rejected on various grounds.

Hearing of his predicament, approximately fifty people, interested both in science and possible remuneration, have offered themselves as subjects. According to Dr. Cornish, most of those offering themselves for "clinical" death are single men. One man from Kansas, in offering himself as a subject stated he considered $300,000 a fair price for the risk involved.

with motion-picture footage. The publicity attracted such attention that the college's administration booted Cornish off the campus. A June-of-1934 report in *Time* magazine describes a saddening follow-through:

> With undying hope in his voice, hollow-eyed young Dr. Robert Cornish last week repeated, over and over, the name of the dog he had killed almost two months ago with ether and nitrogen, revived with chemical and mechanical resuscitants... Lazarus gave no sign that he heard.

> But the bony white mongrel was no longer crawling on his mat. He was walking, slowly, with stiff, dragging hind legs and vacant eyes. He ate regularly but without enthusiasm. Dr. Cornish realized that part of the dog's brain was still dead, might remain so for months or years of apathetic existence.

> Last week, too, Lazarus was no longer in the shabby little laboratory on the University of California campus where he had tasted four minutes of death. He was in the Cornish home in Berkeley, where Dr. Cornish had taken him when the university provost asked [Cornish] to vacate...

Cornish carried on, via a follow–through described in a credulous 1935 report from *Modern Mechanix & Inventions* magazine. (That text is reproduced in the image on Page No. 178.) The descriptions call to mind nothing so much as a 1991 film by Larry Fessenden, *No Telling*, a low-key but nonetheless harrowing indictment of such clinical obsessions.

True or false? No one can say, beyond Cornish's obviously self-interested account and the published suggestions of a stubborn persistence amidst a dreary aftermath. California's prison system later denied Cornish access to Death Row cadavers, and the biochemist appears to have abandoned the effort. Rumors of further such developments circulated over the long term, inspiring such fantastically conceived movies as 1936's *The Walking Dead*, 1946's *Decoy*, and 1956's *Indestructible Man*—all involving executed convicts. *The*

Walking Dead features a laboratory set modeled after Cornish's equipment; Cornish also served as a consultant on 1939's *The Man They Could Not Hang*, which imagines an artificial-heart mechanism.

But before 1934 had run its course, Dr. Cornish had worked a direct influence upon the motion-picture industry. His declaration of success inspired a well-connected filmmaker named Eugen Frenke to develop a movie that would involve Cornish and his laboratory footage.

The resulting film, *Life Returns*, is a poorly made but nonetheless fascinating relic of a short-lived *cause célébre*. This one does not conform to the model of a science-fictional or horrific film, as such, but its cast includes two players essential to those genres: Valerie Hobson moved along to *Bride of Frankenstein* (1935), and Onslow Stevens would at length play a very Frankenstein-like research physician in 1945's *House of Dracula*.

In *Life Returns*, Cornish himself, Stevens, and Lois Wilson portray scientists seeking to conquer death. "I will have the formula that will start the blood circulating again, and with it breath, and with it life!" declares Dr. John Kendrick (Stevens). He accepts a corporate-research assignment—only to be rejected as a crackpot. Just when it seems matters cannot grow worse, Kendrick must face the death of his wife (Hobson).

The film might have turned more sensational if Stevens' character had sought to resurrect his wife. But no. The story detours into a social-problem subplot involving Kendrick's rebellious son (Georgie Breakston). The boy's pet dog runs afoul of an animal-control officer (Stanley Fields) and is gassed. This is the melodramatic set–up for the insertion of Dr. Cornish's laboratory film, placing the purportedly documentary footage at the service of fiction. The results lead to as hopeful a finale as circumstances can permit.

There was no upbeat ending, though, for *Life Returns*, which had been bankrolled at a modest $40,000 by big-time Universal Pictures but then pronounced "not suitable for the regular Universal program" by production chief Carl Laemmle, JR., following ill-received preview showings. Eugen Frenke, as director and co–writer, threatened legal action against Universal and acquired the distribution rights. *Life Returns* finally came into release in 1938. (See also: Page No. 91.)

BACKWATER TEXANA AND A MUSIC–BIZ DIGRESSION

August 26, 2007: The songwriter and guitar–builder Greg Jackson, a key music-making cohort of mine since 1981, has taken the occasional hand in the comics racket, as well, as a consequence of the affiliation. Greg is the life–model, for example, for the character of Jackson Walker in Timothy Truman's *Scout* books, and Greg supplied the lap-steel guitar riffs for a funnybook-soundtrack recording that accompanies a chapter of Truman's and my *Prowler* series, first as an Eva–Tone Soundsheet insert and eventually as a digital file.

Greg and I have a rambunctious Texas Plains upbringing in common, too—our hometown areas sit within half–an–hour's drive from one another, and we attended West Texas Suitcase University during the late 1960s and had many of the same musical accompanists—although we never met until after both of us had resettled in North Central Texas. A steady influence overall has been the work of the Oklahoma-to-Texas balladeer Woody Guthrie, whose rough-hewn autobiography of the 1940s, *Bound for Glory*, once inspired Greg and me to begin thinking about a composite memoir. Guthrie's equally rough-hewn cartoons had

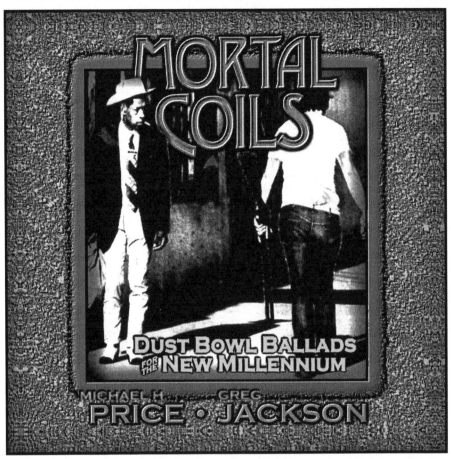

suggested that a comic-book composite memoir might suit the Jackson–Price agenda just fine: Call it *Rebound for Glory*.

A worthy thought, but the music-making imperative has taken prior claim to such an extent that what stories Greg and I have managed to tell together have all turned out to be songs. Postmodern folkie-scare material, for the most part, but with nods all along to a shared family-band tradition. Our first album of Texas Panhandle ballads—*ballards*, as Greg calls 'em—arrived in 2006 under the title *Mortal Coils*, with as emphatic a nod to Aldous Huxley and Mr. Shakespeare as to Woody Guthrie. The origins of some such material predate Greg's and my efforts by a good many years, including quite a bit of resurrected ancestral music from the 1930s–1950s.

Did I say, "predate"—?!? Back in 1934, the silent symphony of a Southwestern dawn inspired two music-making brothers to begin a song called "Mornin' on the Desert." One of the composers, Manny Jackson, eventually became the father of Greg Jackson, a like-minded soul who eventually would retool the verses into a coffeehouse ballad. "I can smell the sagebrush smoke," reads one stanza, lamenting the inexorable spread of urbanization: "I hate to see it burnin', but the land, they say, must be broke." Greg Jackson's decisive version of

"Mornin' on the Desert" retains much of the vision of his father, and of Manny Jackson's brother Paul Jackson: "The air is like a wine... It seems that all Creation has been made for me and mine..." The piece, long a staple of Greg's folksong repertoire, has figured since the 1980s in our collaborative efforts. We preserved "Mornin' on the Desert" on Greg's 1989 solo album, *Faraway Friends of Mine*, and gave it a fresh veneer for the *Mortal Coils* sessions.

With the Mortal Coils song-cycle, Greg and I were wondering, in essence, how Woody Guthrie might have carried on, had he lived into the turbulent present day. The Jackson–Price material descends in a skewed tangent from Guthrie's famous *Dust Bowl Ballads* collection of the Depression era—itself something of a turbulent time.

ROY CRANE AND THE MAN WHO WAS EASY

September 2–9, 2007: Back during the middle 1960s, my newsroom mentor George E. Turner and I became acquainted with the Texas-bred cartoonist Roy Crane (1901–1977), whose daily strip, *Buz Sawyer*—a staple of the local newspaper's funnies section—had recently landed a Reuben Award from the National Cartoonists Society. Like some Oscar-anointed filmmaker with a current box-office attraction, Crane was visiting his syndicate's client–papers, one after another, to help promote this shred of newfound momentum for *Sawyer* as a circulation-builder.

Now, George and I were admirers of Crane's storytelling artistry from 'way back, and we were as interested in an earlier example called *Wash Tubbs*. Crane had shepherded *Tubbs* during the 1920s from a gag-a-day feature to a full-fledged high-adventure vehicle of sustained force, then entrusted it in 1943 to his boyhood pal and studio assistant, Leslie Turner, when the opportunity came to develop *Buz Sawyer*.

For a good many readers, the greater attraction of *Wash Tubbs* lay not so much in its title character—a boyish adventurer with an affinity for trouble—as in Washington Tubbs' cohort, a man of action known as Captain Easy. Easy seemed to George Turner and me an essence of resourceful heroism, and we had wondered: Who might have been the life–model for the rough-and-ready Southerner? (Wash Tubbs' origins seemed an easier call—in part, a wish-fulfillment projection of Crane himself.)

So while visiting with Crane, we asked about Easy. One of us set forth the theory that Easy was based upon either Richard Dix or Jack Holt, square-jawed, hawk-nosed figures who were noted for their tough-guy movies at the time Easy had appeared. Crane smiled and changed the subject. George and I were hardly alone in the wondering. Historian Ron Goulart also had asked; Crane had replied simply that his brother-in-law had suggested that Washington Tubbs needed a strong sidekick, and that he, Roy Crane, had concocted Easy in response to the idea. Goulart had said that Easy seemed reminiscent of Tom Mix, the cowboy star, but Crane had dismissed the idea by saying that he had used his brother-in-law as a model.

But according to separately collected but unanimous opinions from school-days friends of Crane, Mr. William Lee, A.K.A. Captain Easy, was modeled after a college pal. Journalist–turned–novelist Carlton Stowers put us on the track after he had visited with another friend from Crane's youth.

Roy Crane recalled college days as happy days. As a University of Texas *alumnus*, sort of, during the 1940s, he spent several days on cam-

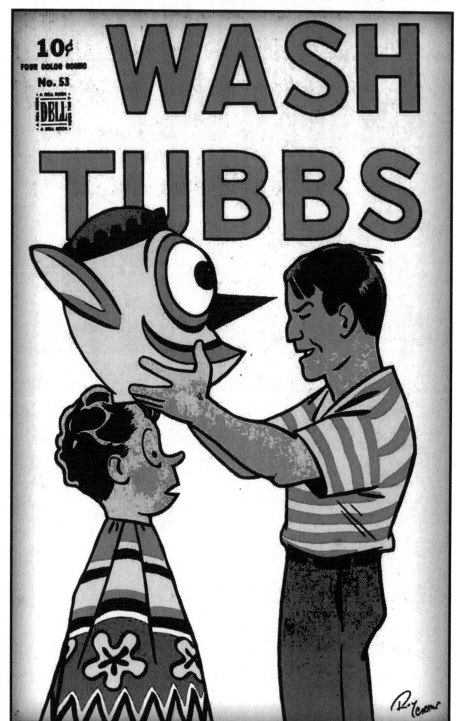

pus painting a finely wrought mural at the Phi Kappa Psi fraternity house. In 1969, he funded the Roy Crane Award in the Arts at UT.

Many souls within his circle wondered why Crane persisted with such loyalty. Crane had been expelled in the middle of his fourth college year for drawing too many pictures and ignoring too many lectures. And because that frat-house mural depicted, amongst other images, a nude woman, the administration later forced the inmates to bury the work under layers of paint.

From the late 1960s into the 1980s, Carlton Stowers, George Turner and I spoke with several prominent Texans whom Crane had mentioned as having been close friends at the University of Texas at Austin. All recalled him with fondness.

"He was a bright sort of fellow," said Deskin Wells, who had become publisher of the *The Ledger* at Wellington, Texas. "He was always far more interested in his drawing. Several times, the Dean of Men called him in to tell him he was going to have to get to work or be dismissed from school. The last time they called him in, it was to talk to the president of the college, and from what I heard, Roy pretty well let him know what he thought about having to take a lot of the courses he was required to take.

"We learned that they were going to dismiss him from school, so he was initiated into Phi Kappa Psi in the middle of the night. He left school the next day." Wells paused for a chuckle, then added: "He came back a few years later for a visit, and he was making more money drawing his cartoons than the president who threw him out."

And did Wells have any ideas about the model for Captain Easy?

"George P. Hill, a fraternity brother from Fort Worth, looked a great deal like Captain Easy," Wells replied. Another fraternity chum, rancher Beaumont Stinnett, told us this: "Roy was a smallish, retiring

sort of man ... more Wash Tubbs than Captain Easy. I've always felt that George Hill ... was the model for Captain Easy, and of course Buz Sawyer is a more realistically conceived carryover from Easy."

Three other fraternity buddies from Amarillo, Texas—lawyer Jude Boyce, banker W.S. Smith, and insurance executive Jeff Neeley—also named George Hill as the likeliest prototype of Captain Easy.

Like Easy, Hill was a man of purpose and vigor—qualities that figure in Crane's work overall. Hill was born in 1898 in the Texas Panhandle near Claude and grew up in Fort Worth, where he became a prominent schoolboy athlete. He lettered in football, basketball, and wrestling as a Crane classmate at the University of Texas, where he completed a degree in mechanical engineering in 1922. Hill's U of T Longhorns football team of 1920 went undefeated and un-tied, an accomplishment that remained unique until the Longhorns' 1963 season. Hill returned to Fort Worth after college and developed a career in the oil industry, in partnership with his father, at the start of a drilling boom in 1926. Hill headed Export Petroleum Co. until his death in 1979.

Hill shunned interviews and sought no corporate publicity, preferring to allow his professional endeavors and charitable deeds to speak for themselves. Apparently he was an unwitting model or, perhaps, too modest to have made much of any connection with the Crane feature's popular acceptance. No such mention appears in his privately published memoir, *Seventy Years* (1968), which Hill crammed with colorful accounts of athletic contests and oilfield adventures into which Easy would have fit comfortably.

Having unraveled this slight mystery to the extent possible, George Turner and I published the results in 1989 in a volume of a *Wash Tubbs* reprint shelf from NBM Press' Flying Buttress Classics Library.

I used the material, as well, in a newspaper article for the *Star-Telegram* of Fort Worth. That story prompted a letter from a West Texas reader—who insisted that a certain small-town personality from Crane's boyhood must have been the life-model for Wash Tubbs. Some mysteries are more to be appreciated than solved. (An elaboration upon this commentary, with the bonus of a word-for-word reminiscence from Crane, appears in *Roy Crane's Captain Easy Vol. 4*, from Fantagraphics Books.)

THE FOLKLORE–INTO–FICTION CONNECTION

September 16–23, 2007: Recycling–in–action: Herewith, an encore of a presentation I delivered earlier this month at Tarleton State University's Langdon Weekend arts-and-farces festival:

If it was good enough for Aesop and Shakespeare and Mark Twain, then it should suit the rest of us—as tradition-bound storytellers with roots in the Old World and in early-day Americana, that is—just fine and dandy. I am speaking of folklore—the oral-tradition narrative medium that encloses and defines any and all cultures and stands poised as a Chronic Muse (often ill-heeded or, if heeded, ill-acknowledged) for anyone who attempts to relate a tale for popular consumption. This is a self-evident truth so obvious as to go overlooked.

Yes, and the barrier between folklore and commercial fiction is as slender as the upper E–string on a guitar, and just as sensitive. Pluck that string and watch it vibrate, and the blurred image suggests a vivid metaphor. The inspiration, at any rate, is as close within reach as air and water, and often less subject to pollution.

"So! Where do you–all get your ideas, anyhow?" The question, vaguely indignant, crops up every time a published author goes out communing with the readership. Stephen King has long since perfected a suitably dismissive reply: "I get mine from an idea-subscription service in Utica." He's woofing, of course, and even the most cursory reading of the humongous body of work that King represents will find the author tapped into a lode, or load, of rustic folklore. Witness, for example, *The Shining*, a 1977 novel-become-movie in which a key supporting character takes notice of a precocious child's thought-projecting abilities: "My grandmother and I could hold conversations ... without ever opening our mouths. She called it 'shining.'"

I grew up in close quarters with two grandmothers like that—not in Stephen King's sense of "shining," as such, although with each I felt a communicative bond that ran deeper than articulated speech. Each, that is, seemed to sense what might be burdening my thoughts at any given moment, whether or not I might care to put any such thoughts into words. And each grandmother, too, was a prolific and spontaneous storyteller, dispensing colorful family-history tales, fables in the Aesopic tradition, and hair-raising horrors divided more-or-less equally between waking-life ordeals and dreamlike supernatural hauntings. With such living-history resources at hand, who needed Little Golden Books?

My maternal-side grandmother, Lillian Beatrice Ralston Wilson Lomen (1895–1982), characterized her ghostlier yarns as "haint stories"—*haint* being a back-country variant of *haunt*. She knew by heart James Whitcomb Riley's famous moral-lesson poem of 1885, "Little Orphant Annie" (*sic*), with its recurring admonition that "the Gobble-'Uns'll git you ef [*if*] you don't watch out!" And she could concoct—or recollect, or fabricate from combined experience and imagination—stories and verses every bit as horrific, and as absurd and uproarious.

When I would inquire as to the truthfulness or factuality of a tale, such as the conjure-woman story she called "Hansel and Gretel in the Piney Woods," my grandmother would reply: "Well, now, I reckon it's all true except for the parts that's not—and if them parts ain't true, then they ought to be." When I would urge her to put these accounts into writing, she would demur: "Well, I ain't no writer—that's how come we pass these stories along, 'mongst our peoples."

Robert Bloch.

Or perhaps the purveyors of spoken-word folklore were the truer writers, inscribing their legends and histories and imaginative flights onto the scroll of Tribal Memory. Nowadays, Tribal Amnesia seems to have become more the norm. Years after her passing, I undertook to transform one of my grandmother's oral-tradition stories, "The Man Who Wouldn't Stay Dead," into a comic-book piece. I sent the script to its assigned illustrator, Frank Stack, the Texas-bred cartoonist-turned-professor of art at the University of Missouri. Frank replied with an inquiry: "Is this supposed to be scary? Or funny?" The answer on both counts: "*Yes.*" The finished result possesses precisely that dichotomy of supernatural terror and slapstick hilarity; it appears, as "Rude Awakening!" (eyes right), in the anthologies *Southern–Fried Homicide* (Cremo Studios) and *Frank Stack's Foolbert Funnies* (Fantagraphics Books).

My Grandmother Lillian kept in mind any number of twists on that "Man Who Wouldn't Stay Dead" theme, which she first related to me around 1955 as "one I l'arned as a young 'un in the Old Country." (The "Old Country," in her perception, was Indian Territory, her native Oklahoma Hills, geographically near Texas' Central Panhandle where my nearer ancestors had resettled but a world apart in terms of rural-*vs.*-urbanized society.) In one account, the titular figure was a defunct farmer who returned from the grave to annoy his widow and thwart her would-be suitors. In another telling, he became a backwoods patriarch who hauled off and croaked in the midst of a family gathering—only to deny his demise and hang around to torment his kinfolks and their visitors. Each version had the same climax and denouement: *rigor mortis* and discombobulation.

In a late revelation, I found the October 1976 issue of *The Magazine of Fantasy & Science Fiction* to contain essentially that same "Man Who Wouldn't Stay Dead" story, under the title "A Case of the Stubborns"—complete with backwoods setting and dialect to match. I read Robert Bloch's short story to my grandmother, who found it familiar: "Well, I *sw'a'n!*" she said. "That feller must've growed up 'mongst the same peoples as *me!*"

Well, hardly. Bloch (1917–1994), a Chicago-born Germanic Jew who remains most widely known for the 1959 novel Psycho, simply had developed the ability to breathe the atmosphere of folklore, and to exhale it, constructively, into cold print. Bloch and I became cordially acquainted during the waning 1970s, as fellow writers in the arenas of horror, humor, and motion-picture lore, and he made plain his affinity for plain-folks mythology as a source of fascination and inspiration.

RUDE AWAKENING!

From an Old and Beloved Folk Tale
SCRIPT & BREAKDOWNS
MICHAEL H. PRICE
ILLUSTRATIONS
FRANK STACK

"So where do you think *Psycho* came from?" Bloch asked me. "Modern-day folklore and gossip, that's where, from sources so far removed from one another that a lot of people wouldn't find them compatible." His story of Norman Bates, a mother-dominated loner of murderous instincts, owes as much to the exploits of Edward T. Gein, a secretive predator of rural Wisconsin whose crimes had come to light in 1957, as it does to Bloch's connections with another fellow altogether, a spooky-literature enthusiast and critic–historian whose every move seems to have been superintended by an overbearing mother.

"Folklore doesn't have to be ancient, y'know," averred Bloch. "The minute ol' Ed Gein was found out to be a dangerous character—the folks around Plainfield [Wisconsin] had considered him something of a weirdo, all along—then the folk–tales started proliferating. He became the new Boogeyman, in those parts. Parents started warning their misbehaving children that 'Ed Gein is gonna get you if you don't watch out!' just like that Whitcomb Riley poem had cautioned the youngsters to watch out for 'the Gobble–'Uns.' "And the Gein jokes, sick jokes, to be sure, cropped up, one after the other, like this one: 'Why did Ed Gein's girlfriend quit him?' And the answer: 'Because he was such a cut–up.'"

"There got to be so many of those 'Geiners,' as the locals called their little nervous riddles, and so many ghastlier details about the Gein case had gone unreported [in the newspapers and the wire-service dispatches], that I figured it was just a matter of time before this hideous legend a–borning would get turned into a piece of fiction. So I stepped up to the plate and made it my story and called it *Psycho*. Of course, it helped Norman Bates' development that I knew this other fellow ... who couldn't seem to untie himself from his mother's apron–strings—nice guy, too, and certainly no menace to society, but the circumstances seemed to fit. And as it turned out, the deeper the authorities went poking into the Gein case, the more evident it became that ol' Ed had suffered more than his share of pernicious Mom–ism, too."

Bloch cited, as an influential example, a motion picture from 1935, Frank R. Strayer's *Condemned To Live*, which fellow film historian George E. Turner and I had discussed in the original volume of the *Forgotten Horrors* books: "Y'know, every culture, no matter how primitive or civilized, has its variations on the vampire legend, the walking dead who prey upon the living. And literature, and then the movie business, they've lunched out on that tradition since who–knows–when. But most of the *Dracula*-type movies are content to hang onto the Mittel European mythology and let it go at that.

"But this one little movie, now, it reached out in a broader sense— to suggest a Third World origin for the superstition, and then to suggest that such a condition might even stem from a prenatal influence. Raised the stakes, you should pardon the expression, on the whole fantasy, and remained unique among the vampire pictures until *Blacula* came along [in 1972], with its parallels between the vampire scares and the institution of slavery. That's what I mean about reaching out to the greater range of folk-tale traditions to beef up your fiction."

Bloch added: "Where I'm coming from, anyhow, is someplace bigger than just the horror-fiction market. I came up, as a teenager, under the direct influence of H.P. Lovecraft and that whole *Weird Tales* [magazine] community of pulp scribes. Lovecraft's greater body of work, y'know, has to do with that ancient race of cosmic monstrosities that got themselves kicked off the planet, with their bad breath and their antisocial conduct, but hung around the fringes, anyway, looking for a way back in. Lovecraft took the germ of mythology—and doesn't every society have its myths about why–for those Bad Old Days were so bad?—and incubated it into a whole new strain.

"It was that long-winded essay of Lovecraft's, *Supernatural Horror in Literature* [1927], that helped to steer me toward all that business," Bloch continued. "Waked in me an awareness of my own *Yiddishe* storytelling heritage, it did, and got me interested in the Southern folk-tales, in particular. And it was Lovecraft who hipped me to Irvin Cobb, the *Saturday Evening Post* writer from Kentucky whose humorous pieces I already knew, but whose Southern Gothics—Cobb called 'em his 'grim stories'— were kind of obscured by his greater fame as a funnyman."

• • •

We had left Robert Bloch hanging in mid–conversation last week, speaking of Irvin S. Cobb as a forerunner of the "bizarre pulp" movement in popular fiction. Irvin Shrewsbury Cobb (1876–1944) was a crony and occasional collaborator of Will Rogers, and a key influence upon Rogers' droll sense of humor. Cobb can be seen as an actor in such Rogers-starring films as *Judge Priest* (1934; deriving from Cobb's folksier tales) and *Steamboat Round the Bend* (1935), both directed by John Ford. It was for other works entirely that Robert Bloch remembered Cobb.

"Have you ever read Irvin Cobb's 'Fishhead'?" Bloch asked me around 1979–1980. "Well, if it was good enough for Howard Lovecraft to single out as a nightmare–on–paper [in the 1927 monograph *Supernatural Horror in Literature*], then I was ready and willing to tear into it. Which I did. Changed my entire direction, that one story did."

I can relate, all right. In 1995, independent publisher Lawrence Adam Shell and I set about to adapt as a graphic novel Cobb's 1911 tale of righteous vengeance, "Fishhead," in which a swamp-dwelling hermit of grotesque aspect runs afoul of malicious neighbors. If Irvin Cobb had drawn upon regional folklore to lend his title character a gift of supernatural communion with the wildlife, then our crew reckoned we must treat Cobb's story itself as folklore—subject to sympathetic reinterpretation and elaboration as a condition of respect.

And otherwise, why adapt at all? Cobb would have done a greater service to scholarship than to popular literature if he had contented himself merely with compiling the various old-time rumors about reclusive souls presumed to possess spiritual bonds with the wastelands. The audacious job that Cobb called "Fishhead" backfired at first, accumulating rejections from one magazine after another on account of its unabashed gruesomeness and its sharp contrast with Cobb's gathering reputation as a humorist. One editor, Bob Davis, of an adventurous magazine called *The Cavalier*, wrote to Cobb in 1911: "It is inconceivable how one so saturated with the humors of life can present so appalling a picture."

But after Davis had relented and published the yarn in 1913, "Fishhead" proved a watershed, helping to trigger the so-called bizarre pulp explosion that would gerrymander the boundaries of mass-market fiction during the decades to follow. By midcentury, when Cobb's light-

FISHHEAD

IN A SHUNNED REGION KNOWN AS THE *BIG SPLAYFOOT*, SOMEWHERE BETWEEN THE UNCHARTED PROVINCES OF *WEST HELL* AND *DIDDY WAH DIDDY* — THERE DWELLED *FISHHEAD*.

AFTER THE STORY BY IRVIN S. COBB
ILLUSTRATIONS MARK EVAN WALKER
ADAPTATION MICHAEL H. PRICE & LAWRENCE ADAM SHELL

hearted and bucolic tales had become by-and-large forgotten, "Fishhead" was still reappearing as a magazine-and-anthology favorite.

But as to the matter of adaptation and assimilation of narrative elements: The entertainer and folksong historian Henry "Taj Mahal" Fredericks has argued that the Southland's traditional blues and gospel idioms can remain vital only if their modern-day practitioners will resist what he calls "arthritic reverence." Co–author Larry Shell and illustrator Mark Evan Walker and I would be remiss not to address an old-favorite story in comparable terms. (Our version anchors the Cremo Studios edition of *Fishhead & Other Carney Gothic Horrors.*)

Robert Bloch also singled out the Texas writer Robert E. Howard (1906–1936) as a particularly effective interpreter of folk inspirations: "You remember Bob Howard's story, 'Pigeons from Hell,' from *Weird Tales*?" asked Bloch. "The one about the birds flocking around the house to capture the departing souls of the newly defunct? Pure deep-Southern folklore, filtered through a good solid melodramatic story–arc."

While wondering all along why my storytelling Grandmother Lillian Wilson Lomen had neglected to set her wealth of hair-raising folk–tales into writing, I also began to notice the gathering evidence that a good many, and maybe even most, published writers must be tapping a similar vein, whether consciously so or not. And how else to explain such diversified examples as Joel Chandler Harris' *Uncle Remus* tales? Or Roark Bradford's similarly dialect-riddled *Ol' Man Adam* takeoffs on the Old Testament? Or the greater body of Biblical lore itself? To say nothing of the legendary hauntings and intrigues that abound in Shakespeare and Mark Twain, and in Margaret Mitchell's strange and self-contradictory work of affectionate bigotry and stubborn nostalgia, *Gone with the Wind.*

And then there is the Ike Turner–Eugene Fox recording of "The Dream" (1954)—in which yet another Man Who Wouldn't Stay Dead, like that sentient-zombie character from my grandmother's yarns, barges in upon a tryst between his widow and an interloper. And there came in 1959 a pop-chart hit record called "Stagger Lee," in which the New Orleans singer Lloyd Price re-enacts a criminal *cause celébre* of the prior century: "Why, we had a record of that same song on our wind-up Aeolian [phonograph, *i.e.*], back when your mother was just a little girl," said my grandmother, alluding perhaps to Mississippi John Hurt's 1928 version. I had pegged Lloyd Price, anyhow, as a vessel of folklore via an earlier recording called "Lawdy, Miss Clawdy"—and how many times had I heard that expression, signifying astonishment or dismay, from one or another of my family elders? Nobody in the here–and–now was likely just to make up such declarations out of Whole Cloth; the thoughts must be floating about in the Communal Dream Stream, waiting for someone to grasp them as a basis of some new and vital concoction. "Where do you–all get your ideas?"—indeed!

SHOCK! THEATRE, 50 YEARS LATER

October 7, 2007: The 40TH anniversary of the Beatles' arrival in North America occurred in 2004. So what else is new? That occasion could hardly be treated as commonplace nostalgia, so urgent has the influence remained. Nor can mere nostalgia account for the significance of the 50TH anniversary of a similarly intense cultural phenomenon known as *Shock! Theater.* [See also: Page No. 75 *et Seq.*] The likening of *Shock!* to the Beatles' impact, and to rock music as a class, will become more evident, so bear with me.

ZACHERLEY

will host
a vulture's
feast on
**SHOCK
THEATER**

The main course will be
SON OF DRACULA

11:15 TONIGHT

WABC-TV CHANNEL **7**

Depending upon one's hometown locale, some folks might remember *Shock! Theater* under some other proxy local-teevee title. My North Texas home-base readership recollects the syndicated-television breakthrough of *Shock! Theater* under the localized name of *Nightmare*. That Fort Worth–Dallas version premiered in September of 1957 over a scrappy and innovative independent channel—a distinctive presentation of a nationwide syndie-teevee blitz.

In reviving a wealth of Depression-into-WWII movie chillers from Universal Pictures, Columbia Pictures' Screen Gems syndicate left the style of presentation up to the individual stations. A channel typically would assign a local-market announcer to pose as a creepy personality (such as John "the Cool Ghoul" Zacherle, in Philadelphia and New York) who would introduce the various *Frankenstein*s, *Dracula*s and so forth and then intrude at intervals to present blackout gags.

At Fort Worth's Channel 11, chief writer and announcer Bill Camfield took a grimly earnest approach. He portrayed a severe character named Gorgon, who took the movies seriously enough to reflect their no-joke nature in his preambles and interludes.

"I had majored in English literature at Texas Christian University," Camfield (1929–1991) told me in 1984, "and I had developed a keen appreciation for the Gothic origins of *The Wolf Man* and *Dracula* and *Frankenstein* and suchlike.

"Most of the other horror-show hosts around the country were playing it tongue-in-cheek with the *Shock! Theater* package—but I wanted to play my version for all the menacing mood I could muster," added Camfield, relishing the alliterative wordplay.

I was a grammar-schooler in Amarillo, Texas, when *Shock! Theater* arrived in 1957. My classmates and I sensed a connection between these ferocious movies and the emerging phenomenon of rock 'n' roll music, if only because our parents and teachers seemed distrustful of both influences. (Horror movies and rock 'n' roll records appeared routinely on the Roman Catholic Church's official roster of Bad Influences Guaranteed To Send the Viewer and/or Listener Directly to Hades. And never mind the pious arguments for Judaeo–Christian Normalcy that figure implicitly in the likes of *Frankenstein* and *Dracula*.) The kinship was cinched when John Zacherle released a chart-climbing recording called "Dinner with Drac," competing for airplay with Elvis Presley and Jerry Lee Lewis.

My town's *Shock!* host, an Amarillo Little Theater hambone and TV announcer named Fred Salmon, billed himself as Mr. Shock and played his Friday-night *Shock!* segments for grotesque slapstick effect. I found the character a distraction from the movies but kept watching, anyhow. Boris Karloff's Frankenstein Monster, Bela Lugosi's Count Dracula, and Claude Rains' tormented Invisible Man were too good to miss. To the target–audience that my schoolboy contingent represented, the movies seemed as new—indeed, *Shock! Theater* marked their teevee débuts—as those fresh-from-Hollywood big-screen sensations *I Was a Teenage Werewolf* (1957) and the ostensibly futuristic *Frankenstein 1970* (1958).

A movie-biz and ComicMix colleague, Robert Tinnell, writes in a recent memorandum: "While the fallout from the release of the *Shock! Theater* package cannot compare with, say, the Beatles, in scope, it absolutely can in terms of intensity. The reverberations of the showering of kids with those films is still being felt today—in everything from breakfast cereals

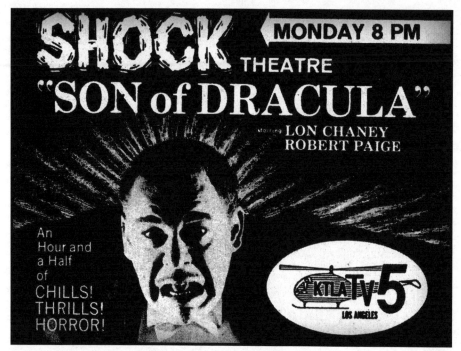

[an allusion to General Mills' Count Chocula and Frankenberry, no doubt] to big-budget films like [2004's] *Van Helsing*." (The influence is particularly evident in Kerry Gammill's heavy-traffic Web site, www.monsterkid.com, and its affiliated Classic Horror Film Boards.)

"What's more," adds Bob Tinnell, "It's undeniable that a significant portion of fandom was born of the [*Shock!*] experience... I still feel very connected to the phenomenon. I'm just grateful I grew up with a horror host like Chilly Billy Cardille out of Pittsburgh—he took seriously the job of warping my impressionable mind."

Such warpage in my experience included the *Shock!*-ing spectacle of watching my hometown's horror-picture host nearly electrocute himself on live television with an unshielded microphone cable, while staging a remote broadcast alongside the duck pond of a cemetery. Hence the name *Shock! Theater*, one supposes.

The popular bearing of such programs was as widespread as the then-48 United States and colonies thereof. Such *Shock!* hosts as Los Angeles' Jeepers Creepers and New Orleans' Morgus the Magnificent followed John Zacherle's example of taking a stab at the hit-record market. (The Jeepers recordings feature the work of a young Frank Zappa. A Morgus record showcases New Orleans rockers Frankie "Sea Cruise" Ford and Malcolm "Dr. John" Rebennack.)

"I had thought about maybe making a Gorgon record, back then," Fort Worth's Bill Camfield recalled, "what with our fine local community of rock 'n' roll talent, like Delbert McClinton and his band, available to back me up. Never quite got around to that. TV was plenty—and I had some other specialty-show characters that kept me busy, as well."

Camfield's Gorgon held forth on *Shock! Theater* into the 1960s, then staged periodic revival appearances during the 1970s. Those "other specialty-show characters" that Camfield mentioned included a resolute goofus known as Icky Twerp, of Fort Worth/Channel 11's *Slam Bang Theater*. Camfield–as–Twerp helped to spearhead a revival of interest in the Three Stooges during the 1950s and 1960s. Lured out of retirement by the newfound popularity of their short-subject theatrical laff–riots, surviving Stooges Moe Howard and Larry Fine thanked Camfield and a bunch of other TV kid-show hosts by casting them in a valedictory movie called *The Outlaws Is Coming!* (1965). Various *Slam Bang Theater* revivals during the 1980s found Camfield—in civilian life, a serious writer and level-headed suit-and-tie businessman—as generous as ever with the unbridled silliness.

Camfield could be just as generous with the low-key ominous presence, although he preferred to retire Gorgon rather than to venture beyond Old Hollywood's acknowledged classics. "Without the *Frankensteins*, the *Draculas*, the *Mummy* pictures, etc.," as Camfield told Elena M. Watson, author of a 1991 book called *Television Horror Movie Hosts*, "you would have a mishmash of cheap SF, splatter pictures, and some mysteries."

During his last years, Camfield became a newspaper columnist and cable-television developer, and a reliable source for my own efforts to write persuasively about the business end of the broadcasting industry. Yes, and no strictly-biznis luncheon conversation with Camfield was complete without his occasional split-second lapse into character as Icky Twerp or the hollow-voiced Gorgon. Camfield would begin to address a dead-earnest state-of-the-industry question by saying, "Now, here's how *I* look at it..." And then he'd cross his eyes and crane his neck at an awkward angle: "Yeah, here's how I look at it!" (The gag was as old as Vaudeville—but it seemed to become fresher every time Camfield pulled it.)

Camfield's fleeting transformations invariably were greeted with amused delight and, sometimes, befuddled stares from our fellow diners seated within gawking range. Bless the man. (One can see him elsewhere on the Web at www.ickytwerp.net.)

COWPUNCHER CARTOONIST: J.R. WILLIAMS

October 14, 2007: Great cultures yield great artists, and I'm not talking necessarily about Ancient Rome or the Renaissance periods of either Italy or Harlem. The Southwestern Frontier has spawned its share of artistry, from poets and musicians to painters and, yes, cartoonists.

Conventional wisdom holds that Charles M. Russell (1864–1926), was the most gifted of the Western cartoonists. Russell's illustrated correspondence helps to shore up this belief. But Russell's leanings toward the presumably finer arts prevented him from pursuing cartooning as a career. A near-contemporary, James R. Williams (1888–1957), took a different tack and became a working cartoonist who based a long-running daily newspaper feature upon his younger days as a ranchhand. I get a chronic kick out of reminding the readership that the cartooning profession has yielded some fine borderlands artists who haven't wound up enshrined in any highfalutin' museums. (A pal in Montana, Stan Lynde, also comes to mind, with his extensive run of Western-themed comic-strip work including *Rick O'Shay* and *Latigo*, and a newer career as a frontier novelist.)

J.R. Williams is largely a forgotten figure today, although his comics feature, *Out Our Way*, served to motivate a next-generation cowboy cartoonist from Northwest Texas named Asa "Ace" Reid. And

Reid's *Cow Pokes* series—authentically Western though derivative and simplistic—remain well known over a decade after his death.

The gulf of artistry is vast between such an accomplished master as Charley Russell and so glib and casual an imitator as Ace Reid. But it is not merely the distinction between Fine Art and Commercial Art that makes it so. For cartooning can become a higher art, if motivated by urges greater than rattling off an easy gag or beating the next deadline. Thus do any perceived barriers between Russell and Williams prove irrelevant. Williams' mass-consumption newspaper cartoons come from a font of artistry and inspiration as deep and personal as anything that drove Russell.

Jim Williams' *Out Our Way* is the great sustained masterwork of cowboy cartooning. The feature draws upon the writer–artist's personal background as a muleskinner (and industrial machinist, and prizefighter, and family man) in ways that make the individual episodes—each self-contained panel suggesting a larger story—as resonant today as when new.

Williams, at 34, was working as a lathe operator in Ohio when a packet of cartoons he had sent to the Newspaper Enterprise syndicate clicked with the right editor. A month later, in March of 1922, *Out Our Way* appeared in half–a–dozen small-market newspapers.

"It was just this little knack I'd developed for drawing things," Williams told *The Saturday Evening Post* in 1953. "Nobody outside the bunkhouse or the machine shop had ever seemed to want my style of small-town humor, but I was too stubborn to give up." By the 1950s, *Out Our Way* had attracted a readership in the millions.

Williams' range of experiences, coupled with a gentle sarcasm and a keenly observational sense, made his work unique. He tapped into the commonplace happenings of everyday life—childhood in a hick town, the earthy humor that lightens the rigors of ranch life and the factory floor—and became an entertaining chronicler of a day before the 20TH Century had come of age.

He had no compunctions about humiliating his characters, subjecting his cowboys to bad horses and worse weather and his machinists to the industrial perils of a pre-OSHA day. But his affection for his players, and his understanding of their circumstances, is genuine: Williams knew these people because he had been one of them. He became a timeless artist by refusing to pander to changing tastes and trends. His situations rely upon a past–life bracketed by the first 25 years of a century. He was current when he started—but already he looked upon cowboy life as a vanishing phenomenon—and his style never changed.

Williams also proves him to have been a capable cowboy–poet. In a 1925 piece, a cowhand has just gunned down a coyote and stops to examine the carcass, only to find a number of the creature's pups nearby. The caption muses:

Born t'be a cattle–killer,
Thief an' genrul all-'round pest.
But I hate t'kill yuh, pardner,
'Cause yo're part o' our Old West.
You an' me is sorta brothers
With our backs ag'in' th' wall,
In a' act that's nearly over
An' th' curt'in 'bout t'fall.

Born in Nova Scotia, Jim Williams grew up Michigan and Ohio. He quit school to become an apprentice machinist. He spent six years drifting around Oklahoma and Texas, laboring as a chuck-line rider until he found a chance to work the cattle. From this background, Williams picked up on the distinctions between ranch life in the Real World and ranching as glamorized in popular literature, equipping himself to create a popular literature of his own with a truer grasp.

In one early *Out Our Way* panel, a rancher introduces a citified novelist to three rugged cowhands, explaining: "He wants to work right with you boys so he can git the romantic atmosphere of cowpunchin' into his book." One of the hired–hands is preparing to bury two horse carcasses, another is whitewashing the bunkhouse, and the third is changing the engine in a T–Model Ford.

During the 1940s, well established as a prosperous cartoonist, Williams tried to reconnect with the Westerner's life. He purchased a 40-acre spread north of Los Angeles but soon wised up to the speciousness of the role of a suburbanite rancher. No longer a hungry cowboy, he now found ranch life merely a pose. Williams resettled in Pasadena for the longer term.

Out Our Way, with its crucial cowhand and small-towner characters looking ever more like throwbacks to a vanished age, finally faced a new generation of editors, pressing for modernization. Williams refused. His audience remained loyal. Williams' death in 1957 gave the syndicate its cue to revamp the feature along modernized lines. One posthumous successor, Neg Cochran, sought to little avail to resurrect the classic Williams style. *Out Our Way* soon lost its following, a casualty of such impatient tampering and nostalgic back–pedaling.

Which is just as well. No heir to the feature could have recaptured J.R. Williams' ingrained knowledge of the Cowboy Way.

THE PERILS AND PLEASURES OF MOVIOLA

October 21, 2007: I've been sorting through the newspaper-cartoon backlog lately, beefing up the digital-image archive while determining whether anything from a busy stretch at the drawing board during the 1990s might bear resurrecting for fresh publication. Much of this material involves a Hollywood-lampoon strip called *Moviola*, which originated as a weekly feature for the *Star-Telegram* of Fort Worth, during its last years as a higher-minded publication.

The first movie parody I ever encountered—and thus, a building-block of my long-stretch involvement in cartooning and film scholarship—came from my Uncle Grady L. Wilson, a theatre-chain manager. Grady could concoct the damnedest jolly nonsense from the flimsiest of material, and keep a straight face in the bargain. He announced to me one day in 1954 that he had booked a picture called *Preacher from the Black Lagoon.*

Now, I was six years old at the time and as impressionable as Silly Putty, and so I found it necessary to witness the arrival of Jack Arnold's *Creature from the Black Lagoon* on the big screen before it dawned on me that my uncle had been just woofing. Once enlightened to this cornball jive, I found my Uncle Grady's Vaudevillian sense of wordplay as addictive as the films from which he earned his living. We developed a routine of it. We rechristened the 1958 jungle epic *Tarzan's Fight for Life*, for example, as *Tarzan Fights His Wife*. Things as a class seem funnier when you are a kid, or when you are an adult who declines to grow up entirely.

And my uncle hipped me to *MAD* magazine, which would spoof not only the movies' titles—but also their substance or lack thereof. And Grady led me back via the Time Machine of repertory cinema to the heyday of the two-reeler slapstick comedy, an age when respectable feature–films routinely had provoked the creation of such short-subject laff riots as "Arabs with Dirty Fezzes" (after 1938's self-serious *Angels with Dirty Faces*), "Andy Clyde Gets Spring Chicken" (after 1939's *Andy Hardy Gets Spring Fever*), "Strange Innertube" (after 1932's *Strange Interlude*, with or without apologies to Eugene O'Neill),

Moviola   MICHAEL H. PRICE & TODD CAMP

and the Three Stooges' "Violent Is the Word for Curly" (a variant upon the 1936 weeper *Valiant Is the Word for Carrie*).

Later on, Harvey Kurtzman, the founding editor of *MAD* and other publications too humorous to mention, became a friend via our involvement in the comics-convention scene. And don't go thinking he didn't encourage this title-spoofing business. "Once you've got a grasp of parody," Harvey averred, "satire can't be too far out of reach. Or *can* it?"

Some movies' titles, as my uncle had pointed out, were unintentionally hilarious—to wit, such he-man sagebrushers of the 1920s and 1930s as *Riders of the Cactus* (*ouch!*) and *Three Texas Steers* (how's *that* again? an emasculate conception?) and *The Fighting Boob* (*mmm–hmm*). Discoveries of this nature were free shots in the game, fully as valuable as any original lampoon.

Even John Carradine took a hand in it: When I met the Great Actor in 1962—the encounter is discussed in some detail in *Forgotten Horrors Vol. 2*—Mr. Carradine told me with a straight face that he was preparing for what could only be his greatest enactment this side of *The Grapes of Wrath* or at least *Voodoo Man*. The role would be that of a ghost harboring a grudge against the entirety of humankind. And its title? *The Gripes of Wraith.*

All of which goes a long way toward explaining why *Moviola* (1992–1997) plays out like such a hokey throwback despite its concentration upon films of its immediate day: Good ham never goes stale—it just leaves you groaning.

• • •

During the formative stages of *Moviola*, my wife and I attended a USA Film Festival reception for a visiting dignitary from the International Consortium of Film Snobs. A fine way to kill a Saturday night, especially if one is attuned to fatuous discourses on the deeper meanings of Bergman (Ingmar or Ingrid) and Truffaut. Christina and I were there for the usual professional–political reasons—and also in order that I might absorb a bit of wisdom from the guest of honor, a gent whom I'd long regarded as a fine role model for a career in film scholarship and criticism. At least the buffet met the expectations. The Great Man His Ownself proved arrogant and stuffy. And although he bothered to acknowledge my one (at the time) published book of moviemaking history as "something I wish I had written myself," still I got the impression that his comment had more to do with Territorial Resentment.

The Big Moment of the evening took place when one couple announced they must be leaving: "We must rise early, for church."

"Church—*feh!*" replied our visitor. "The cinema is my only religion!"

So sour an encounter is of course better forgotten—unless one can find a Practical Use for it. That Important Personage left with me an

Moviola   MICHAEL H. PRICE & TODD CAMP

impression (apart from the value of his writings and his lectures) that I found best dealt with by working it into a cartoon character.

Whereupon that character manifested his own snooty self, spontaneously enough, as a player in *Moviola*. The cartoon version took the character down a few pegs by making him not a respected film scholar, but rather the proprietor of a video-rental shop where (presumably) the guy could look straight down his needle–nose at any customer whose tastes failed to approximate his own.

But not to confront the character with just any old procession of shirtsleeves movie-buff patrons, *Moviola* gave him an annoying client whose cracked perceptions and undiscriminating appetite for entertainment would test the tolerance of even the least militant Film Snob.

Had *Moviola* lasted—more about that presently—its central characters no doubt would have developed a narrative continuity and a sense of camaraderie beyond the glib one–liners that characterize their appearances in the strip as it exists. Kindred souls are always more interesting when oddly matched, and as *Moviola* starts winding down to the Final Curtain during the 1996–1997 episodes one can see a vague semblance of a Character Arc starting to build.

But I digress. The specific prehistory of *Moviola* dates from 1990 and my introduction of a Saturdays-only gag comic called *What Next?!* to the comics page of Fort Worth's *Star–Telegram*. A new hire that year, a newly minted journalism-school graduate named Todd Camp, came along at the right time to pitch in on *What Next?!*, contributing much of the inkwork over my pencilled breakdowns. During this same period, Camp worked as co–illustrator on my studio's *Carnival of Souls* graphic novel (Malibu Graphics; 1991), and helped to compile a horror-comics anthology called *Holiday for Screams* (Malibu; 1992), among other projects.

Moviola came about in 1992 after a larger space had opened on the Saturday funnies page. *Moviola* thrived long enough to develop its two leading characters in addition to the recurring element of Hollywood lampoonery—and long enough, too, to attract the attention of a New Generation of editors who fancied themselves more sharply attuned to the readership than the cartoonists responsible.

Where I was writing in the assumption of an intelligent and hip-to-cinema readership, the New Prevailing Thought in journalism held that a typical reader must be a middle-school dropout, interested enough in the movies as a herd-mentality force but more keenly attuned to celebrity-gawking interests and that shallower strain of humor that can be grasped and let go in a three-second browse. A memo from one of these New Breed Editor–Boors reads as follows: "Like cartoon. But too many words. Can we dumb it down?" Yes, and as Tonto said to the Lone Ranger: "Whaddaya mean, 'We,' white man?"

MOVIOLA
By Michael H. Price

DOESN'T *EDDIE MURPHY* EVER TIRE OF PLAY-
ING THE **SAME OLD ROLE** IN ONE MOVIE
AFTER *ANOTHER?* WHAT DO *YOU* THINK?

Todd Camp remained a mainstay of *Moviola*. He also became essential to the *Telegram*'s weekly kid-stuff magazine. There, he supervised design, composed much of the editorial content, conducted mentoring programs, and produced a solo comics-panel series, *Rimshot*. In a sideline, Camp also began dealing in independent gay-issues journalism, via a comic strip called *Life Underground*, for *The Texas Triangle* at Austin. This dichotomy was something of a thumb–of–the–nose to the First & Best Effort Doctrine by which a newspaper staffer determines how extensively to work as a freelance. As such, *Life Undergound* proved tricky and stressful, though productive and courageous (no pseudonym), for nearly four years.

MOVIOLA

By Michael H. Price

Then things turned weird: A campaign by the holier-than-thee-or-thou American Family Association targeted Camp as a fabricated Menace to Society and began assailing the Fort Worth *Star–Telegram* with calls for his removal, threatening loss of revenue via pressure upon advertising clients. The timing was awkward for all concerned— and disastrous for the paper's school-kids supplement, which relied not only upon Camp's versatility but also upon his gift for working productively with children.

Whereupon the Big Cowardly Newspaper's management cratered to threats—economic, mostly, but also just-plain menacing—from the American Family Association. The incident drew an uneasy parallel with the sorry treatment that the Dallas *Times Herald* had administered to the humorist John Bloom, A.K.A. Joe Bob Briggs, in 1983 after a Briggs column had been accused (falsely so) of conveying a bigoted attitude.

Camp's lot at the lily-livered *Telegram* became that of expulsion from the children's magazine and reassignment to a generic features-reporting post. An outright firing, though hardly deserved, might at least have triggered a more constructive outpouring of massed indignation. A few of us newsroom–types protested the cowardly banishment, incurring in the process the passive-aggressive wrath of those Managerial Geniuses who already had begun an irreversible dumbing–down of the *Telegram*, seeking trendiness at the sacrifice of sense and substance. ("Mass Man must be served by Mass Means," as a cousin of mine, the pedigreed satirist Roger Price, had summarized an ill-heeded warning from the social critic José Ortéga y Gasset.)

In the process, I started finding various of my movie-review columns censored and/or altered to reflect a pandering religious-fundamentalist bias, slightly rightward of Mussolini and/or Falwell. There also came orders, which I defied, to condemn in writing such marquée-value talents as Laura Dern and Renée Zellweger for their involvement in such "evil" movies as (respectively) Alexander Payne's abortion-issues satire *Citizen Ruth* (1996) and Kim Henkel's *Texas Chainsaw Massacre: The Next Generation* (1996). The newsroom environment was fast becoming toxic, except perhaps to methane–breathing Roobs.

Moviola had sprung its last sprocket by 1997. I busied myself from there with the founding of the Fort Worth Film Festival, Inc., left the newspaper racket entirely for a few disgusted years in search of breathable air, and kept up the film-review involvement through the *Forgotten Horrors* books and so forth. [Todd Camp and I have resumed the comic-book activities in times more recent, with new stories and resurrections of early work, and None Too Damned Soon.]

And had I mentioned there's No Accounting for Taste? A workable rule, though often fortunately so for that thuggish lot who prefer to have everyone else account for their rancid tastes.

R. CRUMB'S MUSIC MADNESS

October 21, 2007: The life and times of R. Crumb, a *mensch* amongst men and one of the more steadfastly brilliant practitioners of American (resident or expatriate) cartooning, have been sufficiently well covered in Terry Zwigoff's documentary film, *Crumb* (1994), and in Peter Poplaski's *The R. Crumb Handbook* (M.Q. Publications; 2005) and innumerable column–inches of *The Comics Journal*, that I feel no particular need to pursue any generalized biographical tack here. In a recent letter, Crumb brings things somewhat up to date: "I'm in the middle of a big project—comic-book version of *The Book of Genesis*, approximately 200 pages when finished." This involvement had prevented his traveling to Texas in 2006 to take part in a new experimental-theatre staging of *R. Crumb Comix* with director Johnny Simons and Yrs. Trly. I have joined with Simons' Fort Worth-based Hip Pocket Theatre troupe to adapt Crumb's stories on several occasions since 1985.

Robert Crumb's larger career might reasonably find itself crystallized in warring viewpoints: The authoritative critic Robert Hughes' earnest likening of Crumb to Pieter Brueghel the Elder, greatest of the 16TH Century's Flemish painters, stands in opposition to this declaration from Crumb His Ownself: "Broigul I ain't... Let's face it."

The greater concerns here are those of Crumb's music, and of how he came to apply that interest to one concentrated span of fertile and fevered activity 22 years ago in Texas, in collaboration with Johnny Simons and me. It stemmed from our shared perception of cartooning

and drama and music as intertwined processes. Probably has a great deal to do with my discoveries as a little kid of such music- and cartoon-driven motion pictures as the Fleischer Bros.' *Betty Boop* and *Popeye* short subjects of the Depression years, the Disney studios' *Song of the South* (1946), and a waterlogged MGM musical called *Dangerous when Wet* (1953). All these hinge to one extent or another upon a combination of live-action cinema with animated cartooning and jazzy music.

Crumb's cartooning, which began surfacing in a commercial arena during the early 1960s, is of a style that causes the observer to sense music. I had picked up on that quality straightaway when I first noticed Robert's gag-card work for American Greetings' *Hi-Brows* line. (The department-store shoe boutique where I worked during high school, no doubt anticipating a cue from *The ProJunior Manual of Career Strategies*, stood right across an aisle from the stationery counter.) I found that same implied musicality in Robert's contributions to Harvey Kurtzman's *HELP!* magazine.

Robert's increasingly audacious, ultimately taboo-busting, work of the later 1960s made the musical connections patent: Who else but a devotée of deep-rooted American music would devote entire pages of cartoons to the slogan, "Keep On Truckin'"?

The Texas connection with Crumb began shaping up in 1981, when I dropped the artist a letter in response to one of his more recent publications, an issue of *Weirdo* magazine. A lively correspondence followed, predicated largely upon Robert's interest in the indigenous music of Texas. I mentioned a recent encounter with Fred "Papa" Calhoun, the Fort Worth groceryman who had played piano with Milton Brown & His Musical Brownies during the Depression years. Crumb seemed fascinated by my proximity to such a cultural well-head: "You're certainly in a good area for hot music traditions!"

I mentioned this correspondence at one point or another to Johnny Simons, whose Hip Pocket Theatre was already a going concern with an international following. Johnny mentioned, in turn, his fondness for Crumb's work and inquired whether I might pitch the idea of a collaboration. One thing led to another, and in mid–1985 Crumb traveled from Winters, California, into Texas to begin work on Hip Pocket's first production of *R. Crumb Comix*.

Accompanying Johnny to the airport was John Murphy, the actor assigned to handle the portrayal of Crumb both as a working artist and as one of his own cartoon characters. Through some prankish pre–immersion in character, Murphy had macked himself out as Crumb for this first face-to-face encounter, right down to the finer detail of a prosthetic overbite—what with Murphy's being a practicing dentist and manufacturer of tailor-made porcelain chompers.

At Dallas/Fort Worth Airport, Murphy parked his carcass at a pub on the concourse while Johnny Simons staked out the gate where Crumb's flight would be arriving—this, in a friendlier and less anxious age of airborne comings and goings. Soon enough, Simons and Crumb were en route to the luggage depot. Crumb, a relentlessly searching observer, spotted the impersonator from a distance. Startled by the apparition, Crumb gestured toward the airport barroom, tugged at Simons' sleeve, and whispered, urgently: "There's a guy—sitting there, at the bar—who looks just like me." Prank accomplished.

One must get cracking pretty early in the morning to put one over on R. Crumb, so from the success of their welcoming stunt we might conclude that Simons and Murphy had achieved a running start on that summer's day in 1985. A masquerade sufficiently accurate to halt Crumb in his tracks must be right, as well, for a dramatization aiming to capture both the spirit and the letter of the artist.

• • •

R. Crumb Comix seems to have begun assuming its form some 20–odd years before Simons, Crumb, and I started hammering out the adaptation and setting it to music. It all dates from my first encounter with Robert's then-anonymous series of greeting cards, and then to the revelation of identifying that rambunctious style with the signed pieces that soon followed. For here, in this relentlessly striving body of work, Crumb kept sending out secret signals that whatever his subject matter—erotic obsessions, spiritual and economic chicanery, the counterculture as a class—his steadfast inspiration lay in music.

My first direct communications with Crumb yielded this observation from him about the entertainment racket: "I quit the music business," he wrote in 1981, referring to the disbanding of his old-fashioned string ensemble, the Cheap Suit Serenaders. "Comics are crazy enough... The music business—forget it! I still enjoy playing music, but no more professional jobs, records, tours, *et cetera*... I just couldn't take it..."

When Johnny Simons brought up the idea of a Crumb play, I reckoned the thought a good one. I balked nonetheless, mindful of Robert's stated distaste for show business—and particularly for the execrable misrepresentation of his work in two *Fritz the Cat* movies of the 1970s. I

felt certain that Johnny Simons would do Crumb justice and suggested that Johnny just write Crumb without my middle-manning an approach.

"Naw," said Johnny. "I'd feel better if you brought it up, got me an intro. I don't want to just hit him up, out of the blue."

So we left it at that until—with a friendly correspondence well established—I dropped Johnny's idea into one of my letters to Robert. Crumb wrote back on March 20, 1985:

A friend of yours wants to do a stage production of my work?? Wow! I'm flattered (?) Just tell him to line up those big-leg women and I'll be right down to do some 'collaboratin'. Yuck hilk guhilk... Is the guy any good? Does he have a sense of humor? Will it be sexy? What works of mine is he interested in using? Will there be any pay? Do they have a lot of money to spend on budget? "Hip Pocket" doesn't make it sound too promising in the bank-account department. Will he pay my way to Fort Worth to work on it with him? Well, give him my phone number if you really think this clown is "on the ball"...

Johnny Simons was not only on the ball, but also keen upon snatching up the opportunity. By mid–April, he had enlisted me to develop a musical score, confirmed principal casting, scheduled a long summer-season run, and budgeted for Robert to come in as a collaborator.

R. Crumb's Music Madness • Part No. 2

October 21, 2007: Robert Crumb and I began in April of 1985 to develop a musical accompaniment for the first stage production of *R. Crumb Comix* at Hip Pocket Theatre. We consulted by telephone between my digs in Fort Worth and his home near Winters, California, and Robert prepared numerous reference dubs from his collection of 78-R.P.M. phonograph records. These, I augmented with musical sources from my library, plus original compositions. I recruited an orchestra from within guitarist Slim Richey's and my jazz trio, Diddy Wah Diddy, and from our affiliated string band, the Salt Lick Foundation, with which I had recently completed a string of record albums for Slim's Ridge Runner/Tex Grass labels.

Band rehearsals commenced in May of 1985, with all concerned fore-warned to buck up for a three-hour show scored with what Crumb wanted to be "constant music—just like in those ol' Hal Roach comedy films." Yes, and never mind that the Roach pictures (including the Depression years' *Laurel & Hardy* and *Our Gang* series) ran to just 20 or 30 minutes apiece in length. Well, at least there would be an intermission.

So Robert reached Texas on schedule, got settled in, and found the progress agreeable. He warmed especially to the women (consistent with Crumb's vision) whom director Johnny Simons had cast. Robert took issue with some of the music as sounding "too modernistic—that 1940s swing stuff" (No Accounting for Taste) but found the score workable overall, enjoying the sound well enough to commandeer a plectrum banjo from Salt Lick's D. Lee Thomas and perform as a member of the orchestra on the opening weekend that June. Crumb's banjo–playing fit right in, evoking memories of Eddie Peabody and the Light Crust Doughboys' Marvin "Smokey" Montgomery. I had composed one of the show's tunes, "Save Me a Slice of That," as a Doughboys pastiche.

Hip Pocket Theatre's principal venue in those days, Oak Acres Amphitheatre northwest of Fort Worth, was an overwhelmingly rustic site, seemingly an outgrowth of the very woods surrounding Lake Worth. (The theatre has since relocated to a similarly woodsy area.)

Here dwelt spirits, including one legendary Lake Worth Monster, whose exploits Johnny Simons had chronicled in a cycle of autobiographical plays that, by turns, celebrate and betray the self in ways reminiscent of Crumb's cartoons—and with the same strategic extremes of candor and obliqueness.

This climate of unbridled expression proved sufficiently hospitable to the spirits of Crumb's stories—the lovable charlatan Mr. Natural, the gumption-deficient Flakey Foont, the satyristic troglodyte Mr. Snoid, *et Al.*—who cavorted before capacity turnouts on through July. A scattered few showgoers, walked out in indignant response to the overt, though hardly explicit, eroticism and/or neuroticism of the production.

The stories thus adapted ranged from vignettes first seen in such underground publications of the 1960s as *Zap Comix*, *Yellow Dog Comics*, and *Yarrowstalks*, to newer sustained narratives including "Uncle Bob's Mid-Life Crisis" and "R. Crumb's Modern Dance Workshop." Some of the characters were Bunraku puppets designed and brought to a persuasive imitation of life by James Maynard. Some of the human players, including Ric Swain as the bulb-nosed Mr. Natural, essentially puppetized themselves with extravagant jobs of makeup. Yet others, such as Dwight Welsh as Crumb's eternal

Everyman-as-nebbish, Flakey Foont, just naturally looked the part.

The musical set–pieces included the familiar hokum-blues "Keep On Truckin'" (of course!) and such traditional items as "Alabama Jubilee" and "The Arkansas Traveller." The highest of high points occurred during Robert's opening-show appearance, when actor John Murphy, portraying Crumb, yanked Crumb himself bodily out of the orchestra pit, confronting the crowd with the spectacle of twin Crumbs. The fans who had joined the audience as well-intentioned stalkers were duly astonished to learn that Robert had been hiding in plain sight, plunking away on the banjo.

Robert hauled out soon thereafter for France, where he connected with a splendid Continental jazz outfit known as Primitives of the Future—very much in the *musette* tradition, with Robert playing mandolin—and began contemplating a move for keeps.

This accomplished, Robert and his family revisited America in 1992, stopping in Texas long enough to catch up with the Hip Pocket players and to perform an impromptu blues-and-country jam with the guitarist Josh Alan Friedman and me during the comic-book industry's Harvey (as in *Kurtzman*) Awards ceremonies at the Dallas Fantasy Fair.

We found time, elsewhere during the Dallas sessions, to screen a videotape of the 1985 show, with a sizeable crowd. I figured the viewing would be a snoozer for Robert—but no such thing. Instead, he hyucked it up all through the thing, recalling backstage antics and humming along with all that "constant music," as he had called for to begin with.

"What a wacky troupe!" said Crumb.

LI'L ABNER: LOST IN THE HOLLYWOOD SHUFFLE

November 11, 2007: Sustained flashback to 1940, and to an early stage of confidence and high promise for Al Capp's long-running comic strip, *Li'l Abner*. Conventional wisdom, bolstered by accounts from Capp His Ownself, holds that the name *Yokum* is a combination of *yokel* and *hokum*. That would be Yokum, as in Abner Yokum and his rural Southern lineage. Such an explanation also might seem to demean the resourceful gumption that Li'l Abner Yokum and his family represent. Capp established a deeper meaning for the name during a series of visits during 1965–1970 with George E. Turner and Yrs. Trly.

"There are many real-life Yokums around the South," explained Capp. "Some spell the name like Abner's, with variations including Yoakam and Yokom, and so forth. It's phonetic Hebrew—that's what it is, all right—and that's what I was getting at with the name *Yokum*, more so than any attempt to sound hickish. That was a fortunate coincidence, of course, that the name should pack a backwoods connotation.

"But it's a godly conceit, really, playing off a godly name—*Joachim* means "God's determination," something like that—that also happens to have a rustic ring to it," Capp added. "When I came up with that 'yokel-plus-*hokum*' bit in some early interviews, I was steering clear of any such damned-fool intellectualism. It helps to keep things looking simple for the massed readership, when you're trying to be subversive with a cartoon." (One such "*yokel/hokum*" reference appears in an article on Capp's success in the November 1942 issue of *Coronet* magazine.)

A.D. 1940 is a significant point, here, in that the year marked *Abner*'s first leap from the funnypapers onto the moving-picture screen. Capp's strip was beginning to hit its stride as a consistently inventive fusion of suspense and biting wit. Capp could not have arrived at this convergence of artistry and self–assurance in expecta-

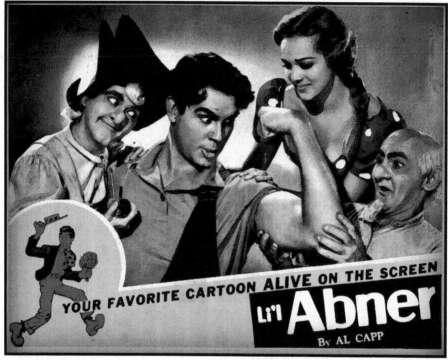

tions of being insulted. He had known enough of that as a workhorse in the Associated Press' cartoon stable, and as an assistant on Ham Fisher's *Joe Palooka*. But in seeking prospects for *Abner* beyond a patch of daily-newspaper real estate, Capp neglected to reckon with the power of popular cinema to corrupt and trivialize a literary source.

As readership mounted for Capp's imaginative twist on Voltaire— Abner Yokum conveys the determined innocence of *Candide*, ranging at large amidst intrigues and treachery—the feature inevitably attracted the attention of the motion-picture industry.

Hollywood had long since found the newspapers' comic strips (*Joe Palooka* among them) to yield properties worth adapting. The movie that resulted from Capp's inspiration, Albert S. Rogell's *Li'l Abner* (1940), suggests that Capp and United Features Syndicate connected with the wrong company of screen artists. Prints that have survived from distribution by RKO–Radio, to more extensive circulation by tiny Astor Pictures, offer a revealing look—more confoozin' than amoozin', and often quite stupefyin'—at how Capp's graceful command of one narrative form was knocked askew by those responsible for adapting it to another. The principal debit is an overall sacrifice of tension and a satiric edge to knockabout comedy.

"I liked the idea of a *Li'l Abner* movie," Capp told Turner and me. "But that first attempt missed the point—all hokum, and no grasp of my attempts to commit satire."

Capp's misconnection with the movie business established a precedent that was echoed only four years later, when Columbia Pictures issued five unimaginatively literal cartoon shorts based upon the strip (Page No. 218). A dozen years then passed before a dramatization more

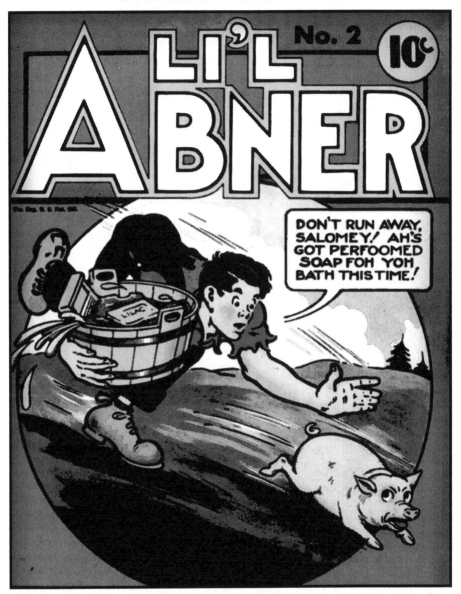

sharply attuned to Capp took shape: The bombastic Broadway production of Gene DePaul and Johnny Mercer's duly satirical musical, *Li'l Abner*, opened in 1956 and found its way onto the screen in 1959.

Al Rogell's 1940 version, little known today though a mainstay of one-lung cable-teevee stations and off-brand video labels, is nonetheless of interest in view of its gathering of Old Hollywood character players and lapsed pioneers of picture-show comedy—to the exclusion of star-caliber players. The absence of big-name leads is not so much a crippling factor (although that element worked against the film's marquée prospects) as it is a giveaway that the production company,

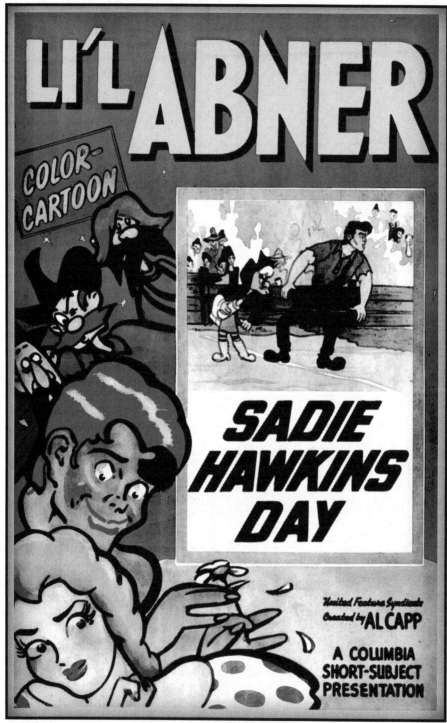

Vogue Pictures, approached the project with modest resources and an incomplete grasp of Capp's rambunctious intellect. Capp's participation in the marketing campaign nonetheless bespeaks keen expectations on his part; the publicity materials include drawings that Capp had keyed specifically to the film.

Failings aside, this *Abner* serves any number of intriguing functions—as a footnote to quite a few careers, as an outcropping of a craze for hillbilly photoplays, and as a commentary on how far Capp had come in ability to define a vivid milieu. The denizens of Dogpatch, U.S.A., and their surroundings seem faithful to Capp's visual sense, but screenwriters Charles Kerr and Tyler Johnson scarcely bother to contrast the hill-folk caricatures with representatives of urban civilization—a crucial part of the strip's makeup since its beginning in 1934.

The movie draws a helpful intensity from Abner's (Granville Owen) conflicting fears of marriage and death. A redeeming element of menace is supplied by a rampaging Earthquake McGoon, as played by Charles A. Post, an exhibition wrestler who billed himself as Man Mountain Dean. (Post's role amounts to gimmick–casting: Capp had modeled McGoon after Man Mountain Dean.)

Clashing romantic interests surface among leading lady Daisy Mae Scragg (Martha O'Driscoll), her manipulative Cousin Delightful (Billie Seward), and an aggressive nature-gal type named Wendy Wilecat (played with undue sophisticated refinement by Kay Sutton). O'Driscoll, a former juvenile player en route to modest stardom, makes an appealingly vulnerable and determined Daisy Mae—practically a ringer for Capp's drawings before the character developed a buxom aspect. Granville Owen, who in the same year impersonated Pat Ryan in a Columbia Pictures serial based upon Milton Caniff's *Terry & the Pirates*, looks the part of Abner and conveys the right mixture of genial vigor, indignation and (*gulp!*) apprehensive disorientation.

Some clever banter figures in a sequence where Abner praises Daisy Mae's charms while pretending to insult her, and in a subsequent confrontation with a chronic annoyance named Abijah Gooch (Frank L. Wilder)—an embellishment upon a memorable set–piece from the strip's earlier days. The dialect, however, is taken with over-literal directness from Capp's "yo'"-means-"you" modifications of the language. This usage becomes a tiresome distraction.

Few superficial liberties are taken with Capp; his proclamation-happy Mayor of Dogpatch, Prometheus McGurgle, is rechristened Mayor Gurgle for Chester Conklin's enactment. But the pageantlike exposition and the costume-party looks of the performers signal an annoying departure from Capp's greater substance.

Gone is the immersion in storytelling that one can take for granted in the published yarns. Only seldom does Rogell, a prolific director of small-change Westerns and whodunnits, capture the urgency with which Capp kept his newspaper readers wondering what would happen tomorrow. Rogell achieves tension with a creepy sequence involving Abner's lone-commando raid on hostile Skunk Hollow, or Holler. Likewise for Rogell's pacing of a husband-capturing tournament, in which Abner's plight is kept in suspense via frequent cutting to other participants, all in the midst of a posse's pursuit of badman Earthquake McGoon. Such moments of assured handling are obscured by an overabundance of inconsistently amusing slapstick.

One catalytic element for all that silliness is the approach of Sadie Hawkins Day, an event that places Abner at risk of being roped into

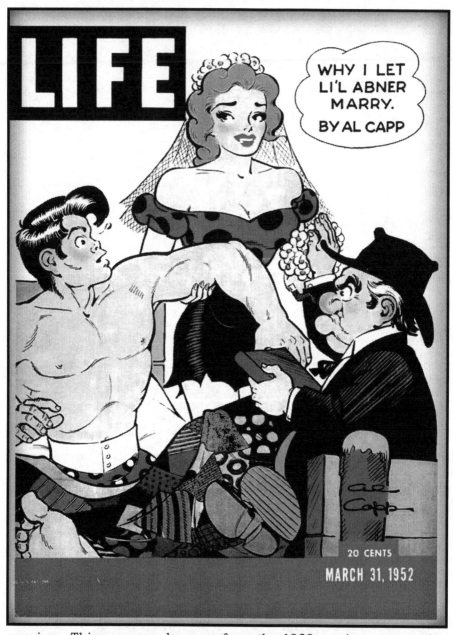

marriage. This sequence borrows from the 1939 comics-page version of the Sadie Hawkins Day race. Other plot propellants include a posted reward for McGoon, "daid or alive—better daid," and the announced arrival of a doctor named Barbour.

   When Abner develops a bellyache after devouring a "Yokum starvation preventer" (a sandwich that might give Dagwood Bumstead pause) he and Hannibal Hoops (Winstead "Doodles" Weaver) set out to consult the visiting Dr. Barbour. In an ineptly developed bit of confusion, Abner instead meets a barber (grouchy Walter Catlett), who takes advantage of the mountain boy's confusion to make a mocking diagnosis.

"You've got Scrombosis," declares the barber as he boards an outbound train.

"Will ah die?" Abner shouts.

"You're dead now, from the neck up!" returns the barber.

"How soon will the rest of me be daid?" asks Abner.

"In 24 hours!"

Abner accepts this pronouncement of doom with relief: He can make known his affectionate feelings for Daisy Mae without risking marriage; he can capture the fugitive McGoon and leave Mammy and Pappy Yokum (Mona Ray and Johnnie Morris) secure with an "ee–normous" $25 reward; and he can repay a kindness done him by McGoon's intended, Wendy Wilecat, by promising to marry her. The conflict between Daisy Mae and Wendy becomes patent just as Abner comprehends that he is not about to die, after all. Mayor Gurgle declares Abner off–limits to all Sadie Hawkins Day contenders but Daisy Mae and Wendy.

While the situations and their pacing are hardly compelling, the film exercises a perverse fascination in several ways. Musical scoring is wildly inconsistent, ranging from clichéd (even in 1940) cues that might fare better in an animated cartoon, to instrumental "stings" applied in the manner of sound effects, to honestly effective mood-building passages. A peppy main-title song (credited in part to Milton Berle) is recapped in a minor mode at one foreboding moment and is retooled elsewhere, by turns, as a string-band piece and as a bravura underpinning for chase footage. The juxtaposition of unremarkable stock music with Lud Gluskin's original orchestrations is consistent with Rogell's inconsistent direction.

Of more troubling unevenness is the failure to deploy eccentric makeups across the board—or to do away with them entirely. Mona Ray, a child player of the silent-screen years, was no stranger to an altered appearance, having portrayed a convincing Topsy in blackface for a 1927 filming of *Uncle Tom's Cabin*. Ray's Mammy Yokum is sufficiently tough in attitude to render her makeup—an exaggerated nose and chin—beside the point. And yet Mammy's counterpart, Daisy Mae's Granny Scragg, appears without comparable physical exaggeration. Maude Eburne, a stocky matron-type best remembered for her fussbudget comic relief in 1933's *The Vampire Bat*, supplies a satisfactory impersonation without looking anything like Capp's drawings.

This visual *non sequitur* continues in the pairing of Hairless Joe (Bud Jamison) and his Indian cohort Lonesome Polecat (Buster Keaton, still game despite a lapse as a major-league comedy artist). Joe's bushy countenance and bulbous schnozzola are pure Capp—except for the drawings' suggestion of expressive facial mobility beneath all that hair. Polecat looks like Buster Keaton with long hair and a suntan.

Keaton's role is hardly crucial, but the brilliant comic makes much of his few scenes, especially at points where Lonesome Polecat makes a raucous display of attempting to build a fire by primitive means, and where he and Hairless Joe are the only men trying to get nabbed in the Sadie Hawkins race. Keaton's career had declined a decade earlier in a tangle of ill-suited movie assignments, marital woes, alcoholism, and deteriorating health. The *Abner* performance, seven years before Keaton's rediscovery began in earnest, finds him capable of enlivening unchallenging material and foreshadows his contributions to the similarly absurdist cycle of *Beach Party* movies of the early 1960s.

There are other memorable faces. As Mayor Gurgle, Keystone Kops alumnus Chester Conklin is as blustery as when he had played second banana to Charles Chaplin. Edgar Kennedy, master of the slow-burn comic-reaction device and star of a run of domestic-farce short subjects, shares a funny interlude with Granville Owen in which Abner imagines himself "daid" and in heaven. Johnny Arthur, former silent-screen lead and whining father–figure of the later 1930s' *Our Gang* shorts, plays a victim of Earthquake McGoon. Al "Fuzzy" St. John, another Keystone veteran who had retrenched as a grizzled sidekick in low-budget Westerns, takes a small turn. Lucien Littlefield, a familiar face behind a generally unfamiliar name, handles two distinct characterizations. And Mickey Daniels, another *Our Gang* alumnus, deploys his signature braying laughter in an incidental scene.

Given its ties with a hugely popular comic strip, the failure of *Li'l Abner* to register much of an impression in its year of release resists explanation. It is substantially more likable than a better-remembered picture of its countrified ilk from 1940, Harold Young's schmaltzy and schizoid *Dreaming Out Loud*, a screen début for the *Lum & Abner* (no kin to Yokum) radio act of Chester Lauck and Norris Goff. And this *Li'l Abner* lacks the tone of condescension that is held in common by many other backwoods gag–movies of 1940.

These films—the likes of *Barnyard Follies*, *Comin' 'round the Mountain*, *Grand Ole Opry*, *Scatterbrain*, and *Friendly Neighbors*—may be forgiven their ham–handedness if only because they have no distinguished source-works against which they must be compared. The first filming of *Li'l Abner*, for all its good nature and many points of interest, fails Capp entirely.

GEE NAUTRY'S EMPIRE, PHANTOM OR OTHERWISE

November 18, 2007: "So *how* did I get to be a movie star, anyhow?" Gene Autry (1907–1998) asked George E. Turner and me in 1985. George and I were consulting with Old Hollywood's preeminent make-believe cowboy about his donation of a large collection of motion-picture footage to the Southwest Film & Video Archive at Southern Methodist University in Dallas. (I had begun working with the SMU film library in 1983 in connection with the preservation of an extensive batch of black-ensemble movies from the 1920s –1950s that had been salvaged from an abandoned warehouse in East Texas. Hence the Tyler, Texas, Black Film Collection—a story for another day.)

Anyhow, on this 1985 occasion, Autry had recognized George and me as the authors who had taken him to task a few years earlier for his having usurped the greater celebrity that had belonged to an authentic cowboy–turned–movie star, Ken Maynard.

Now, being admirers of Maynard, George and I had assumed a resentful attitude toward Autry in the first edition of *Forgotten Horrors* (1979–1980). The movie that at once cinched Autry's stardom and signaled Maynard's decline is *The Phantom Empire* (1935). And yes, *The Phantom Empire* is a horror movie, with nuclear-age science-fictional foreshadowing. And a Western adventure. And a country-music showcase, on top of all that. Only in Hollywood.

"Well," Autry was saying, "I reckon I wasn't fit to polish Ken Maynard's boots. He was a real ranchman and a rodeo champ, besides. Neither of us could really act, not hardly, but Ken had the

edge, and the physique and the experience, where I had started out as kind of a pudgy ol' boy who knew just enough about horsemanship to be a danger to myself. And the only thing Western about me, really, was where I came from [Tioga, Texas] and the fact that I had made a mark, singin' cowboy songs.

"But these things happen—don't you know?—and I just happened to find myself in the right place, at the right time, to pick up a movie role that Ken was about to get himself fired from," continued Autry. "I'd never have strategized any such development—heck, I was a fan of Ken's, too, y'know—but luck kicks in at the doggonedest moments."

The meeting with Autry proved sufficiently cordial and productive to lead to George Turner's and my involvement as consultants in the development of Autry's own Western Heritage Museum (now part of the Autry National Center) in Los Angeles, where Turner had become editor of *American Cinematographer* magazine. It helped that Autry had a deep-seated fondness for the Fort Worth–Dallas metropolitan area—my home base in the newspaper racket—stemming largely from a happy experience at shooting *The Big Show* (1936) on location at Dallas' Texas Centennial grounds, and from his status as the first movies-and-radio big–timer to headline Fort Worth's Fat Stock Show & Rodeo, in 1944. Autry was on temporary leave from the movie business that year, having joined the Army Air Corps as a munitions transporter in the Sino–Indian Theatre of Operations.

Name-brand entertainers had graced earlier Stock Shows—including the great blues singers Gertrude "Ma" Rainey and Bessie Smith, during the 1930s—but Autry's appearance raised the ante considerably on mass-audience appeal: At 33 in 1940, he had become one of Hollywood's top-10 box-office draws—ranking fourth after Mickey Rooney, Clark Gable, and Spencer Tracy.

And Autry already had outstripped all the other horse-opera heroes of the Depression-into-wartime years to become the movie industry's *Public Cowboy No. 1*, as the very title of an Autry film from 1937 gloated. (The year 1944 also marked the Fort Worth Fat Stock Show's move to the Will Rogers Memorial Center, lending a sense of homecoming for Autry—whom Rogers had helped to achieve a breakthrough into radio broadcasting and the phonograph-record business.)

Autry had not exactly come out of nowhere to win such distinction. For as early as 1929—a time when, for example, the Western Swing pioneer Bob Wills was still playing back-country hoedowns around Fort Worth as a more-or-less obscure fiddler—Autry had become a protégé of the down-home humorist Will Rogers and gained a berth as "Oklahoma's Yodeling Cowboy" on Tulsa-based KVOO-Radio. A major-label recording deal had followed, along with a move to the National Barn Dance program at WLS Radio in Chicago.

But the movie business in those days was a world apart from the broadcasting and recording industries, and Autry had found it necessary to crack Hollywood the hard way—starting at the bottom of the bit-player ladder at the smallest of studios, and trusting to a combination of dumb luck and hopeful ambition.

The fans who turned out in 1944 to catch Autry's Fat Stock Show act might not have noticed him in *Mystery Mountain* and *In Old Santa Fe*, low-budget productions built around the biggest Western star of the early 1930s, the exhibition rider Ken Maynard. Maynard's devotées, though, might have pegged an unbilled Autry as the ornery owlhoot who shoots Maynard out of the saddle at one tense moment in 1934's *Mystery Mountain*. Likely few people had given a second thought to that small scene, which would prove prophetic for both actors.

But that earliest generation of Autry's fans had sure–enough noticed him in *The Phantom Empire* (1935)—the basis of Autry's stardom, and perhaps the unlikeliest springboard to recognition that any actor could find. Nat Levine's Mascot Pictures was a big-time moneymaker among Old Hollywood's Poverty Row studios, specializing in serialized films—one new chapter a week, 12 weeks or more at a stretch—that dispensed gee-whiz thrills as opposed to dramatic weight.

By the time of Autry's arrival in Hollywood, Mascot had launched John Wayne toward stardom with *The Hurricane Express* and *The Shadow of the Eagle*. And Mascot had made movie stars, briefly, of football champ Harold "Red" Grange (in 1931's *The Galloping Ghost*) and circus entertainer Clyde Beatty (in 1934's *The Lost Jungle*). The company also had become a candidate for absorption by an upstart bigger studio, also specializing in serials and Westerns, called Republic Pictures. Meanwhile, the mighty Ken Maynard had so thoroughly alienated big-time Universal Pictures, with his ill temper and his demands for creative autonomy, that he was fortunate to get work on Poverty Row.

Nat Levine announced Maynard as the star of *The Phantom Empire*, whose wild scenario screenwriter Wallace MacDonald had

dreamed up while under the influence of nitrous oxide in a dentist's chair. Or so MacDonald told George Turner and me, anyhow, around 1970, while we were researching that first *Forgotten Horrors* collection. The story would have been ideal for Maynard, whose fondness for off-beat themes already had yielded such films as 1932's *Tombstone Canyon* (a frontier takeoff on *The Phantom of the Opera*) and 1934's *Smoking Guns*, which takes place on a Halloween night in a purportedly haunted house. The formula-busting audacity of *Smoking Guns* got Maynard fired at Universal Pictures (see also: Page No. 89).

Maynard seemed right for Mascot Pictures, where weirdness was a cherished commodity.

But Nat Levine found Maynard "a temperamental cuss," as the producer described the actor in a late-in-life interview. Levine, aware of Gene Autry's major-league recording career and grateful to have the singer under contract for $100 a week, took a rare gamble and sacked Maynard—replacing him with Autry in *The Phantom Empire* and throwing in Autry's singer-comedian pal, Lester "Smiley" Burnette, for good measure. Produced for $70,000 (an epic, by Mascot standards), *The Phantom Empire* laid the foundation of a lucrative career for Autry; changed the course of Hollywood's cowboy-picture sector, by popularizing the musical Western; and established a vogue for science-fiction serials that would last into the 1950s.

• • •

Our story, so far: Gene Autry's Radio Ranch is a resort famed for its musical broadcasts. The property is invaded by radium pirates—nuclear claim–jumpers—who in turn disturb the underground kingdom of Murania, which dispatches an army of steel-masked Thunder Riders to menace the surface world. The criminal mob frames Gene for murder, but he eludes a posse in time to get home to Radio Ranch and stage his usual show. Eventually, Gene finds himself at large in the phantom empire of Murania, where he dies in a radium explosion but is brought back to life by Muranian super–science. And so forth for a whopping 245 minutes of screen time, until a rebellion in Murania moves Gene to attempt to rescue the ruler (played by Dorothy Christie). Queen Tika chooses, however, to remain enthroned as a disintegrating ray melts the subterranean kingdom in a barrage of primitive special effects. Gene makes it home in time to clear his name and stage a big musical finale.

If *The Phantom Empire* should sound like an Acquired Taste, its drug-induced pageant of make–believe is nonetheless a delight for those who have acquired the taste. Autry's music, including the early million–seller "That Silver-Haired Daddy of Mine," is as spirited as anything he ever delivered at Columbia Records, and Smiley Burnette's comedy relief is pure corn-fed hokum. The film resurfaced during the 1940s in three condensed versions of an hour–and–change each: *Radio Ranch*, which emphasizes the musical element; *Men with Steel Faces*, which emphasizes the SF qualities; and an edition that played in England under this droll title: *Couldn't Possibly Happen.*

• • •

So how *did* Gene Autry get to be a movie star, anyhow? He lacked the robust presence that one associates with the likes of John Wayne, Buck Jones, and Ken Maynard. He started out as a poor horseman, but he learned fast and well under the tutelage of movie-stunt experts Yakima Canutt and Yancey Lane. And Autry's bland screen personality took on an edge of resilience with experience before the cameras.

Autry's surge to an enduring stardom is proof that only the stars and their fans—and not the studios, or the critics—can define the elusive concept of Star Quality. Many of his nearly 100 movies and 600-or-so phonograph records remain in circulation, and his namesake museum makes a point of showcasing the other movie cowboys and the Real World trailblazers who defined the mythology and the history of the Western frontier. Which makes it a Foregone Conclusion that Gene Autry's restless spirit should hover yet.

AND NOW FOR SOMETHING COMPLETELY HONKY-TONK

November 25, 2007: Some recent installments of this so-called *Forgotten Horrors* feature—the title suggests a resurrection of obscurities more so than it proclaims any particular shivers—have established the music-making imperative as essential to the standing of Robert Crumb (Page No. 209 *et Seq.*) as a Great American Cartoonist. Other such pieces have touched upon the kinship that I have perceived over the long haul amongst comics, movies, and music. This inclusive bias was cinched as early as the moment I noticed, as a grammar-school kid during the 1950s, that a honky-tonking musician–neighbor named Honest Jess Williams was (unlike most other grown–ups in my orbit) a comic-book enthusiast.

The connection was reinforced around this same time, when I met Fats Domino backstage on a Texas engagement and learned that the great New Orleans pianist included in his traveling gear plenty of issues of *Little Lulu*, *Archie*, and *Tales from the Crypt*. Later on, as a junior high–schooler, I discovered that a stack of newsstand-fresh funnybooks always seemed to exert their thrall more effectively with a hefty stack of 45-R.P.M. phonograph records on the changer. (DC Comics' *Flash of Two Worlds* plus Charlie Blackwell's Warners-label recording of "None of 'Em Glow like You," augmented with a 12-ounce bottle [frosted] of Frosty Root Beer and a doublte–wad of Bazooka Bubblegum, add up to undiluted pleasure. Well, the combination worked for me, anyhow.)

Honest Jess Williams.

This latest unearthed obscurity has more to do with music—and a peculiar strain of indigenous Texas music, at that—than with any other influence. But the parallel tracks of American roots music, comics, and motion pictures tend to cross spontaneously. There is only one Show Business, and if not for the early revelation that such a fine Western swing guitarist as Jess Williams followed the comic books avidly (his favorites were *Tomahawk* and *Blackhawk*, the comics' great *Hawks* after Will Eisner's *Hawk of the Seas*), I doubt that such a conclusion would have struck home with me.

I have written extensively about Williams and his steel-guitarist cohort, Billy Briggs, in a book called *Daynce of the Peckerwoods: The Badlands of Texas Music* (Music Mentor Books of Great Britain; 2006). [And after this column first appeared, in an expanded edition for the U.S. market called *Thick Lights, Loud Smoke, and Dim, Dim, Music: The Honky–Tonk Badlands of Texas.*] Now comes a late discovery that bears amplifying:

The gruff vocalist and inventive steel guitarist Billy Briggs, with his and Williams' X.I.T. Boys ensemble of post-WWII Texas, had blazed a trail from Western swing toward rockabilly—with just few enough breakout-hit recordings to leave the late-arriving admirers wondering why the band had not persisted long enough to gain a foothold in rock 'n' roll. The X.I.T. Boys' rambunctious shuffle beat, their grasp of part-countrified and part-doo–wop harmonies, and their fondness for play-

THICK LIGHTS LOUD SMOKE AND DIM, DIM, MUSIC

ful novelty songs and romantic laments, by turns, had pointed assuredly in such a direction.

Ambitious persistence, as it turns out, was hardly lacking among the X.I.T. Boys. Both Briggs (1919–1984) and his chief collaborator, the rhythm guitarist Jess Williams, held forth on a provincial level for a good many years beyond their brief span as national-profile recording artists foreshadowing a breakout for rock.

The 1950s found their ensemble sound essentially unchanged from the progressive fusion of idioms they had developed during the 1940s with a Bob Wills satellite band called the Sons of the West. Neither Briggs, with his taste for coaxing bizarre, stinging chords and a jazz-rooted shuffle-boogie pattern from his long-leggéd and home-made nine-string steel, nor Williams, with his blues-based heartbeat strumming, could be pegged as a typical hillbilly artist.

But Briggs and, especially, Williams found rhythm–and–blues and prototypical rock 'n' roll appealing enough to explore, even within the resolutely anti-rock confines of their principal showplace, a diehard honky-tonk nightclub called the Avalon Ballroom, out on the wild-side-of-life northeastern fringes of Amarillo, Texas. The X.I.T. Boys' 1947 independent-label recording of "X.I.T. Song," combining a romantic complaint with a salute to an annual reunion of cowhands from the historic X.I.T. Ranch, proves downright subversive in retrospect: A review in the show-business tradepaper *Billboard* characterized "X.I.T. Song" as "very close to playing race swing." It helps to know that Briggs and Williams were frequent after-hours sit-in players at the La Joya Hotel, a black nightclub and gambling den at the northwestern edge of Amarillo.

Briggs, a disappointed man since the lapse in 1953 of a mass-market contract with Los Angeles' Imperial Records, became ever more reclusive despite his hometown acclaim. The Avalon and, later, a maverick enterprise called the Briggs Nightclub, kept Briggs playing while serving as perpetual retreats from civilian, and civic, life. He stuck with Williams, and with the Avalon, until 1955, when he opened the Briggs Nightclub. The site lay close by Amarillo's honky-tonk district, along a little-traveled spur route called the Fritch Highway. (Jess called the road the Son-of-a-Fritch Highway. He also noted that, somewhere between the towns of Twitty and Fritch, there must be a settlement called Twitch.) The nightclub lasted until 1963—an instance of awkward timing, given that the early-middle 1960s saw a surge in traffic along the Fritch Highway in response to new recreational and residential developments northward from Amarillo. When Briggs dropped out during the 1960s, he did so in a decisive manner, quitting Texas for California, where he settled at length into a make-do career as an industrial security guard and retired in 1981.

Williams was grateful to be back home in Amarillo after his wartime experiences. His European Theatre service had left the genial extrovert with a chronic-to-acute case of shell-shock anxiety that could be triggered by something as commonplace as an automobile's backfire. In becoming ever more the local celebrity, Williams branched into television, beyond the X.I.T. Boys' radio-and-teevee appearances, as an after-school kid-show host. He furthered the "Honest Jess" monicker as a Chevrolet salesman and a horse–trainer and riding coach. From Williams and Funk, by turns, I learned to ride and to swim in competition. And Williams raised musically inclined offspring, including guitarist Ron Williams and drummer Lynn Williams, who would become prominent sidemen on the rock-band scene around and beyond Texas' Panhandle region.

Williams' service as a mentor extended to my attempts to form a blues-and-rock band as early as the waning 1950s—his, and Briggs', friendships with the Price family dated from the Depression years—and Williams demonstrated a willingness to rock out with such 45-R.P.M. releases of his own as "Suzanne (Stop Rockin' to the Can–Can)" and a variant called "Suzanne (Quit Twistin' to the Can–Can)." These oddities surfaced while Jess was still holding forth at the Avalon Ballroom with a post-Briggs band called the Western Cavaliers.

I eventually began working with Jess' sons Ron and Lynn Williams around 1978 on various road-band and studio-based projects, with the guitarist and producer Billy Gene Stull. In 1979, Stull and I brought Jess Williams out of retirement as a featured artist on a postmodern honky-tonk engagement combining Stull's country-rock quintet, Billy & The Kids, with the Gairrett Bros. Band, a Montana-based outfit that had settled into Amarillo.

Briggs and Williams, right foreground, with the Sons of the West.

But we were talking about Billy Briggs, and about the rediscovery of an episode from the heyday of Billy Briggs & His X.I.T. Boys. The resurrected story has to do with one of Briggs' several attempts to approximate the commercial success of a signature song called "Chew Tobacco Rag," which became a widely covered hit early in 1951 for Imperial Records and its Commodore Publishing division. Briggs sequelized the piece with "Chew Tobacco Rag No. 2"—each tune is distinguished by its deployment of rhythmic spitting noises— only to find himself locked into a spiral of diminishing returns.

Billy Briggs.

The indulgent cycle of bad-habit songs must have seemed like a good idea at the time, but the recurring novelty also proved a distraction from Briggs' wider interest in writing verses about romance, failed or otherwise, regional color ("Coyote Shuffle" and "Texico, New Mexico, Joe"), and ironic declarations of down-home machismo ("The Sissy Song").

Briggs ordinarily wrote verses and melodies as a solo artist, bouncing ideas off Jess Williams as a matter of routine while serving a similar sounding-board function for Williams' own original compositions. A remarkable collaboration with an unlikely outside partner proves to have been responsible for one of Briggs' earlier attempts to sustain the image fostered by "Chew Tobacco Rag."

The song is 1951's "Dip Snuff Stomp." I often had wondered about the Imperial pressing's BMI composer credit, which cites "Briggs & Juniper." The solution to that slight mystery reinforces the notion of what a small world this is, after all.

It turns out that the "Juniper" half of a spontaneous songwriting team is one Dr. Walter Juniper, a dean at West Texas State College—whom I encountered in 1970 when I enrolled in a course on Græco-Roman antiquities at that same academy, since upgraded from college to university. Dr. Juniper had schooled three generations of Panhandle-area collegians. Although the students knew him as a spirited and humorous intellectual (he signed his memoranda as "Dr. Jupiter" and referred jokingly to himself as "an egghead"), still his interests in popular music hardly figured in his classroom sessions.

The key to that "Briggs & Juniper" composer credit surfaced by chance while I was sorting through some scrapbook clippings from the Price household in Amarillo. Of course, my late father, being an old-time pal of Billy Briggs, would have kept the occasional memento on file. This one stands out. It comes from the *Daily News* of Amarillo—a March 10, 1951, installment of a recurring column called *From A to Izzard*, from the newspaper's editor–in–cheese, Wesley S. Izzard, who usually wrote as a right-wing ideologue. (The piece may have been ghost–written by Izzard's second–in–command, Paul Timmons, who often served such a function.) The column follows:

THAT'S HOW SONG HITS ARE BORN

If, a few weeks from now, your favorite jukebox should start jumping with a new song called "Dip Snuff Stomp," you'll be interested to know that the composer is Dr. Walter Juniper, classical scholar, dean of the college, and professor of Latin at West Texas State College in Canyon.

In defense of the Good Dean's reputation as a scholar, we hasten to explain that the whole thing is an accident. It happened yesterday [March 9, 1951, that is]. *Here's the story:*

Dr. Juniper, as a hobby, conducts an old-time record program over KGNC [radio] *every Sunday afternoon. He calls it* Jukebox of Yesteryear.

Yesterday, Dr. Juniper was in KGNC's studio transcribing his program for next week. Also in the studio were Billy Briggs & His X.I.T. Boys, getting set to tape their morning show.

Briggs, it should be explained, is a songwriter. Just a couple of weeks ago, he hit the big time with a tune called "Chew Tobacco Rag." Dr. Juniper and Briggs got to talking. Dr. Juniper told Briggs that he had tried his own hand at composing, turning out a parody of Briggs' "Chew Tobacco Rag." He called his parody "Dip Snuff Stomp."

Briggs demanded that the professor sing it.

Now, Dr. Juniper is a fair country tune–carrier, and he warbled "Dip Snuff Stomp," accompanying himself with a few piano chords. Just as he finished, the phone rang.

It turned out to be a long-distance call for Briggs, from his Hollywood agent, Lew Chudd, of the Imperial Recording Company. Chudd wanted a list of new tunes that Briggs had promised to have ready for the agent's consideration. [Chudd, who had founded Imperial in 1946 at Los Angeles, was more boss than agent to Briggs.] *Briggs rattled off a dozen, and then, on the spur of the moment, added, "and 'Dip Snuff Stomp.'"*

Chudd asked for the list again. Briggs repeated, but played it straight this time, omitting mention of "Dip Snuff Stomp."

But Chudd demanded, "What was that last one you mentioned before?" ... Briggs tenored through a few swift bars... "Great!" shouted Chudd. "Make that one and send it out right away!"

Briggs and Dr. Juniper immediately went into a huddle. And they came up with a new songwriting team—Briggs and Juniper. That's the way it will be on the record...

The moral of this little tale is: If you are a Latin professor, don't poke fun at the hillbillies by writing parodies on their songs. You may find yourself in business...

• • •

And so ends the on-the-spot account of an intriguing, if hardly pivotal, moment in the history of an oddly transitional period in American roots music. The Amarillo *Daily News'* interest in Billy Briggs had primarily to do with Briggs' affiliation with KGNC–Radio, which in turn was a corporate affiliate of the *Daily News,* and with Briggs' status as a favored entertainer at rich-folks ranch-house parties thrown by the Ruling Class oil-and-cattle owners of those publishing and broadcasting companies.

Briggs could sing persuasively of "oil, cattle, and wealth" on one of his last mass-market Imperial sides (1953's "Full Blooded Texan"), but his lot remained that of the hardscrabble working-class musician.

The *Daily News* columnist's show of admiration for Briggs ran more toward local-boy-makes-good condescension than toward any sharper understanding of Briggs' inventive drive. The local newspaper soon lost interest as Briggs lapsed from name-brand recording artist back to the rank of a strictly hometown entertainer.

A 1984 obituary notice in that same Amarillo *Daily News* acknowledged Fort Worth native Briggs' larger career as dating from 1938 in Amarillo and cited such other X.I.T. Boys recordings as "Panhandle Shuffle" and Jess Williams' sentimental "Blue Bonnet Waltz." But the memorial piece reserved its greater attention for "Chew Tobacco Rag"—the song that had signaled Briggs' breakout, even as it consigned him to typecasting as a gimmick-song specialist.

MY COUSIN VINNIE VS. THE VAMPIRES

December 2, 2007: Right about now, my cousin Vincent Price would be grumbling about a new film called *I Am Legend*—reminding anyone within earshot that he had been the first to star in a movie based upon that apocalyptic story and muttering, "You'd think we hadn't done it right, the first time." Price (1911-1993) had said as much about another movie during our last get–together, in 1986 during a college-campus lecture-tour visit to Fort Worth. David Cronenberg's Oscar-bait remake of *The Fly* was about to open, and Price—who had starred in the original *Fly* of 1958—was exercising his prerogative, as a Grey Eminence of Hollywood's horror-film scene, to cop an indignant stance: "Hmph! You'd think we hadn't done it right, the first time." Like I said...

Francis Lawrence's *I Am Legend*, starring Will Smith in a role corresponding to that which Price had handled, is the third filming of Richard Matheson's 1954 novel about an epidemic of vampirism. Price's version, belatedly issued in 1964 with little fanfare, bears the title *The Last Man on Earth*. Price might have grumped about a 1971 remake called *The Omega Man*—if not for the presence of his friend Charlton Heston.

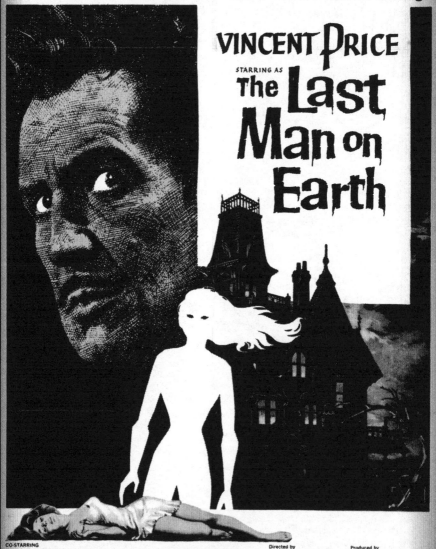

In a benevolent side-effect, the heavy promotion of *I Am Legend* has prompted a classy widescreen-DVD release of *The Last Man on Earth.*

Vincent Price: The name conjures images as varied as the roles he tackled (romantic, comical, heroic, tragic) before typecasting kicked in to distinguish him as the baddest of bogeymen. Price was as prominent a champion of Gracious Living—gourmet chef, cultural scholar, published author, and discerning collector of art—as he was a reliable movie menace. Having followed his pictures since my schoolboy days, and imagining him a possible uncle or some–such via the surname in common, I finally met Price in 1974. The occasion was a newspaper interview in connection with Price's popular stage show, *And the Villains Still Pursue Me.*

"Price, *eh*?" he asked.

"Yessir," I said.

"Ever trace your family tree? Back to West Virginia, maybe?"

"*Uh*, yessir, Mr. Price."

"Any particular ancestors?" he asked. "A planter and military man named Sterling Price, maybe?"

The name registered, sure enough. Gen. Sterling Price had turned up in a genealogical search conducted by a great–great–aunt of mine, and I had learned quite a lot about him through a shelf of scholarly books on the Civil War, as published by the Riverside Press of Chicago.

"Why, yes, sir!" I answered.

"Well, then, shake, Cousin!" said Vincent Price, extending a grand theatrical handclasp.

We never quite figured out the specific kinship, third– or fourth–cousins or whatever, but we developed a friendship that persisted. Price's frequent visits to Fort Worth brought him often to my newsroom office in Fort Worth. He lessened such touring as the 1980s trailed off into the 1990s.

That last Fort Worth visit in 1986 coincided with Price's involvement with two motion pictures, both issued the following year, that would effectively cap his career: Price considered a compassionate role in Lindsay Anderson's *The Whales of August* to be his valedictory. He dismissed an appearance in Jeff Burr's *The Offspring* as a demeaning exploitation. ("They pitched that one to me as something more nearly akin to Poe," Price complained. "I found out after the fact that it's one of those gory splatter movies.") Less assertive work, including a mournful extended cameo in Tim Burton's *Edward Scissorhands*, dates from 1988–1990.

But we were talking about *The Last Man on Earth* and its sparkling new DVD edition—as opposed to innumerable bootleg copies from ill-preserved teevee-syndication prints. (American International Pictures, which had handled sparse theatrical distribution in the first place, had allowed the copyright to lapse. What remains of AIP, long since absorbed into the ghostly afterlife of MGM Pictures Corp., can be found primarily in the many AIP productions and acquisitions that have surfaced on video under that MGM identity.) There was in 2005 a decent widescreen-DVD release of *The Last Man on Earth,* paired with 1962's *Panic in Year Zero,* a director–star vehicle for Ray Milland. The new edition is the first to treat *Last Man* as a sharply restored, self-contained attraction.

Typecast as a villainous presence since 1953's *House of Wax,* Vincent Price had settled by the 1960s into a productive cycle of E.A. Poe adaptations (*House of Usher, Tales of Terror,* and so forth) at AIP, with the producer–director Roger Corman. (See *Forgotten Horrors Vol. 8*). These assignments dovetailed with the heroic leading role in *The Last Man on Earth*, which the low-rent Hollywood producer Robert L. Lippert picked up as an independent project after Hammer Films of England had taken a Pasadena on the story–property. Filming took place during 1961 in Italy, where Price had landed on a working sabbatical.

Lippert teamed a native-born director and screenwriter, Ubaldo B. Ragona, with an Old Hollywood workhorse director, Sidney Salkow, to help bridge the language barrier for Vincent Price. Salkow would direct Price again in 1963 on the portmanteau film *Twice Told Tales*, which attempted to do for Nathaniel Hawthorne what Roger Corman had accomplished on behalf of Mr. Poe. The Lippert production of *Last Man* languished for three years before it became a desultory pick-up acquisition of American International Pictures.

The story, thus far: Immune to a plague that has transformed humankind–at–large into a race of bloodthirsty predators, Dr. Robert Morgan (Price) carries on through some unexplainable reserve of will. Price delivers a nuanced portrait of a resourceful survivor, struggling as much with the pain of isolation as with an incumbent threat.

"That one, now—quite a change of pace for me," as Price recalled *The Last Man on Earth*. "I had pretty well made my mark as a Grand Manner actor—which is a polite way of saying, 'a ham'—and a perpetual villain, on top of that. When occasionally I got to play the Good Guy, as in *The Fly*, the role was usually not as emotionally demanding as I'd like. So this *Last Man on Earth* thing allowed me a sympathetic role that also called for some intensity. Very welcome, although I was disappointed that it never played all that widely."

The influence of *The Last Man on Earth* proved striking, nonetheless. The film is generally perceived—along with such titles as Herk Harvey's *Carnival of Souls* (1962) and Edward L. Cahn's *Invisible Invaders* (1959)—as an inspiration to George A. Romero's breakout film of 1968, *Night of the Living Dead*.

And of course, Price and his associates treated *I Am Legend* right the first time, barring some disagreements that provoked source-author Richard Matheson to disown his collaborative script for *The Last Man on Earth*. (Matheson assigned himself a bogus name, Logan Swanson, for the finished project. He took no hand in 1971's *The Omega Man*, apart from source-author credit; that same credential applies to 2007's I Am Legend.) Ironic, though, that such a remake as my Cousin Vinnie professed to despise should wind up calling belated attention to his original version.

TIPPY TACKER'S YULETIDE TRAVAILS

December 9, 2007: December of 1938 saw the arrival of an *ad hoc* comic strip called *Tippy Tacker's Christmas Adventure*, signed by one Robert Pilgrim and distributed to the daily-newspaper trade by the Bell Syndicate. The feature appears to have run its month-long course with little fanfare and only desultory, though complete, documentation of its passage. The microfilm archive in which I had found *Tippy Tacker* shows no advance promotion, no front-page come–ons, and no particularly prominent placement. The daily installments appear away from the formally designated Comics Page, plunked down at random amongst the general-news and advertising columns. Just a business-as-usual, matter-of-fact deployment, with no attempts to steer the reader toward a special attraction.

The piece came to light around 1990. I was rummaging through

the files of the Fort Worth *Star–Telegram*, my home-base newspaper during its last years as a Real Newspaper, in aimless pursuit of who–knows–what. The Depression Era back issues had yielded considerable raw material for my contributions to the original *Prowler* comic-book series, along with motion-picture advertisements relevant to the *Forgotten Horrors* series of movie-history books. Robert Pilgrim's *Tippy Tacker* cropped up during one such eyestrain marathon at the microfilm station.

Sometimes, obscurity alone is cause for a resurrection, even though many outpourings of the Popular Culture ("history in caricature," as the novelist and cultural historian James Sallis puts it) will lapse deservedly into obscurity. But I happen to have built a career around the defeat of that Old Devil Obscurity—starting with the *Forgotten Horrors* books and progressing, or digressing, from there—and *Tippy Tacker's Christmas Adventure* seemed to fit that pattern..

And besides, here was a sustained comics narrative that patently had represented a significant burst of creative energies; that had merited syndication to who–knows–how–many American newspapers; and that now represented a keen challenge of restoration and new utilization. The Dickensian story concerns a scrappy waif who finds himself transported to Santa Claus' headquarters.

I started with hard-copy prints from microfilm and found the artwork more vivid, when enlarged, than its hand-lettered captions and dialogue. Where retouching would suffice for the drawings, the lettering demanded a thorough job of *re*–lettering, complicated by the urge to approximate the original style of lettering.

The objective was to present the *Telegram*, where I held forth as an editor and columnist–cartoonist, with a unique feature for whichever Christmas season might coincide with the completion of a *Tippy Tacker* restoration. It proved easier to reconstruct the individual strips than to persuade the unimaginative Powers That Did Be to devote the space and promotional resources necessary to make *Tippy* a renewed attraction.

Yes, and already, newsroom management nationwide was gleefully succumbing to the idiocy that prizes shallow glamour and faddish trend–gawking over any rediscoveries of misplaced gems.

By the time the restoration was ready to roll, during the waning 1990s, the *Telegram*'s transformation to a celebrity-gossip and scandal-sheet/window-peeking organ had been rendered complete via a buyout by the consummate dumb-it-down publishing concern of Knight Ridder and the ascent of a managerial *junta* whose idea of Good Journalism began and ended with *People Weekly* and *USA Today*. Seeking a graceful exit but dead–set upon seeing some version of *Tippy Tacker* in print as a gesture of defiance, I condensed and re-drew the 30-strip restoration into a four-page colorized version, with the help of staff artist Dale Taylor. This, Dale and I sneaked into *Class Acts*, the Telegram's weekly Kid Stuff supplement. I jumped ship shortly thereafter and spent five years in the property-management racket. Finally rejoined the publishing business in a niche-market sector where celebrity-gossip snarkery is irrelevant.

Yeah, well, and So There, already. The readers' response to that condensed version proved enthusiastic, including a handful of reminiscences from old–timers who had encountered *Tippy* during their childhood days. Samples from both the original run and the restoration are reproduced here. That unassuming little comic, having outlived its original stewardship, had become a marginally obsessive interest. *[The full-length restoration surfaced in 2009 in my* Great Big Crock of Christmas *anthology.]*

And the elusive Robert Pilgrim? Likely a Bell Syndicate pseudonym—or so suggests the comics historian Bill Blackbeard. In any event, the artwork bespeaks not so much a distinctive personal style, as it nails a distinctive 1930s style. And more power to it.

THE POSTHUMOUS PERSISTENCE OF GEORGE E. TURNER

December 16, 2007: George E. Turner is a familiar name among serious movie buffs—a pivotal figure in the realm of film scholarship, as influential these many years after his death as he was during a lengthy prime of productivity. George's authorship alone of a book called *The Making of King Kong* (and known in a newer edition as *Spawn of Skull Island*) would be sufficient to cinch that credential.

But add to that George's hitch during the 1980s and 1990s as editor of *American Cinematographer* magazine and resident historian of the American Society of Cinematographers, and you come up with a pop-cultural impact of formidable staying power, beyond the reach of trendy distractions. Where George preferred to limit his interests to the prehistory of filmmaking and the first couple of generations of Old Hollywood, he nonetheless kept a hand in current developments: His last job in a seven-year span of purported retirement was that of storyboard artist and second-unit director on the hit network teleseries *Friends.* a taste for which there is no accounting. And as a fan, he was as fluent in the continuing story–lines of *The X–Files* and *Buffy the Vampire Slayer* as he was in the history of RKO–Radio Pictures or the careers of Boris Karloff, Claude Rains, Tod Browning and Val Lewton.

The *Friends* storyboarder hitch is significant: Even those who are most familiar with George Turner's film scholarship—for example, a genre-history series that he and I launched in 1979 with *Forgotten Horrors*—scarcely know of his parallel career as a commercial artist and gallery painter, a comics artist and newspaper illustrator, and overall an accomplished talent in practically any medium one might

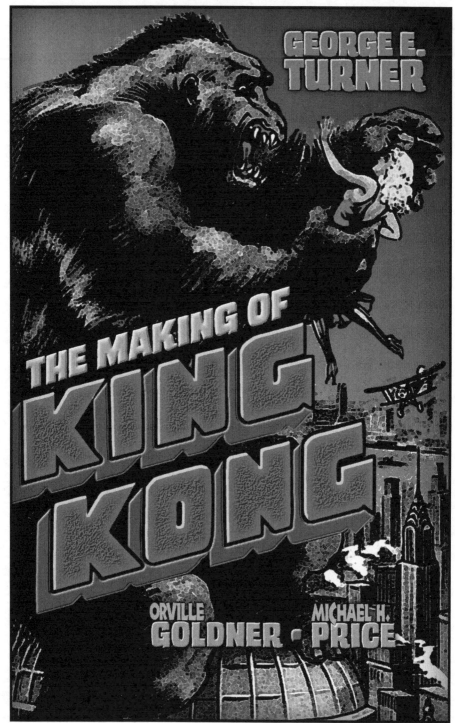

GEORGE E. TURNER

THE MAKING OF KING KONG

ORVILLE GOLDNER · MICHAEL H. PRICE

care to mention. His higher degrees, after all, were in commercial illustration (from the American Academy of Art and the Art Institute of Chicago), and before he reinvented his career in Hollywood during 1978–1980 he had spent 27 years as the editorial art director of a daily newspaper in Northwest Texas.

This is where we began working together during the 1960s, at the *Daily News & Globe-Times* of Amarillo. I had grown up reading George's exclusive-to-the-*Globe* cartoons and comic strips, and as a schoolkid I had recognized his distinctive style in a locally produced series of tourist-trap postal cards bearing the signature of one Tex Lowell (an example, with George's self–caricature, appears above). The bogus name was necessary to survival at a pinchpenny newspaper whose management frowned upon freelancing, and I found it astonishing that nobody in charge ever seemed to make the connection between the dignified newspaper art of George E. Turner and the roughhousing gag-card cartoons of Tex Lowell.

When George cashed in unexpectedly at 73, early in the summer of 1999, a bunch of us *American Cinematographer* cohorts got together for a memorial roast at Society of Cinematographers' clubhouse in Los Angeles. I brought up the topic of George's seminal work in the postal-card racket. Scarcely anybody out there in the Far West was aware of this early sideline. Indeed, although George had spent much of his time in Hollywood as a storyboarder (on Carl Reiner's *Dead Men Don't Wear Plaid* and Francis Ford Coppola's *One from the Heart*, amongst others) and a cartoon animator (on the *SHAZAM!* series, *etc.*, at Filmation), few within his film-scholarship circle knew George's cartooning interests to consist of much more than a habit of place-mat doodling while awaiting service in restaurants.

So I cited a particularly ripe example from George's Postcard Period. Most of those in attendance were amused; some found the joke undignified and pronounced it just as well that George had outgrown that scrofulous phase of his career before he could set foot in the

FOR SHANE, WITH ALL THE BEAST WISHES FROM SKULL ISLAND!

A G. Turner
autograph.

Motion Picture Capital of the Known World.

Except that George never cared to outgrow much of anything that interested him. As late as 1999, he was working on a new series of gag cartoons as innocently vulgar as anything from the postcard years.

He never outgrew much of anything, that is, with the patent exception of Amarillo, Texas, where a comfortable professional groove had gradually turned into a rut. Linwood Dunn, a Cinematographers honcho who had been a leading camera-effects artist with RKO–Radio Pictures during that big studio's Depression-into-wartime heyday, had met George during the 1960s while George was conducting research for *The Making of King Kong*. Having visited Amarillo during the book's preparation, Dunn had found George to be "withering on the vine," as Dunn put it. He began contriving a way to lure George to Los Angeles. The Amarillo newspapers' newer chain–ownership had proved oppressive, and George's new wife, newsroom editor Jean Wade—was on the hunt for an exit, anyhow. So George accepted a tentative gig with a Dunn-related outfit called Film Effects of Hollywood (the position was fuller of promise than of immediate stability) and parted ways with his native Texas.

The move threatened to play Holy Hades with George's and my

writing-and-drawing partnership, which had started in the newsroom and then branched into international publishing, with the first *Forgotten Horrors* book contracted to London's Tantivy Press and its Barnes & Co. affiliate in New Jersey, and a follow-up book in progress called *Human Monsters*. *The Making of King Kong*, which had provided me with an apprenticeship, had made a big splash in 1975, and during the next few years the book resurfaced in a Ballantine paperback edition and a translation into Japanese.

But George made a point of keeping the collaboration perking, and by the 1980s I had followed his lead out of Amarillo, landing in Fort Worth at a bigger newspaper, where I found all manner of opportunities to travel to Los Angeles on journalistic assignments. These always managed to transform themselves into movie-biz and cartooning excursions with George, and I seldom returned to Texas without a portfolio crammed with new research notes and comic-book roughs. George contributed many ideas to the *Prowler* comic-book series that Timothy Truman and John K. Snyder III and I developed at Eclipse Comics during the late 1980s, and George and I rough-sketched and rough-drafted any number of comics pages and film-scholarship essays that—as late as the here-and-now—are still finding their way into various projects.

Some saw print during George's lifetime, including a 20TH-anniversary edition of *Forgotten Horrors*, which appeared in print a few days before George's death. Others published posthumously, including our expanded version of *The Making of King Kong*. For a new *Prowler* escapade, I've worked a four-page Turner & Price story into the overall script.

I've continued the *Forgotten Horrors* books, meanwhile. The original edition had covered the independent horror-movie scene from 1929 into 1937. The recently published [as of 2007] *Forgotten Horrors Vol. 4* (in collaboration with the novelist and critic John Wooley) brings that coverage well into the post-WWII years, and *Forgotten Horrors Vol. 5* is stretching into the 1950s as a fertile period for low-budget horror and science-fiction movies.

Somewhere along the way, I figure a companion volume will be in order—might call it *Horrors beyond Forgetting*—that will document more fully George Turner's earlier efforts as an illustrator and hopeful moviemaker. I have restored his earliest published comic strips, from the 1950s, for a book called *The Ancient Southwest* (TCU Press), and I have compiled a selection of our earlier frontier-history pieces into an anthology called *The Cruel Plains* (Zone Press). Together, such artifacts serve to demonstrate that George Turner was ready for Hollywood long before Hollywood knew it was ready for him.

KING OF THE COW BONES

December 23, 2007: Texas' Fort Worth Fat Stock Show & Rodeo, a hardy and adaptive survivor of the 19TH Century, marks not only a continuation of the region's most emphatic reminder of its economic basis in agriculture. The occasion [as of 2008] also nails the 50TH anniversary of a major-league show-business breakthrough for the Fat Stock Show. Roy Rogers and Dale Evans arrived in Fort Worth in 1958 to serve as hosts for the first comprehensive network-television coverage of an authentically Western rodeo.

The presence of the King of the Cowboys and his Queen of the West in Fort Worth marked a showy progression from the name-brand entertainment presence that the Fat Stock Show's main-event rodeo had

begun developing during World War II, starting
with an appearance by Texas-bred Gene Autry
(Page No. 224). Both Autry and Rogers had
been on furlough from the movie industry at
the respective times of their visits to Fort
Worth—Autry, on military duty, and
Rogers, in hopeful preparation for a new
teevee series. Both had pursued a friendly
rivalry since the 1930s.

*Roy
Rogers.*

By the middle 1950s, too, both Autry
and Rogers had lapsed from competitive
movie stardom to more of an symbolic
presence within the Popular Culture, with
comic books and signature toys and appar-
el and schoolkids' lunchboxes to show for
their influence. Autry's Flying A Productions
had discontinued a long-running *Gene Autry
Show* during 1955-1956, and Rogers' independent company had wrapped the final episodes of *The
Roy Rogers Show* in 1957. A briefer *Roy Rogers & Dale Evans Show*
surfaced during the early 1960s. Such programs remained in syndi-
cated-teevee play well into the 1970s—as would the stars' numerous
big-screen movies, retooled for television.

The Rogers & Evans appearance in Fort Worth in 1958 distinguished an NBC extravaganza, a live-and-in-person rodeo presentation
with such featured stars as George "Gabby" Hayes, Rogers' longtime
comical sidekick, and the harmonizing Sons of the Pioneers, with whom
Rogers and Evans had appeared in numerous films and recordings. As
a result of their breakthrough at the Fort Worth Fat Stock Show—as if
Roy & Dale needed another breakthrough, at that stage of a successful
shared career—Rogers and Evans found themselves launched into a
cycle of stock-show appearances throughout the Southwest. They continued with such showcase performances well into the 1970s, often
headlining Amarillo, Texas' Tri–State Fair, among other such exposi-
tions. The frontier image suited Roy Rogers and Dale Evans, despite his
city-boy origins and her greater background as a pop-jazz singer.

• • •

Rogers (1911-1998) was born in Cincinnati. His christened name
was Leonard Slye. His father, Andy Slye, soon moved the family to
rural Ohio and gradually settled into the farming life.

"Some farm!" Rogers told me during the early 1970s on a tour-
date stop in Amarillo. "We never raised much more than rocks!

"And sooner or later, my Dad realized that he'd have to go back into
factory work if he intended to support a household. He left me at home
to handle the chores while he began commuting back to Cincinnati, back
to his old job at the U.S. Shoe Co., and spending weekends with us on
the farm at Duck Run. Yep, that's some name for a town! We lived so far
out in the sticks that they had to pump sunlight out to us.

"Not that I minded, y'know," Rogers grinned. "And my becoming
the man of the house, so to speak, at such an early age surely helped
my mother, Mattie, who was a powerhouse of a woman despite a lingering lameness from when she had contracted polio as a youngster.
Raised four kids, she did—me, and my sisters."

On weekends, Andy Slye would play host at household dances.
Leonard—Roy, that is—had learned to play the mandolin and the gui-

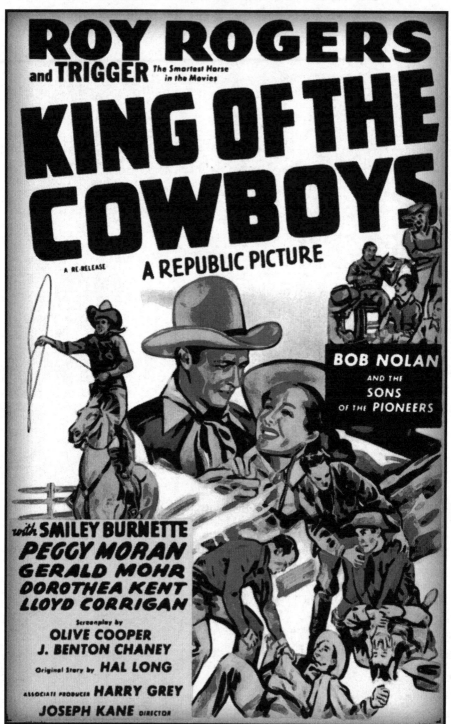

tar, and he became a skilled square-dance caller. He also became a yodeler; the eccentric singing style had come to him through cylinder phonograph records of Swiss- and Welsh-tradition yodeling.

"Y'know what 'yodel' means?" Rogers asked me during one visit backstage at Amarillo's Tri-State Fairgrounds Coliseum. "It means, 'to pronounce the word *yo*.' Now, the kind of yodeling that the American countrified singers do—that's kind of a far cry from the original purpose of yodeling, which was what the European mountain folk did to communicate amongst themselves over great distances.

"My Mom and I, now, we developed a system of yodeling that was a whole lot like Morse Code—she had a yodel to call me in for dinner, and I had another yodel to let the folks back at the farmhouse know that there was a thunderstorm a–comin', and I could modulate my yodeling to let my sisters know where I was. Many variations, there, and when I yodel in a song, nowadays, it always takes me back to my childhood."

Rogers left high school about midway toward graduation and joined his father on the shoe-assembly line at Cincinnati. Older sister Mary Slye had married by now and moved to the Los Angeles area. On a visit to her new home, the Slyes decided to quit Ohio for California.

"Man, it felt just like John Steinbeck—*The Grapes of Wrath*, y'know what I mean?" said Rogers. "The Depression had hit California, 'land of plenty'—*ha!*—as hard as it had socked the rest of the country, and by 1930-1931 I was drivin' a gravel truck, pickin' peaches in the Tulare Farm Belt—anything to keep body and soul, and the family, together."

A radio station at Inglewood, Calif., sent out a call for amateur musicians. The Slye family had a candidate.

"Mary, now, she made me a cowboy-style shirt to wear for the occasion," said Rogers. "And I—well, I was so shy, apart from parlor-singin', that I'd never've tried a radio appearance without her pressuring me—I just got up there and blurted out some tunes and some yodeling, just as if I knew what I was doin'."

The guest-shot generated an invitation during the summer of 1931 to join a band called the Rocky Mountaineers. This connection led to alliances with such vocalists as Bob Nolan and Tim Spencer—laying groundwork, in the process, for the eventual development of the Sons of the Pioneers. Roy married a radio-show fan, Arline Wilkins, in 1936 while establishing a sturdier basis in show business. Rogers had re-aligned himself with Tim Spencer and Bob Nolan as a powerhouse act known as the Pioneer Trio. Their harmonic yodeling on a song called "'Way Out There" cinched a distinctive style, defining the sound that would come to characterize not only the Sons of the Pioneers but also commercialized Western music as a class.

"It was our radio host, Harry Hall, who gave us our lasting identity," Rogers told me. "One day, Harry hauled off and declared that we all looked too young to be pioneers, so reckon how come we didn't just call ourselves the Sons of the Pioneers?" The addition of the jazz-influenced fiddler Hugh Farr, followed by his guitarist brother Karl Farr, sealed the ensemble sound. A progressive new broadcast-syndication company, Jerry King's Standard Radio, helped to break the band out of California toward nationwide recognition.

Radio, in turn, brought the players to the attention of Hollywood. While singing in Dallas during the Texas Centennial of 1936, the Sons of the Pioneers appeared in an on-location Gene Autry movie called *The Big Show*. Autry's success in Hollywood since 1935's *The Phantom Empire* had prompted other studios to seek cowboy crooners. A dispute between Autry and Republic Pictures Corp. provoked the company to begin scouting for some likely replacement. Roy Rogers—now billing himself as Len Slye—heard about the opportunity and barged in on Republic's casting office without an appointment. In 1937, Republic Pictures signed him, first, under the name of Dick Weston and, then, as Roy Rogers. Republic and Autry resolved their conflict, and by 1938 the small but ambitious studio had two big-time singing-cowhand stars under contract.

The career-making movie for Rogers was *Under Western Stars* (1938), which also introduced Rogers to his famous Palomino, Trigger. Savvy management strategies established Rogers as a trademark beyond the movies-and-music recognition. Republic announced him as Hollywood royalty with 1943's *King of the Cowboys*—an answer to 1937's Autry–starrer, *Public Cowboy No. 1*.

Roy Rogers loved a good corny joke, often at the expense of his popular image. During the first of several interviews he and I conducted, he told me about a new brand of dog food that he was developing, manufactured from bone meal: "Reckon that'll make me the 'King of the Cow-Bones,'" he said. Just woofing, of course.

His pictures tend to be just as lighthearted in tone, but Rogers also appreciated the Western Gothic style of mystery and suspense and indulged this taste for scary business with such films as 1940's *The Ranger and the Lady* (with a murderous giant at large) and 1948's *Eyes of Texas* (with a pack of predatory wolf–dogs on the loose). Even *King of the Cowboys* hinges upon a menacing presence—a mad bomber (played by Gerald Mohr) in the service of the Third Reich.

"I enjoy a good scare as much as the next guy," Rogers told me. "And there's no rule that says you can't have your harmonies and yodelin' and your smoochin' on your leading lady in the same picture where there's a monster on the loose. I reckon there must have been plenty of monsters on the loose, back in the frontier days. Most of 'em were thieves and murderers who, really, must have seemed about as normal as the guy next door—but there must have been some subhuman brutes around, too.

"'Course, now, Republic wanted me to deliver a certain quota of pictures that'd play things mostly light and adventurous, with lots of singin' and smoochin' and comedy relief, along with the shootin' and fistfightin'. But once in a while, they'd let me make somethin' *really* dark. There was this one I did in the late 1940s called *Eyes of Texas*, which had this mean ol' crooked lawyer–woman [played by the usually grandmotherly Nana Bryant] with a pack of trained-killer dogs.

"And in 1940, we did a kind of a *Most Dangerous Game* type of thing—*The Ranger and the Lady*, except I reckon we should have called it *The Ranger and the Lady and the Monster*. Because we even had Noble Johnson in it, playing the kind of brute he had played in the real *Most Dangerous Game* [1932]—only scarier, I like to think." (A re–edit for television of *The Ranger and the Lady* minimizes Noble Johnson's formidable presence; in its 1940 cut, the film is a *bona fide Forgotten Horror*.)

"And then there was *King of the Cowboys*—*whew!*—some way to treat a King, if that's what I was s'posed to be," Rogers continued. "Man, I took some heavy-duty bullyraggin' and beatin's in that one, tryin' to fight back against those wartime home-front bad guys!"

Rogers' teaming with Texan Dale Evans (*née* Frances Octavia Smith; 1912–2001) occurred with 1944's *The Cowboy and the Señorita*. She completed an extended family for Rogers' Hollywood image—Dale,

Trigger, the Sons of the Pioneers and ornery sidekick Gabby Hayes.

The death of Arline Rogers in 1946 left Roy a widower with three children. He and Dale Evans married in 1947—a logical extension of their popular image. The family grew considerably.

Republic Pictures carried on with the Rogers-starring films until 1951, ending the association (as Rogers explained it) "on account of, I was keener on moving into television, and television at the time was considered a threat to the movie industry." Rogers responded by developing his own teevee show and signing with big-time Paramount Pictures for a co–starring turn with Bob Hope in 1952's *Son of Paleface*.

Later ventures included the Roy Rogers Family Restaurant chain and a Roy Rogers Museum (since moved from California to Branson, Missouri). The museum, in turn, helped to inspire the development of the Gene Autry Museum in Los Angeles. Both stars insisted upon celebrating historical Western heritage and the Hollywood-cowboy traditions.

"I'm just an old boy who doesn't really change all that much over the long haul," Rogers told me. "I've had good times during my bad times, and bad times during my good times, and somehow it all seems to even out so that the good times tend to outweigh the bad.

"It helps to have a loyal audience, and that's what Fort Worth showed to me and Dale and our bunch—a loyal audience—at a time when I felt I was gettin' a little too old to play cowboy any longer, but too fond of the music and the Cowboy Way to just hang it all up.

"In many ways," said Roy Rogers, "I've owed this whole later phase of my career to the Fort Worth Fat Stock Show, which Dale and I enjoyed every bit as much as the Sons of the Pioneers and I had enjoyed playing Dallas' State Fair, 'way back in 1936. Both those appearances were turning–points."

BAMBOOZLED BY BAT MASTERSON

December 30, 2007: Every time I backtrack to some 20TH Century comic book or movie or teevee show that purports to portray Bat Masterson, I come away with a greater appreciation of the historical model. Granted that some of Masterson's Real World exploits and con–games aren't quite the stuff of sensationalized melodrama, I'll take the genuine article for Puckish wit and adaptability to strange environments.

Back in the not-so-long-ago 1960s, the Standard Oil Company unearthed a hidden mess when it undertook to lease a great deal of property around the townsite of Old Mobeetie, in Texas' Northward Panhandle region. The transactions proved abnormally complicated because, as an executive from Standard's Oklahoma City office complained: "It cost us a fortune to get those land titles straightened out because of all those crooked survey lines."

One of the old-time landowners said the Standard Oil bigwigs might be surprised to learn who had been responsible for all that erratic surveying. The surveyor in question was Bat Masterson, one of many colorful and controversial denizens of Mobeetie's earliest days.

William Barclay Masterson was born in Illinois in 1856 and moved to Kansas as a youngster. The Plains tribes were resisting the decimation of the bison herds by the settlers when Masterson joined a band of buffalo-hide predators. A fun-loving kid who never quite grew up despite constant pressures to do so, Masterson became a hero at age 18 when he helped to hold off a Kiowa–Comanche raid at the Battle of Adobe Walls in Hutchinson County.

Now, buffalo hunters were the most profane, belligerent, and evil-

smelling men in the West. Masterson, who preferred the citified life, decided to look for a new career. When he rode into Sweetwater City, which had been established on the site of an abandoned hide-hunting camp in Wheeler County, he found the town in need of a surveyor. So Masterson declared himself a civil engineer and was assigned a surveying job for which he was eminently unqualified. The town became known as Mobeetie in 1879; the term is a tribal equivalent of *Sweetwater*, which had already been claimed as the name of another Northwest Texas town.

Masterson began keeping company with an 18-year-old saloon dancer named Molly Brennan. Thus did Masterson arouse the ire of the entertainer's former consort, Melvin A. King, a disgraced soldier who had been stationed at nearby Ft. Elliott. A known deserter who had proved too elusive and tough for the military to recapture or drive away, King served the town as its resident bully—a Bluto to Masterson's Popeye, with Molly Brennan as an ultimately tragic Olive Oyl.

Masterson and King tangled in Mobeetie's Lady Gay Saloon, and after some preliminary fisticuffs King pulled a hunting knife. Masterson drew his six–shooter and persuaded King to crawl from the saloon into the street. King returned after the saloon had closed. Finding Masterson and Molly Brennan enjoying an after-hours drink, King burst in on them, brandishing a pistol and cursing. He fired at Masterson, but Molly leapt between the men and took the lethal impact. The bullet traveled on to inflict upon Masterson a permanent limp. Masterson returned fire just before he lost consciousness, putting a decisive end to King's thuggish career.

The wound caused Masterson to begin carrying the walking–stick that would become his trademark. Masterson could not be certain whether King's demise was the result of marksmanship or accident. In either case, the killing in wild-and-woolly Mobeetie of a dangerous renegade, by a youthful hero of Adobe Walls, became a *cause célébre* throughout the frontier and formed the basis of a classic Western legend. The legend and the man, as usual, bear but slight similarities to one another.

Because in a brawl he wielded his cane with devastating efficiency, Masterson became known as "Bat." Because, after leaving Mobeetie, he became a peace officer in the notorious trail town of Dodge City, Kansas, it became natural to think of him as a gunslinger in the tradition of his predecessor, Wild Bill Hickok. The legend held that Masterson had killed 30 desperadoes—if not more.

Masterson preferred the peaceable pursuits of gambling, women, liquor, and practical jokes. There was little gunplay in Dodge City during Masterson's regime because Masterson enforced Hickok's established ban against firearms. Masterson was part–owner of the fabled Long Branch Saloon, and he numbered among his friends such widely feared tough eggs as the Earp Bros., Doc Holliday, Luke Short and Charlie Bassett. Masterson's political fortunes, however, were dependent upon those of Mayor Dog Kelley. When Kelley became involved in a noisy scandal involving a slaying at his home, Masterson left Dodge and went to Tombstone, Arizona, with the Earps.

Masterson drifted from one town to another, working as a rule in gambling halls and relishing the irony of his legend as a bloodthirsty killer. He developed friendships on both sides of the law. One friend on the better side of the law was Theodore Roosevelt, who persuaded Masterson to accept appointment as a deputy marshal in New York, beginning in 1902. In New York, Masterson became such a devotée of boxing and baseball that he resigned his lawman's commission to become a sportswriter for the *Morning Telegraph*. He found himself as comfortably at home on Broadway as he had been in Mobeetie or Dodge or Tombstone, and he enjoyed the company of Damon Runyon and Louella Parsons as much as he had relished life among the Earp clan.

On random occasions, Masterson would file 30 notches onto the handle of an old Colt .45 and sell the weapon to a dealer in antiques. No telling how many such counterfeits remain in the hands of collectors.

On the evening of October 25, 1921, Masterson was seated at his typewriter when he collapsed in death. He had just written this line: "Everybody gets about the same amount of ice in his lifetime. The rich get theirs in summer time, and the poor in winter." Masterson had come a long way for a fun-loving kid who never tired of a joke.

Masterson's New York friends spoke long and late of the frontiersman's boasts about the bluff that had landed him a civil engineering job, 'way out on the desolate Plains. The Standard Oil Company's discovery of the Mobeetie surveys' eccentric nature doubtless would have appealed to Masterson's sense of humor, had he been able to foresee the long-term outcome of his feat of fraudulent engineering.

A DEEPER ORIGIN OF THE ASIAN HORROR-FILM PHENOMENON

January 6, 2008: Blame it on Bud Pollard, for want of a more readily identifiable scapegoat: Hollywood's prevailing obsession with remaking scary movies from Japan seems to have caught fire with Hideo Nakata's *Ringu* (1998), which led to Gore Verbinski's *The Ring* in 2002, with sequels and imitations from either side of the planet.

Old-time hack filmmaker and Directors Guild co–founder Pollard (1886–1952) helped to seed the movement 'way back during 1932–1933, though, when a domestically unreleasable flop of his called *The Horror*—involving an Eastern curse placed upon a Western thief—became a well-received attraction when exported to Japan.

Ignored by the Depression Era American critics and seldom shown in the U.S., *The Horror* garnered thoughtful, if dumbfounded, coverage in its day from Japan's influential *Kinema Junpo* magazine. As translated from the archaic prewar Japanese grammar and syntax, the *Kinema Junpo* review finds the critic–of–record as fascinated with the rambling, surrealistic presentation as he appears flabbergasted by the film's refusal to follow a coherent narrative arc.

Leslie T. King—who had played the Mad Hatter in Pollard's similarly odd 1931 *Alice in Wonderland*—serves *The Horror* as a traveler who steals a sacred idol, only to find himself besieged by weird apparitions and a disfiguring transformation. Pollard re–edited *The Horror* during the 1940s to convey a temperance lecture, changing the title to *John the Drunkard* and explaining the ordeal as a nightmare brought on by an alcoholic stupor. Where *The Horror* had gone largely unreleased in America as a theatrical attraction, its preachy condensation played long and widely in church-and-school bookings.

But as a commercial release in Japan, Pollard's *The Horror* helped over the long term to inspire the dreamlike, often incomprehensible, style that distinguishes Japan's present-day contributions to the genre. Seen today in surviving footage at the Library of Congress, *The Horror* looks like nothing so much as a genetic template for modern-day Asian horror cinema.

This preamble points toward Eric Valette's *One Missed Call*, latest [as of 2008] in a string of U.S. remakes of Japanese hair–raisers. Any

sharper appreciation of some Americanized version requires a familiarity with the original. The source–film in this case is Takashi Miike's *Chakushin Ari* (2003); it, and various spinoffs, can be found DVD editions. There is a resemblance to *Ringu*, or *The Ring*; to Japan's similarly conceived *Ju–On* series of recent years, known in America as *The Grudge*; and to the South Korean *Phone* (2002).

One Missed Call stars Shannyn Sossamon as Beth Raymond, a cellphone user (and who isn't?), who has good reason to associate some disturbing voice-mail messages with the close-together deaths of two friends. These missed calls"appear to have been made from the near future, foretelling disaster. Though dismissed as a crank when she attempts to report this impossible information to the police, Beth finds a sympathetic listener in a detective named Jack Andrews (Edward Burns), who has lost a sister under similar circumstances. Drawn inexorably into the mystery, the characters appear to be approaching a solution—when Beth's telephone begins to register that same ominous signal: *One Missed Call.*

Apart from the self-evident truth that a telephone is not all that creepy an implement, *One Missed Call* in either version does a fair job of generating the shivers. The absorbed viewer might gain a richer context for watching this one by backtracking to catch 1939's *The Story of Alexander Graham Bell*. More sinister uses of Mr. Bell's invention can be found in 1930's *The Laurel–Hardy Murder Case* and 1932's *The Thirteenth Guest.*

The emotional depth, crucial to a tale of suspense, is either half–full or half–empty in the Hollywood version. Shannyn Sossamon brings little dramatic conviction but a great deal of vain self–consciousness to her role. Edward Burns, however, is very good as the lawman with a personal stake in the case. French director Valette seems more concerned, at any rate, with driving the audience to the edge than with achieving any sense of identification with the characters beyond their desperate situation.

Original-version director Miike, best known for an unnerving picture called *Audition* (2000), deals more ambitiously with the story of *One Missed Call.* Miike places a greater emphasis upon the emotional instability of the leading character (played by Kou Shibasaki), and he makes somewhat more of the *Ring*-like notion that some vengeful ghost is responsible for all those threatening 'phone calls. Miike plays the yarn up to a point as a conventional psychological thriller—then launches into a bolder array of Shock Value.

And *The Horror*'s Bud Pollard? More about that shabby Grey Eminence in *Forgotten Horrors: The Original Volume.*

CLOVERFIELD: BIG–MONSTER PICTURE, OR 9–11 ALLEGORY?

January 13, 2008: Ringed with popular anticipation in view of its producer's involvement with the hit teleseries *Lost*, director Matt Reeves' Cloverfield proves to be something more than the moviegoing customers might have expected. The film is an American *Godzilla*, and I don't mean the bloated Hollywood *Godzilla* of 1998. A larger-than-life disaster film, Cloverfield addresses the terrorist attacks of September 11, 2001, in much the same way that Inoshiro Honda's *Gojira*, or *Godzilla*, of 1954, helped Japan to come belatedly to terms with the bombings in 1945 of Hiroshima and Nagasaki.

And yes, I know: Giant-monster movies are dime-a-dozen fare, and

so what do we need with another one? We don't so much need another one, as we need somebody capable of doing one right—the way Fritz Lang did with *Siegfried* in 1924, or Honda with the original *Godzilla*. *Cloverfield* makes the cut, okay.

Such impossible menaces, after all, have served since ancient times to literalize humanity's fears of threatening forces beyond reasonable control, from the Tiger Demon mythology of primeval Siam through the Germanic and British legends of *Siegfried* and *Beowulf*. (Robert Zemeckis' 2007 version of *Beowulf* is more a matter of digital-effects overkill than of mythological resonance.)

Never mind that the American movie-import market had treated the 1954 *Godzilla* as merely another creature-feature extravaganza, drive-in escapism with trivialized English-language insert–footage and enough re–editing to diminish the myth-making allegory. In its authentic Japanese cut, *Godzilla* is a national epic on a par with Akira Kurosawa's *The Seven Samurai*—same year, same studio. It took a while for America to catch on: The fire-breathing creature known as Godzilla is the A–Bomb, re–imagined in mythological terms.

Yes, and it takes time for the Popular Culture to get a grip on a Real World disaster. Hollywood dealt at first with the 9/11 destruction of New York's World Trade Center by dodging the issue, then gradually addressing the loss in such lifelike dramas as Spike Lee's *25TH Hour* (2002), whose allusions to Ground Zero pointed toward an explicit depiction of the crisis in Oliver Stone's *World Trade Center* (2006). There have been other such striking examples—but you get the idea.

Producer J.J. Abrams has shaped *Cloverfield* as a New York-under-siege story that catches its characters as thoroughly off–guard as the 9/11 attacks caught civilization–at–large. Its major-studio distribution deal aside, *Cloverfield* radiates the spontaneous, searching attitude one expects from an independent production. The swath of destruction is immense, but the viewpoint feels intimately personalized. The counterpart to the collapse of the World Trade Center is a combination of generalized devastation with a singularly unpleasant fate for a still more hallowed landmark—the Statue of Liberty.

An ensemble cast of little-known players, including *Black Donnellys* supporting actor Michael Stahl–David and *The Class'* Lizzy Caplan, likewise enhances the indie-movie texture. Director Reeves, though a busy television-series talent in recent years, remains best known as a feature-filmmaker for 1996's *The Pallbearer*, an ordinary-people drama in the debt of Mike Nichols' career-defining film of 1967, *The Graduate*.

Taking a cue from such tales-of-terror enchmarks as Robert Bloch's 1951 short story, "Notebook Found in a Deserted House," and Daniel Myrick and Eduardo Sánchez' *The Blair Witch Project* (1999), *Cloverfield* hangs upon the discovery of an abandoned video camera in the wake of a catastrophe. The camera's operator appears to have been shooting a festive private occasion—only to be distracted by a breaking-news report involving a capsized ship.

A gigantic creature proves responsible. The situation proves urgent in short order as the attack moves inland. With the understanding that there is not much dramatic impact to be derived from a force of nature as large as a skyscraper and as impersonally menacing as a hurricane, Reeves and screenwriter Drew Goddard concentrate upon fearful anticipation and individual misadventures more so than upon the source of the threat. On a ghastlier near-human scale, the creature appears to be afflicted with parasites that serve to compound the terrors.

Cinematographer Michael Bonvillain renders persuasive the illusion of watching a video-camera document. Viewers predisposed to motion sickness may find the darting, frenzied images *too* convincing. Few amateur videographers, however, could manage such consistently smart visual-narrative compositions. Well-placed flashbacks ground the situation in a plausible reality: The better such movies aren't actually about the cause of all that extravagant desperation—they're about the human response, and about the combined fragility and resourcefulness that define the species.

JOE PALOOKA AS A WEIRD–MENACE VEHICLE

January 20, 2008: One connection leads to another and then another, whether via the proverbial Six Degrees of Separation or by means of random-chance Free Association. Which explains how the moviemaking Coen Bros., Joel and Ethan, and Ham Fisher's strange trailblazer of a comic strip, *Joe Palooka*, come to be mentioned in a single sentence. The Coens' current [as of 2008] motion picture, *No Country for Old Men*, took Best Picture honors the other day in a vote amongst members of my Southwestern branch of the National Society of Film Critix. A re–screening seemed in order, particularly because the film—an unnerving combination of crime melodrama with Existential Quandary—contains a bizarre murder gimmick that had triggered a vague memory of some other movie from 'Way the Hell Back When. I figured that a fresh look might complete the connection between the lethal device in *No Country for Old Men* and whatever other picture I was recalling.

And sure enough: The compressed-air cattle-slaughtering implement that Javier Bardem wields in *No Country* proves akin in that respect to Charles Lamont's *A Shot in the Dark*—a fairly conventional whodunit from 1935, rendered weird by the use of industrial machinery in lieu of conventional weaponry. George E. Turner and I had devoted a chapter to *A Shot in the Dark* in our first volume of the Forgotten Horrors movie-history library, figuring that although murder *per se* might or might not render a film horrific, murder by unconventional means is a qualifier.

That slight recollection, in turn, pointed toward a batch of other weird-gizmo murder pictures, leading at length to 1947's *Joe Palooka in the Knockout*, part of a series of movies spun off the Fischer strip. When odder random associations are made, the *Forgotten Horrors* franchise will make 'em.

Did I say "unconventional means"—? Try murder by frozen-liquid missile, as in 1936's *A Face in the Fog*. Or murder by toxic fumes, from 1935's *Rip Roaring Riley*, amongst others. Or murder by poison-saturated sweat-rag, as seen in 1936's *Prison Shadows*. All of which lead toward *Joe Palooka in the Knockout*, which posits the notion of a prize-fight killing via a tainted mouth–protector. That the implement of death is a trusted tool of the pugilist's trade, lends a black irony beyond the forcibly wholesome insipidity of Fischer's original comics yarns.

This third of Monogram Pictures' 10 *Palooka*s stars dependable Leon Errol, one of Old Hollywood's great grouches and a favorite foil of W.C. Fields, as manager Knobby Walsh; and Joe Kirkwood, JR., as heroic pug Joe Palooka. Things start looking grim for Joe when opponent Jackie Mathews (Tom Garland) drops dead, apparently from a blow landed by Joe. In fact, Mathews had been overdosed with a sneak drugging that was supposed merely to have left him zonked out.

Mathews' manager, Max Steele (Whitford Kane), had played along with the scam under threat of blackmail, but now he is furious to learn that things have turned lethal.

Joe Palooka swears off fighting (a foreshadowing of John Wayne's withdrawal from the sport in John Ford's 1952 film *The Quiet Man*) and drifts about aimlessly—until an encounter with Mathews' fiancée (Trudy Marshall) leaves him convinced that Mathews had met with foul play. Another bearer of clues turns up defunct, and finally Joe finds himself marked for murder. Gambler John Mitchell (Marc Lawrence) and henchman Pusher Moore (Danny Morton) are caught tampering with Joe's gum-protector plate; they leave a locker-room attendant (Benny Baker) beaten nearly to death. Steele, fed up with it all, guns down Mitchell and Moore. Ringleader Howard Abbott (Morris Carnovsky) remains at large until confronted by the bereaved fiancée, who intends to shoot him. She is spared the trouble by Abbott's dog, whose ill-timed boisterous entrance causes the killer to shoot himself. Joe re–enters the ring and slugs his way to a championship.

Joe Palooka had come to the screen in 1934 as *Palooka*, a respectable one-punch job from the coalition of little Reliance Pictures and big United Artists Corp., starring Jimmy Durante as Knobby Walsh and mild-mannered Stuart Erwin as the sweet-natured rube prizefighter Joe. *Palooka* is remembered fondly today, when remembered at all, as a showcase for Durante's signature song, "Inka Dinka Doo."

The Monogram series ran from 1946 into 1951. In addition to the viciousness at large in *Knockout*, the films would touch on such harrowing fare as sniper attacks (1946's *Joe Palooka, Champ*); kidnapping and child exploitation (1948's *Joe Palooka in Winner Take All*); inflicted blindness (1948's *Joe Palooka in Fighting Mad*); and druggings and more druggings (1949's *Joe Palooka in the Big Fight* and 1950's *Joe Palooka in the Squared Circle*). In 1954, the Monogram series' Joe Kirkwood, JR., returned to the ring as producer–star of a low-rent television series called *The Joe Palooka Story*.

The character's origins and back–story ran sufficiently deeper and darker as to suggest a scenario for some Coen Bros. film: The Hack cartoonist Ham Fisher had launched *Joe Palooka* in 1928 as a sentimentalized romance-adventure piece for the McNaught Syndicate, crudely drawn (Fischer was more a conceptual artist and pitch–man than an accomplished illustrator) and written for full measure of corn—except for a Depression Era stretch when a young Al Capp, as Fischer's anonymous assistant, took gradual anonymous charge with more intelligent results.

Having raised *Palooka* to levels of sardonic wit beyond Fischer's grasp, Capp jumped ship and launched his own comic strip, the vividly satirical *Li'l Abner*, in 1934.

Prevailing antagonisms kept Fischer and Capp at odds for years—a common scenario in which a supposed apprentice out–performs an oppressive boss. The *Joe Palooka* comic strip continued apace as a happy-sappy popular favorite, spawning movies and licensed toys and other such cultural detritus.

(*Li'l Abner* found itself adapted sporadically to film during its earlier years—a 1940 grotesquerie that captured only the superficial attributes of Capp's brilliance, followed by a disappointing run of animated cartoons. The 1950s would see the Gene DePaul-Johnny Mercer musical Li'l Abner become a smash on Broadway, followed by a splendidly bombastic movie version. See also: Page No. 215.)

The backstage hostilities culminated in Fischer's attempt to drum Capp out of the cartooning profession by calling their colleagues' attention to (forged) examples of camouflaged obscenities in *Li'l Abner*. His treachery having backfired, Fischer dealt with the loss–of–face by committing suicide in 1955.

Joe Palooka continued dispensing its reactionary wholesomeness well beyond Fischer's lifetime, finally fading away in 1984. Capp, who nursed a grudge as relentlessly as Fischer but proved too honorable to resort to ambush defamation, had told his side of the story in a bitterly hilarious essay called "I Remember Monster," never once mentioning his mentor–turned–tormentor by name. (The title, "I Remember Monster," is Capp's sarcastic evocation of John Van Druten's famous family-saga play, *I Remember Mama*, filmed in 1948. Which might suggest a Free Association exercise for another day.)

INGAGI: GORILLAS IN OUR MIDST

January 27, 2008: If a long-mislaid but vividly documented Depression Era motion picture called *Ingagi* should ever re–surface—in the manner that such lost-and-found titles as the 1931 Spanish-language *Dracula* or the 1912 *Richard III* have cropped up, in unexpected, out-of-the-way locations—its rediscovery alone would justify a monumental curatorial celebration and an overpriced DVD edition. [*Since this installment's first appearance, a censored print of 1930's* Ingagi *has surfaced, hiding in plain sight in the U.C.L.A. Film Archive.*]

The film probably does not deserve as much, except perhaps on grounds of sheer obscurity and an ironically monumental influence. Never having viewed the picture intact, I am of course ill prepared to dismiss *Ingagi* as an unwatchable trifle. But primary-source screening notes from my late mentor, the film archivist and historian George E.

Turner, describe a muddled combination of silent-screen expeditionary footage with staged bogus-safari scenes.

Ingagi is hardly the first of its kind, but it appears to have established a precedent for representing an imaginary journey into unexplored regions as an authentic record of a scientific expedition. As such, it collected a reported $4 million in box-office returns—back in the day when a buck was still a dollar—and inspired numerous imitations.

The cryptic title (*Ingagi* = *gorilla*) became a household word: Such comedy acts as the Three Stooges and Hal Roach's *Our Gang* ensemble devoted throwaway gags to *Ingagi*, and as late as 1939–1940 the actor-turned-filmmaker Spencer Williams, JR., invoked the term with an otherwise unrelated picture called *Son of Ingagi*. During a visit at Dallas in 1993, comic-book pioneer Julius Schwartz cited the original *Ingagi* and a 1937 knockoff called *Forbidden Adventure in Angkor* as inspirations for the recurring "Gorilla City" subplot that distinguishes DC Comics' *The Flash* funnybooks of the 1960s.

Ingagi, when pronounced if uttered at all, is pronounced as "in–*GAD*–ji," although some speak it more like "in–*GAGGY*." The film is a gag, all right—a smirking hoax that appears to have been taken altogether too seriously by organizations as oddly matched as the American Society of Mammalologists and the Ku Klux Klan.

The scenario concerns an expedition into Africa to investigate legends of a gorilla-worship tribe. The credits state that *Ingagi* was written by Adam Hull Shirk, a melodramatic playwright whose filmography also includes such ape-escape escapades as 1934's *House of Mystery* and 1940's *The Ape*, but the presentation suggests authenticity. Having outlasted various perils of the wilds, the explorers find the colony and witness the abduction of a woman by an ape. The safari moves along to find a tribe of gorillas and human females. The gorillas attack, and the explorers kill a 600-pound specimen. One of the women mourns the death of what appears to have been her mate. The scientists (term used advisedly) return home with evidence of incredible discoveries.

The marketing campaign appealed more directly to the science of mass-appeal sensationalism: "HALF–APE HALF–HUMAN—WILD WOMEN … QUEER HALF–BREED CHILD…," along with such claims as "AMAZING DISCOVERIES OF JUNGLE LIFE! THE SCIENTIFIC MARVEL OF THE AGE!" Such ballyhoo was the stock–in–trade of studio chief Nathan "Nat" Spitzer, an old-time carnival impresario.

Intercut with the genuine safari footage (pirated from Lady Grace Mackenzie's expeditions of the 1910s) are fictional episodes filmed in California. George Turner's notes from the 1940s describe a purportedly venomous reptile as a tortoise, with laminated wings and the armor of a scaled anteater. Various creatures and botanical specimens from the Americas are seen in the mock-African setting.

Members of a preview audience in Los Angeles in 1930 recognized *Ingagi*'s abducted tribeswoman as a bit player well known at Central Casting. The principal gorilla is played by Charles Gemora (1903–1961), whose string of ape–impersonations in 1930 also included *The Unholy Three* at MGM Pictures, an *Our Gang* short called "Bear Shooters" at Roach Studios, and *The Gorilla* at First National Pictures.

A combination of emphatic advertising and widespread controversy made *Ingagi* a tremendous commercial success. *Screenland*, a show-business tradepaper, railed: "Not only is [*Ingagi*] the greatest movie hoax …, but the most offensive." Dr. William C. Gregory, of the American Museum of Natural History, announced that the Society of

Mammalologists "expresses its utter disapproval." The American Nature Association characterized the film as "an imposition on the public, a blot on the moving-picture industry, and a serious threat to the usefulness of moving pictures" but in the same breath acknowledged the film to be "good entertainment."

Various regional boards of censors condemned and sometimes banned the film. The family of Lady Grace Mackenzie, whose safaris had yielded much of the authentic imagery, filed suit against Nat Spitzer's Congo Pictures, LTD., and won a $150,000 plagiarism judgment. Spitzer persisted with a nationwide release on March 15, 1931, overcoming even a New York censors' ban on grounds of "nature faking." A profitable run followed during the fall at NYC's Central Theatre.

Seldom has so much ruckus been raised over so little. Charles Gemora, in a late-in-life interview with George Turner, said he had staged the gorilla-enclave scenes for $5,000 and sold the filmed results to Spitzer for $7,000. The moneymaking accomplishments of *Ingagi*, in turn, inspired such imitations as *Forbidden Adventure in Angkor* and *Love Life of a Gorilla*, both from 1937.

By 1937, of course, the machinery of institutionalized censorship had changed appreciably, what with a 1934 takeover by the Roman Catholic Church's Legion of Decency of the Motion Picture Producers & Distributors Association and its affiliated Production Code Administration.

The producers of *Forbidden Adventure in Angkor*, which transplants the apes-and-women scenario to Southeast Asia, maneuvered around the Production Code by showing chief censor Joseph I. Breen a tamed version while putting a different cut into distribution. (A memorandum from Breen to *Angkor*'s Dwain Esper forbids "dialogue which in any way brings up the idea of possible sexual intimacy between women and monkeys." Breen appears to have been incapable of telling a mobilized gorilla suit apart from a monkey—although it bears noting that *Angkor*'s own narration neglects to distinguish between the great apes and the lesser primates.)

I had mentioned the odd kinship between *Ingagi* ET SEQ. and the "Gorilla City" element of the *Flash* comic books. Said Julius Schwartz: "We just took out the women-love-apes business and gave the gorillas a higher intelligence. If the Comics Code Authority had known where we were coming from with that idea, we've never have gotten away with it!"

• • •

One persistent account suggests that *Ingagi* had been misappropriated, well into the last century, as a tool of indoctrination by the Ku Klux Klan, whose bigoted leaders would have relished the outlandish depiction of African tribal life. This notion would seem consistent with the Klan's known usage of D.W. Griffith's race-baiting *The Birth of a Nation*, from 1915, for comparable purposes. So corrupt a use, however, cannot have been part of the strategy of *Ingagi*'s producers, who were more interested in luring a thrill-hungry mass audience than with advancing any crackpot social-political agendas.

The persistence of *Ingagi* as an influential film, in any event, proved such that found-object tribal footage, with or without gorillas, was still finding its way into new pseudo-documentary pictures beyond the midcentury mark. In 1959, a theater-manager uncle of mine named Grady L. Wilson booked a movie of this tantalizing nature called *The Mating Urge* into one of his classier downtown venues in Amarillo, Texas. A police raid followed, scandalizing our family with its on-the-spot news coverage while provoking heavy-duty box-office traffic from customers who figured they'd better hurry up and catch this attraction before the print could be confiscated. The booking was one of those limited-run roadshow engagements—outside the conventional channels of film distribution. By the time the case, such as it was, could be formally dismissed in Misdemeanor Court, the film had run its intended course at a profit.

Every time I would attempt to bring up this topic with my Uncle Grady, thereafter, he would laugh it off and change the subject. By the time of his death in 1968, the mystery of that notorious showing had compounded itself immeasurably. Then during the 1980s, George Turner and I chanced to find a press kit for *The Mating Urge* at a movie-memorabilia shop in Santa Monica. This reminded, I sought out Amarillo's since-retired chief of police, Wiley Alexander, and asked whether he might remember anything about his vice-squad raid on *The Mating Urge* at my uncle's State Theatre.

Alexander grinned, as if caught off-guard by the ghost of a memory. Then he burst out in a horselaugh: "Well, y'know, yo' uncle and I—we were old-time pals, and he was a great prankster.

"So he had this chancy ol' picture comin' in. And a pretty tame li'l' ol' thing, it was, too, about courtship rituals in the Third World. Had a good lurid title but not much in the way of an advertising budget.

"And so ol' Grady and I, now, we figured it out that if that picture could get itself raided, so to speak, then it'd stand a better chance of makin' some money," said Chief Alexander. "That 'raid,' as our ever-vigilant local newspaper called it—why, that was nothin' but an old-fashioned publicity stunt! And it worked, too!"

By 1962, a more radical re-invention of the *Ingagi* phenomenon had asserted itself for a fresh wave of big-screen exploitation mania: The commercial success of the Italian-made patchwork film *Mondo Cane* triggered a fresh craze of gawking at Forbidden Images from a safe distance. Recommended viewing: Ted Bonnitt and Eddie Mueller's 2001 documentary film *Mau Mau Sex Sex*, which addresses the bogus-safari expeditionary films as crucial elements in the history of exploitation cinema.

CAPTAIN MARVEL AND SERIAL RETRO–MANIA

February 3, 2008: Apart from some chronic bouts of concentrated cliffhanger enthusiasm in visits with the Texas cartoonist–turned–fine artist Frank Stack, I haven't paid a great deal of attention in recent years to the extinct form of Hollywood filmmaking known as serials, or chapter-plays. I've overcome that neglectful tendency lately with an assignment to deliver a foreword for IDW Publishing's *The Complete Chester Gould's Dick Tracy, Vol. 4*, which covers a stretch of 1936–1937 and thus coincides with the early-1937 release of the first *Dick Tracy* serial by Republic Pictures Corp. George E. Turner and I had covered the Republic *Tracy* in our initial volume of the *Forgotten Horrors* books—but a great deal of information has come to light since then.

The transplanting of *Tracy* from the newspapers' comics pages to the big screen figures in an earlier installment of this ComicMix column. (Page No. 137.) So no point in re-hashing all that here, or in spilling any fresher insights that appear in the IDW *Tracy* edition.

Anyhow, I had expected that these strictly-research refresher screenings of Republic's *Dick Tracy* and *Dick Tracy Returns* and so forth would bring on an attack of Serial Burnout Syndrome—but no such. If anything, the resurrected *Tracy* cliffhangers have stoked a

level of interest that I hadn't experienced since I had been granted my first looks at the Republic serials via teevee in 1966. (Those attractions were feature-length condensations, roughly half or less the running time of a theatrical serial, prepared for broadcast syndication, and re-titled to compound the confusion: 1936's *The Undersea Kingdom*, for example, hit the tube as *Sharad of Atlantis*.)

I had wondered aloud while comparing notes recently with Frank Stack, whose lifelong fondness for the serials influences his own approach to storytelling, as to how *Dick Tracy* in particular could have adapted so brightly to movie-serial form—given that Republic's adaptation had altered many key elements of Chester Gould's comic strip. Frank's lucid reply:

> *Yes, I think Gould was the greatest popular master, outside the movie business, of the serial cliffhanger... He said his technique was to kill his character first and then start cudgeling his brains about how to get him out of the scrape. The particularly original cliffhanger quirk ... was to treat the villains ... with the same concern that [Gould] had for his heroes. And sometimes, villains, or marginal characters, really did buy the farm. You might remember also that [Alley Oop author–artist] V.T. Hamlin's dictum was: "Shoot your character in the first chapter. Then get him out of it."*

Like I said: Chronic bouts of concentrated cliffhanger enthusiasm.

In this light, it might seem that the comics-based serials would hold up more effectively than those taken from original-screenplay conceptions. Republic Pictures' *Adventures of Captain Marvel* bolsters an argument in this direction, but a fresh look at Columbia Pictures' *Batman* serials suggests otherwise. Producer Sam Katzman's *Superman* serials, also for Columbia, exert a peculiar charm quite

apart from their offering neither a particularly sharp interpretation of the character nor any advancement of the serialized storytelling idiom.

The two serials I'm rediscovering just now are Columbia's *The Monster and the Ape* (1945), with some persuasive acting from Ralph Morgan and George Macready and a scary if hardly realistic gorilla impersonation from Ray Corrigan; and Republic's *Adventures of Captain Marvel* (1941). And inasmuch as *Marvel* is a comics-based serial and this venue is, after all, ComicMix, I figure that film must call for the greater attention:

Adventures of Captain Marvel ranks among the more polished and relentlessly entertaining of Republic's serials, though hardly in a class with Universal's splendid *Flash Gordon* adaptations. The *Marvel* project came about by default when an attempt to adapt *Superman* to live-action cinema fell through in preproduction. Republic's switch can only have exacerbated a war of nerves between the characters' respective publishers, whose lawyers sniped at one another for years over the simplistic accusation that *Captain Marvel* represented an infringement upon *Superman*. The *Superman* camp finally won—a feeble victory, after all that sabre–rattling—by strong–arming control of the *Marvel*'s trademarks and then neglecting to do anything constructive with the properties until many years after the fact. (A new-century resurgence of the Captain, under Jeff Smith, bears mentioning.)

Of course, all the comic-book superheroes, from whatever publishing companies, were imitations of one character or another. *Superman* merely claimed pride–of–place as an inventive takeoff upon heroic legends dating from antiquity and pop-literary world–beaters of times more recent. *Captain Marvel*'s great originality is that his first-generation stories pack an overriding sense of humor: Principal creator C.C. Beck was a master of childlike drollery and absurdities.

An aftertaste of Republic's abortive *Superman* serial found its way into Adventures of *Captain Marvel*. Veteran Western star Tom Tyler, who landed the title role, was quite the image of a funnybook super-hero—but leaner and sterner than Beck's version. This Marvel's ruth-lessness in dealing with criminals can be quite scary, and Tyler's clipped speech is calculated to intimidate. And what a grim Superman Tyler would have made!

The story retells the familiar fantasy about an urchin named Billy Batson (Frank Coghlan, Jr.), who is granted the ability to transform himself into the World's Mightiest Mortal, Captain Marvel, upon speak-ing the name of an ancient wizard, Shazam. In the film's closest resem-blance to the comic-book yarns, Nigel de Brulier looks as though he might have stepped directly from one of Beck's drawings of Shazam.

The tale concerns a forbidden expedition into a burial ground along the Burmese borderlands, where a simmering volcano, a dor-mant curse involving the secrets of alchemy, and the mixed blessing of Shazam's gift lie in wait. The otherworldly thrills become gradually more attuned to modern-day civilization as the serial progresses, what with a cloaked badman called the Scorpion on a rampage, Billy Batson's chums in near-constant peril, and Billy/Marvel himself sub-jected to explosions, falling blades, floods of lava, electrocution, bombs, machine-gun barrages, and the like.

Plot is beside the point: The interest lies in the pageantry of gee-whiz visual effects, the stirring musical cues that lend dramatic momentum where there is no actual drama of which to speak, and the breathless pacing that kept the kids of 1941—and of 1953, when a full-scale reissue took place—coming back for each new chapter.

The masked villain known as the Scorpion only looks hokey. His voice, supplied by Gerald Mohr, is appropriately menacing, and his murderous devices bring out the best in Republic's crackerjack spe-cial-effects team. The props by brothers Howard and Theodore Lydecker include an astonishingly realistic mannequin, which repre-sents Captain Marvel in flight. The action–stunting by Dave Sharpe includes numerous bone-rattling drops and leaps: Such organic, real-time effects and stunts still pack a greater wallop than anything in the realm of CGI. Republic was especially attentive to realism in the effects-and-stunts department, lest any one youngster in the audience holler, "Fake!" and trigger a massed outcry.

Later on in 1941, *Superman* fared well with the start of a series of animated cartoons, launched by the Fleischer Bros.' studios for Paramount Pictures. The Columbia *Superman* serials, from 1948 and 1950, represent Sam Katzman's cheesemaking skills more effectively than they represent the *Superman* franchise.

GEORGE A. ROMERO'S 'DIARY OF THE DEAD' IN REVIEW

February 10, 2008: The film-trade press tends increasingly to hail Pittsburgh's George A. Romero as "the godfather of gore," in a smirking nod to his new picture, Diary of the Dead, and to the persistent influence of Romero's breakout film of 1968, Night of the Living Dead. The facile assumption, here, is that Romero's films must rely more upon visceral shock value than upon narrative ferocity or scathing social criticism— qualities that constitute his larger impact as a filmmaking artist.

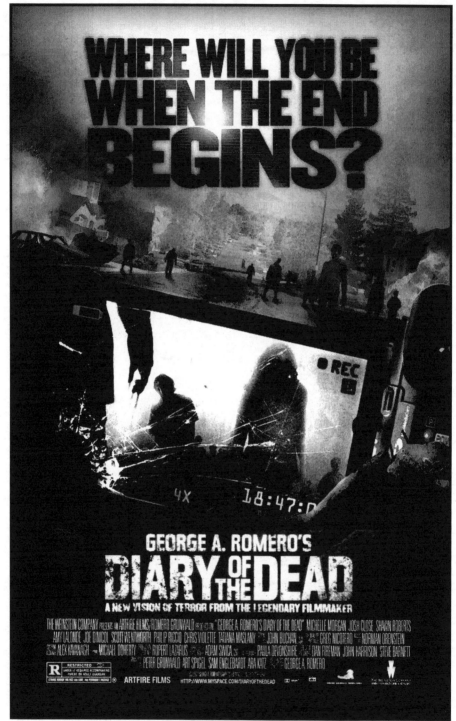

The idiom is outright and unapologetic horror, of course—a perennially hardy escapism-or-allegory genre that had embraced gratuitous gore as a ticket-selling commodity several years before Romero had seasoned *Night of the Living Dead* with such incidental excesses. If any human agency counts as a precursor, it must be the short-lived partnership of Herschell Gordon Lewis and David F. Friedman, whose first-of-a-kind collaborative films *Blood Feast, Two Thousand Maniacs!*, and *Color Me Blood Red* (1963–1965) had championed the pageantry of bloodletting spectacle to the near–exclusion of storytelling values. (Interesting to see a tribute-to-Lewis sequence crop up in Jason Reitman's indie-film Oscar-bait hit, *Juno*. Enough with the digressions, already.)

Romero's investment in the genre, however, involves a steadfast commitment to bigger and more troubling ideas about the fragile state of civilization. Imitations, remakes and homages abound, but Romero stands apart as the Genuine Article. (Among the more sharply attuned nods to Romero: Danny Boyle's *28 Days Later*, from 2002; Edgar Wright and Simon Pegg's *Shaun of the Dead*, from 2004; and Robert Kirkman's comics-chapbook novel *The Walking Dead*, from 2003 *et seq.*) [Kirkman declared a homage to Romero with *The Walking Dead*, but that series' television spinoff has nodded no further to the Master.)

Romero's previous such picture, *Land of the Dead*, goes so far as to channel the humane, defiant desperation of John Steinbeck, suggesting a *Grapes of Wrath*-like prophecy of America as a Third World country—harshly divided amongst a small monied class, an impoverished mass population, and a gathering horde of once-human predators, with no remedies in sight and no perceptible middle-class buffer zone. Romero, like Francis Ford Coppola with his *Godfather* suite or Ingmar Bergman in his film-by-film search for a Meaning of Life, has accomplished more with one recurring concern, so outlandish that it becomes plausible, than many another writer–director from either the maverick or corporate ranks could perform with any succession of self-contained ideas.

The essential Romero-series films, after *Night of the Living Dead*, include 1978's *Dawn of the Dead*, 1985's *Day of the Dead*, and 2005's *Land of the Dead*, first of the series to boast a Corporate Hollywood pedigree. With *Diary of the Dead*, Romero pulls back to a simpler balance between social commentary and audacious jolts. The emphasis here is upon a youthful ensemble cast of technology-smart survivors—proving Romero at 68 to be as thoroughly in touch with a discerning new-generation audience as he had been with that first film during a period of popular unrest over such Real World concerns as the Civil Rights Movement and Vietnam.

It helps, too, that *Diary* shares an element of Web-and-video savvy in common with a big youth-audience hit of the moment, Matt Reeves' *Cloverfield* (Page No. 254), and with 1999's inordinately successful *The Blair Witch Project*. As civilization disintegrates in an outbreak of some hideous plague, the college-student protagonists (more perceptive and resourceful than their camera-wielding counterparts in *Blair Witch*) find themselves growing ever more distrustful of the corporate news media—and in possession of video-recording capabilities and Internet documentation that might yield a truer account of the catastrophe. The age of do-it-yourself amateur video suggests, after all, a polemic with the homogenized and manipulated "facts" (term used advisedly) of the mass-consumption media: I shoot, therefore I yam.

Aspiring filmmaker Jason Creed (played by Josh Close) is at work on a fictional shooting project in Mr. Penn's Woods—guerrilla filmmaking of convenient portability and desperate vulnerability. Word reaches the troupe about episodes of actual terrors, if not calculated terrorism—suggesting that the project's make-believe crisis might have some basis in precognitive imagination. The troupe includes Jason's impatient girlfriend, Debra (Michelle Morgan); a combative fellow student named Tony (Shawn Roberts); actress Tracy (Amy C. Lalonde); tech-crew fixit–man Eliot (Joe Dinicol); and a doubtful professor (Scott Wentworth).

Seeking a haven at Debra's home, the crew finds such ominous indicators as an abandoned hospital, countryside folks determined to take a stand against encroachment, soldiers–turned–vigilantes–and–worse and, at length, a seemingly fortified stronghold occupied by another member (Philip Riccio) of the filmmaking bunch. Where *Cloverfield* tells persuasively of a disaster from a viewpoint of amateur video-camera footage, *Diary of the Dead* compounds such an illusion with a keener emotive intimacy and a heightened realism.

The characters' distrust of government and the mass media advances the attitude that Romero's films have conveyed all along, beginning with the depiction of on-the-spot news–reportage as a dumbfounded bluff in *Night of the Living Dead*. Diary cuts deeper yet, winding up in a tough-minded antiwar stance that might move the Absorbed Viewer to tears of rage.

Amongst a smartly arrayed ensemble cast, Michelle Morgan delivers the most emphatic heroic presence. Amy C. Lalonde conveys the right mixture of spirited wit and fearful response. The special-effects shocks, all the more startling for their randomness, combine old-school prosthetic effects with digital enhancements. The location-shooting scenery, in Ontario, passes convincingly for East-by-Northeastern Pennsylvania.

BLUES POETRY: ROUGH & RAW

February 14, 2008: Fort Worth, Texas' Wesley Race is a businessman in much the same way that the Chicago blues singer Little Walter Jacobs once proclaimed himself a businessman: "I'm a business man," Jacobs growls on a 1964 recording called (what else?) "I'm a Business Man," allowing songwriter Willie Dixon's lyric to leave the nature of the business open to suggestion but permitting no doubt of a businesslike attitude.

Walter Jacobs had died, a casualty of a busy sideline in streetfighting, a year before Wes Race's arrival in 1969 on Chicago's blues-club scene in search of raw emotive authenticity. Jacobs, among such others as the singer-guitarists Muddy Waters and Howlin' Wolf, had embodied the urbanized and electrified Deep Blues style that had drawn Race to Chicago—perhaps less for the raucous nightlife, than for the poetic ferocity that Race had long perceived in the blues.

Race's path, winding but decisive, has led to the release of a début compact-disk album of his original poetry, recited with real-time spontaneity against a blues-rooted musical backdrop. The recording, *Cryptic Whalin'* (Cool Groove Records), is a production of the guitarist and engineer Jim Colegrove, with instrumental contributions from such additional mainstays of Texas' roots-music scene as saxophonists Johnny Reno and René Ozuna, guitarists Sumter Bruton and James Hinkle, drummers Steve Springer and Larry Reynolds, steel guitarist David McMillan, and keyboard artists Jeff Gutcheon and Ruf Rufner.

I fell in with the project two years ago as pianist and organist on a few selections—yeah, the usual B.F.D., or Belated Full Disclosure—in

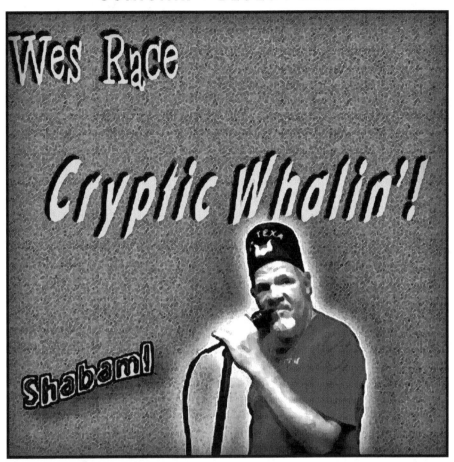

light of a lengthy affiliation with Colegrove and Bruton, and a cordial acquaintanceship with Wes Race.

Many enthusiasts over the long term, from the dramatist and poet Leroi Jones to the seminal cultural historian Samuel Charters, have sensed what Charters called "the poetry of the blues." And America's Beat Poetry movement of the last century had tapped into the blues' defiant attitude of "laughin' to keep from cryin'," often inspiring musical outpourings in response.

It is a temptation to characterize Race as an artistic descendant of such Beat figures as Jack Kerouac and Lawrence Ferlinghetti, but Race's amused sense of wordplay and rhythmic lyricism suggest a distinct strain of blues-inspired verse. Race cites Nelson Algren's 1956 novel of innocence–under–pressure, *A Walk on the Wild Side*, among influences, and Race mentions a particular admiration for the poetic rock 'n' roll ramblings of Don Van Vliet, A.K.A. Captain Beefheart.

"While growing up in Wichita, Kansas," says Race, "I had found myself captivated by jazz—started out as a Dixielander, then got into a correspondence back-and-forth with Bob Koester, there at the Jazz Record Mart in Chicago. And Bob steered me toward the Chicago-style blues artists, beginning with Muddy Waters.

"Seems funny to a lot of people to think of Wichita, Kansas, as having any kind of a hipster scene—but that was very much the case, there. And in 1965 I started attending poetry readings ... Somehow, the poets resonated with me, and so did this increasing interest in the blues as a means of poetic expression.

"Of course, I was bound and determined to get to Chicago, expecting to soak up all those older sounds that had appealed so strongly to me," adds Race. "Visited in 1969—moved there in 1970—and of course it wasn't 1953 any longer, and a lot of commercialization had crept in."

The death of Little Walter Jacobs in 1968 represented a significant loss to an indigenous American musical form. This general period also found Old Schoolers Muddy Waters and Howlin' Wolf under recording-company pressure to modernize their respective styles. Meanwhile, the guitarist Buddy Guy, formerly of Muddy Waters' band, began dealing in less traditional approaches to the blues, prompted in part by the crossover-to-pop success of James Brown and a broadening assimilation of blues elements into the psychedelic-rock movement.

"But a lot of more traditional developments were poised to happen, too," says Race, "and my timing was such that I could take part."

The blues guitarist Theodore "Hound Dog" Taylor (1915–1975) became an early beneficiary of Race's interest. Largely unknown outside Chicago, Taylor and his band struck Race in 1970 as "the real thing, untouched by commercialism."

"I approached Bob Koester [via Delmark Records] about recording Hound Dog," recalls Race. "Volunteered to put up $1,000 of my own money for that purpose, yes, I did. The idea went nowhere until Bruce Iglauer, who was working for Koester at the time, started thinking about it—and Bruce and I wound up taking on Hound Dog as a project of our own."

The début recording, *Hound Dog Taylor & the Houserockers* (1971), launched Iglauer's upstart Alligator Records as an influential label. Race cites his role as "mainly, that of just researching and codifying all the original instrumental compositions that Hound Dog had never bothered to assign titles to." Race also traveled with Taylor as the band's popular acclaim broadened; a tense account of a combative backstage situation appears as part of a digressive monologue on Race's *Cryptic Whalin'*.

Race's influence also extended to the signing of guitarist Frank "Son" Seals (1942–2004) with Alligator Records, in 1972. Race returned to Kansas in 1975, prompting a fondly remembered farewell from Chicago guitarist Louis Meyers: "That's too bad. You've been a good blues spectator."

More participant than spectator, probably. But the observational gifts of the devoted observer–of–humankind clearly have figured in Wes Race's ability to transform seemingly mundane experiences into riveting poetic recitations of unabashed frankness. There is a kinship, here, with Harvey Pekar's autobiographical American Splendor comics pieces, and with Charles Bukowski's jagged-edge style of storytelling. Race's poetry is sometimes harshly worded and confrontational, a timely study in First Amendment Absolutism—and sometimes nostalgic or colored with sentimental longing. The pieces tend to resolve themselves in a tone of jovial absurdity, often with the garnish of a punchline or a *non–sequitur*.

In "Bright Boy's Boogie" and "T–99," Race tells of pub-crawling, thrill-hunting excursions that might tax anybody's stamina. A backfired curse triggers the crisis of "Voodoo–ola." "Ragmop Reality" recalls a job Race once held as a psychiatric nurse's aide, in terms of the healing possibilities of music. He weaves a rhyming commercial slogan for Thunderbird Wine into a wild filibuster called "Shot Time." His "Cryptic Cocktail Mix" lays out a floor plan for a museum enshrining the blues. And in "Madam Fufu's Dream Book," Race turns for inspiration to a self-help manual for superstitious small-time gamblers: "If those lucky-number dream books aren't poetry," avers Race, "then I don't know what is."

Settled in Fort Worth since 1994, Race has operated his own Race Records label—the name plays off an old-time recording-industry term for black music—notably with the late guitarist Robin Sylar's *Bust Out* CD in 2000. Race deals with the workaday world as both a security guard and a relentlessly supportive participant in the city's blues-and-jazz scene.

"I learned early on, as a youngster, to find constructive ways to entertain myself," says Race. "The sheer joy of words has come in very handy, all along. And in the language of the blues, I found a way to communicate on levels 'way beyond pointless small talk.

"The language, of course, strikes some people as cryptic and inaccessible—but it really speaks to lots of other people," he adds. "That's where I'm comin' from, anyhow, and this CD is something of a document of the way I've always interpreted the blues in its truer form. Pure, unaffected poetic expression."

ON THE WAVELENGTH OF 'THE SIGNAL'

February 17, 2008: The *dramatis personae* roster for a three-author film called *The Signal* lists a multitude of roles identified only as "random bodies," "struggling people," "deranged people" and so forth. If the casting, as such, suggests chaos, then such must be precisely the intent. From a premise of frenzied malevolence, writer–directors David Bruckner, Jacob Gentry, and Dan Bush have crafted a smart and orderly, if cryptic, chiller that owes many debts of influence but also brings some welcome new twists to an old and over-familiar formula.

The menace appears to stem from the electronic gizmos that have dominated civilization since the middle of the last century—television as a murderous influence, compounded by telephones and computers and anything else capable of transmitting a disruptive signal. The Bruckner–Gentry–Bush screenplay might trace its ancestry as far back as a 1935 movie called *Murder by Television* (back when TV, still a dozen years away from commercial acceptance, was popularly regarded as a science-fictional concept), in which a high-tech breakthrough yields "the interstellar frequency that is the death ray."

The Signal is, of course, creepier and hipper by far than the bland and stodgy *Murder by Television.* The new film imagines a force that transforms ordinary working-class souls into maniacs—borrowing extensively from hither and yon, although co–director Gentry hastens to point out that "our killers are not mindless zombies."

Point/counter–point. The prevailing influences, nonetheless, must include George A. Romero's *Living Dead* series (1968 *et seq.*) and, particularly, Romero's 1973 film *The Crazies*. There is a nod to the Japanese *Kairo* (A.K.A. *Pulse*, from 2001), with its tale of Internet-borne mayhem. One might be reminded of Lamberto Bava's *Dèmoni* (Italy; 1985), about a movie that affects its audience adversely; or Stephen King's 2006 novel *Cell,* envisioning the ubiquitous cellphone as an infernal device.

The Signal, its prospects bolstered by favorable responses at the Sundance and South by Southwest festivals, is poised for an opening that may presume too great a general appeal for so quirky a low-budget

THE SIGNAL

COMICMIX • THE SIGNAL • MO' DERN' ART

picture. Excesses aside, the film also packs a wealth of ironic humor and a belief in the persistence of tenderness amidst ghastly circumstances.

Bruckner, Gentry, and Bush, as the respective directors of three distinct acts, achieve a unified narrative tone that allows little in the way of distinctive flourishes. Other team-directing efforts, such as Quentin Tarantino's guest–shot on a portion of 2005's *Sin City*, usually display sharper distinctions of style. Gentry's midsection of *The Signal* applies a keener edge of gallows humor to its tale of a party ruined by an outbreak of jealousy and homicidal mania, but overall the directing style is homogenous.

Which is not to say *homogenized*—far from it. The setting is a slum-town enclave, where people dwell in squalor but seem nonetheless in possession of expensive home-entertainment devices. The film opens with what appears to be a conventional 1980s-style horror film, which turns out to be a movie–within–the–movie, on a teevee screen. The picture breaks into static, and the camera draws back to reveal leading characters Ben (Justin Welborn) and Mya (Anessa Ramsey) in an adulterous rendezvous. Ben urges Mya to leave this grimy town with him, but she insists upon returning home.

Mya finds plenty of static at home, too, from both the TV set and her possessive husband, Lewis (A.J. Bowen). The mysterious, quivering TV signal appears to send Lewis on a killing spree, which Mya escapes by dodging their similarly homicidal slum-dweller neighbors and ducking into a neighboring apartment.

The filmmakers dart back–and–forth in time to relate differing viewpoints, but a headlong momentum prevails. The intrinsic violence is tempered throughout by an infusion of absurd comedy, which figures in the secondary tale of another wife (Cheri Christian) who cannot come to terms with having her New Year's party plans derailed by the outbreak. A bewildered landlord (Scott Poythress) struggles to keep matters, and his own impulses, under control.

The little-known players lose themselves in the roles, with a savvy combination of theatrical and naturalistic mannerisms. A.J. Bowen is particularly effective as the wronged husband, radiating sadness while growing ever more the menace. Justin Welborn conveys a sane determination to outlast the crisis, and Scott Poythress leaves a lasting impression as the bewildered innocent who figures out an awkward way to block the mind-altering signal.

The eventual escape of Mya and Ben seems a foregone conclusion—but don't let's presume too much. The telling blurs the line between perception and reality, and the film ends on as enigmatic and troubling a note as it had begun. The storytellers hint, here and there, at an underlying cause, but they wisely take a cue from Samuel Taylor Coleridge's famous critique of Shakespeare: "The motive-hunting of motiveless malignity." In other words: Sometimes, the inexplicability of evil can be more fascinating than any pat over-explanation.

Mo' Dern' Modern Art

February 24, 2008: The Fort Worth Circle—a fabled and enduringly relevant colony of artists who transcended their provincial Texas bearings to help redefine art as a class during the 1940s and 1950s—comes full–circle in a massive exhibition at the Amon Carter Museum in Fort Worth, Texas. The styles of painting and etching—often veering toward cartooning, like their European counterparts in the somewhat earlier dawning Age of Picasso—are too wildly diversified to allow

From the Fort Worth Circle's Dickson Reeder.

any simple description: One might say the members shared an impulse to describe how it felt to be alive at a time of unbridled creative enthusiasm and reciprocal encouragement.

The display of nearly 100 striking examples is called *Intimate Modernism: Fort Worth Circle Artists in the 1940s*, the first such industrial-strength retrospective in more than 20 years. (More than 50 years is more like it, in the case of many of the featured works. Some privately held pieces have gone that long without a public-viewing showcase.)

If some of the works suggest music to those discovering the Circle for the first time, it might be helpful to mention that Stravinsky and Ravel, as modernists in their own right, were among the members' preferred composers; at the time of the Circle's launching, the larger movements toward modern jazz, progressive jazz, and free-form jazz had yet to take a decisive form.

The selections suggest a parallel with musical influences in yet another respect: Southern-bred, New York-modified jazz of the 1920s affected the work of such European instrumentalists as the guitarist Django Reinhardt and the violinist Stephane Grappelli. Their Quintette of the Hot Club of France, in turn, rebounded upon America during the 1930s to shape, like the crease in a Stetson, a Texas-bred offshoot of jazz known as Western Swing—reflecting most vividly in a Fort Worth–Dallas band, the Light Crust Doughboys, and a Texas Plains ensemble, the Sons of the West. (See also: Page Nos. 228 *et Seq.*) Texas' rustic provinciality has long masked a subcurrent of hipsterism, whether in music or in the painterly pursuits.

The styles of the Fort Worth Circle are as varied as the personalities involved. Taken together, the selections tell nothing less than "the tale of how progressive art came to Texas," as curator Jane Myers puts it. To Texas, and through Texas, one might add. If the Fort Worth Circle had begun to close ranks after the 1950s, its influence persisted in Texas' deeper backwaters, charting a course for such developments as the monumental sculpture-garden works of Stanley Marsh III—as in Amarillo, Texas' perpetually changing Cadillac Ranch installation.

"The history of art in Fort Worth goes back more than 100 years," as the historian–exhibitor Glenna Crocker wrote to herald a 2005 private-gallery show that placed the Fort Worth Circle in context with Texas' earlier artistic movements. "The social and political posturing of those eras [since the 1940s] forever changed the creativity of the art world... [The influence of the Circle] continues today, although somewhat obscured by the influx of a multitude of modern contemporaries." Adventurous artists, that is, without direct ties to the specific hometown background.

The advancement of the Circle's influence into a new century had rested largely with the abstract painter Cynthia Brants (1924–2006)—a primary-source bearer of the European Cubists' influence—who remained a working artist despite her retrospective, somewhat contemptuous regard of the Circle as a relic.

"It was natural and inevitable that our work was relegated to history and no longer considered relevant to Fort Worth's ambitions for continuing cultural prominence in the visual arts," Brants said in connection with that 2005 showing. "It was, however, sufficient for us to have opened some eyes to a wider range of possibilities in painting and sculpture than had been previously accepted." The most lasting direct localized tangents have surfaced in the performing arts, largely via the deeply rooted Fort Worth troupe known as Hip Pocket Theatre—with which I have produced a recurring cycle of stage-plays based upon the comic-book stories of Robert Crumb.

The Fort Worth Circle radiated during the 1940s from a nucleus of four locals, then in their middle 20s, who had met as students: Lia Cuilty, Veronica Helfensteller, Marjorie Johnson and Bror Utter. Just prior to America's involvement in World War II, Dickson Reeder, a school-days friend of Utter's, assumed leadership. Reeder and his New York-born wife, Flora Blanc, provided the social-milieu bonds. Also in the sphere were Sara Shannon and William P. "Bill" Bomar, JR.

And Reeder, Bomar and Helfensteller shared a background in private instruction. Kelly Fearing entered the circle as a newcomer to Fort Worth during the war. In 1945, Cynthia Brants became the youngest female member. George Grammer, youngest among the artists, joined in 1946.

Drawn together by a painting, dance, music, theater, and myth–making, the artists of the Fort Worth Circle sought radical tangents of expression as a departure from a prevailing popular preference for bucolic, nostalgic regionalism and more conservative styles. They also shared a fascination with fantastic, enigmatic, imagery that infiltrates otherwise lifelike vistas with skewed perspectives, anatomical exaggerations, and unexpected textures. Members of the Circle responded to Modernism by creating a unique aesthetic based upon contemporary Surrealism and Abstraction—drawing upon imagination.

Their ascent proved lasting, as well. By the mid–1950s, the æsthetic gave way to newer ideas, even while the shared view of art without regimented boundaries persisted. The members became, in turn, significant as teachers and educational administrators. Individual works can be found today in various museums and private collections; the Carter Museum's exhibition presents a unique opportunity to view the works in context with one another, as if to suggest an imaginary regathering of the tribe.

The Modern Art Museum of Fort Worth.

STILL MO' DERN' MODERN ART

March 2, 2008: If any one outcropping of the cultural skyline of Fort Worth, Texas, can be said to state a case for a Bold New Millennium, it is the 2002 landmark address of the Modern Art Museum, designed by the architect Tadao Ando as a sculptural statement in itself. The Modern Art Museum of Fort Worth is at once the oldest such museum in Texas—chartered in 1892—and handily the newest in aspect. I spend a great deal of time there for both workaday and leisurely purposes: The Modern's art-film theatre is descended from a film-society program that I developed during 1996–2002 at one of the downtown movie houses, and my jazz trio performs at the Modern as a matter of routine. Full disclosure, and all that.

As befits a monumental sculpture of architectural pedigree, the building that houses the Modern of Fort Worth has fared particularly well as a showcase for internal exhibitions of sculpture. The exhibit of the moment [*as of 2008*] is called *Martin Puryear*. The retrospective survey of works by a celebrated American artist features nearly 50 sculptures in an arc reaching from Martin Puryear's first solo museum show in 1977 to the present day.

Working primarily in wood, Puryear has maintained a commitment to manual skills and traditional building methods. His forms derive from everyday objects, both natural and fabricated, including tools, vessels, and furniture. His sculptures are rich with psychological and intellectual references, examining issues of identity, culture, and history. Key influences can be traced to his studies, his work, and his travels through Africa, Asia, Europe, and the United States.

Curator Michael Auping explains: "Puryear's work has a way of sneaking up on us perceptually... Partially through his surfaces, we are drawn in, invited to inspect more closely, as one would a more intimate construction, through the subtlety of inflection that he imparts to the surface." Puryear's most striking forced-perspective work, *Ladder for Booker T. Washington* (1996), is part of the permanent collection—and as such, an ideal element of familiar leverage into the greater range. This towering object was inspired by homemade ladders that Puryear had noticed in the French countryside while working at Alexander Calder's studio.

In a conversation five years ago with Auping, Puryear explained the monument: "It just occurred to me that this would be an interesting project to try to do, to make a very tall or long ladder... I had been interested in working with a kind of artificial perspective through sculpture, which if you think about it is not so easy to do. With a ladder, a very long ladder, I could make a form that would appear to recede into space faster, visually, than it in fact does physically."

And like the functional ladders that inspired it, *Ladder for Booker T. Washington* is made from a single sapling that the artist had split down the middle. He added rungs to form a 36-foot span that narrows to just over an inch in width at the top. This sculpture has been one of the museum's steadier draws.

Other sculptures include *Greed's Trophy* (1984), a 12-foot net of wire mesh; *Desire* (1981), a wooden wheel measuring 16-by-32 feet attached to an eight-foot-tall basket; and *Some Tales* (1975–1978), six wooden segments of varying lengths, some of which resemble saws, spanning 30 horizontal feet. The sculptures examine a chronological evolution, demonstrating how the artist refers, repeatedly, to earlier ideas for the sake of reinterpretation. Among these works are Puryear's *Ring* series of the late 1970s, his *Stereotypes* and *Decoys* sculptures of the 1980s, the vessel-like forms of the 1990s and the more allegorical works of times more recent.

From childhood into adolescence during the 1940s and 1950s, Puryear constructed and crafted such objects as bows and arrows, furniture, and guitars. As a teacher with the Peace Corps in the Sierra Leone, he learned the craft of carpenters. Puryear spent two years at the Swedish Royal Academy of Art in Stockholm, where he began sculptural investigations of craft traditions and modern Scandinavian design. Upon returning to the United States, Puryear resumed his studies during the 1980s, centering upon Japanese architecture and garden design. He has concentrated exclusively upon his own artistry since the late 1980s.

ALLAN TURNER'S FOLKLIFE TREASURES

March 9, 2008: The measurable results of bare-knuckled research, like gold and luck, will turn up where you find 'em. Folks often think of cultural research in academic terms—the Ivory Tower stereotype, alone in the realm of uninterrupted thought and empirical fact–sifting, or the aloof egghead at large amongst the tribes—but a truer basis must rest with the very folks whose thoughts and dreams and deeds form the foundations of any Popular Culture.

Or should the term be *populist*, as opposed to *popular*, culture? No matter—the root word means "of the people," in any event. And some of the most lasting such research has come from the efforts of working-civilian folks whose interest in the down-to-earth lives of other folks drives them to venture among the masses with a companionable attitude, laden with note–pads and recording devices, to take down impressions for the long term. (Pete Seeger has a good term for such excursions, research-driven or not: "a political vacation.")

The Allan Turner Collection at the University of Texas provides a memorable example of this people-to-people imperative. The name-

Fred "Papa" Calhoun at the time of the Turner–Price interviews.

sake of the archive is a news-biz colleague of long standing, and several of these conversational interviews date from a collaborative push that Turner and I accomplished during the 1970s and 1980s.

Deep-rooted sources of this influence include Thomas Edison (1847–1931). Eager to popularize and perfect his version of the 19TH Century phonograph, Edison reconciled note-taking anthropological research with sound-recording technology by sending crews into the streets to capture the crowd noises and pushcart-vendor cries of the turning of a century. Then, in a more focused campaign of the early-middle 20TH Century, the father-and-son team of John and Alan Lomax concentrated upon the preservation of American folk music—starting with the songs of prison inmates and field–hands in the Deep, Deeper, and Deepest South.

Alan Lomax (1915–2002) helped in particular to forge new commercial possibilities for traditional folksinging during the 1950s and 1960s—advancing a Voice of the People urgency during the reactionary post-WWII years, on the one hand, and arguing the case for a purer folkloric expressiveness during the 1960s' craze for a more commercialized dilution of folk music.

• • •

Only at a certain stage of accomplishment does one start thinking of such efforts as research, or oral history, or whatever other highfalutin' label one might attach. I caught the Lomax bug as a grammar-school kid around 1956, encouraged by a combination of the Lomaxes' preservation of the story–songs of Huddie "Leadbelly" Ledbetter and my own family's purchase of a Sears & Roebuck Silvertone-brand tape recorder. The clincher was the realization that one of my grandmothers knew some of the same cottonfield-holler work songs that Leadbelly had sung.

Thus inspired to compile a family-album collection of recordings—war stories, early-times reminiscences, prairie ballads and such—I soon learned that the tape recorder provided a reliable means of annoying the kinfolks. They would pose, grinning, for a snapshot-camera, which had long since become a household commonplace. But the tape machine was imposingly larger than a Kodak Brownie, and unfamiliar on top of that, and people seemed not to know what to make of hearing their own voices from a playback.

"Who's that ol' hillbilly woman yackin' her mouth off?" asked an aunt.

"Why, that's you," I answered.

"*What*?!" she yelled. End of session.

Allan Turner and I met during the 1970s as newspaper staffers in Amarillo and soon recognized a shared interest in field-recording activities. Turner had invested in an industrial-grade machine and, by this time, had entered what he calls "my Alan Lomax phase" of ranging throughout Texas and Louisiana to capture the words of cowboys, crawfish farmers, blues-and-ballads singers, back-country sin-killer preachers—anybody with a story to relate. We teamed first on a career interview with the veteran journalist A.F. "Tex" Kiersey, there at the Amarillo *Daily News*, where church-page editor Kiersey regaled us with tales of his early adventures as a pistol-packing crime reporter.

And Allan and I ranged the Panhandle area in search of folks who had lived through the catastrophic Dust Bowl of the Depression years. We huddled in a backroom of Fred "Papa" Calhoun's North Side Fort Worth store, to document the pianist-turned-groceryman's impressions of the origins of Western swing as a musical force. (Calhoun, pictured on the facing page, had played during the 1930s with Milton Brown's Musical Brownies.)

And Turner and my wife, Christina, and I road–tripped to Southwestern Louisiana to make tapes and moving pictures of a rural Mardi Gras celebration. We visited the historic black community of Boardhouse, Texas, to capture the Amen Corner hoo-hah frenzy of a circuit-preacher's Sunday-morning visit. Some projects came with institutional commitments, but most were spontaneous exercises in the preservation of Tribal Memory. Even a microphone-shy grandmother of mine came around gradually to take part, speaking expansively of her childhood in Indian Territory.

Turner, later of of the Houston *Chronicle*, has maintained such one-of-a-kind sessions in their original spooled ribbons of magnetic tape, hedging the bets for longevity with digital-audio transplants. And at length, these organic-research documents have found their way into the academic realm, as the Allan Turner Collection at UT–Austin's Center for American History.

The Institutional Abstract cites "interviews and musical recordings with musicians spanning a wide range of musical genres, including *conjunto*, blues, country-and-Western, Czech and German." The non-musical topics are similarly extensive.

Allan's entrenched interest in South-by-Southwestern folklife also has yielded contributions to publications of the Texas Folklore Society and a collaborative book (with Richard Stewart) called *Transparent Tales: An Attic Full of Texas Ghosts*. Alongside a fine and elongated newspaper career, the centerpiece of this substantial body of work is the collection at UT–Austin—the generous results of that 10-year "Lomax phase," during which Turner criss–crossed Texas and Louisiana in search of authentic folk expression.

'SUPERHERO MOVIE' IN REVIEW

March 23, 2008: The superhero, and I don't mean sandwich, has been a staple of the Popular Culture since well before the Depression-into-wartime beginnings of *Superman* and *Batman*. Those characters' nascent comic-book adventures of 1938–1939 served primarily to focus a popular fascination with superhuman struggles against extravagant menaces—but similarly conceived protagonists had existed all along in ancient mythology and mass-market popular fiction. And how better to explain the superior heroic intellect of Conan Doyle's Sherlock Holmes and Seabury Quinn's phantom-fighting Jules DE Grandin, or the beyond-the-normal escapades of Robin Hood and the Scarlet Pimpernel?

People need heroes. Such characters spur the imagination to assume hope in the face of fearful Real World circumstances, even if their activities and abilities (and allegorical antagonists) seem patently outside the realm of possibility. And the spiritual generosity of superheroism is such that people are willing to fork over either hard-earned cash or Daddy's Money to experience the fantasy: Hence the proliferation of superhero comic books in the immediate backdraft and long-term vapor–trails of *Superman* and Batman, and hence those characters' fairly prompt leap into motion pictures during the 1940s.

Many people regard the superhero movie phenomenon as a fairly recent development, traceable as far back as Sam Raimi's *Spider–Man* breakthrough of 2002, or maybe to the perceived antiquity of Richard Donner's *Superman* pictures of 1978–1980. Not by a long shot.

Nor are the inevitable parodies—as seen in David Zucker's collaborative production of *Superhero Movie*—any particular innovation. Just as there is something awe–inspiring about some guy in long-john tights, hurdling buildings or piercing the veil with a blast of X–ray vision, there also is something innately ridiculous about such a spectacle. Even some of the earlier superhero films, such as Columbia Pictures' *Batman* serials of the 1940s, emerged as unwitting parodies despite (or because of) their more earnest aims.

The formal parodies are a rarer breed. Zucker had proved himself a capable spoofer with 1980's *Airplane!*—a well-received lampoon of the large-ensemble Disaster Movie subgenre—much as Mel Brooks had parodied such genres as the Western epic and the Gothic horror film (with *Blazing Saddles* and *Young Frankenstein*) to pleasing effect. Both artists sprung from the influence of Harvey Kurtzman's *MAD* magazine of the midcentury, with its recurring demonstration that a parody must harbor an affectionate understanding of the story it intends to spoof.

Zucker has suffered the occasional lapse in recent years, and his involvement as director of two *Scary Movie* sequels (2003–2006)—with their skit-like pageantry of send–ups, as opposed to a sustained narrative—suggests a general decline in Hollywood's ability to turn a popular genre inside–out with ridicule. With *Superhero Movie,* co–producer Zucker and writer–director Craig Mazin have recaptured a vibe very much like that of the original *Airplane!*

Recalling the genre-savvy sensibilities of Kinka Usher's impressive *Mystery Men* (1999; from Bob Burden's comic-book stories), *Superhero Movie* re–exaggerates the stock-in-trade exaggerations of such recent comics-based hits as the *Fantastic Four* and *Spider–Man* and *Batman* movies to an extent that one Weblog reviewer likens to "watching *Spider–Man* in a fun-house mirror." A basis in sustained storytelling—

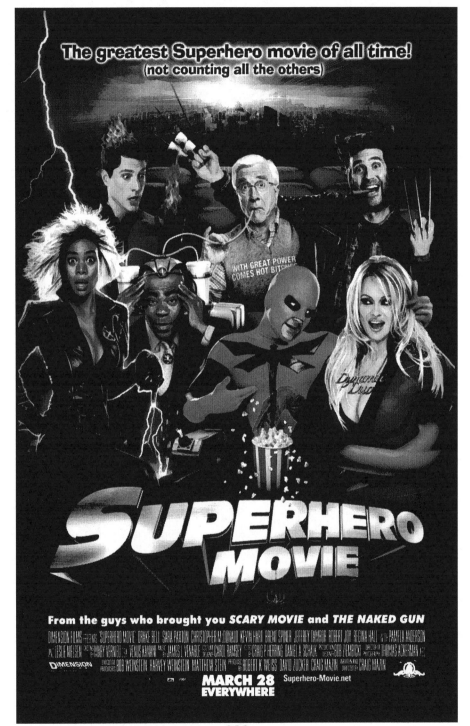

Drake Bell's leading character, Norman Normal, develops superhuman powers, which render normalcy irrelevant—recalls the tribal-memory story-arc of the *Spider–Man* series but leaves room for references to various other costumed-hero franchises. Mazin's screenplay bespeaks a fondness for the idiom in its natural state.

A well-cast ensemble follows suit. Sara Paxton appears as a spirited romantic interest for Bell's costumed Dragonfly. Chris McDonald makes a suitably absurd surrogate for the first *Spider–Man* picture's chief villain. Brent Spiner takes a Mad Scientist role beyond madness. Leslie Nielsen, a Zucker-troupe mainstay since 1980, steals the show as an arrogant Big Shot, patterned after Marvel Comics' grandstanding figurehead, Stan Lee.

Technical credits, too, are up to snuff, particularly in a jaw-dropping what-the-hell-next? set–piece built around a runaway train and its obstacles. Jerry Zucker's long-term influence is sufficient to validate his career; that influence is particularly evident in recent films by the English parodists Edgar Wright and Simon Pegg, notably *Hot Fuzz* and *Shaun of the Dead*. But it is especially rewarding to find Zucker reasserting his mastery with Superhero Movie. The film is as funny as its generally flagging subgenre needs it to be. And heroically so, yet. High time an *Airplane!*-calibre example got itself put forth.

MEL BROOKS AND WOODY ALLEN AND DREW FRIEDMAN

April 6, 2008: I met Drew Friedman in 1990 through a friendship with his brother and then-frequent collaborator, the songwriter and social critic Josh Alan Friedman, while we were attending a cartoonists' convention in Dallas as working artists and comic-book developers. Drew had built a reputation within the industry as a meticulously lifelike portraitist, capable of arraying tiny dots of ink into images of dreamlike accuracy that captured the soul—unflatteringly so, as a rule—as unerringly as it suggested a physical reality.

Poised for a leap into mass-market commercial illustration, Drew had brought to the Dallas Fantasy Fair a work-in-progress assignment for a video-box edition of a trailblazing television series, *The Honeymooners*. The portrait of star player Jackie Gleason shone forth from the oversized Strathmore page—Drew was working on a scale larger by far than the size of a videocassette sleeve—like some impossible photograph. The piece was too richly caricatured to be a photo, but it captured an essence of Gleason in a way one seldom sees in ink–on–paper.

"Needs some cleaning up," Drew said, surveying the results. He set aside his Rapidograph, a fountain-pen drawing tool capable of dispensing near-microscopic quantities of ink, and went to work with an X–Acto knife, chiseling at one ink–speck after another with unerring precision. Gleason's face, already as convincing as if reproduced by a halftone engraving camera, seemed to engage the observer in direct eye-contact animation under Friedman's touch.

The intervening years have found Drew Friedman moving ever deeper into pop-mainstream acclaim via such publications as *MAD* and *Los Angeles Magazine* and *Entertainment Weekly*—a far cry from the compassionately acerbic show-business satires that he and Josh Alan once produced for various under-the-counterculture and arts-revue publications.

But Drew has remained devoted to the soul-capturing interest that he once applied to such figures as Bud Abbott & Lou Costello, nostal-

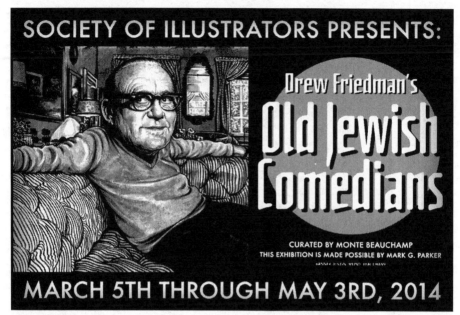

SOCIETY OF ILLUSTRATORS PRESENTS:

Drew Friedman's

Old Jewish Comedians

CURATED BY MONTE BEAUCHAMP
THIS EXHIBITION IS MADE POSSIBLE BY MARK G. PARKER

MARCH 5TH THROUGH MAY 3RD, 2014

gic talk-show schmoozer Joe Franklin, Shemp Howard and his fellow Stooges, and the foredoomed horror-movie stars Bela Lugosi and Rondo Hatton. (The titles of two perennial Friedman Bros. books serve notice that their words-and-pictures portrayals must be as sardonic as they are affectionate: *Any Similarity to Persons Living or Dead Is Purely Coincidental* and *Warts and All.*)

Drew found an ideal groove a couple of years ago with a handsome solo book called *Old Jewish Comedians: A Visual Encyclopedia*, its bright-eyed cover painting of an aged, still-antic Milton Berle serving as an irresistible come–on. The seemingly esoteric volume wound up triggering a popular sensation, and Friedman has now delivered a sequel. [*And more extensive such coverage since 2008.*]

More Old Jewish Comedians (Fantagraphics Books) is a comparable delight—as much for its array of personalities, as for the showcase it affords for Friedman's evolved ability to transform paint into seemingly animated flesh. Drew has moved long since from ink-on-Strathmore pointillism into confident, densely layered brushwork, and the fine-art reproduction technique allows the textures of the paints, the very fingerprint of the brush–tip, to command as keen an attention as the subjects themselves.

The format places such household-name figures as Mel Brooks and Woody Allen in meaningful context with the since-obscure likes of Bert Gordon—once a celebrated radio voice known as "the Mad Russian" and star of one of the out-and-out weirdest of Old Hollywood comedies (Page No. 147)—and Bill Dana and Soupy Sales and Three Stooges pinch–hitter Joe Besser.

As the technique has matured to an Old Masterly combination of classical environmental portraiture (the occasional street-scene and dressing-room surroundings are as revealing as the central figures) and cartooning and caricature, Friedman has retained the gift that makes his much earlier work so arresting: That is, the illusion that each of his subjects is looking the Absorbed Viewer directly in the eye. Gaze upon Friedman's visions of Joe E. Ross, or Belle Barth, or the forgotten Marx Bros., Gummo and Zeppo, and you come to sense the artists' tragicomic glory.

"Loving portraits of people who do not fit the bill of classic American loveliness," as one Web reviewer characterizes the new book. The same could be said of all Drew Friedman's images over the long term.

In a 2006 *Jewish Journal* review of the first *Old Jewish Comedians*, Hank Rosenfeld invoked a traditional Yiddish saying: "Weep before God. Laugh before people." Say no more.

Drew Friedman certainly needs to say no more but must do so, anyhow. Both books are appropriately light on text, with a first-volume introduction by the critic–historian Leonard Maltin and a second-volume foreword by the screenwriter and funnyman Larry Gelbart, who delivers essentially a stand-up monologue in print: The Jewish humorist's pursuit of "a life that is essentially a Kvetch–22," writes Gelbart, deploying a heavy-artillery pun for a higher purpose, "means never letting desperation have the last word ... humor as a weapon and a shield."

The pictures, of course, are sufficient to tell the greater story. The *Old Jewish Comedians* books add up to an essential document of show-business history—all the more eloquent for their near–wordlessness.

YUH GOTTA BE A JUGGLER TUH WOIK IN DIS RACKET

April 13, 2008: "Yuh gotta be a juggler tuh woik in dis racket," a senior-staff powerhouse named Frosty Sloane informed me after I had landed my first job in a competitive marketplace, back around 1965.

"I thought we were selling shoes," I answered him. Which of course we were. I had a fleeting mental picture of some *Ed Sullivan Show* juggling act involving wingtipped brogand clodhoppers and stiletto heels. Took a while for Frosty's metaphor to sink in—but once I had experienced my first stampede of customers and watched Sloane accommodate 10 or 15 prospective buyers while I attempted to deal with one or two of 'em, I caught his drift, all right.

Frosty Sloane was so effective, with consistently high sales tallies to show for it, that he could afford to be overconfident. He would juggle products while juggling customers: If a shopper should ask to see one style, Sloane would bring out half–a–dozen selections and wind up selling two or three of those. And he was such a *weisenheimer* that I wondered how he could get away with some of his sales-floor stunts.

"Y'see, haffa th' customers who come in here durin' a slower stretch—they don't even *know* they're customers, yet," Frosty counseled me, as if dispensing the Wisdom of the Ages. "They're jus' sleepwalkin', browsin' away like as if they knew what they were doin'. An' yuh gotta figger out how t' get their attention." No sooner had he spoken, than a woman wandered into the department, browsin' away—just like the man said.

"Watch dis," Frosty said, "an' I'll show yuh what I mean by 'sleepwalkin.'" He strolled toward the browser, nodded in her direction, and then spoke: "Tickle your ass with a feather, ma'am?" He paced the question just rapidly enough to blur the words.

"No, thank you," she replied. "Just looking."

Within half an hour, Sloane had waked this sleepwalker sufficiently that she wound up spending a couple of hundred frogskins.

Our manager, Byron Motley—he referred to the staff as his Motley

Crew—had another term for the ratio of a few sales–clerks to any number of simultaneous shoppers and just-browsing loiterers: "Doubling up," Byron called the process, although it often was more a matter of "quadrupling up," if not more so.

Now, "doubling up" sounded to me a whole lot like an onslaught of abdominal cramps—a natural response, perhaps, to such responsibilities in a short-staffed workplace with a heavy-traffic clientele—but once I had tackled a few such crunches and rung up more sales than no–sales, the process became a snap. The equivalent modern-day lingo, "multi-tasking," sounds downright anemic by comparison with "juggling" or "doubling up."

It dawned on me soon enough that I had been practicing similar tactics since childhood, anyhow—pursuing parallel interests in cartooning and music and writing, juggling school-day and after-school activities—and when I left the retail-fashion trade in 1968 to become a newspaper reporter and editorial cartoonist, I took the lessons of the shoe-store treadmill with me. This experience, combined with a school-days music-biz involvement with rock-and-country producer Norman Petty's recording-studio activities in Texas and New Mexico, translated well to a newsroom-deadline setting: One reporter might expect to compose a dozen brief stories and a couple of bigger ones, from multiple informative sources, in an eight-hour stretch. The task of answering to one City Editor, one Chief Copy Editor, and one Opinion Page editor on any given shift seemed a great deal like the opening of a seasonal clearance sale at the department store.

The juggling abilities came in especially handy as I moved from news reporting into newsroom management while helping out, as well, in the editorial-cartoon department and developing a comics feature of my own. A busy freelance regimen, including the launch of a series of movie-history books with a colleague, George E. Turner, developed from there, along with a continuation of the recording-studio activities.

The juggling grew to seem less a conscious effort than an automatic response to a busy marketplace. I didn't think specifically about Frosty Sloane and his benevolent wiseacre wisdom, so much as I kept it as an anchoring presence in the back of the mind. If it works on the sales floor, then it's bound to apply to the arena of communications. Then there was Sloane's corollary observation: "Tuh do *dis*, yuh got tuh know *how*."

• • •

That shoe-store counsel came to the conscious foreground again in 1986, when a fortunate encounter with Timothy Truman during a book-promotion tour drew Tim and me and fellow author–artist John K. Snyder III into a serialized project called *Prowler*, at Eclipse Comics. Eclipse had recently published a new edition of George Turner's and my first *Forgotten Horrors* book. Tim's involvement with Eclipse at the time included such heroic-adventure comics as *Scout* and *Airboy*.

And could my newspaper and music-business commitments accommodate the addition of a comics-production schedule? Well, why not? *Ya gotta be a juggler to woik in dis racket.*

Turned out that the second-nature juggling act lent a greater momentum to the comics venture than I might have expected. Since our first meeting during the earlier 1980s, during Timothy Truman's breakthrough stretch on *GrimJack* at First Comics, Tim and I had found in common an interest in indigenous American music as a class, and the blues in particular. Blues–plus–comics—how to com-

bine the influences to lasting effect? Tim was already blazing some trails in that direction with the *Scout* stories, and we determined to carry such hybrid thinking further with the *Prowler* books. (There was a B-movie influence at work, as well, but I've already got too many digressive topics in play, here.)

And hence not only the phonograph-record comics-soundtrack inserts that graced both *Scout* and *Prowler* at one point or another, but also an overall blues–consciousness within both series. Tim Truman and John Snyder and I, along with Prowler backup artist Graham Nolan, conceived enough blues-rooted storylines to account for a few dozen issues if not more.

The *Prowler* series had run its published course by 1989, however, before most of these plotting strategies could come into play. One blues-as-comics element left hanging stemmed from a true-crime *cause célèbre* of the early 20TH Century—the so-called "Axeman of New Orleans" case. Tim and I had imagined that our masked-vigilante character, Leo Kragg, alias the Prowler, might find himself drawn toward a new siege of Axeman murders, recalling the historic rampage of 1918–1919 and picturing the perpetrator as a deathless spirit more so than any merely mortal menace.

That Axeman storyline never materialized as a *Prowler* adventure (not yet, anyhow)—but Tim composed and recorded an intended "Axeman" instrumental track, and I retooled the basic tale into a self-contained short story called "Blues Passover." That yarn saw print in 1998 in a preliminary version, in an anthology called *Southern-Fried Homicide*.

And so why "Blues Passover" as a title? Well, the Biblical allusion has to do with a letter that some fool had mailed in 1919 to the editor of the New Orleans *Times–Picayune*, purporting to be the elusive serial killer known as the Axeman and making this promise: "I am going to pass over New Orleans... Every person shall be spared in whose home a jazz band is in full swing." You get the picture. There must have been plenty of jazz cranked out in response (assuming a willingness to buy into the myth), for that night passed with nary a severed noggin.

• • •

A generation later in the here-and-now [*2008, that is*], I find myself back in harness alongside Tim Truman and John Snyder on a fresh run of new-and-resurrected Prowler stories for ComicMix. Plenty of ground to cover, in both a re–presentation of the original serialized yarns and some new directions. Amidst preparations to repatriate the Prowler property during the last few years, a reminder of New Orleans' Axeman scare has come to light in a Real World natural disaster—The Great Southern Coastal Panic of 2005. A forcible allegory, perhaps, but an allegory all the same: The act of storytelling often requires a imaginative stretch or two.

That coastal situation, of course, sent many residents of New Orleans ranging far afield in advance of the onslaught of Hurricane Katrina. My home-base city of Fort Worth, prominent among the first Southwestern cities to lend refuge, became as a result a new home base for a latter-day jazz traditionalist from New Orleans named Adonis Rose. And Rose, in turn, is an artistic descendant of those 19TH-into-20TH Century musicians who had formed the sonic levee that kept the Axeman at bay during one dark night of 1919. (Still assuming that willingness to honor the myth, natch.)

Adonis Rose, a drummer and composer acclaimed for his work with such artists as Harry Connick, JR., and Wynton Marsalis, has returned Fort Worth's welcome by settling in as founder of the Fort Worth Jazz Orchestra, an ensemble dedicated to a combination of preservation and newly commissioned artistry. In his relentless juggling, or doubling–up, of career interests—he also operates a smaller outfit called the N.O. Vaders and has worked on Spike Lee's disaster documentary, *When the Levees Broke*—Rose has served as something of an inspiration to my efforts with the new *Prowler* book. That is, in presenting a new multiple-tasker Role Model and in presenting a steadfast reminder of the blues' value as a defiant response to urgent, perpetual struggle as a way of life.

But I digress. So what else is new? The short version is that, yes, there is a new *Prowler* book in the works. And yes, it picks up where the original Eclipse series leaves off, raveled plot–threads and all. And no, it hasn't skipped a beat in staying apace with the hard-bitten, living-the-blues conception that Truman and Snyder and I had formulated during 1986-1987.

And Tim and John and ComicMix editor Mike Gold and I are collaborating as furiously just now as if it were still 1987 and we lived within stumbling distance of one another. (Actually, we've never resided within stumbling distance of one another, but such comparatively newer developments as eMail and up-and-download technology bring us somewhat closer together.) I'm still doubling and tripling up with the traffic, with newspapers to feed in Texas and Pennsylvania and that chronic sideline in the music business. There's a new album in preproduction for guitarist Sumter Bruton's and my blues ensemble, and I'm busy with preparations for the 2009 installment of the Van Cliburn International Piano Competition. Nice woik if you can get (away with) it.

Not to mention that new *Prowler* opus. Working title: *Blood Kin*. Not to spill too much, y'know. Ya gotta be a juggler to woik in dis racket. And thank you, Frosty Sloane.

Recommended reading: *Gumbo Ya-Ya* (Bonanza Books; 1984), containing art and essays from the Federal Works Progress Administration's Louisiana Writers' Project of the 1930s—and including a detailed account of the Axeman case.

[*A managerial lapse at ComicMix left the* Prowler *venture dangling, damn it all to hell, whereupon Tim Truman and John Snyder and I reclaimed the original* Prowler *stories and developed a maverick reprint project. That new episodic installment remains at this writing one of those proverbial Stories for Another Day.*]

'SKIPALONG ROSENBLOOM' BLOOMS ANEW

April 15, 2008: "In the days before the cultural faucets of radio and television had become standard equipment in each home," wrote the social critic Gunther Anders in 1956, "the [American public] used to throng the motion-picture theaters where they collectively consumed the stereotyped mass products manufactured for them... The motion-picture industry ... continues the tradition of the theater ... a spectacle designed for simultaneous consumption by a large number of spectators. Such a situation is obsolete."

Anders' influential gadfly manifesto, The Phantom World of TV, came fairly late in the initial outcropping of a Cold War between movies and teevee. Earlier during the 1950s, the movie industry had begun arraying such competitive big-screen ripostes to television as widescreen cinematography, three-dimensional projection—and such passive-aggressive lampoons of television as Arch Oboler's *The*

Twonky and Sam Newfield's *Skipalong Rosenbloom*. Anders' perception of obsolescence for moviegoing has proved No Such Thing over the long stretch, of course—despite many movie theaters' best efforts during the past generation to render the experience overpriced, inconvenient, and unsanitary, with cheapened operational standards and automated film–handling procedures. And yet film exhibitors as a class continue to raise the question, "Is moviegoing dead?" This, as if the post-WWII threat of mass-market television had never gone away despite a sustained détente between the big auditorium screen and the smaller home-viewing screen.

Television and the movie business have long since forged an uneasy peace. But a long-term alliance between the moviemaking studios and the movie-showing theaters has eroded steadily since the cable-television and movies-on-video booms of the 1970s and 1980s. A movie that might play for a few weeks, with diminishing returns, in the theaters can count on an infinite afterlife on the cable networks or DVD/Blu–Ray/HD video.

The most striking new [*as of 2008*] change in the theaters' historic role may rest with one unconventional feature-length attraction of 2008: *Hannah Montana/Miley Cyrus: Best of Both Worlds Concert Tour.* That digital 3–D musical event–film grossed some $65 million in limited theatrical play (682 auditoriums, primarily in North America), impressing one industry analyst in Los Angeles, Jeff Bock, as "the sign of an overwhelming change in the film-exhibition industry." *Best of Both Worlds*, built around a Disney Channel pop-country franchise aimed at a schoolgirl audience, represents a new breed of theatrical event-video programming—ranging from sports tournaments to opera to sensationalized 3–D adventure films. This development, in turn, represents the theaters' gradually diminishing dependency' upon the conventional feature-film medium.

Such fresh outcroppings as *Hannah Montana* recall nothing so much as the big-screen rallying of the earlier 1950s. Without the (perceived) menace" of teevee as a provocation to the theaters, the moviegoing masses might never have seen such competitive big-screen spectacles as Merian C. Cooper's something-for-everybody spectacle *This Is Cinerama* (1954), with its intense sight-and-sound imagery and its swooping aerial photography; or Jack Arnold's *It Came from Outer Space* and *Creature from the Black Lagoon* (1953–1954), with their confrontational arrays of 3–D Shock Value. (Between *It Came from Outer Space* and *Creature from the Black Lagoon*, Arnold had addressed the encroachment of television upon Hollywood, with another 3–D-effects film called *The Glass Web* [1953]—a murder yarn with a teevee-studio setting.)

Such timely and explicit responses to the movies-vs.-television rivalry are rare. The most emphatic of these, though hardly a competitive blockbuster in its day, is a 1953 film called *The Twonky*—in which the movies-and-radio producer Arch Oboler condemns teevee as a mind-controlling medium. Two years earlier—when such Hollywood cowboy-movie stars as Gene Autry, Roy Rogers, and Bill "Hopalong Cassidy" Boyd were moving away from film and into television in a self-preservation strategy—director Sam Newfield and prizefighter–turned–comedian Maxie Rosenbloom had delivered a stinging parody of teevee-based Westerns with an outlandish big-screen picture called *Skipalong Rosenbloom.*

Neither *Skipalong Rosenbloom* nor *The Twonky* caused any box-office sensations—much less, left their viewers with any anti-teevee leanings—and both titles wound up in short order as feed-the-monster fodder for late-show syndicated television. So there.

The renewed availability of *Skipalong Rosenbloom* (proxy title: *Square Shooter*) via various Web catalogues suggests a fresh appraisal. The upstart film (small studio, big snide attitude) betrays more silliness than satire on the part of screenwriters Eddie Forman and Dean Riesner, but the depiction of television as a vehicle for pandering commercialism has a resentful edge. (Sam Newfield, a tenured mainstay of the low-budget Hollywood sector known as Poverty Row, would find himself sidetracked increasingly into television assignments during the 1950s.)

The title's suggestion of a *Hopalong Cassidy* spoof aside, *Skipalong Rosenbloom* runs short on lampooning references to Bill Boyd's *Cassidy franchise* but compensates with slapstick re–enactments of such standard Western-movie devices as extravagant gunplay, haymaker fistfighting, and the shopworn crooked-banker plot. Max Rosenbloom (1904–1976) plays himself, more or less, as a teevee-Western hero at odds with a frontier mobster named Butcher Baer (heavyweight boxing champ Max Baer). A Rubber Reality framing story concerns a household argument as to which television program wants watching—as though there were all that many channel choices in 1951.

Butcher Baer, upon learning that Skipalong Rosenbloom has been summoned to help his grandfather, Tex Rosenbloom (Raymond Hatton), avoid a mortgage foreclosure, sends a hireling known as Sneaky Pete (Fuzzy Knight) to ambush Rosenbloom. The genial hero dodges the pitfalls with more oafish dumb luck than skill. Arriving in the town of Buttonhole Bend, Rosenbloom dazzles the locals with a show of gunplay—shooting at a tossed coin and transforming it into a shower of small change. The bad guys' truer objective proves to be a hidden map that might lead to a forgotten gold mine.

Rosenbloom accepts the job of sheriff—in a town where lawmen represent an endangered species. The purported map turns out to be a sheet of dance instructions. Rosenbloom, captured and placed near a lighted keg of explosives, proves allergic to gunpowder and blows out the fuse with a monumental sneeze. Triggering another explosion aimed at the Baer gang, Rosenbloom inadvertently reveals the location of the mine. The ordeal ends in capture for the surviving crooks and prosperity and Happily Ever After for all who deserve it. Except for Rosenbloom, who finds that sidekick Jackie Coogan, assuming Skipalong dead in a shoot–out, has wooed and won Skipalong's schoolmarm sweetheart (Jacqueline Fontaine). Rosenbloom resigns as sheriff and rides away in search of new adventures.

Eagle Lion Films, an ambitious but over-prolific independent studio descended from an old-line low-budget outfit called Producers Releasing Corp., found itself cash–strapped in 1951 and sold *Skipalong Rosenbloom* to a larger old-line releasing company, United Artists, which kept the film—barely—in small-market theatrical distribution before selling it to the enemy camp, syndicated television. The change of title to the generic *Square Shooter* deprived the picture of a chief point of attraction, given the original title's sideways reference to the household-name familiarity of the *Hopalong Cassidy* series.

The film plays inappropriately well on the small screen, given its origins as a snipe at teevee. For those postwar filmgoers old enough to have caught a theatrical showing, it must have been a hoot to watch Maxie Rosenbloom subject himself to such surreal absurdities, like a Three-in-One Stooges act, on the big screen. (Rosenbloom had co-starred during the 1940s, with Billy Gilbert and founding Stooge Shemp Howard, in a brief run of imitation-Stooges features for producer Sam Katzman.)

And of course, the stuff of which *Skipalong Rosenbloom* is made is dreadful if one attempts to take it as anything more than slapstick absurdity. The film's greater success lies in Rosenbloom's smarter-than-the-character combination of innocence and indignation, and in the obvious delight that supporting players Jackie Coogan, Fuzzy Knight, and Hillary Brooke (playing to exaggerated *film noir* (or *femme noir*) type as a villainous townswoman) take in the opportunity to spoof themselves.

THE OCTOPUS STRIKES

April 20, 2008: In his frank and provocative column, *Writing under the Influence*, for ComicMix, John Ostrander speaks of imitation as "the starting point for what you eventually become" as a storyteller: "Nothing is created in a vacuum," Ostrander avers.

Writing may often seem the loneliest of professions—and certainly so, if one lacks a Reality Check communion with one's customers and kindred preactitioners—but who has the time to wallow in loneliness when besieged by the insistent Muses of Narrative Influence? Derivative thinking can make for an ideal springboard, given an ability to narrow the onrush of influences and a willingness to seek new tangents of thought and deed.

I have spent the past several months—with a stretch yet ahead—on a 20-years-after return to a comic-book series called *Prowler* for ComicMix, starting with a digital-media remastering of the original Eclipse Comics stories (1987–1989), moving into a short-stack file of unproduced scripts and raw-material ideas from that period, and settling in at length with a new novelistic *Prowler* yarn that will tie up some raveled plot–threads from the Eclipse episodes and then head off in other directions.

The reunion of the primary creative team (Timothy Truman, John K. Snyder III, and Yrs. Trly.) re–summons the influences with which we had sought to develop 4Winds Studios' 10 *Prowler* books as a Mulligan Stew of such persistent interests as ancient Hebraic Law and American frontier vigilantism; the Deep Southern blues and gospel-music traditions as a response to repressive social and economic conditions; the now-horrific, now-heroic irrationalities of Depression Era pulp fiction; and the bizarre extravagances of Old Hollywood's low-budget horror-movie factories.

Truman and Snyder had defined two vigilante Prowler figures, each representing a distinct generation of indignant humanity, by the time I signed on with the project, late in 1986. While Truman and I were sharing a bookstore tour to promote our respective titles at Eclipse—Tim, with *Scout* and *Airboy*, and my ownself with the movie-history book *Forgotten Horrors*—Tim came up with the idea of twisting the plots of some of those 1930s-period *Forgotten Horrors* titles to accommodate the early-day exploits of the first-generation Prowler.

Hence the appropriation of Bela Lugosi's hoodoo-man character from *White Zombie* (1932) as a recurring annoyance for Leo Kragg, alias the Prowler. And hence the adaptation of such movie yarns as *The Vampire Bat* and *The Sphinx* (both from 1933) as *Prowler*-series vehicles. References to Republic Pictures' Saturday-matinee cliffhanger serials crept in, as well, as did another Lugosi character, the benevolent sorcerer known as Chandu the Magician. A recurring back-story allusion to

an elusive world-beating Chinese Mandarin bespoke a shared fondness for the *Fu Manchu* tales of Sax Rohmer and such Tong War movies as William A. Wellman's *The Hatchet Man* (1932) and William Nigh's *The Mysterious Mr. Wong* (1933). Such points rode a ragged edge between inside-joke overkill and heartfelt homage—with a saner middle-ground objective of crafting something new and unusual from a mixed bag of abiding influences. (Our nods to Lugosi garnered a favorably amused response from the actor's son, Bela G. Lugosi, when I presented him with a run of the Eclipse Prowlers during the 1990s.)

The new *Prowler* story, in development, taps such influences anew—alluding here to a true-crime *cause célèbre* of the last century and delving further, there, into a tense if long-dormant relationship between Leo Kragg and his Lois Lane/Vicky Vale surrogate, a pure-gumption journalist named Geraldine Crane. No plot–spoilers, here, although it bears mentioning, too, that one element owes a tangled debt to a spontaneous-combustion combination of Richard Connell (1924's "The Most Dangerous Game") and H.P. Lovecraft (1937's "The Thing on the Doorstep") and Popeye's E.C. Segar, by way of David Cronenberg's film *Scanners* (1981). Mulligan Stew, okay, if not Creole Gumbo. My overriding narrative attitude combines the social-critic bearings of a lengthy career in newspaper editorializing—coupled, perhaps, with family ties to the satirist Roger Price—and an ancestral background in oral-tradition storytelling. To say nothing of a long-term admiration for the acerbic laughing-to-keep-from-crying wit of such comics masters as Walt Kelly and Steve Gerber. But I digress.

Yes, and lest I lapse into laundry-listing all the influences under which I write, I should cut to a single point of reference that cropped up, unbidden, a few weeks ago while *Prowler* artist John K. Snyder III and I were discussing how best to portray the conflict of two personalities inhabiting a single mind. I happened to notice a teevee-grid reference to a Turner Classic Movies marathon of octopus movies—1955's *It Came from Beneath the Sea*, 1948's *Wake of the Red Witch*, 1933's *Below the Sea*—and wondered if this package might include an oddity from 1937 called *Sh! The Octopus*.

Elspeth Dudgeon.

Now, that Warner Bros. film is renowned (term used advisedly) primarily for its arresting title, and for its pageant of slapstick absurdities in the service of a murder yarn. In the midst of the concentrated foolishness, however, there lies one of the most jarring split-personality transformations ever to grace the screen. A fresh look at this sequence might yield a suggestion or two about how to play a similarly conceived moment in the new *Prowler* yarn. *Writing under the influence*, like the man said.

So I turned the teevee-book page and found a fourth title in the Turner lineup: The fine-print listing cited only *Octopus*, but a look at the Turner Classic Web site affirmed the selection as William C. McGann's *Sh! The Octopus*. Time for a rediscovery.

Sh! The Octopus springs from the Broadway-to-H'wood genre known as the Mystery Farce, which contains such essential titles as *The Cat and the Canary* (1927), *Black Waters* (1929), *The Bat* and *The Bat Whispers* (1926–1930), and two versions of *The Gorilla* (1927–1930). *Sh! The Octopus* takes place in a presumably abandoned lighthouse, which has attracted an oddly matched gathering. A master criminal known as the Octopus is at large, but there also appears to be a marauding tentacled octopus lurking about. A corpse hangs from a high beam. Hidden passageways and peep-hole hiding–places abound. Two loopy detectives (Hugh Herbert and Allen Jenkins) are among the inmates. An ill-tempered caretaker known as Capt. Hook (George Rosener) seems to have wandered in from a *Peter Pan* troupe.

The tale veers off toward espionage and death-ray science fiction but goes nowhere in particular until Hugh Herbert finds himself in a weird, almost poignant, interlude with a sweet little old granny-lady stereotype (Elspeth Dudgeon, from James Whale's *The Old Dark House* of 1932). A gathering of the ensemble cast follows, with an outburst of violence that provokes a transformation in the old woman. Her pleasant face contorts itself into a grimace as her flesh rots and her teeth turn to fangs—seemingly in Real Time, without cutaways or stop-motion effects. (And of course it's in real time: Camera chief Arthur L. Todd accomplished the trick with graduating lens–filters, revealing layers of grotesque makeup. This device is a variant upon the techniques that cinematographer Karl Struss had employed on the healing-of-the-lepers sequence in the 1925 *Ben–Hur*, and on Fredric March's transformations in the 1931 *Dr. Jekyll & Mr. Hyde*.)

The Rubber Reality ramblings of *Sh! The Octopus* point toward a finale, following a climactic disaster, in which the fidgety comedian Hugh Herbert wakes from a dream—cringing from Elspeth Dudgeon's hideous transformation, only to be reminded that she is his mother–in–law. One movie-buff blogger, Scott Ashlin, characterizes the film as "nearly impervious to synopsis, let alone analysis" and suggests "the disconcerting possibility that its creators understood exactly what they were doing," noting, after all, "Isn't that exactly the way dreams really work?"

Exactly, if not more so. And sometimes, one's forgotten or dis-remembered dreams—whether in the slumbering mind or on the night-owl movie screen—will intrude upon the storytelling imperative to suggest new possibilities. So stay tuned for further developments, already. And stay attuned to those lurking influences.

AMOS 'N' ANDY IN CINEMATIC EMBRYO

April 27, 2008: An earlier installment of this column (Page No. 259) had examined a 1931 gorillas-at-large movie called *Ingagi* as an unlikely long-term influence upon the Popular Culture as a class. *Ingagi*, a chump-change production built largely around misappropriated African-safari footage and staged mock-jungle sequences, tapped a popular fascination with apes as a class even as it fostered a generalized anti–enlightenment toward natural history and racial politics.

Strange, then, that the film should have inspired a sequel (unofficial, of course, and certainly in name only) from a resolutely Afrocentric sector of the motion-picture industry. The production resources behind 1940's *Son of Ingagi* stem from white-capitalist niche-market corporate interests—but the screenwriter and star player, and his supporting ensemble cast, all represent a trailblazing movement in black independent cinema.

From momentum that he had developed beginning with *Son of Ingagi* at Alfred Sack's Texas-based Sack Amusement Enterprises, Spencer Williams, JR., attained recognition that would lead him to a role-of-a-lifetime breakthrough in 1950, with his casting as Andrew Brown on a CBS–Television adaptation of a long-running radio serial called *Amos 'n' Andy*. Though created by white-guy talents Freeman Gosden and Charles Correll, *Amos 'n' Andy* needed black artists for its on-screen representation. (Gosden and Correll had gotten away with blackface portrayals in 1930's *Check and Double Check*; the tactic would not have borne repeating in 1950.) The partners hired a pioneering showman of the pre-Depression Harlem Renaissance period, Flournoy E. Miller, as casting director for the CBS–TV project, and Miller came through with such memorable presences as Williams, Tim Moore as George "Kingfish" Stevens, and Alvin Childress as Amos Jones, Andy Brown's business partner.

Popular acceptance (since 1928) of *Amos 'n' Andy* gave way gradually to controversy and cancellation of the teleseries (by 1953), even though the teevee version had tempered its broader caricatures with resourceful likability and affectionate warmth while granting mass-media exposure to an under-employed sector of Hollywood's talent pool. As a general-audience attraction, *Amos 'n' Andy* also helped to signal a gradual end to segregated moviegoing. Which amounted to good news for the Popular Culture—and a career-wrecking development for Spencer Williams.

What had seemed a bold strategy for Williams in 1950 proved at length to have been a misstep upon the cancellation of his starring teleseries. He could not turn back to the off-Hollywood movie studios, for producer Al Sack—who had granted Williams creative autonomy since the small-market watershed of *Son of Ingagi* in 1939–1940—had

STAR THEATRE
Bancroft, Iowa

MATINEE AND NIGHT
THURSDAY, THANKSGIVING

NOV. 27

! **Thrill** !

Follows

Thrill !

INGAGI
(GORILLA)

WAS DARWIN RIGHT?

See Wild Women who live with Gorillas—
• • •
Children who are half-human atrocities! Plunge into the dim mysteries and savage horrors of Jungle Life!
• • •
Chill your blood by seeing Actual Scenes of Bestiality and Savagery that has all America interested, and the Scientific World agog!

'INGAGI'
(Gorilla)

...Shambling giant Ape Brutes...Strange, tearing, clawing Half-Men...Leopards speared on the run ...A Living Wooman sacrificed to Man-Killing Apes before your Very Eyes... Learn of the Customs of Savage African Tribes... Listen to the Weird Chant of the Congo!

See and Hear Creatures, Half Ape and Half Human!

by 1953 edged away from the movie business, sensing the approaching collapse of the black-neighborhood theater circuits that had been his primary marketplace. Nor could Williams move forward in the major leagues of network television or Hollywood–at–large: The industry was damnably slow to open such doors, such mass-appeal powerhouse talents as Lena Horne, Eddie "Rochester" Anderson, and Dorothy Dandridge notwithstanding.

Williams' isolated creative prime of 1937–1946 had begun finding its shape in 1910, when the Louisiana-born artist landed a messenger job with Oscar Hammerstein in New York. Williams became a songwriter and recording artist, an audio engineer for the emerging talking-picture industry, and a scenarist and actor in collaboration with the Yiddish Southerner humorist Octavus Roy Cohen on a late-1920s series of comedies about black-neighborhood life. If Cohen's yarns indulged in blatant stereotypes, still Williams' involvement seasoned the adaptations with a sense of authenticity that is lacking in the larger studios' similarly concerned films of the same period. (A representative title is 1929's *The Framing of the Shrew*.)

After Williams had contributed dialogue and a supporting-role presence to Herbert Jeffries' black-ensemble cowboy movies of the waning 1930s, distributor Al Sack bought Williams' original script for *Son of Ingagi* and hired him to play a bumbling but ultimately helpful police detective. Sack was so pleased with the result that he enlisted Williams as a producer–director–writer–star for a nine-film stretch.

Where Herb Jeffries' Harlem-out-West movies follow frontier-adventure formulas very like those that had served the white-guy likes of Ken Maynard, Gene Autry, and Roy Rogers, Williams' screenplay for *Son of Ingagi* is no more a conventional horror movie than it is a formal sequel to the 1931 *Ingagi*.

The film boasts a monster and a Mad Doctor—of course. But the renegade physician is a woman (played by the distinguished stage actress Laura Bowman), in an inversion of traditionally masculine casting of such roles. (*Son of Ingagi* foreshadows two major-studio B–picture productions of 1942–1943: *Dr. Renault's Secret*, with George Zucco as the crazed scientist and J. Carrol Naish as an ape–become–human; and *Captive Wild Woman*, with John Carradine and Acquanetta Davenport in the respective roles.)

In *Son of Ingagi*, the forbidden objective of Laura Bowman's character has less to do with outlaw laboratory shenanigans than with luring an innocent young woman (Daisy Bufford) into a forcible tryst with a captive ape–man (Zack Williams, no kin to Spencer, though both had origins in Louisiana). The most nearly direct nod to the original *Ingagi* involves a suggestion that the ape–man comes from Africa. He bears the name of N'gena, which might sound something like *Ingagi*.

Williams' screenplay concerns itself primarily with establishing a lifelike domestic situation between Daisy Bufford and Alfred Grant, as the romantic leads, and with Williams' comical portrayal of a cop who seems incapable of detecting the monster at close range. The story has as much to do with a hidden fortune in African gold, sought by the scientist's crooked brother (Arthur Ray). Amidst the search through a house riddled with hidden passageways, N'Gena abducts his quarry but accidentally sets the place afire. Williams and Grant perform the necessary rescues, salvaging the treasure in the process.

Williams' deft comic timing accounts for much of the appeal, and so does Laura Bowman's portrayal of the ape–man's foredoomed keeper as an impatient grouch. Williams' script is rich in the finer points of middle-class household life, dwelling upon the hospitable details of a wedding reception, reveling in a love of music, and establishing early on that the doctor has conflicted reasons—some friendly, some sinister—for wanting to see the young woman inherit a gloomy house and its laboratory. Bufford and Grant make convincing newlyweds, even to the point of an outbreak of bickering.

Spencer Williams' greater body of work as an off-Hollywood filmmaker, including such high points as *The Blood of Jesus* (1941) and *Dirty Gertie from Harlem, U.S.A.* (1946), is preserved in the Tyler, Texas, Black Film Collection, Southwest Film & Video Archive, at Southern Methodist University in Dallas.

IAN SHAUGHNESSY EMERGING

May 4, 2008: From V.T. Hamlin in the 1920s and Etta Hulme during the midcentury, through the *Superman* books of Kerry Gammill in times more recent, Fort Worth, Texas, and its environs have long yielded a wealth of storytelling artistry to the comics industry at large.

An ambitious new representative of that regional-breakout scene is graphic novelist Ian Shaughnessy, of Arlington, Texas. Shaughnessy's books for Portland, Oregon-based Oni Press—including an edgy comedy–of–errors called *Shenanigans*, with the Canadian illustrator Mike Holmes—bespeak a childhood fascination with comics, filtered through a lifelong love of language and an interest in taking the words-and-pictures medium to provocative literary levels more commonly associated with the independent filmmaking sector.

"I find myself writing under the direct influence of Billy Wilder," says Shaughnessy, 24, invoking the name of a great screenwriter–director whose career spanned from 1929 into the 1980s. "I discovered Wilder during the 1990s with *The Apartment* [1960], then with *Double Indemnity* [1944], and found myself very inspired—in a lasting way.

"With *Shenanigans*, I found myself attempting to honor the spirit of Billy Wilder—that mastery that he had of romantic tensions, with finding the humor in awkward situations—as a key influence."

Any such talent needs a practical springboard. With V.T. Hamlin, the creator of a famous comic strip called *Alley Oop* that has survived him by many years, the springboard was a cartooning job at the Fort Worth *Star–Telegram*. Hamlin spent much of the 1920s at the daily paper, generating such local-interest attractions as a serialized feature about a formidable minor-league baseball club, the Fort Worth Cats. (A retrospective collection of Hamlin's *Oop*-prototype *Panther Kitten* cartoons is in preparation, along with an earlier Hamlin gag strip called *The Hired Hand*, whose booklet edition has been out of print since the 1920s.) [*That collection arrived in 2015 as* Alley Oop's Ancestors, *from Cremo Studios.*]

For Etta Hulme, the *Star–Telegram*'s signature opinion-page cartoonist since 1972, an early breakthrough lay in a post-WWII comic-book series about a cowboy critter, *Red Rabbit*. Graphic designer–turned–publisher Kerry Gammill spent the 1980s and earlier 1990s as an illustrator with Marvel Comics and DC Comics, then moved into motion-picture conceptual art on such productions as 1998's *Blues Brothers 2000* and 1999's *Storm of the Century*.

Ian Shaughnessy traces his springboard to a fortunate connection, as a schoolboy, with Oni Press. Shaughnessy represents not only a new generation of niche-market comics talent, but also a fondness for mainstream comic-book influences—although he favors the independent-publishing arena—that he traces to one childhood favorite, an issue of *Batman*.

"I grew up reading," Shaughnessy recalls, "with strong encouragement from my parents—and I've always read comics. But that one issue of *Batman*, with its powerful interpretation by Matt Wagner—I bought it at an airport newsstand, and it left me with an impression that this would be the kind of storytelling that I'd like to do." Wagner has remained a direct influence, Shaughnessy adds, although "the business of writing my own stuff has left me with little time to read the newer comics as extensively as I might like."

His family encouraged the interest early on with a trip in 1999 to the Chicago Comics Convention. The upstart publishing firm of Oni Press was touting a comics-spinoff version of that year's most lucrative independent-film release, *The Blair Witch Project*.

Shaughnessy found the Chicago expo "more mainstream than indie" but felt drawn to the Oni booth, where he met such talents as Greg Rucka and his wife, *Blair Witch* comics scripter Jen Van Meter, and editor Jamie S. Rich.

"They kind of took me under their wing, you might say, and by the time I had completed high school I had been offered a summer internship at Oni Press in Portland," says Shaughnessy. "One internship led to another, and although I knew that I wanted to write, more so than to work as an editor, I enjoyed the experience a great deal—a real turning–point. Turned out, too, that Jamie Rich also wanted to create, as opposed to working as an editor. And so we've both ended up in that creative realm.

"But I also believe that what writing strengths I may have developed owe a great deal to the editorial internship at Oni," Shaughnessy adds. "I found a publisher that had dedicated itself to stories of a certain human dimension—as opposed to the mainstream's overall greater interest in sensational adventures—and ... a publisher willing to provide not only a learning experience but also a creative outlet over the longer term.

"And that has been my real education beyond high school," he says, "although I won't rule out the prospect of a college-degree plan. One of these days."

A pivotal assignment has involved a graphic-novel project called *Strangetown*, with the writer-artist Chynna Clugston. Planned as a series involving a disoriented central character at large in a city of mystery, *Strangetown* has been interrupted by other commitments for Clugston. She and Shaughnessy plan to resume the serial in due course.

"In all, just now," says Shaughnessy, "I've got three graphic novels in preparation. Mike Holmes and I have tightened our collaborative skills to a point where we can communicate instinctively.

"When Mike started drawing the pages for *Shenanigans*, we had not yet met in person and I had written only 50–or–so pages of the finished script. And as Mike's illustrated pages started coming in and we moved closer to completing the book, I found that I was writing less exhaustive stage-instruction descriptions and he was sensing more and more of the situations from my dialogue among the characters."

Shaughnessy devotes about half his working time to the writing process, preparing scripts as if writing a stage-play or a screenplay but reserving the right to resort to pencil-and-paper notes to test the credible flow of his characters' dialogue. He envisions a generally young readership, given *Shenanigans*' array of college-age characters, but often finds himself surprised to find his audience leaning toward middle age.

"So who's the audience, anyhow?" Shaughnessy asks. "People who can relate to committed storytelling."

As to technique, he mentions: "A lot of people look at me kind of weird when I say I'll test–write a dialogue sequence in pencil. But it's a system that works for me. If an exchange reads well in longhand, then I'll key it into the script.

"I'm really bad about self–editing," he adds. "Sometimes, I'll set aside a sequence and try not to think about it for a while—but of course then it'll prey on my mind until I go back to try to get it right. Sometimes, a spontaneous rush of words will work as a finished product. But sometimes I'll scrap it and start over."

Shaughnessy devotes about half a workday to the writing, setting no page–quota but pursuing a regimen of plotting and outlining, which he considers necessary to the development of a finished script.

"The graphic novel, unlike the traditional comics magazine, gives you a good 100 pages and more to tell a story," he explains. "With the graphic novel, you don't have to worry about writing to fit into a fixed page–count, and your story can unfold more naturally—less episodically."

The long-term commitments anticipate Shaughnessy's objective of making comics a full-scale career.

"The comics career is finding its way," says Shaughnessy. "I'm concentrating on the writing, on polishing the skills with dialogue and life-like situations and character development, and not worrying about commercial prospects beyond the delivery of a book that's worth publishing. A lot of comics nowadays, especially with the current rush of movie-studio interest in comic-book properties, read as though they were written as movie pitches more so than self-sufficient stories. The bigger comics conventions, too, like San Diego's, seem to have become less about a love of comics than about movie-studio hype.

"And, too, the publishers have their own people who deal with movie-development prospects, if a book should come to that. My job is just that of telling a good story.

"I'm in it for the love of comics—that's the basis," says Shaughnessy, "and for my belief in the medium as an area of great potential for telling stories about real people in credible situations."

HILLBILLY LOVE SLAVES OF THE OZARKS

May 11, 2008: Sixty-five years after a double-edged sword of a movie called *Child Bride of the Ozarks* professed to indict the custom of underage marriage—while courting a leering, voyeuristic audience, naturally—the issue remains urgent. The April-of-2008 raids upon a polygamist sect in Texas demonstrate that such persistence, involving girls scarcely into their teens, belongs as much to the presumably Civilized World as to the more thoroughly well-hidden corners of the planet: The Yearning for Zion Ranch had hidden in plain sight, a Third World concentration camp, bunkered in alongside Mainstream Amerika.

Meanwhile in the Dominant Culture, a Florida-based plastic surgeon named Michael Salzhauer has published a cartoon–storybook testament to female objectification called *My Beautiful Mommy* (Big Tent Books) that purports to "[guide] children through Mommy's [cosmetic] surgery and healing process in a friendly, nonthreatening way"—nonthreatening, that is, until one grasps the deeper message: Looks are everything, and you get what you can pay for. The greater objective would appear the preconditioning of a next generation of face-lift addicts: Better start saving up now, girlie, and maybe develop an eating disorder as a prelude.

So which sector, or sect, is the less civilized? The backwater zealots who propose to wait out the Apocalypse in round-robin conjugal confinement with brides young enough to be their granddaughters? Or the proponents of glamour–at–a–price?

Dr. Salzhauer's idealized *Beautiful Mommy*, as pictured on the cover of that scrofulous little book, calls to mind nothing so much as an over-glamorized Britney Spears or Miley Cyrus, perhaps a Bratz–meets–Barbie: Never too young to aspire to such artificiality, never too old to lay claim to it, given a loaded checkbook. Photographs from the Yearning for Zion round–up suggest nothing so much as some 19TH Century agrarian-society re–enactment, but the forcibly modest attire of the young women involved conveys an aspect more ominous than bucolic.

About that movie: My lingering impression of Harry Revier's *Child Bride of the Ozarks* has hinged more upon featured player Angelo Rossitto (1908–1991) than with any social-agenda implications. Rossitto, a pioneering dwarf player of Old Hollywood, had reminisced fondly about *Child Bride* during a series of late-in-life interviews for the *Forgotten Horrors* film-history books. George Turner's and my chapter on *Child Bride* in *Forgotten Horrors Vol. 2*, in turn, deals as much with Rossitto as with the picture itself.

"I especially liked the part I was lucky enough to get in a little picture called *Child Bride*," Rossitto told us in 1990. "That was one that could've been just the usual creepy-dwarf business"—and indeed, the advertising campaign emphasizes Rossitto's grotesque make-up—"but they let me *do* some things with it. Unusual, that a picture will let a little guy step in and save the day."

Exploitation producer Raymond Fridgen made *Child Bride* as a roadshow attraction, for release outside the conventional film-distri-

bution channels. As such, the film was issued without a Production Code Administration Purity Seal—destined for those smaller theatres that occasionally ran adults-only shows, for burlesque houses, and for four-wall situations in which the distributor would rent (literally speaking) the four walls of an auditorium for as many weeks as the film could draw a crowd.

Unlike many others of its kind, *Child Bride* boasts competent work from Hollywood-based professional tradespeople. More surprisingly, the film presents a fairly realistic story—a sort of poor-relations composite of 1941's *Swamp Water* and *Tobacco Road*, with foreshadowings of Elia Kazan's once-notorious *Baby Doll* (1956)—and captures the naturalistic horror that comes with the territory among inbred and isolated communities. The tale is related grimly, with scant conscious humor, although laughter might be a sensible response to Frank Martin's foppishly enacted city-slicker romantic lead and the overplaying of a courageous schoolteacher by Diana Durrell (who was the wife–to–be of producer Fridgen).

The cast is peopled largely with unknowns, but Warner Richmond, well cast as the lustful villain, was a veteran of the 1921 filming of *Tol'able David* and a popular Bad Guy presence in Westerns and serials of the 1930s. The title player, Shirley Mills, fares well enough in a difficult role, displaying a defiant mettle to offset her more demeaning moments of conspicuous nudity. (Mills had appeared as Ruth Joad in John Ford's 1940 filming of the John Steinbeck *The Grapes of Wrath*.)

Likewise familiar, though more as a memorable presence than as a marquée name, is two-foot-ten Angelo Rossitto, who had graced the screen since the waning 1920s and claimed a prominent role of heroic vengeance in Tod Browning's *Freaks* (1932). During the 1940s,

Rossitto also operated a newsstand at the busy corner of Hollywood Boulevard and Wilcox, made a run for mayor of Los Angeles ("finished seventh in a field of eight, yes, I did," he told us) and appeared now and again as a skulking accomplice to career badman Bela Lugosi. *Child Bride* bills Rossitto under a pseudonym, Don Barrett, although his character bears the name of Angelo.

Child Bride finds Shirley Mills playing Jennie Colton, schoolgirl daughter of a moonshiner (George Humphreys) whose business partner, Jake Bolby (Warner Richmond), also serves as the town bully. A schoolteacher, Miss Carol (Durrell), begins a campaign to end the hill-country tradition of grown men marrying young girls, with the help of her fiancé (Martin), a lawyer. Bolby orders the abduction and torture of Miss Carol. Angelo, who works at Bolby's whiskey still, provokes a raid to rescue the teacher.

Bolby kills Jennie's father and threatens to accuse Jennie's mother in the slaying—the better to claim the girl as his wife. A schoolboy (Bob Bollinger) with a crush on Jennie threatens to kill Bolby, but Angelo intervenes and guns down the bootlegger. None too soon. Miss Carol's efforts are rewarded with the passage of a law banning child marriage.

"It all became very real to me," Shirley Mills said during the 1990s. "The only hard part was displaying fear of the villain [Richmond] because he was so kind and considerate to me... But suddenly he became very ominous because of his own acting ability."

Filmed considerably earlier than its formal release date in January 1943 (Mills recalls a shooting schedule in 1938), *Child Bride* feigned a socially influential position consistent with the lofty objectives of its schoolteacher character. The film was hardly in such a position, however, and Raymond Fridgen was more interested in selling tickets than with advancing reforms.

Fridgen went through the motions of applying for a Purity Seal, but the film industry's Production Code Administration refused the credential. Of course, nudity and rude misconduct abound, not to mention the overriding air of degeneracy implicit in the very title. Then, too, Hollywood's built-in censorship machine would have preferred to see Rossitto's character punished for his murderous act of heroism: No penalty, no Purity Seal.

Although director Harry Revier paces the yarn briskly, he dwells nonetheless upon the earthier details of backwoods life. A particularly queasy element is a skinny-dipping sequence for Shirley Mills—this, for the benefit of any viewers who might have entertained the same perversity that the picture condemns. A similarly glaring dual standard occurs in a prologue stating that the producers seek to improve the lives of the mountain folk, and that no disparagement is intended. Oh, yeah, *right*. Such excesses are, even so, tied to what dramatic strengths the film possesses, in an unusual display of integrity among pictures of this slum-cinema class.

The film's professed interest in derailing a demeaning tradition proves to have been no such thing—not back then, and certainly not in the enlightened (term used advisedly) here–and–now. The aim was to peddle Gawker Bait, plain and simple, and reforms be damned. The present day's comparable situations, from reclusive U.S. outposts, to foreign provinces, to a metastasized resurgence of mass-media objectification, render a rediscovery of *Child Bride of the Ozarks* all the more unnerving, as much a prophecy as a crass relic.

Etta Hulme: Self–caricature.

WOMEN IN COMICS: ETTA HULME

May 18, 2008: During 1992–1993, my newspaper-of-record became a sponsor of a traveling exhibition of art tracing the centuried history of editorial-opinion cartooning in Texas. Curators Maury Forman and Bob Calvert, seeking to preserve the display as a book, enlisted me to edit their program notes into manuscript form. The finished result, *Cartooning Texas* (Texas A&M University Press; 1993), boasts a cover design by my cartooning cohort (and Pulitzer Medalist) Ben Sargent. The book has outlived the exhibition by a good many years—but of course could use an updating by now.

One timely offshoot was that our expo-opening ceremonies involved such Working Cartoonists as Sargent himself, of the Austin *American–Statesman,* and Etta Parks Hulme, of the Fort Worth *Star–Telegram,* in panel discussions and sketch-demonstration sessions that served to bring the exhibition into the here–and–now. Or the there–and–then, as it were. Etta and I officed within shouting distance of one another at the *Star–Telegram,* and I had been pressing the Powers That Did Be for a couple of years about devoting a *Telegram-*spinoff book to her cartoons.

The leverage of the exhibition proved sufficient, if only just, to encourage a Hulme book from the *Star–Telegram.* More of a pamphlet, actually, but it compiled a fairly generous selection of 'toons, with a page for each piece. I had suggested that we call the thing *Ettatorials,* but the newspaper's marketing office preferred *UnforgETTAbly Etta.*

And *UnforgETTAbly Etta* went promptly out of print as a subscription premium, priming the pump for a Pelican Publishing Co. collection of Etta's work. That one surfaced in 1998 as *The Ettatorials: The Best of Etta Hulme.* Sometimes it takes a while for a good title to kick in.

Around the time of the *Cartooning Texas* exhibition, I also had been visiting with Trina Robbins in San Francisco in connection with her research for *A Century of Women Cartoonists* (Kitchen Sink Press; 1993), suggesting such Texas talents as newspaper cartoonists Nell Williams, from Amarillo, and Etta Hulme. Trina's interest lay less with editorial cartooning than with comic-book and comic-strip artistry. But I kept pressing the idea that Trina should take a closer look at Etta—who had worked for the Disney Machine during WWII, and who, I sensed, must have something of a comics pedigree. During one of the Cartooning Texas presentations, I asked Etta about a comics background.

"Oh, yeah—you *bet!*" she said. "Did you ever hear tell of *Red Rabbit?*"

"*You* did *Red Rabbit?*" I asked. The title, from Chicago-based Dearfield Publishing, had been an early-childhood favorite of mine—a funny-animal comic with an unusual ring of cowhand authenticity.

"Oh, yeah," Etta said. "One of my more ambitious youthful efforts. Had a pretty good run with it. I was Etta Parks, in those days. Sometimes signed myself as just-plain 'Etta.'

"And ol' *Red Rabbit*, now, those funnybooks gave me good excuse to take off from my Disney-studio experience and combine it with an interest in wild-and-wooly Western adventures."

• • •

Etta Parks Hulme was born Dec. 22, 1923, at Somerville, Texas. She has been a widely distributed opinion-page mainstay, based at the Fort Worth *Star–Telegram*, since 1972.

Having completed a fine-arts degree from the University of Texas at Austin, Etta spent two years in the Disney animation shop during WWII, after military conscription had caused the studio to relax its barriers against the hiring of women. Etta returned to Texas during the postwar years as a commercial artist and art instructor. She spent a late-1940s/early-1950s stretch with Dearfield in Chicago, working on the *Red Rabbit* comics. Back in Texas by the waning 1950s, Etta began cartooning for *The Texas Observer*. She and her husband, a coal-company executive named Vernon Hulme, settled in Fort Worth.

Etta Hulme.

"Mr. Hulme and I made a good team," Etta told me several years ago, "what with my left-of-center political-cartooning career and his corporate-industrial career—coal-mining exploration, at that, during a time [the 1970s] when Texas was just starting to develop an environmental conscience.

"But Mr. Hulme also was ahead of his time, in that regard," she added. "He had a policy of taking great care to minimize the damages of any mining operation, and when his company [Texas Industries] located one huge vein of coal in 1977 at Thurber, Texas, he even took pains to protect the migratory route of a rare breed of bird in that area." (Vernon Hulme died in 1983.)

The lapse from the Old Guard Liberalism of *The Texas Observer* to the provincial *Star–Telegram* might have found Etta's readers expecting a softening of her social-critic voice. The Hulme cartoons have retained their edge, from then to now, at the mainstream daily.

"Good old-fashioned ridicule—that's the ticket," Etta says. "And a lot of absurdity, too. Let the readers know you're having fun, poking fun at the politicians and taking a stand on the issues, and they're likely as not to get a kick out of a cartoon even if they disagree with it. All except for those miserable souls who can't take a joke.

"I love gettin' disagreeable letters," she adds. "I just love stirrin' the pot until it boils over. Objections from the readers, disagreements with whatever stance I might take—nothin' to 'em. Just give me some Real World abuses of power or political absurdities to work with, and I'll find the humor necessary to point up the seriousness of a situation. The only obstacles I've ever encountered have been the occasional editors who are leery of my gettin' 'too opinionated,' as they'll say, and want to slam on the brakes for me.

"Well, y'know, there's a reason we call these things 'editorial opinion cartoons,'" says Etta Hulme. "I'm in this business to dispense opinions, and—if the job gets done right—to get people stirred up while keepin' things on the funny side."

[*Etta Hulme retired from the newsroom later on in 2008 but carried on with the cartooning. She died in 2014.*]

STUART GORDON'S 'STUCK,' UNSTUCK

May 25, 2008: A general release has been too long in coming for *Stuck*, Stuart Gordon's mordant and mournful film about a traffic accident and its criminal aftermath. I began picking up on the raves shortly after a film-critic comrade, Joe Leydon, caught the picture at 2007's Toronto Film Festival and published a favorable review in the show-biz tradepaper *Variety*. Joe suggested a "carefully calibrated theatrical roll-out" but added: "Difficult to tell whether the sardonically edgy pic will reach many mainstream auds before fast–forwarding to homevid."

Now comes word of a belated, slightly broader, opening for *Stuck*—three months after a well-received showing at the American Film Institute/Dallas Festival. ThinkFilm, the distributor, keeps hedging about general distribution. I have pressed for a film-fest slot or a commercial engagement in Fort Worth because that is where my newspaper's core readership dwells. And because *Stuck* owes its dire inspiration to a Real World ordeal that took place in Fort Worth.

"Why, we couldn't show a movie like that in Fort Worth's very own film festival," one Leading Light of the FW-based Lone Star Film Society told me last fall after I had recommended *Stuck* as a centerpiece for a November 2007 event. "We're here 'To Preserve and Present the Art of the Moving Image'—just as our Mission Statement declares—not to dredge up any horrible memories."

"Yeah, well," I answered—once that "yeah, well" injunction kicks in, any such exchange is doomed to deteriorate—"an occasional reminder might do us all some sobering good. And besides, the film uses the local case only as a springboard. Changes the setting and fictionalizes a lot. More an inspiration than an explicit reflection."

"I'd be careful how I used that term, *inspiration*, if I were you," came the reply. "Anyone who would find inspiration in such a ghastly occurrence has no business being allowed to make movies." (Guardians of the Culture, take note.)

"*Hmmm*," I said, unable to resist. "So then how do you explain the selection of [Sidney Lumet's] *Before the Devil Knows You're Dead* or [György Pálfi's] *Taxidermia* for the current festival? Some pretty 'ghastly occurrences,' there."

"Those pictures are fictional," said the Cultural Gatekeeper. "Or outright fantasy. And besides, they're not local." End of discussion: Those superior debating skills get 'em every time.

• • •

One night in 2001 in Fort Worth, a nurse's aide and after-hours hedonist named Chanté Mallard was driving home after a night of overindulgence when her automobile struck a pedestrian named Gregory Glenn Biggs. Thrown head–first through the windshield, Biggs pleaded with Mallard to summon help. She drove home, instead, garaged her car,

Stuart Gordon.

and left Biggs to die. With secretive assistance from a fellow degenerate, she had the body moved to a neighborhood park, to leave the appearance of a hit-and-run fatality. Some loose talk and a tipster eventually led the police to Mallard, who landed a 50-year prison sentence.

The shock registered communitywide—Fort Worth, despite an increasing population and cosmopolitan airs to match, still likes to consider itself one of those it-can't-happen-here towns—and resonates yet. Robert Wilonsky, who writes for the *Dallas Observer* branch of Village Voice Media, acknowledged *Stuck* with a facile snark: "Fort Worth, you're stuck with this one," while appraising the film's likelier commercial prospects along "the sick-and-twisted cult circuit."

The ivory-tower critical conceit that crime-and-horror films as a class have no business addressing a "mainstream" audience is nothing new. Such figures as Martin Scorsese and Jonathan Demme and Sidney Lumet, who often draw upon such inspirations, appear exempt—but mention the name of Stuart Gordon or various of his signature pictures (also including the H.P. Lovecraft adaptations *Re–Animator* and *From Beyond*), and the Critical Brethren will resort mechanically to such dismissive terms as *sick-and-twisted* and *campy*. One prominent critic's response to *Stuck* at the AFI/Dallas Fest hailed "serious guilty-pleasure potential," invoking one of the more cowardly expressions in the film-reviewing arsenal. Another offered condescending praise as "enjoyably trashy" and "breezy camp."

Gordon, of course, has no such sleazy bearings. His films since 1985's *Re–Animator*, a confrontational elaboration upon Lovecraft, bespeak, rather, a willingness to jar his viewers out of a state of passive complacency in order to state a case for the Human Condition as an abyss of obsessive susceptibility. Allegory, underscored in crimson. The attitude seems made to order for the exploitation-film industry. This self-evident truth was especially so at that time, a generation ago, when the boundaries of the horror-movie genre were ripe for some serious gerrymandering—shortly before the major corporate studios began annexing the territory of grindhouse cinema and forcing the genuinely audacious low-budget studios to retrench into either extinction or home video.

But Gordon's moviemaking career has been more an extension of his loyalties to the legitimate stage than any bid for film-industry prominence or notoriety. Our one face-to-face visit, during a promotional tour for his 1987 film *Dolls*, proved more concerned with Gordon's seminal involvement with the broadly experimental and influential Organic Theatre Company of Chicago. That connection, in turn, signifies deep ties to the present-day ComicMix ensemble.

• • •

The tragic absurdities of *Stuck* were in place well before screenwriter John Strysik set to work on the tale. Its parallels with the Chanté Mallard case capture vividly the bleak paths of two ordinary citizens forced onto a collision–course by bad timing, bad habits, and a New Depression Economy. Tom (played by Stephen Rea) seems a bright middle-class businessman, rendered an outcast by a chain–reversal of fortune. Brandi (Mena Suvari) appears a dedicated sort, though inordinately fond of dope and booze.

Faced with joblessness and homelessness and a bureaucratic brush–off, Tom finds himself wandering the area where Brandi is attempting to drive home while under a buzz. Their violent crossing leaves her shaken, but not so much so that she cannot ponder how a D.U.I.-with-injury arrest might affect her brilliant career. She hides her car, and the victim with it. Tom lingers in a pained attempt to rally for an escape. Brandi enlists a low-life boyfriend (Russell Hornsby) to dispose of Tom, who remains long enough among the living to account for the film's ore harrowing moments.

The film draws its greater unnerving power from the interest of Gordon and Strysik in the emotional toll of violence, embodied in Mena Suvari's depiction of Brandi as a caregiver–by–convenience—devoted to a career of going through the humanitarian motions, but incapable of responding with compassion or practicality to an emergency of her own making. Her panicked response seems pitiable until, by subtle degrees, Suvari reveals the vicious impatience behind her apparent distraction. Hers is a courageous performance, matched by Stephen Rea's persuasive impersonation of a hard-luck sort determined to beat some formidable odds. Russell Hornsby lends a cruel absurdity as a Tough Guy *poseur* out of his depth.

Gordon and camera chief Denis Maloney frame the story with a dismal aspect reminiscent of Edgar G. Ulmer's low-budget *noir* masterwork, Detour (1947)—a similarly conceived, though more palpably contrived, tale of a hapless wanderer who finds himself entrapped by harsh circumstance.

EDGAR G.
ULMER

Detour on Poverty Row

EDITED BY GARY D. RHODES

AN UNPRECEDENTED PERSPECTIVE ON EDGAR G. ULMER

June 1, 2008: I had mentioned Edgar G. Ulmer, the Grey Eminence of Old Hollywood's Poverty Row sector, in last week's column, in attempting to draw a thematic similarity between Ulmer's most vivid example of low-budget *film noir*, 1945's *Detour*, and a newly opening picture called *Stuck*, from the dramatist–turned–filmmaker Stuart Gordon. The cause-and-effect response here was an urge to take a fresh look at *Detour*. Right about that time, the mail brought a copy of Gary D. Rhodes' new book, *Edgar G. Ulmer: Detour on Poverty Row* (Lexington Press).

Gary Rhodes is a colleague of long standing, a filmmaker, educator, and journalist whose work has intersected with mine on several fronts. Such Rhodes volumes as *White Zombie: Anatomy of a Horror Film* and *Horror at the Drive–In* relate strategically to the *Forgotten Horrors* books that George E. Turner and I originated during the 1970s, and Gary and I have long acknowledged a shared interest in Ulmer (1904–1972) as a talent essential to any understanding of maverick moviemaking.

With *Edgar G. Ulmer: Detour on Poverty Row*, Rhodes takes that interest to an unprecedented extent. Editor Rhodes and his contributing writers consider Ulmer in light of not only his breakthrough film, 1934's *The Black Cat* at big-time Universal Pictures, or such finery-on-a-budget exercises as *Bluebeard* (1944) and *Detour*, but also Ulmer's tangled path through such arenas as sex-hygiene exploitation films (1933's *Damaged Lives*), Yiddish-language pieces (1937's *Green Fields*), well-financed symphonic Soap Opera (1947's *Carnegie Hall*; see also: Page No. 333), and ostensible schlock for the drive-in theatres (1957's *Daughter of Dr. Jekyll*).

There emerge several distinct portraits of Ulmer. A perceptive chapter from Christopher Justice ponders whether the writer–director might be considered "the godfather of sexploitation," in view of the "new æsthetic terrain and ... core prototypes" that can be observed in such films as *Damaged Lives* and Girls in Chains (both from 1943) and *The Naked Venus* (1958).

Tony Williams regards Ulmer as an advancer, rather than a follower, of the "psychobiography" approach that Orson Wells had defined with *Citizen Kane* in 1941—on the evidence of an often-maligned, oftener-ignored Ulmer picture called *Ruthless* (1948). (*Ruthless* stars

Zachary Scott as an industrialist who might make Welles' Charles Foster Kane look like Fred Rogers by comparison.)

And Williams' chapter, and Tony Tracy's examination of *Carnegie Hall*, explore Ulmer's ability as an outside-the-system talent to make the occasional big-budget independent feature that resembles the products of the major corporate studios.

It helps to remember that Ulmer had broken through as a major-studio artist, fallen almost immediately from grace. Call it Bad Timing, multiplied: Ulmer's *The Black Cat*, an ambitious and morbidly comical star vehicle for Bela Lugosi and Boris Karloff, had the unconditional blessing of Universal Pictures until an adulterous affair came to light between Ulmer and the wife of a junior executive who also happened to be a nephew of the hellbent-for-nepotism studio chief.

The in-house penalties would have been sufficient, but Universal's Laemmle family preferred to brand Ulmer as *persona non grata* within the big-studio industry–at–large. Then, too, 1934 also was the year in which Hollywood's institutionalized-censorship machinery kicked into overdrive—targeting the lucrative genre of horror in particular. (See also: James Whale's *One More River*, Page No. 87.) Universal was only too delighted to offer *The Black Cat*, with its undercurrents of necrophilia and demon-worshipping fanaticism, as a sacrificial goat. It is astonishing that the film emerged from the censors' butchery–shop with any coherence; perhaps even more so that *The Black Cat* has attained acknowledgment over the long term as a classic of its kind.

The Austro–Hungarian Ulmer remained drawn toward horror films over the balance of a small-studio career, though just as readily identified with crime melodramas, ethnic-interest pictures, psychological ordeals, and—essentially, any productive assignment that might pay the rent and keep his name in view.

Many enthusiasts might find it absurd to regard Ulmer's work at Producers Releasing Corp., or PRC Pictures, with any recognition of artistry, but the innate shabbiness of PRC seems to have challenged Ulmer to seek some higher level. *Bluebeard*, which reconnected Ulmer with a story that he might once have developed at Universal if not for that career-crippling indiscretion, emerged at PRC as a delicate study of a deteriorating mind, affording John Carradine a role that the actor would count among his few favorites. *Detour*, also from PRC, succeeds as a tale of blind-alley entrapment more because of its technical limitations than in spite of them.

One of the more insightful strokes of Gary Rhodes' book is its examination of *Daughter of Dr. Jekyll*—a title that seems more readily to invite derision. Essayist Robert Singer finds deeper currents here, however, to the extent of some vivid parallels between *Daughter of Dr. Jekyll* (a film whose bankrollers expected nothing more than grist for the grindhouses and the drive–ins) and a more generally respected Ulmer title, from PRC in 1945, called *Strange Illusion*. Writes Singer: "Strange Illusion reveals a preoccupation to which Ulmer will return some 10 years later [with *Daughter of Dr. Jekyll*], the haunted adult–child, who bears the responsibility of the family name and its historical implications." Smart leverage, there, for a smart discussion.

Edgar Ulmer remains a challenging figure, almost too versatile and sometimes too undiscriminating a talent for the good of his reputation. In recent years, the Turner Classic Movies cable network has taken pains to showcase Ulmer in a more enlightening perspective, devoting festival-like blocks of programming to a range of titles from various of the Yiddish entries, to the big-league false start of *The Black Cat*, to the unlikely occasional finery of the PRC assignments and the much later, noticeably less polished, drive-in attractions. Rhodes' book brings the perspective into sharper detail yet, establishing Ulmer as a Compleat Filmmaker and perhaps the most influential forebear of the new century's independent-cinema movement.

POPEYE AND THE LANGRIDGE OF HEROISM

June 8, 2008: The breakthrough of the season, as far as superhuman heroism goes, might lie beyond such big-screen spectacles as *Iron Man* and *The Incredible Hulk*. The watershed lies, in part, in a set of *Popeye the Sailor* cartoons that have gone largely unseen—in authentic form, anyhow—since the late 1930s and the earlier 1940s.

A companionable development is a new series of hardcover books reprinting the original *Popeye*, or *Thimble Theatre*, comic strips of writer–artist E.C. Segar. The current volume is *Popeye Vol. 2: "Well, Blow Me Down!"* (Fantagraphics Books). The elaborately packaged Fantagraphics shelf commences at the commencement with *Popeye Vol. 1: "I Yam What I Yam."*

The books qualify as near-architectural marvels in their own right—towering, heavy-stock packages with die-cut front-cover windows and an interior design that showcases many days' worth of the newspaper feature with each spread. A full-color section devotes a page to each of what originally had served as Sunday-supplement episodes, complete to the extent of reproducing Segar's subordinate feature, *Sappo*, about a household in perpetual turmoil.

The stories in *Vol. 2* include a wild Frontier Gothic pitting Popeye's entourage against a mob of cattle rustlers; and a scathingly funny commentary upon charity at odds withgreed, in which Popeye attempts a banking career in defiance of all practical sense. There surfaces a gemlike example of Segar's gift for mangling and/or improving upon the langridge: When Popeye uses the adjective *liberous*, does he mean *liberal*, or *generous*, huh? Neither—he means *liberous*, and So There. The book also sports a touching tribute to Segar from *Beetle Bailey*'s Mort Walker.

Together, Segar's comic-strip novelettes and the Fleischer Studios' Popeye films reveal all that anyone could hope to know about an essentiable cartoon character. Everything post-Segar and post-Fleischer has proved inferior, despite occasional rallyings of greatness from such Segar-loyalist successors as Doc Winner, Bela Zaboly, and Bud Sagendorf. Segar's newspaper feature, in turn, is stronger than the animated cartoons in terms of plotting and characterization. But the early movies boast a gritty allure and a consistency with Segar's rambunctious style of drawing.

The short films are hardly unknown—long having circulated on television, though in degraded copies—but their DVD restoration from master film-vault elements is a revelation. The visual design, with an astonishingly rich palette of black-and-white shadings and the occasional indulgence in Technicolor, packs almost a palpable range of textures.

For anyone who has wondered how a Fleischer *Popeye* cartoon must have looked in its first-run prime, some answers lie in a forthcoming DVD box called *Popeye the Sailor: 1938–1940, Vol. 2* (Warner Home Video). The restorations, as with the *Popeye Vol. 1* set of 2007, render useless any number of off-brand video releases that purport to represent the series but often blur the line between the Fleischers and the post-

Fleischer *Popeye*s from Paramount Pictures' Famous Studios subsidiary. The difference is basically a matter of the organical vs. the synthetical.

Vol. 2 continues to track the Fleischer Studios' *Popeye*s in chronological stride. The series reached a sustained plateau of accomplishment during the later 1930s, with increasingly inventive variations on the standard theme of Indignant Everyman Popeye vs. the Eternal Thug, Bluto, with a stringbean romantic interest named Olive Oyl usually caught in the middle as the scrappy third leg of an inexorably shifting triangle. Key titles are "It's the Natural Thing To Do," in which Popeye and Bluto attempt gentlemanly behavior with awkward results; "Females Is Fickle," in which Popeye attempts a death- and dignity-defying rescue; and a Technicolor variation, *Popeye*-style, on the *Arabian Nights* fantasy of Aladdin.

Bonus tracks include a documentary account of the rocky history of the Fleischer Studios, profiles of voice–actors, and an example of the Fleischers' kindred *Superman* series. The more nearly realistic *Superman* cartoons demonstrated the studio's versatility while drawing a likeness between *Superman* and *Popeye*: Both characters helped to define the concept of the superhuman protagonist at a crucial stage. (A revealing insight lies in *Time* magazine's early-day perception of *Superman* as a crossbreed of Segar's *Popeye* and Al Capp's *Li'l Abner*.)

Matters are hardly so simply laid out in the original Popeye yarns of Elzie Segar. Spinach, supposedly the source of the Sailor Man's might, plays a lesser role in Segar's grim-but-uproarious tales, and so does Bluto—whom Segar had arrayed among a procession of grotesque troublemakers. (Bluto the Terrible will enter in a third volume from Fantagraphics.) The Fantagraphics editions make patent Segar's mastery of desperate suspense and biting humor as essential components of storytelling, combining serialized ordeals with the imperative of dispensing a gag every day.

Segar had introduced Popeye during the late 1920s in a comic strip called *Thimble Theatre*. The Sailor Man soon sidelined such characters as Castor Oyl (Olive Oyl's conniving brother) and Harold Hamgravy (Olive's suitor, later known as Ham Gravy) in terms of popular appeal and narrative possibilities. Popeye's credo, "I yam what I yam and that's all what I yam," is a succinct manifesto of self-effacing confidence. His handling of the English language reflects the resilient restlessness of Immigrant America, assimilating by improvisation.

In simplifying Popeye for the screen, the Fleischers also took pains to capture an essence of Segar's vision, retaining the working-class outlook and keeping the characters attuned to the scrappy resourcefulness that was the only sensible acknowledgment of the harsh economic realities of the day. The overall look is colorful, figuratively speaking, as only black-and-white photography can allow, displaying a shades-of-gray depth unequaled by Walt Disney's or the Warner 'toonshop's rival B&W products of the general period. (Only three Fleischer-shop *Popeyes* were produced in Technicolor.)

Warner Home Video prefaces the works with a disclaimer cautioning the viewer to beware of rampant Political Incorrectness. This fatuous reminder—presumably accounting for such elements as reciprocal violence, occasional ethnic caricatures, and Popeye's appetite for tobacco—hardly diminishes the Fleischers', or Segar's, brilliance at suggesting plain gumption as a response to dehumanizing economic circumstances. The cartoons yam what they yam, and that yam more than enough to render them relevant to a massed audience of this ill-acknowledged New Depression. The Segar *Popeye* books prove still more so.

Recommended Listening: *Smiley Burnette: Country Songs & Comic Cuts* (British Archive of Country Music), contains the largely unknown "I Can Whip Any Man but Popeye"—with the singer's recurring deployment of a persuasive Popeye voice.

DOIN' THAT DOLEMITE SHUFFLE

Something of a preamble, here, so sit tight and Now Dig This: The comics-censorship ruckus of the post-WWII years had begun to peter out, if only just, as the phobic 1950s gave way to the larger struggles—expression vs. repression, in the long wake of the Depression—of the presumably more free-wheeling 1960s. All were rooted in a popular urge to embrace the freedoms that the close of World War II was supposed to

have heralded; a contrary urge to confine such freedoms to a Privileged Few was as intense, if not necessarily as popularly widespread.

Everybody wants freedom, but not everybody wants freedom for everybody: Hence the entrenchment of Oligarchy within Democracy, like that essential flaw in Green Lantern's otherwise limitless Power Ring.

The comic-book flap was an element of a larger insurgency-and-putdown cycle that pitted, for example, Cavalier Hollywood against a Roundhead Congress in the purges of the House Committee on UnAmerican Activities. Within the microcosm of Hollywood itself, struggles erupted over whether individual films—such as Dore Schary's production of a pacifist fable called *The Boy with Green Hair* (1948) at hawkish Howard Hughes' RKO-Radio Pictures—should convey instead a war-preparedness message in those days when much of America was still looking for another Axis to whip.

Might as well seek that next Axis within the mottled cultural fabric of America: And hence the right-minded War on Comics, and the Congressional siege upon liberal-by-convenience but economically conservative Hollywood, and the censors-gone-wild bans upon such free-expression poets and novelists as Allen Ginsberg (1956's "Howl") and William S. Burroughs (1959's *Naked Lunch*). The uprisings were as inevitable as the Thought Police actions.

Humor, a favored mechanism of challenge and rebellion, is of course irrepressible. And furthermore hence the survival of *MAD* magazine at a safe distance from the "Hey! Kids!" comic-book racks. Lenny Bruce, once the most forthright of rebellious comedians, plied his trade straight into a run of early-1960s obscenity investigations and busts, leading with his jaw to such an extent that he became punch-drunk—and forgot how to be funny as a consequence.

Slightly later, in 1969, a similarly emphatic comedian named Rudy Ray Moore emerged as a comparable voice of ribald candor and caustic hilarity. Moore hedged his bets against Bruce-like obscenity busts by avoiding politics and religion, and by confining his appearances to his own black community. The Dominant Culture authorities in those segregationalist days preferred to leave the African–American sector to its own devices—provided that the influence did not impinge upon the cultural mainstream. A significant exception was a sustained outcry of the midcentury, driven by Big Religion and Big Politics, against rock 'n' roll music and especially its black taproots.

Moore's recordings, however, knew no ethnic dividing–lines—and neither did an appreciative niche–audience of white youngsters who knew where to find the record stores that dealt in such under-the-counter products. (As the social critic Robert Warshow pointed out during the 1950s, in an influential essay about the comics-censorship commotion, kids need a secret cultural life outside the range of Parental Sanctions as part of the gradual process of coming to terms with grown-up responsibilities. The odd gratification of shock and bewilderment—*how much can you stand?*—is necessary to the ritual.)

Shock and bewilderment aren't what they used to be, of course. One can only wonder whether the Free Speech movement of the last century might have expended its energies merely so that some shopping-mall kiosk can peddle rude-slogan T–shirts without fear of getting busted. And what new impact can the pioneering underground diatribes of a Lenny Bruce or a Rudy Ray Moore exert upon a society that has accepted the neurotic-booshwah sanitized quasi–pornogra-

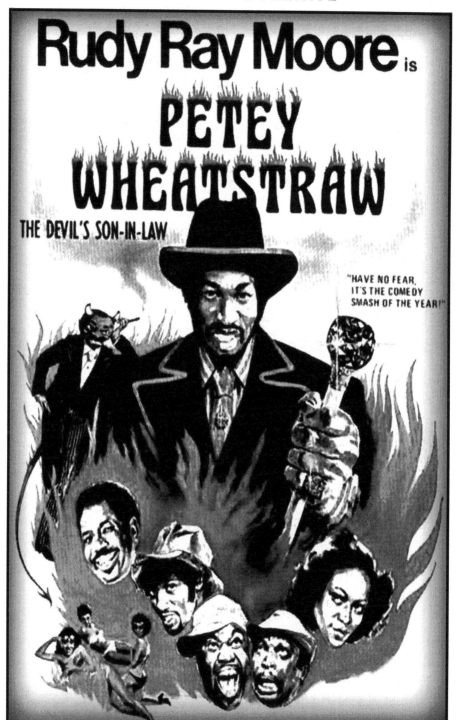

phy of *Sex and the City* and *Two and a Half Men* as family-hour teevee fare? For my part, I suspect a Puritanical conspiracy to devalue the coinage through overfamiliarity.

• • •

Twenty years have passed since two art-broker and show-business friends, the brothers Thomas and Peter Rainone, and I began taking steps to bring Rudy Ray Moore, long since retired by 1988, back to a semblance of prominence. The restoration has lasted. Rudy's 1960s tactic of ranting in rhymed couplets, like a foulmouthed Edna St. Vincent Millay, represented a 19TH Century black-tradition idiom known as *toasting* but also foreshadowed the emergence of rap. A sobriquet bestowed during the 1990s by Arsenio Hall hails Moore as the Godfather of Rap, and don't go thinking Moore hasn't capitalized upon the recognition.

If Moore, the Human Tornado his Ownself, was born in 1937—as he, and the Internet Movie Data Base, have declared in times more recent—then he'd be about 9 years old in the accompanying photograph, here (eyes left), which Moore himself has dated at A.D. 1946. Mighty mannish for a 9-year-old kid. Or might he be that precocious homewrecking juvenile philanderer of whom the bluesman Elmore James once sang with such taboo-tempting indignation?

But no, the Arkansas-born singer–turned–comedian looks to be somewhere around 20 in this publicity photo for his early-day rhythm-and-blues revue. That aspect would peg Moore's nativity at something more like 1927, the year that Moore had mentioned to me in 1988 during a backstage conversation on the occasion of a small-scale comeback from an enforced obscurity.

Now, the concept of backstage at the HOP, in Fort Worth, Texas, was a relative consideration: The HOP's stage, such as it was, was more of a glorified platform, wide but shallow and affording its performers no exit except straight into the ringside-seating area. So Moore and my wife and I settled for a back-booth as a refuge between sets, as far back as we could get without barging in on the grease-pit kitchen.

Moore had come there from Los Angeles, to this whitebread-collegian venue as an unlikely showcase for his resolutely black artistry, at the behest of a small coalition including Tom and Pete Rainone, second-generation fine-art dealers and film-and-music talents from nearby Arlington, Texas, and Yrs. Trly.

The Rainone Bros. and I had met a few years earlier at movie-industry event, and we had found sufficient interests in common to stay in touch. Among these interests was an abiding curiosity as to whatever had become of Rudy Ray Moore, whose forbidden party-record albums I had discovered as a college kid in Amarillo, Texas. My hometown's Go–Low Records ran a lucrative sideline in such fare—peddling as many of the things to taboo-busting white pseudo–hipsters as to the black customers who provided Moore (and such kindred souls as a newly ambitious Redd Foxx and a fading Mantan Moreland) with a built-in audience.

Moore long had been a chronic failure at showmanship—not in the sense of giving up, but rather in the fact of his being a striving entertainer whose every Next Breakthrough had proved illusory since around 1950. This condition persisted until he dropped the pretense of mass-market compatibility and began exploiting a Lower Common Denominator as leverage to commercial acceptance.

Now, Moore is hardly the first to have tried such a route, but he is patently the first to have made a career of committing explicitly bawdy material to commercially issued phonograph records. Although Moore would undermine such material with a smirk, a self-caricatured presence, and the tacit assurance that he meant no harm greater than a barrage of jolts, still he served to encourage imitators whose entire point became that of talking dirty with no sense of irony. A distinction is Moore's understanding of the dividers between Art and Life, along with an instinctive sense of where those lines blur.

"Ol' Rudy just dropped out of sight after that *Disco Godfather* thing he did," Tom Rainone had said, referring to Moore's swan-song starring movie of 1979.

"Good provocation to drop out of sight," I had returned. "That movie wasn't a patch on *Dolemite* or *The Human Tornado*." The visit took place at Rainone Gallery, with its backdrop of Old World and American Modernist canvases. Hardly the place to be discussing the *oeuvre* of Rudy Ray Moore. But to continue:

"No, really. I mean, the man was some kind of a genius—in his way," said Tom.

"Yeah, well, raunch requires a certain genius, I reckon. That is, if you want to walk that fine line between comedy and shock value. So how do you rate him by comparison with Lenny Bruce?"

"About equal, what little I've heard of Lenny Bruce's stuff," said Tom. "But didn't Lenny lose touch with the humor, there, toward the end?"

"Yeah, well, that period hardly counts, except as natural melodrama," I said. "So how does King Rudolph the First, Second & Third stack up against Redd Foxx?"

"More in the same class," said Tom. "I mean, in terms of comedy aimed at a black audience."

"Okay, and so how does that apply to white guys? Like us?"

"Well, I happen to think that the black comedians' material is funnier than white-folks comedy—edgier."

"Edgier than Lenny Bruce? In his prime, I mean."

"Not satirically edgy," said Tom. "I mean, that kind of raw edginess that makes you cringe and laugh both at the same time."

"How about the newer crop? Richard Pryor? Eddie Murphy?"

"Pryor built on Moore's foundation, okay. On Lenny Bruce's, too. Odd combination of influences. And Murphy's not fit to shine Rudy Ray Moore's boots.

"And as for Redd Foxx," Tom added, "he hasn't made anybody cringe in years. Not since he went mainstream with *Sanford and Son*. Sold out, that's what Foxx did. He's a regular teddy bear, now."

"Better to sell out than drop out, maybe. Wonder what ol' Rudy Ray's doing these days?"

"How's about we find out?" asked Tom in reply.

Whereupon we set out to do so, drawing upon my newspaper-editor interests, Tom's connections with the independent-film underground, and a certain enthusiasm that had more to do with Outlaw Nostalgia than with any particular Cultural Imperative. The only recent outcropping of Rudy Ray Moore had been a digital-audio sampling of his material (without authorization or compensation) in 1986 by the raunch-rap act 2 Live Crew.

So Tom Rainone and blues–rock drummer Pete Rainone and I called in some favors from friends in Los Angeles. We touched base with a few old-time exploitation filmmakers who would have kept in touch with the pandering schlockmeisters who had helped, with strings attached, to underwrite Moore's brief run of motion pictures of the 1970s. At length, Tom and I came up with a telephone number known to few souls this side of Ma Bell. Rudy Ray Moore answered the call without so much of a buffer as an agent or a secretary.

He wasn't working much nowadays, he explained. Just some church-group comedy, he explained, emphasizing that not all his routines rely on scrofulous material. A video-reissue deal seemed poised to materialize. Moore had taken a Pasadena on the moviemaking business after *Disco Godfather* (1979), he said, dropping a broad hint that that snakebit production had left him in debt to some investors with criminal-underworld leanings. Anyhow, Moore would be visiting Texas soon to administer his general-audience scriptural humor at a church-folks convention in Dallas. He wondered aloud whether any commercial venues in North Texas might have an interest in his Old School black-on-black comedy routines.

"I used to play the old Guys & Dolls [*nightclub*] in Fort Worth for weeks at a stretch, back in the '60s and '70s," Moore said. "That place is prob'ly long gone, by now. [*And so it was.*] But there's got to be *somebody* out there besides you boys and that Eddie Murphy guy that'll remember who Dolemite even *was.*"

Dolemite is Moore's stock-in-trade fictional character, a badder-than-bad anti-heroic sort who, in his prime, could have out–shafted John Shaft, out–flown Superfly, and staked Blacula clean through his blacker-than-black heart. Stagger Lee incarnate. Say no more: If Rudy Ray Moore was coming to town for one narrow and vaguely evangelical purpose, then we would broaden the agenda and guarantee him a payday or two in the process.

Rudy Ray Moore.

Many come-lately enthusiasts trace the resurgence of Rudy Ray Moore to such mass-market touchstones as an appearance of the early 1990s on television's *Arsenio Hall Show*, to a CD-album duet of dueling insults between Moore and the suave rapper known as Big Daddy Kane (Antonio Hardy), and to a running gag about the *Dolemite* movies in a hip-hopper picture called *House Party* (1990).

The beginnings of a larger popular rediscovery, to Moore's direct benefit, date from Sept. 2, 1988, and the comedian's arrival at a Rainone-clan birthday party in Arlington, midway between Dallas and Fort Worth. Here, between outbursts of comedy-routine warm–ups, Moore told us his life story with all its promises and disappointments and false starts at cracking any bigger leagues. The next night would mark the first time in its several years' existence that Fort Worth's HOP had seen more than one or two black patrons in a single evening. Moore strolled into the place, gray–haired and leaning on a shiny black walking–stick, then ducked into the Gents' Room and emerged, without the cane, wearing a dense black modified-Afro wig: Mr. Dolemite, the Human Tornado, reborn. The following weekend, Moore appeared at Dallas' predominantly black Blues Alley club.

The Popular Culture is predisposed to Tribal Amnesia in its blind headlong rush toward the latest fleeting trend, but the genuine enthusiasts never forget. Most of the HOP's turnout on that occasion consisted of middle-class, middle-aged black couples who remembered Moore from the heyday of the Guys & Dolls Club. He recognized many of them, in turn. These patrons he treated to customized insults and pre-emptive counter–heckling as a condition of dispensing a familiar brand of entertainment. "*Hey,* brother," Moore called to one boisterous customer, "is them yo' *lips,* or are you wearin' a *turtleneck sweater?*" Moore did a great deal of *a cappella* singing that night—a reminder of a rhythm-and-blues record-making career that had prefaced his more lasting foray into comedy. Pete Rainone provided drum-kit accompaniment, timing the rolls and crashes to Moore's spiel.

Backstage—in the back–booth, that is—between the acts, Moore turned to my wife, Christina, and spoke in a soothing, grandfatherly voice quite unlike the assertive rasp of Dolemite: "If anything in my performance might have offended you, please feel free to inform me of any objections you might have."

Christina considered a moment and replied that, no, she had expected precisely what he had delivered and found it all perfectly amusing.

"You think *hard*, now," Moore pressed. "Because if anything, *anything at all*, that I might have said has offended your sensibilities in *any way at all*, then I want you to tell me frankly"—a studied pause, here, then a roughening of the voice—"so that I can get out there for the next set and see if I can be *twice as raunchy!*"

[*Rudy Ray Moore died at 81 in 2008.*]

THE VAN CLIBURN FILM FESTIVAL

We lapse from the confrontational, bawdy wit of Rudy Ray Moore to the Old World Pianistic Classicism of Van Cliburn. The names probably should not be uttered in the same breath, but so what of that? There is only one Show Business, after all.

I had signed on to manage theatrical properties for a highfalutin' entertainment district in Fort Worth in 1998, right around the time that the city's Van Cliburn Foundation was making preparations for its 11TH Van Cliburn International Piano Competition of 2001. The tournament had taken shape during the 1960s, a few years after Harvey Lavan "Van" Cliburn, JR. (1934–2013), had aced the Tchaikowsky Piano Competition in Moscow. The Cold War's most benevolent volley of statesmanship had found Cliburn "unlocking the Iron Curtain with 88 keys," as the Texas newspaperman Elston Brooks remarked the occasion.

Now, I had become acquainted with Cliburn around 1956 through a friendship between his domineering career-manager mother, Rildia Bee Cliburn, and my piano tutor, Mary Elizabeth Wilson. Miss Wilson stood in awe of the Widow Cliburn's Svengali-like influence over her offspring–turned–cash cow. Having no offspring of her own, Miss Wilson settled for a procession of lesser cash-cow pupils from whom she might coax the occasional outburst of artistry. Van Cliburn, even as a provincial Texas talent, already had become a Rising Star before the Tchaikowsky Competition, and it seemed that every other bourgeois mother in Texas now wanted to raise another Van Cliburn. I preferred to play boogie–woogie but tolerated the regimented Euro-classical tutelage as a means of learning to navigate the keyboard.

Cliburn and I found few interests in common, what little conversation we shared and what with his being 13 years older than my schoolboy self. He cringed at my mention that he must be to RCA Victor Records' highbrow Red Seal label what Elvis Presley was to Victor's shirtsleeves pop-music machine (both artists were million–sellers, and each had a controlling mother). Yes, and Cliburn seemed downright insulted when I informed him that another RCA act, the country-music parody team of Homer & Jethro, had mentioned him in a throwaway gag on a recent album. "I do not listen to country music," Cliburn said, "or to that rock 'n' roll. All due respect."

Of course, I harbored a greater respect for Cliburn's preferred idiom than he for mine, and we left it at that, and cordially so. Strange, then, that he and I should have wound up working together during 1998–2001 in the production of a Van Cliburn Film Festival as an offshoot of the Cliburn Competition.

The event was a brainchild of the Cliburn Foundation's president, Richard Rodzinski, a descendant of Carnegie Hall royalty. The project dovetailed with a collaborative production of mine, the Fort Worth Film Festival (1997–2003), and Rodzinski concluded that Van the Man His Ownself and I should curate this *ad hoc* exhibition from a selection of narrative motion pictures dealing with the lives of the Great Classical Composers. One film title flashed to mind: Will Jason's *The Soul of a Monster* (1944), whose musical score embraces the extremes of an extract from Franz Liszt's *The Mephisto Waltzes* (1859–1885) and a boo-gie-woogie improvisation by Clarence Muse. "No horror films!" demand-ed Cliburn. Which also ruled out Paul Wendkos' 1971 film, *The Mephisto Waltz*, about a frustrated pyrotechnical pianist's descent into occultism and soul–snatching. I nonetheless sneaked in a screening of a dark Dr. Seuss fantasy from 1953, *The 5,000 Fingers of Dr. T*, in which a mania-cal teacher conscripts an army of pianists to activate a monumental instrument in the service of a nuclear strike. Cliburn was jake with that one. Go figure. We also chose 1947's *Carnegie Hall*, by a director, Edgar G. Ulmer (Page No. 314), who is more generally known for horror films and crime melodramas. Subversiveness has its practical applications.

Meanwhile in my property-management career, I was helping Richard Rodzinski and the Cliburn Foundation's marketing chief, Sevan Melikyan, to prepare Fort Worth's Bass Performance Hall for the competition. Rodzinski and I were aghast to learn that an overzealous downtown Big Shot had booked a raucous outdoor C&W festival into a nearby parking lot to coincide with the Cliburn Competition. (See also: Page No. 153.) Richard and I protested to no avail, and the clash of idioms proceeded, to the chagrin of the culture-conscious Ruling Class swells who would have preferred to take their Cliburn Competition without the intrusion of a Hillbilly Woodstock just across the street. Fort Worth's tourism bureaucracy prizes the slogan, "Cowboys 'n' Culture," but here the juxtaposition proved too close for comfort.

Anyhow, the Cliburn Film Festival, A.K.A. *Hollywood and the Piano*, came off without a hitch during seven days in June of 2001. The event also provided contest–goers with a respite from the bombard-ment of pianistic zealotry. The accompanying program book follows, beginning with...

A WORD OF WELCOME
FROM VAN CLIBURN

Van Cliburn.

Hollywood does indeed love the piano. For where would the movies be, from the silent era to the here–and–now, without that glorious orchestra–unto–itself to supply the evocative melodies, the stings and flourishes and rum-blings, so crucial to the restless moods of the Moving Image?

But this is no one-aided *affaire*: The piano also loves Hollywood. The piano has, in exchange for all that enduring loyalty, given Hollywood such splendid stories as the lives of Chopin, Liszt, Schumann, Mozart, and VON Beethoven.

As often as not, the picturemaking industry has taken extraordinary liberties. Peter Schaffer's celebrated *Amadeus* relies more upon fantasy than upon fact in the serv-ice of a Higher Truth than a straightforward life-of-Mozart story would have approached.

Certain of our selections in this series reduce dry factuality to frothy Soap Opera. (*A Song To Remember*, that pur-ported biography of Chopin, comes to mind.) Hollywood and the piano, their mutual affection notwithstanding, sometimes prove awkward in expressing that fondness.

In association with the Eleventh
Van Cliburn International Piano Competition

HOLLYWOOD and the PIANO

June 4-10, 2001

Which is entirely our point in selecting and presenting these feature-length motion pictures from a lengthy span of American cinema, the 1940s into times much more recent.

However accurate or fanciful these piano-inspired movies may be, they all crystallize the relationship that has not only made the ancient rhythms of the piano integral to the development of the much younger filmmaking art, but also has established filmmaking as a medium crucial to the continued development of the piano.

—VAN CLIBURN
June 2001

INTRODUCTION TO THE SERIES

Conan Doyle said it best, through his own most famous mouthpiece, Sherlock Holmes: "To [those who love] Art for its own sake, it is frequently in its least important and lowliest manifestations that the keenest pleasure is to be derived."

All due respect to the handful of motion pictures that we have gathered here—but there remain legitimate questions: Are these films distinguished by their devotion to a handful of the Great Composers? Or are the Great Composers diminished by their depiction in a popular cinema that remains, ever after a century's striving, one of the lowlier manifestations of Art? Answers are the province of each individual viewer—so *you* tell *us*. The greater point here is to demonstrate the fascination that the piano has exerted upon Hollywood over the past few generations, as a revealing sidelight to the vital Real World drama of the Van Cliburn International Piano Competition.

The insurmountable obstacle in the cinema's long struggle toward a higher-minded acceptance is its very pedigree as a lowbrow form of entertainment, born of the parlor novelty, the carnival sideshow, the amusements pier, and the P.T. Barnum Dime Museum. For every filmmaker since the waning 19th Century who has sought to demonstrate that the moving picture can be a vital art form, for every Georges Méliés or David Lean or Sam Peckinpah, there have been numerous others who can only be characterized as *schlockmeisters* in search of the fast buck: We find the Thomas Edison whose company captured on film a circus's destruction of a rogue beast in the Year 1903, then sold tickets to *The Electrocution of an Elephant* as a cheap-thrills vicarious experience, safely distanced by the moving-picture screen; the make-believe explorers who in 1930 pirated legitimate African-safari footage and jazzed it up with made-in-America dramatizations and a mock-scientific narration as *Ingagi*, the first film to gross multiple millions of box-office bucks via sheer notoriety; and in times more recent, the James Cameron who exhibited the guff and/or gumption to champion his extravagantly brutal *Terminator 2: Judgment Day* as "a violent film about peace."

These are extreme examples, of course. They are hardly devoid of entertainment value, and—like it or not—they stand as valuable accounts of the uses and mis-uses to which our piebald culture has put the art and science of filmmaking over the long stretch. With or without such extreme comparisons, our seven films in this Cliburn series are polite, unquestionably honorable, attempts to craft mass-appeal entertainment from the finer art of the piano. The selections probably have even served to popularize the classics, if not through their use of the music then certainly through their attempts to portray the likes of Chopin, Liszt, Brahms and the Schumanns in universally identifiable terms of human frailty.

Filmmakers, and especially American filmmakers, have sought so to prove their chosen medium a Right and Proper Art Form that (as the film theorists Adam Garbicz and Jacek Klinowski have pointed out) many movies have veered into an academic stiltedness while seeking the course to Greatness. There is a forcible earnesty about most of our present selections that tells us these artists must simply have been trying too hard to Make Art.

And yet, whatever their intellectual or artistic failings, the selections consistently reveal a passion for the subject matter and a blessédly opinionated stance: Even the purely fictional *Deception* and

Intermezzo, a Love Story remark knowingly on the tendency of emotional entanglements to compromise an artist's dedication to a life in music. If Edgar G. Ulmer, that erratic *eminence grise* among Depression-into-wartime screen directors, found it necessary to let *Carnegie Hall* squeak by as what the critics of the day would have called "a weeper," then at least he allowed its self-sacrificing heroine, a sort of music-loving Stella Dallas, a measure of solace within the shelter of a great auditorium. If Robert Schumann had not suffered from a madness as consuming as his own creative brilliance, then Hollywood would probably have found it worthwhile to re-imagine Schumann as a madman; consider the proletarian anti-Czarist compulsions that became the lot of Chopin in the revisionist movie version.

All of which only serve to make Hollywood's affections for the piano all the more revealing, if only one will use the cinema as an odd gateway, grotesquely off-center and strangely illuminated, to the more genuinely self-possessed artistry of the piano. We trust, above all, that our choices will serve a missionary function in provoking the viewer to undertake a deeper personal quest of discovery: Who, after all, *were* these people, whose transformation *by* the piano led them, in turn, to transform music itself for the larger Common Good?

—*Michael H. Price*

Amadeus
(Orion Pictures • 1984)

Peter Shaffer's lavishly reimagined, fetchingly anachronistic depiction of 18th Century Vienna has done more to acquaint a massed audience with Mozart than any volume of academically forced appreciations could accomplish. Shaffer's masterstroke is simply to fancy Wolfgang Amadeus Mozart as a prototypical art–rocker, possessed of cosmic gifts that can only drive the commercial hacks of the music business to an envious rage.

When reviewing *Amadeus* as a fresh Oscar-bait release, the Fort Worth *Star-Telegram*'s Elston Brooks carped with curmudgeonly glee about the title of Shaffer's play–into–movie: By such a standard, Brooks declared, a remake of *Sunrise at Campobello* would necessarily be called *Delano*.

Clever line, that, but it misses the greater point. For *Amadeus* is not so much a fragment of the artist's name as it is the very soul of the story. *Amadeus*, derived from the Latin, translates to "Belovéd of God," and it is that assumption, that perception, of Received Divinity that fuels not only the music but also the irrational hatreds underlying the tale.

We meet Antonio Salieri (F. Murray Abraham) in an asylum. Maddened by years of envious self–torment and accumulated guilt, Salieri contends that his one great accomplishment as a composer was to bring about the death of Wolfgang Amadeus Mozart. Incapable of rising above his own failings as a purely mercenary music–maker, Salieri reveals, he chose the next-best course of action and did away with his unaffectedly artistic rival.

Flashback to 1781: Mozart as a young man (played with a child-like abandon by baby-faced Tom Hulce) arrives in Vienna. Salieri is comfortably situated as composer–in–residence to the court of the Hapsburg Emperor Joseph II (Jeffrey Jones), and both Joseph and the massed undiscriminating citizenry are perfectly happy with Salieri's competent but hardly visionary melodies. Mozart's own music is rather too progressive for the times and the provincial appetites of the

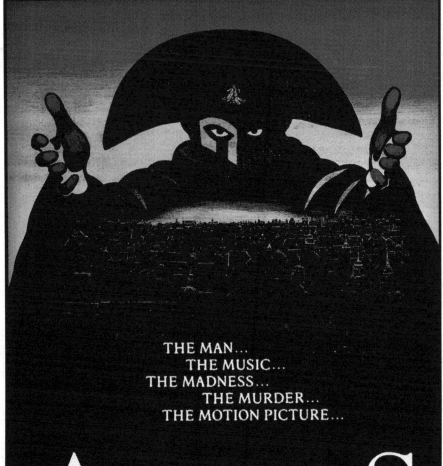

THE MAN...
THE MUSIC...
THE MADNESS...
THE MURDER...
THE MOTION PICTURE...

AMADEUS

...EVERYTHING YOU'VE HEARD IS TRUE

The SAUL ZAENTZ Company Presents PETER SHAFFER'S AMADEUS A MILOS FORMAN Film

F. MURRAY ABRAHAM   TOM HULCE   ELIZABETH BERRIDGE

with SIMON CALLOW   ROY DOTRICE   CHRISTINE EBERSOLE

JEFFREY JONES   CHARLES KAY

Executive Producers MICHAEL HAUSMAN and BERTIL OHLSSON   Director of Photography MIROSLAV ONDRICEK

Music Conducted and Supervised by NEVILLE MARRINER   Production Designer PATRIZIA VON BRANDENSTEIN   Choreography TWYLA THARP

Screenplay and original stage play by PETER SHAFFER   Produced by SAUL ZAENTZ   Directed by MILOS FORMAN

An ORION PICTURES Release   70 mm   DOLBY STEREO   Filmed in PANAVISION®   Prints by TECHNICOLOR®   PG PARENTAL GUIDANCE SUGGESTED
SOME MATERIAL MAY NOT BE SUITABLE FOR CHILDREN

Viennese—and Mozart himself seems a joyously earthy vulgarian at odds with polite society—but Salieri recognizes the underlying brilliance and champions the upstart before the court of the Emperor.

Salieri conceals the anger and cancerous resentments that Mozart has innocently awakened. This anger is directed not so much toward Mozart as toward God, who Salieri believes has pulled a cruel stunt in bestowing such genius upon a crass rival. Salieri vows to destroy Mozart. (From the skewed evidence of the framing story, we are led to believe that Salieri succeeded, only to lose his presence–of–mind over the unkillable essence of Mozart—his music.)

This glorious fantasy is entirely in the service of a truth greater than dry factualism. Shaffer argues persuasively that Mozart *was* his own— and God's own—Magic Flute, a flesh-and-bone instrument of æthereal greatness, however ill recognized. Tom Hulce's title portrayal conveys this argument beyond mere satisfaction.

Shaffer has crafted the account as a pageant of intentional anachronisms, utilizing such repetitive 20TH Century cultural touchstones as pop-rock music-making allegories and television-styled plotting and pacing. Director Milos Forman honors this peculiar rhythm, allowing neither flourishes of directorial style nor showy star-turn affectations to distract from Shaffer's polemic with the mixed blessing of genius. The music is right and correct—including ornate stagings—but the people's response to it is that of a Top 40 radio audience accustomed to the assembly-line hit-record concoctions of the Brill Building.

The bedroom banter between Mozart and his bride (an exquisitely coiffed-and-gowned Elizabeth Berridge) could have been drawn from some situation comedy or daytime-teevee serial. When Mozart's nosy father (Roy Dotrice) intrudes upon this scene or that, one almost expects a laugh–track. The speaking voices are 20TH Century bourgeois American. Of story arc, there is virtually none—just a handful of basic situations, rendered distinctive not by character development or narrative momentum but by changes of costume and setting. The acting is uniformly splendid, with a riveting tension between Tom Hulce and F. Murray Abraham.

The finer concern lies not with any death-of-Mozart histrionics, nor even with any art-vs.-politics intrigues. The point is, rather, to convey not only the pious literalism of the title but also the bitter contradictions of that title. Certainly, one so "Belovéd of God" should have known only triumph. (A 20TH Century rustic Amadeus, the great folk-music fiddler Amadée Ardoin of Louisiana, led a similarly troubled existence.) Shaffer reminds us, however, that genius is also a burden of responsibility, and his depiction of a creative juggernaut is at once inspirational and sobering. The crucial scene where Salieri dutifully transcribes a Requiem as described by Mozart in his death–throes will impress the viewer as indelibly as the music itself.

CARNEGIE HALL
(Federal Films • United Artists • 1947)

It is altogether fitting that we should accentuate the arrival of the Cliburn Competition in Bass Performance Hall with a tale from bygone days about the nurturing presence of another Great Hall. Indeed, a polished and refurbished Carnegie Hall is as much a star of this film as any of the "world's greatest artists" (so designated on screen) who grace the frankly soap-operatic proceedings. All that would seem to be missing is the originally intended Technicolor photography, which was scrapped in favor of a more economical black-and-white shoot after

the independent financing fell short of an announced $1.8 million budget. (Though minuscule in the present day, when commonplace exploitation thrillers cost in the tens of millions, that sum was a whopping figure by the Hollywood accountants' reckoning of 1947.)

The story of Edgar G. Ulmer's *Carnegie Hall* centers upon an Irish immigrant, Nora Ryan (played by Marsha Hunt), who works as a cleaning–woman at New York's mighty Carnegie Hall during its earlier years. Nora loves music and delights in listening to the sounds that accompany her labors. Her co–workers care little about the artistry that surrounds them, but Nora takes every opportunity to listen in on the rehearsals.

Such an eavesdropping session finds Nora overhearing a confrontation between Tony Salerno (Hans Yaray), an arrogant pianist, and the conductor, Walter Damrosch (Harold Dyrenforth). Tony vents his anger upon Nora—but later returns to apologize and finds himself charmed by her story of how she had "found heaven" as a child in the newly opened Carnegie Hall. She idolizes Damrosch, who once permitted her to watch Piotr Ilyich Tchaikovsky in action at the podium. Tony and Nora begin dating, and at length they marry. A son, Tony, JR., arrives, but Nora is suddenly left a widow. Determined to raise Junior to follow his father's path, Nora betters her career prospects and grooms the boy to become a great pianist. Moving into the residential quarters of Carnegie Hall, she becomes an overbearing stage mother. Tony, JR. (William Prince), develops a rebellious streak, and—in a twist that can only have been appropriated from Al Jolson's breakthrough film *The Jazz Singer* (1927)—begins playing jazz.

To his mother's chagrin, Junior falls for a big-band singer, Ruth Haines (Martha O'Driscoll, in her last film before a premature retirement), and strikes up a friendship with Ruth's boss, bandleader Vaughn Monroe (himself). Monroe hires Tony for a tour, and a predictably hostile split results between mother and son.

Tony, JR., finds success in the realm of Tin Pan Alley pop, but his marriage to Ruth begins falling apart. Ruth visits Nora to seek motherly advice. Nora counsels her to tough it out and make the marriage work. A helpful friend (Frank McHugh) surprises Nora and Ruth with tickets to Carnegie Hall to witness Tony, JR.'s first presentation of his own new composition. Seems the boy has been secretly living up to his mama's expectations, after all.

Unadulterated *schmaltz* is what *Carnegie Hall* is, of course. This quality is hardly a crippling flaw, however, for a picture so rich otherwise in artistry and in sheer celebration of music–making. Seldom have the classical and pop idioms co–existed so happily in a single work of cinema; more commonly, as in Walter Hill's 1986 film *Crossroads*, the Euro-classical imperative is seen as an oppressor of indigenous American music. (The cast roster, seen in the poster at left, is a veritable Who's Who. Other celebrated artists, including Benny Goodman, Paul Whiteman, Tommy Dorsey, José Iturbi, Vladimir Horowitz, Duke Ellington, Victor Borge, and Alec Templeton, were announced as participants but did not make the final cut.)

This début production of the independent Federal Films began shooting early in August of 1946, following a massive cleaning and redecorating of Carnegie Hall as the actual shooting site. (The chief purpose here was to assure that the hall would look new for the flashback scenes set during the late 19TH Century.) Filming was completed during mid-October of 1946, but financial setbacks and creative compromises snagged completion until May of 1947, when a New York premiere took place as a benefit for the New York Foundling Hospital and the New York Philharmonic's Pension Fund. Further re–editing delayed the general release until August. (An interim print on file at the Smithsonian Institute is incomplete by comparison with the general-release version.)

Director Edgar G. Ulmer was a curious choice to helm *Carnegie Hall*, given that his once-promising career in Hollywood's major leagues had long since lapsed into a regimen of low-budget (however finely wrought) adventure melodramas, horror thrillers, and ethnic (Yiddish, African-American and Ukrainian) specialty pictures. Ulmer rises admirably to this occasion and seems particularly inspired by the abundance of music. Indeed, *Carnegie Hall* is Ulmer's most musically conscious film since Universal Pictures' 1934 production of *The Black Cat*, a Boris Karloff-vs.-Bela Lugosi star vehicle whose original orchestral pastiches and *hommages* even today are routinely mistaken for the work of Tchaikovsky.

THE COMPETITION
(Columbia Pictures • 1980)

ASIDE FROM M.H. PRICE: *Joel Oliansky's* The Competition *was a scheduled attraction of the Cliburn Film Festival until Van Cliburn pulled a last-minute reconsideration in view of the film's R-as-in-Restricted rating as to audience suitability. I suspect that some Cliburn Foundation insider also reminded Van that the film also takes rather an irreverent view of the Cliburn Competition. Sacred cows, and all that. The listing is restored here from the original program-book manuscript.*

Inspired in part by the Cliburn Competition itself, *The Competition* struggles throughout to fulfill clashing imperatives: It must serve at once as a star vehicle for Richard Dreyfuss and as a rumination upon the pressures that such an event exerts upon its participants. Dreyfuss is essentially playing Dreyfuss here—an ingratiating, often annoying, personality—but that undisguised self is precisely right for the character.

At 30, Paul Dietrich (Dreyfuss) comprehends that his boy-wonder days are behind him, and all that remains to him (or so he believes) is the chance of winning an influential piano competition. Driving himself beyond endurance, Dietrich indulges his more ruthless nature.

Heidi Joan Schoonover (Amy Irving), a rival contestant, is considerably more at ease: Playing, not necessarily winning, is her reward for a lifetime of dedication. She is financially secure, too, where Paul must scrimp on accommodations in order to present himself as a contender. The force behind Heidi is her mentor, Greta Vandemann (Lee Remick), a manipulative and rightfully prideful maestro who can trace her own lineage of teachers as far back as Beethoven His Ownself.

The attraction between Dietrich and Heidi is a foregone conclusion, but director Joel Oliansky cranks the suspense as to whether a triumph for one would force estrangement upon both. Dreyfuss' Dietrich is a volcanic presence, wavering between vulnerable good humor and childish tantrums and conveying most satisfactorily the driven, conflicted nature of a brilliant artist who cannot quite convince himself of his own worth. Especially memorable is his show of astonishment upon realizing that Amy Irving's Heidi is as accomplished a player as he is. (Both Dreyfuss and Miss Irving studied pianistic body language for several months in order to convey the concentration of physical, emotional, and intellectual energies that the instrument

Richard Dreyfuss and Amy Irving.

requires.) The antagonisms between Dietrich and Lee Remick's arrogant Greta also contribute much to *The Competition*—especially in her withering speech about the responsibilities of artistry, his brattish sarcasm toward her, and finally her climactic lapse of academic propriety when overwhelmed with the sheer joy of the music.

Although it works superbly as a three-actor showcase, *The Competition* tries rather too hard to open itself up as a representative chronicle of a tournament. (The scenario is based largely upon the documented backstage intrigues.) Secondary pianist characters are assigned such explicit ethnicity—the African–American, the Italian, the Russian—and such broad quirks of personality as to become commonplace stereotypes in the service of a film that, otherwise, has its sights fixed upon a considerably higher purpose.

THE 5,000 FINGERS OF DR. T
A.K.A.: Crazy Music
(Stanley Kramer Productions • Columbia Pictures • 1953)
"A delightfully funny and fantastic treat."
—RYAN BRENNAN
Program Notes
Fort Worth Film Festival 2000

And no, the film is not related to Robert Altman's *Dr. T and the Women* (2000). But you knew that. Theodore "Dr. Seuss" Geisel and Hollywood scenarist Allan Scott, a veteran of the Fred Astaire–Ginger Rogers musicals, dreamed up Roy Rowland's *The 5,000 Fingers of Dr. T* as an imaginative and sympathetic nod to any child who has ever felt enslaved to regimented learning. A fond appreciation of music courses throughout the film, but so does a defiance toward the despotic stereotype that many conservatory maestros have brought down upon their profession through sheer, *uhm*, despotism.

Bart Collins (played by the *Lassie* teleseries' star–to–be, Tommy Rettig) is a spirited youngster who would rather play baseball with his neighborhood pals than study piano with the tyrannical Dr.

Terwilliker (Hans Conreid, in one of the screen's great Grand Manner caricatures). Seuss' contention here is that a fondness for the instrument must grow of its own accord; to force it is to alienate the child.

At any rate, Bart grows so to dread his sessions with Dr. Terwilliker that he evolves a paranoid fantasy of cosmic proportions: He dreams that he and 500 other boys have been taken captive by Dr. T, who forces them to play at a massive, serpentine keyboard. Their prison is a castle guarded by blindly obedient hoodlums and equipped with a dungeon where other prisoners—who play purportedly lesser instruments, other than the noble piano—while away the hours in a perpetual jam session. Dr. T's master plan is to use the harnessed energy of the piano marathon to touch off an atomic bomb.

The Cold War allegory is less obvious today than it would have seemed amid the Red Menace climate that afflicted America during the post-World War II years. This quality is of a piece with another night-marish kid's-eye view of a hostile world–gone–haywire, William Cameron Menzies' Red-baiting 1953 production of *Invaders from Mars*. But with or without any perceived political baggage, *The 5,000 Fingers of Dr. T* holds up as a delightful phantasmagoria of good humor and resourceful heroism, especially if the viewer happens to be a child or a child–at–heart. The brainwashing tactics of Hans Conried's Dr. Terwilliker might have as much to do with personal quirks as with Communist machinations, and (Freudian McCarthyism to the contrary) sometimes a cloud of red smoke is merely a cloud of red smoke.

Mary Healy and Peter Lind Hayes, a popular married-couple comedy team, complete the principal cast as Bart's well-meaning mother and a friendly handyman who, in both Bart's dream–state and the waking world, will help to save the day. The fanciful cartooning style of Dr. Seuss translates vividly to the live-action setting; the special-effects sequences, vivid Technicolor cinematography, and overall set design compare favorably with the look and texture of Ron Howard's overwrought live-action version of *Dr. Seuss' How the Grinch Stole Christmas* (2000). *The 5,000 Fingers of Dr. T* was hardly a box-office sensation in its day, but by the later 1950s it had found an apprecia-tive audience on television. Its acclaim grows with every new genera-tion of enthusiasts, but of course the picture fares best in a well-pre-served print splashed across the big screen.

The piano-lessons mandate became a Social Imperative during America's affluent and (sometimes) culturally attuned postwar 1950s (still a good many New Deal Liberals around to hold the line against Creeping McCarthyism), with the predictable consequence that many children were conscripted more by parental fiat than by any desire to learn to play. Baldwin's fine parlor-model Acrosonic spinet could be pur-chased for as little as $700; Wurlitzer's ersatz–Acrosonic, tinnier to the ear but adequate, cost substantially less. One result of this popular obsession was the phenomenon of the communitywide Massed Piano Recital, in which a conservatory would assemble as many pianos as a local concert-hall stage could hold—and then have all its students per-form a lock-step ensemble program. The unwitting resemblance of these Group Think ordeals to *The 5,000 Fingers of Dr. T* was astonishing.

Nor is *Dr. T* the only such creation to erupt from the middle-American mania for piano instruction. In 1948, Alan Livingston pro-duced a best-selling record album for Capitol records called *Sparky's Magic Piano*, in which an impatient not–quite–prodigy dreams that his piano has the ability to make him seem a brilliant concert artist.

IMMORTAL BELOVED
(Columbia Pictures • 1994)

ANOTHER MEMO FROM M.H.P.: *Another title axed from the bill–of–fare after Van Cliburn objected to the R Certificate rating: "We must think of the children in the audience." I hadn't the heart to inform him that R-rated films were drawing as many juvenile customers as adults, or that this selection might prove more enlightening to a schoolkid audience than the next installment of Die Hard. Meanwhile, a Cliburn Foundation board member suggested that we might substitute a fairly recent picture called Beethoven, but I felt compelled to mention that that one is about a dog.*

Like the searing questions of the truer identity of Jack–the–Ripper, the habits of the Loch Ness Monster, and how Dickens intended to resolve *The Mystery of Edwin Drood*, the matter of Beethoven's so-called Immortal Beloved is a puzzle more to be appreciated than solved.

Which puts Bernard Rose, the screenwriter–director, automatically on shaky ground with *Immortal Beloved*. This mystery of a veiled reference in the correspondence of Ludwig VON Beethoven provides Rose with a motive to mount a purportedly biographical study of the Great Composer. Pity, then, that Rose let his ambitions lead to a fairly commonplace detective movie, bent upon identifying the elusive personage whom Beethoven hailed as his Immortal Beloved.

Whistle the syllables in the title of *Citizen Kane* to the thunderous opening notes of VON Beethoven's Fifth Symphony, and you will have an idea of the nature of Rose's conceit. In a patent imitation of Orson Welles' famous psychological mystery of 1941, Rose pitches Gary Oldman's seething impersonation of Beethoven as a bombastic Kane–clone. Jeroen Krabbe takes up the Joseph Cotten cudgel as the artist's long-suffering servant–turned–sleuth. Valeria Golino and Isabella Rossellini deliver radiant supporting work as significant women in Beethoven's life.

SONG OF LOVE
(MGM • 1947)

Caveat Emptor: "In this story of Clara and Robert Schumann, of Johannes Brahms and Franz Liszt, certain necessary liberties have been taken with incident and chronology. The basic story of their lives remains a true and shining chapter in the history of music."

So reads a strategic disclaimer scrolled at the beginning of *Song of Love*, Clarence Brown's stirring reinterpretation of a vital stage in the advancement of the piano. The whether-or-nots of historical accuracy were, really, a lesser concern, and in fact the lives concerned are followed with an attention to detail—liberties notwithstanding—that oftener eludes Hollywood.

Song of Love had riskier challenges with which to deal in the Real World of postwar popular cinema: "Its longhair aspects may militate against it," cautioned one influential movie-trade publication, allowing nonetheless that "taking into consideration the general public's growing acceptance of longhair music and grosses rolled up by Columbia's *A Song To Remember*, this one has a good chance of doing well all down the line." Of inadvertent help was *Song of Love*'s preoccupation with the gathering madness of Robert Schumann—whose brooding impersonation by Paul Henried dovetails nicely with the period's accelerating *film noir* style of Existential despair and intimate cataclysm.

A Song To Remember (Page No. 343) had fared well, indeed, just two years previous, with both popular acceptance and accolades from its industry. *Song of Love* performed impressively as a box-office attraction— so impressively, in fact, as to inspire four of Clara and Robert Schumann's grandchildren to mount an opportunistic $9 million lawsuit charging libel, invasion of privacy, and misappropriation of performance rights. This crackpot litigation dragged on until 1954, when the Supreme Court of New York State dismissed it on grounds that Schumann was every bit "as insane as depicted in the defendant's motion picture."

But we're getting ahead of the game, and this game stars Katharine Hepburn as the youthful virtuoso Clara Wieck. At a royal command performance in Dresden in 1839, Clara follows a triumphant interpretation of a Liszt concerto with a forbidden piece, "Traumerei," composed by her lover, the unknown Robert Schumann. Clara's overbearing father–teacher (Leo G. Carroll) has rejected Schumann as unworthy of his famous daughter. Clara is underage, for that matter.

In defiance, Clara takes the issue to court, seeking permission to marry Schumann. The judge (Kurt Katch) is on the point of ruling against her when Franz Liszt (Henry Daniell) intervenes, praising Schumann as a genius and successfully defending the marriage.

Little works out for the better, for although their marriage proves stable enough over the long stretch, Clara finds herself overburdened with children and grants domesticity prior claim over her career. Recognition as a composer eludes Schumann. He is reduced to teaching as a means of providing for his family, and he finds himself awkwardly compromised when one new student—the promising composer Johannes Brahms (Robert Walker)—becomes infatuated with Clara.

This situation aside, Schumann invites Brahms to move into the household. Brahms proves an honorable sort, loyal to his benefactor. During a traditional fortune-telling ritual at a New Year's party, an omen of doom befalls Schumann.

Clara toys with the notion of returning to the concert stage. The overworked Schumann finds himself beset with feelings of inadequacy even as he struggles to complete an epic operatic retelling of *Faust*. His compositions take on a morbidly overwrought texture, prompting Clara to worry that the insanity that had claimed Schumann's sister might run in the family.

Faust meets with rejection at first, but Clara hides this fact from her husband and, with help from Brahms and Liszt, arranges for a public début. Brahms, unable to conceal any longer his unrequited love for Clara, moves away. Schumann collapses while conducting his own premiére and must be committed to an institution. Clara realizes her husband's case is hopeless when he tells her of a "new" composition, his "Traumerei." Schumann dies unrecovered and still obscure.

Five years later, a now-famous Brahms visits Clara and is appalled to find her yet in mourning. Lecturing her about Robert's determination and her own lapsed devotion to the piano, Brahms leaves for Cologne and the presentation of his new symphony. Astonished to spot Clara in his audience at the début, Brahms now finds himself moved to propose marriage. Her loyalty to the memory of Schumann prevails, however, and Clara embarks upon a campaign to bring her husband's music to posthumous recognition.

Katharine Hepburn, Paul Henreid, and Robert Walker—all concerned play the passionate tale for full measure of seething emotion and defiant artistry. The glamorous leads also prove surprisingly convincing at manipulating the keyboard; their seeming command of the instrument is crucial to making the performances appear more than merely the pianistic equivalent of lip–synching. (Artur Rubenstein provided the actual playing.) Through adroit editing, savvy camera placements, and hand-doubling, the miming meshes almost seamlessly with the music.

The film seemed overlong in its day, at 117 minutes; nowadays, when two hours is the average running time, more or less, for a motion picture, this length is unremarkable. The multiple-author screenplay often betrays its origins as an (unproduced) stage play, and producer-director Clarence Brown handles the more actorly sequences with a deliberate, declamatory intensity born more of stagecraft than of film-making, with less cinematic assurance than he brings to the piano-solo presentations. A close collaboration with camera chief Harry Stradling yields some memorable sequences, including a breathtaking swoop at the denouement from a closeup of Miss Hepburn at the keyboard to a long shot of a vast auditorium.

Miss Hepburn is quite good as Clara, whose fiery temperament and ferocious dedication lend themselves to both humor and pathos. Smart techniques of makeup and lighting assist with the character's aging over the film's long course of years, but the greater realism belongs to the actress' immersion in character. Henreid brings to Schumann a pleasing combination of austerity, preoccupation, and hopeful zest for living. Walker cannily underplays throughout as Brahms. Henry Daniell is excellent as Liszt. Costuming and set design are just right for this tale of artistry triumphant over thwarted passions and festering lunacy.

A SONG TO REMEMBER
(Sidney Buchman Productions • Columbia Pictures • 1945)

The operative term in the title is *Song*, for it is the music of Chopin that is the ultimate salvation of Charles Vidor's *A Song To Remember*. In a day when the elaborate production values of Old Hollywood have become passé among the mass audience and the celebrity of the wartime marquée names has shriveled beyond popular recognition, the compositions remain vital and germane. The film itself is more relevant today as a reminder of how Great Art could provoke the moviemaking industry to commit fantasy and then call it biography.

Lest we run afoul of the same reception that greeted *A Song to Remember* as a fresh release, it bears overstating that the film leaves rather a bit to be desired as an account of the life and times of Frèdéric Chopin. ("Perversely inaccurate" is one of the more restrained volleys from the critical brethren of 1945. The film became a hit, nonetheless—though probably more so on grounds of its prevailing sentimentalism than any other attribute.) The music is the *raison d'etre*, and it transcends the *schmaltz* to enthrall the Absorbed Viewer in ways that an overwrought screenplay cannot approach. The film should serve more to interest the viewer in Chopin than to leave any impression of biographical authority.

Chopin (1810–1849) was the progeny of a Polish noblewoman and a French-born merchant—hardly the offspring of peasant stock, as *A Song to Remember* would have it. Chopin's first published work appeared when he was 15, and by the time he had graduated from the Lyceum at 17 he was acknowledged as a gifted composer and the pre-eminent pianist of Warsaw. Chopin had performed successfully as a visitor to Vienna before deciding to leave Warsaw and its imposed Russian military regime. In the Real World, Chopin stormed Paris as an accomplished and acclaimed pianist, rather than as the ill-recognized up–and–comer whom this film offers.

A Song To Remember is, withal, pretty much as *Variety*, that influential tradepaper for movie-biz insiders, described it in a January-of-1945 review: "Abounding in entertainment factors," with "a showmanly presentation of intimate drama and music." Screenwriters Sidney Buchman and Ernst Marischka (working from an unbilled scenario by Frank Capra) introduce Chopin as a prodigy (played as a schoolboy by Maurice Tauzin) and equip him with a gruff but kindly and dedicated teacher in Joseph Eisner (Paul Muni). Denied an audition in Paris on account of his family's poverty, Frèdéric finds himself increasingly engrossed in the Polish struggle against Czarist Russia. Maestro Eisner counsels the boy to concentrate on his music: Fame as a concertist can make him a leader in the struggle for freedom.

Several years later, Chopin (Cornel Wilde) is giving a command performance when he spots the Russian Governor General of Poland (Michael Visaroff) among the guests. Chopin's hostile outburst makes him a political fugitive, and Eisner takes his student to safety in Paris. There, a chance encounter at the keyboard with Franz Liszt (Stephen Bekassy) convinces impresario Louis Pleyel (George Coulouris) that this newcomer is a talent with whom to reckon, and Chopin's future as a concert pianist seems assured. There follows an ill-advised liaison with the manipulative author Georges Sand (played with ferocious and mannish arrogance by Merle Oberon), who takes Chopin away to isolation on the island of Majorca. Afflicted with tuberculosis and driven by Miss Sand to compose rather than to concentrate upon his performing career, Chopin finally heeds his patriotic leanings and breaks free for a concert tour benefiting the Polish Revolution. Which is hardly to give away too much, for the picture has a great deal more to say in its fast-and-loose revisionist approach to history.

Cornel Wilde, who would become associated with more robust and adventurous roles, delivers a passionate yet fragile portrayal of Chopin. (He found it necessary to lobby for the role, Wilde told an interviewer at the time, because Columbia considered him too athletic in aspect.) Paul Muni, Old Hollywood's greatest impersonator of historical figures, steals the show as Chopin's blustering teacher. Merle Oberon, who was better known for her portrayals of vulnerable innocence and romanticism, registers strikingly as the calculating bohemian Georges Sand. Stephen Bekassy offers a sympathetic and rounded interpretation of Liszt. 'Way down among the supporting ranks, Darren McGavin can be spotted in his movie début as a Polish citizen in a crowd scene.

The great unseen star of *A Song To Remember* is the pianist José Iturbi, who provides the performances of numerous Chopin compositions, generously deployed. Iturbi could not take screen credit for the assignment because he was under contract to a rival studio, MGM. Wilde, tutored in physical keyboard presence by the concert pianist Victor Allen, gives a sufficiently convincing display of immersion in the music, with strategic hand–doubling by Shura Cherassky. The editing and the camerawork leave an adequate impression that the actor is playing. The sound engineering is among the best of its day, comparing favorably with the Depression-into-wartime piano-recording techniques developed and refined by RCA Victor/Red Seal and Columbia Masterworks.

Chopin's life—or more pointedly, his relationship with Georges Sand—had been portrayed in a 1927 French film, *La Valse*. *A Song To Remember* also drew inspiration from Doris Leslie's book, *Polonaise*. Columbia Pictures had begun preparations for *Song* as early as 1938, with Frank Capra docketed as director. In 1946, a year after the opening, Capra filed suit against Columbia, maintaining that his original story treatment had gone unacknowledged. The court assigned Capra a 25 per cent share of *Song*'s profits; the award came in handy at the time, which found Capra contending with the box-office failure of his independently produced labor–of–love, *It's a Wonderful Life*.

A Song To Remember landed Oscar nominations for Best Actor, Color Cinematography, Original Story, Sound Recording, Editing and Musical Score. The director, Charles Vidor, would return to this terrain in 1960 with the Liszt-derived drama *Song without End*—another of our selections (below). Other films concerning themselves with Chopin and his troubled orbit include *Notorious Woman* (BBC–TV; 1975) and *Impromptu* (1991).

SONG WITHOUT END
A.K.A.: Crescendo
(Columbia Pictures • 1960)

An absorbing, Oscar-anointed job of musical scoring distinguishes the Liszt bio–picture *Song without End*, which more than anything else demonstrates what a long memory Columbia Pictures had as to the popular success of its 1945 production of *A Song To Remember* (Page No. 343). The earlier film's director, Charles Vidor, was attached in the hope of recapturing that box-office magic, and in a visionary bit of behind-the-scenes casting the company enlisted Jorge Bolet to perform the crucial pianistics. Bolet would develop over the long term into one of the preeminent interpreters of Franz Liszt.

Song without End, however, promptly grew to seem a jinxed production. Vidor had charged into the production, scarcely concerned with allowing the historical record to get in the way of the broadly caricatured soap–operatics and lapsed factuality of Oscar Millard's screenplay. But Vidor died unexpectedly in 1959 after scarcely a month's shooting. Columbia rescued the project by bringing in George Cukor amidships as director. Cukor, a more realistically inclined artist though similarly comfortable with the tale's Grand Manner romanticism, balked at the sheer unreality of a venture that only pretended to depict a crucial span of decades (from the 1830s into the 1860s) in the life of Liszt. Cukor's on-the-spot revisions helped considerably, demanding a more subdued and realistic leading portrayal from Dirk Bogarde than Vidor had envisioned and coaxing from Geneviève Page and the glamorous model-turned-actress Capucine (*né* Germaine Lefebvre) vividly realized impersonations of the women in Liszt's troubled orbit. Other characters fare less well: Patricia

FRANZ LISZT...
his music
as impassioned
as the loves
that inspired it!

COLUMBIA PICTURES
presents a
WILLIAM GOETZ PRODUCTION

SONG
WITHOUT
END
The Story of Franz Liszt

starring
DIRK
BOGARDE

with
GENEVIEVE PAGE | PATRICIA MORISON · IVAN DESNY | and CAPUCINE | Written by OSCAR MILLARD | CINEMASCOPE
MARTITA HUNT · LOU JACOBI | Directed by CHARLES VIDOR | EASTMANCOLOR

Morison's portrayal of the novelist Georges Sand and Lyndon Brook's posturing presence as Richard Wagner are but shallowly realized. (Cukor, incidentally, insisted that Columbia give Vidor's name a greater prominence in the billing and the advertising.)

Bogarde, despite a lacking resemblance to Liszt, fares quite well as an artist distracted from his art by an involvement with the Countess Marie d'Agoult (Miss Page) and a pursuit of the married Princess Carolyne VON Sayn–Wittgenstein (Capucine). The historical context is beside the point, serving chiefly to array the likes of Georges Sand, Wagner and Chopin (played by Alexander Davion) as fodder for name–dropping.

But like such impoverished 'way-distant relatives as *Hillbillys in a Haunted House* (1967) and *Ghost of Dragstrip Hollow* (1959), *Song without End* exists more as a showcase for music—albeit of a superior strain—than as a job of storytelling. The music, generously deployed and often summarized as evocative dramatic underscoring, ranges from the Hungarian Rhapsodies and the *Benediction de Dieu dans la Solitude* to "Mazeppa" and a particularly able reading from *The Mephisto Waltzes*. A popular tune, "My Consolation," surfaced from the film as a free-handed adaptation of Liszt's "Consolation No. 3." The illusion of Bogarde's playing is expertly rendered.

Melodramatic extravagances aside, *Song without End* seems a model of restraint by comparison with Ken Russell's eccentrically bizarre *Lisztomania* (England; 1975). Lizst himself might have preferred over either his entirely fictionalized portrayal in Arthur Lubin's 1943 remake of *The Phantom of the Opera*. Here, as tellingly portrayed by Fritz Leiber, Liszt innocently provokes the transformation of an obscure composer (Claude Rains) into the dreaded Phantom—and then becomes a heroic figure in the entrapment of the menace. In another unlikely outcropping of Liszt in the popcorn cinema of the 1940s, a distillation of *The Mephisto Waltzes* figures as the stirring centerpiece of a nerve-wracking storm scene in Will Jason's *The Soul of a Monster* (1944), a modern-dress retelling of the *Faust* legend from Columbia Pictures' B-as-in-budget unit.

RECOMMENDED ADDITIONAL VIEWING

Our selections are drawn from a list that will serve a similar function during Cliburn Competitions yet to come. (For subsequent Cliburn Film Festivals, Van Cliburn and Richard Rodzinski and I chose from an array of documentary films by Peter Rosen, longtime chronicler of the Cliburn Competition.) That roster also includes, among many others, this representative sampling. Meanwhile, there are video sources as everpresent as the World Wide Web or the shopping mall. (These words were written before the Web and Netflix had rendered excinct the video

storefronts.) The titles are presented in no particular order of preference:

Intermezzo (1939)— This David O. Selznick soaper marks the U.S. début of Ingrid Bergman, who plays a piano teacher to the daughter of a renowned violinist (Leslie Howard), whose accompanist and adulterous lover she also becomes. Guilt vies with some fine music (arranged by Max Steiner) for control of the telling. Cecil Kellaway serves as the conscience, ill heeded, of the piece. The pianistic vircuosity is dubbed by Norma Drury Boleslavsky.

Rhapsody in Blue (1945)—Irving Rapper's highly fictionalized and obsessively sanitized treatment of the life of George Gershwin. The music is almost the entire point. Robert Alda stars.

The Great Lie (1941)— Mary Astor plays a concert pianist in conflict with Bette Davis over the affec-

tions of George Brent. Edmund Goulding's Oscar-anointed film is pure soap, but it packs a rewarding attention to detail in the musical realm.

Rhapsody (1954)—Charles Vidor retraces familiar territory in this overwrought tale of a wealthy patron (Elizabeth Taylor) who finds her affections torn between a pianist and a violinist. The actual playing is the splendid work of Claudio Arrau and Michael Rabin.

They Shall Have Music! (1939; A.K.A. *Ragged Angels* and *Melody of Youth*)—Producer Samuel Goldwyn's well-intentioned attempts to bring the classics to the masses yielded, among many other pretentious middlebrow films, this heart-strings–tugger about a slum child who, inspired by an encounter with Jascha Heifetz (playing himself), undertakes to become a great musician. Walter Brennan stars as a struggling maestro. Archie Mayo directs.

Fantasia (1940–2000)—Walt Disney's pretentious campaign to popularize an Old World musical sensibility had begun much earlier than *Fantasia.* Disney's 1929 breakthrough with "The Skeleton Dance" utilizes Edvard Greig's playful minor-modal *March of the Dwarves* virtually intact; the short subject launched a sustained series of cartoons that Disney called *Silly Symphonies.* With *Fantasia,* Disney codified the approach so strikingly that the original version remains as much a treat to the ear, as to the eye. A revamped and expanded *Fantasia 2000* played theatrically with limited bookings. Either version is recommended, particularly as an introduction for children to the classics.

INDEX OF PERTINENT NOMENCLATURE

INDEX

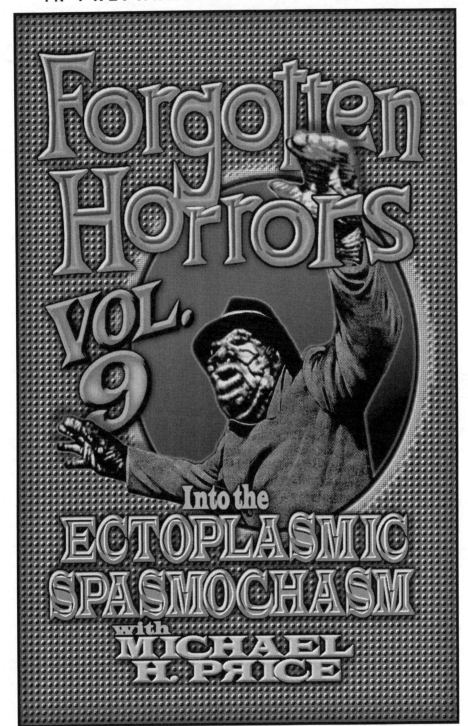

Forgotten Horrors

VOL. 9

Into the
ECTOPLASMIC
SPASMOCHASM

with
MICHAEL
H. PRICE

FROM CREMO STUDIOS

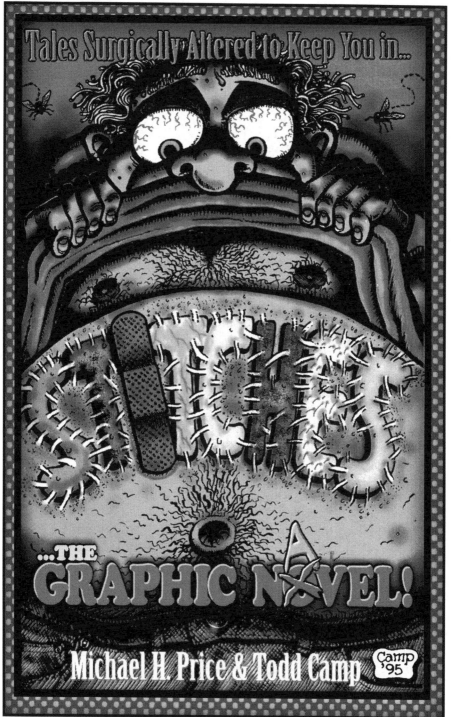

FORGOTTEN HORRORS
PRESENTS...

COMICS FROM THE GONE WORLD!

B&W OMNIBUS VOL. 2

Ghost Gallery

COMPILED & ANNOTATED BY MICHAEL AITCH PRICE

FROM CREMO STUDIOS

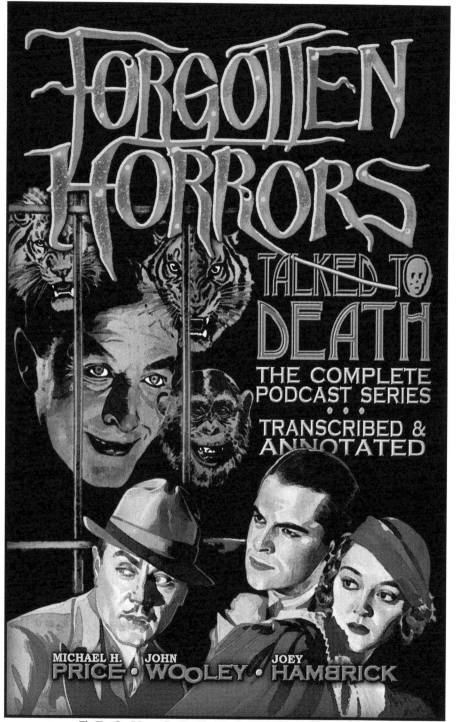

FROM CREMO STUDIOS

Made in the USA
San Bernardino, CA
18 August 2017